Dr. Martin Luther

"Here I stand
and cannot do otherwise. God be my help."
p. 318

In order to preserve the historical nature of this work, British
spellings and the formatting of the text have been kept as they were
in the original book as found.

For information write:
New Leaf Publishing Group, P.O. Box 726, Green Forest, AR 72638.

ISBN-13: 978-0-89051-599-0

Library of Congress Number: 2010934824

Printed in the United States of America

Please visit our website for other great titles: www.nlpg.com

Originally published in 1850 by:

American Sunday-School Union

Now known as:

American Missionary Fellowship

www.americanmissionary.org

THE

LIFE OF LUTHER;

WITH

Special Reference to its Earlier Periods

AND THE

OPENING SCENES

OF

THE REFORMATION.

———

BY BARNAS SEARS, D.D.

———

AMERICAN SUNDAY-SCHOOL UNION:
1122 CHESTNUT STREET, PHILADELPHIA.

PUBLISHER'S NOTE

Barnas Sears (1802 – 1880) served in areas of
education and pastoral ministry for more than fifty
years. He was a promoter of "free schools for the whole
people," helping encourage and provide support of public
schools through adequate taxation, and president of Brown
University from 1855 to 1867. His publications include
A Grammar of the Language in 1842, The Ciceronian: or
the Prussion Method of Teaching the Elements of the Latin
Language in 1844, as well as editor of the Christian Review
from 1838 to 1841.

The ASSU, now called American Missionary
Fellowship (AMF), has been associated with some of
America's most prominent citizens and religious leaders.
Bushrod Washington, George Washington's nephew and heir
of Mount Vernon, who served as Associate Justice of the
US Supreme Court, was vice-president of the ASSU until
his death in 1829. Included among other ASSU officers
or influenced by its mission were Bishop William White
of Philadelphia's Christ Church; Francis Scott Key, who
wrote "The Star Spangled Banner"; D.L. Moody; Laura
Ingalls Wilder; and John Adams (related to both early
American presidents), who personally organized over 320
Sunday schools.

ASSU missionaries carried books published by the
mission in saddlebags to leave with the fledgling Sunday
schools they had started, promoting literacy, education, and
the very best in Christian moral values. Though it stopped
publishing books in 1968, American Missionary Fellowship
continues its missionary work in the United States,
extending beyond Sunday school work to include church
planting, church camps, and numerous other programs.

www.americanmissionary.org

4

TABLE OF CONTENTS

Part I - Birth till beginning of Reformation 1517

Part II - From publishing of the theses 1517
      to the Augsburg Confession 1530

PREFACE.

In an age so distinguished for historical research as the present, it would be remarkable if there were no demand for a Life of LUTHER, founded upon new investigations. In the English language the want of such a work is much greater than in the German. In the latter, the facts newly discovered, though they lie scattered in many different publications, are recorded; while, in the former, they are nearly or quite unknown. To say nothing of Luther's letters, edited by De Wette, and of Melancthon's, by Bretschneider, without which no good biography of Luther can be written, elaborate historical essays, almost without number, on points connected with the life of the Reformer have been published within a few years in Germany, of which hardly a trace can be found in English or American books. The year 1846, the third centennial of Luther's death, was, in this respect, unusually prolific. In the recent histories, too, of old towns and cities, in the publications of learned societies, in the later critical biographies of many of the associates and contemporaries of the Reformer, and in several special and general histories relating to the affairs of Germany in that period, important additions have been made to our knowledge of the life and times of Luther.

About three years ago, the Committee of Publication of the American Sunday-School Union applied to the writer, to prepare a life of Luther, to be published under the auspices of that society. Having, from the time of my temporary residence in Germany, in the years 1834–5, when my historical studies, under the guidance of Neander, commenced, contracted some familiarity with the writings of Luther, and with the history of his age, I was induced by my historical tastes, and my interest in the Reformer, some of whose minor works I had edited, no less than by the hope of doing a service to the young, to engage in the undertaking. During this interval of three years, nearly all the works, amounting to some hundreds of volumes, which cast new light on the subject in hand, have been carefully examined. Many new facts have been brought together, and many obscurities removed, while not a few apocryphal accounts have been discarded.

Persons who are conversant with the sources of information, will not complain that the admirable work of Jurgens on the youth of Luther should be followed, so far as it extends. No other single work, except Luther's letters, has been used so much as this. But from the year 1517, to Luther's death in 1546, no such explorer and guide could be found. Fortunately, from that date,

Luther is his own best biographer. The five large volumes of his published letters, with the supplementary collections, embrace the history of this period of his life with remarkable fulness of detail. The fact that no life of the Reformer had been written, in which was incorporated the body of materials contained in his correspondence, determined the mind of the writer to make that correspondence a subject of particular study with reference to his object. The new colouring which would hereby be given to the narrative would, it was believed, render it both more truthful and more interesting. Luther would appear in his own dress. His thoughts, expressed in his own words, would reveal his true character as nothing else would. Never could such a plan be more justifiable than in the case of one so accustomed as he was, to give unreserved freedom to his tongue and pen, and to speak out all that was in his heart. Indeed, so perfectly does the character of the individual shine forth in his own utterances and actions that a separate portraiture of it has been omitted as superfluous.

It will, I trust, appear that the author has had no theory to establish, no secret purpose to answer, but has studiously laboured to set forth Luther in his real character. His faults have not been concealed, nor his virtues wittingly overdrawn. It seemed irreverent to interrupt the solemn voice of history, and ill-advised to imitate the example of those who transfigure imperfect and erring men into pure saints, for the blind homage of the ignorant and credulous.

In order to give full relief to the picture of Luther's youth and early manhood, for the benefit of the young reader, it was necessary to abridge the latter part of his life. This design was favoured by the consideration that Luther's later years were involved in controversies, which it would be improper to perpetuate in the publications of the Union. Indeed, the biographical interest sensibly abates at the point where it begins to expand into general history, a circumstance which would of itself justify the limited plan of the present work.

B. SEARS.

Newton Centre, Jan. 21, 1850.

DESCRIPTION OF INITIALS AND VIGNETTES.

PAGE 10. Entrance to Luther's House in Wittenberg, with "1540" inscribed at the top.

—— 13. The Electoral or All-saints' Church at Wittenberg, described on page 128.

—— 15. Taken from a medal struck in Saxony, in the year 1617, the first Jubilee of the Reformation. It represents Luther taking a bushel from a lamp or candle— a symbol of the gospel, as is intimated by the open Bible at the side, and the name of Jehovah above, in Hebrew letters.

—— 47. Luther's House, or the Old Augustinian Cloister. His apartment was in the second story, connected with the second and third windows from the right. The entrance was at the door on the right of the tower and near by it.

—— 48. Taken from a medal struck by the city of Worms in 1617. It represents a burning candle standing upon an open Bible, with a serpent endeavouring to extinguish it, and a hand from the clouds pointing to it, and intimating that divine strength feeds the flame. The medal itself has a Latin inscription—signifying, "O Lord! let it shine on for ever."

—— 61. The Ninety-five Theses of Luther on Indulgences, posted up on the door of the Electoral Church at Wittenberg. The hammer is lying at his feet.

11

PAGE 69. The Augusteum, or University, on the left, and Melancthon's house towering high on the right.

—— 119 Luther's Monument, erected in 1817—1821, in the Market-place at Wittenberg.

—— 120. Jubilee-medal struck in Saxony, in 1617, representing the Elector, Frederick the Wise, in his robes of office, holding a sword in his right hand, and pointing with his left to the name of Jehovah. By his side stands Luther, holding a burning light in his right hand, and with the left pointing to the Bible. On the table-cloth is seen the Elector's coat of arms.

—— 270. Luther's seal, described by himself, p. 449.

—— 137. A rear-view of the Parochial or City Church in Wittenberg, where Luther commonly preached.

—— 183. From a medal of the second Jubilee of the Reformation, in 1717, in Saxe-Weisenfels. It represents the Church founded upon a rock—the waves of the ocean dashing wildly around it.

—— 295. Taken from a medal struck by the City of Nüremberg, in 1717, representing a Bible open to the passage—"The word of the Lord endureth for ever." V. D. M. I. Æ. are the initials of the same words in Latin—"Verbum Dei Manet In Æternum." On the left of the Bible is a mason's plummet-rule or level, with reference to the passage (Gal. vi. 16): "As many as walk according to this rule, peace be on them and mercy," &c.

—— 302. The Double-headed Eagle and Crown represent the German Empire.

—— 327. Taken from a medal struck in Saxony, in 1617, representing a brick-kiln on the left; on the right, the brazen serpent, or serpent on the cross, and the name of Jehovah with a pillar of cloud between. The meaning is, that as Moses conducted the children of Israel from the bondage of Egypt, so did Luther conduct the people of God from papal captivity.

PAGE 374. The Castle of the Elector at Wittenberg.

—— 375. Taken from a medal struck at Halle, in Suabia, in 1617, resembling that on page 302; except that it has the city arms or seal.

—— 416. Chapel Corpus Christi (Body of Christ), one of the oldest public buildings in Wittenberg.

—— 417. From a medal of Saxe-Gotha, struck in 1717, representing a palm-tree among thorns, and yet flourishing. Its emblematical import, as applied to the church, is obvious. Upon the medal itself is inscribed a verse from Ovid—"Vixi annos bis centum, nunc tertia vivitur ætas"—"I have lived two centuries, and am now living in the third."

—— 496. The Yard or Court of the Elector's Castle at Wittenberg.

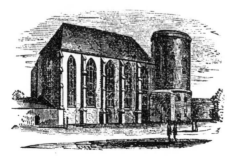

FULL-PAGE ILLUSTRATIONS.

PART I.

CHAPTER I.

LUTHER'S BOYHOOD TO THE FOURTEENTH YEAR OF HIS AGE,
WHEN HE LEFT HIS FATHER'S HOUSE.

SECTION I.—*Luther's Birth place and Parentage.*

OME twenty-five miles north-west of Leipsic is situated the old town of Halle, on the Saale. From this town, the road running to the west, after crossing a fertile plain, leads to a romantic spot, at a distance of ten miles, where the hills of south-western Saxony begin to rise, and the flat lands, extending all the way from the Baltic Sea, reach their termination. Here the road, passing between two beautiful sheets of water, the one fresh and the other salt. enters a vale, with ranges of vine-clad hills on either side, which becomes wider and wider, till at the distance of nearly ten miles, it contracts again, and the heights that bounded it converge and form the varied and pleasant scenery of Eisleben, once the capital of the county of Mansfeld. As the traveller enters this town, he leaves, on the left, before proceeding very far, the house where Luther was born, now converted into an edifice for the accommodation of an orphan school. In the same quarter of the city, a few rods to the east, is St. Peter's Church, where, according to the custom of the times, the boy was, on the very next day after his birth, baptized, and christened Martin, as that happened to be St. Martin's day. This circumstance is highly characteristic of the religious sentiments of that age. The senses and the imagination were employed, more perhaps than the heart, in the service of religion. The infant child was to be brought at once, in imagination at least, into connection with a saint; and it was believed that an association of the name would be adapted to awaken in him a corresponding association of ideas. The font which was used on that occasion is still shown to the curious traveller.

Leaving these places and passing directly on, about half-way through the town, the visiter will reach the point where a broad street, coming from the left, meets at right-angles with the one he is in. Turning in that direction he will see most of the city lying before him, on a rising eminence. At a little distance stands, on the left, the old and somewhat stately house in which Luther died. On the other side of the street, a few rods above, is to be seen the chuich in which he preached his last sermon, the very pulpit in which he stood being still preserved.

Let us now look for that district in Thuringia, or Western Saxony, where the ancestors of Luther re-

sided. We will imagine ourselves at the castle of
Wartburg, about seventy-five miles south-west of
Eisleben, and about twenty-five west of Erfurt.
Before us, as we face the east, we shall have Eise-
nach, in a valley, almost at our feet, and along the
hills and dales beyond, Gotha, Erfurt, Weimar and
Jena, lying respectively at distances of about twelve
or fourteen miles from each other.

To the left, towards Eisleben, we look directly
across four or five ranges of hills, which run parallel
with the Thuringian Forest, with long narrow vales
between them. To the right, or in a south-easterly
direction, lies the Thuringian Forest itself—a romantic range of hills or mountains, extending about forty
miles. Through all this tract of country were scattered different branches of the family which bore the
name of Luther.

Directly south from Wartburg, on the south-
western declivity of the forest, on the way to
Salzungen, lies the hamlet of Mora, where was
the homestead of that branch of the family
from which Martin Luther sprung. Here the
grandfather, Heine Luther, had a small farm, which
he seems to have left to his eldest son Heinz
or Henry Luther, the uncle of Martin. While
Heinz received the small estate and assumed the
maintenance of his parents, Hans or John, Martin
Luther's father, appears to have been dependent
upon his own industry for his livelihood. The most
probable opinion is, that not long after his marriage
he removed to Eisleben, in order to engage in the
business of mining. From the Hartz Mountains,
lying to the north-west, between Eisleben and
Hanover, there runs a vein of copper with a small

ingredient of silver, passing through Mansfeld and extending to Eisleben. At this last place, Hans Luther, Martin's father, took up his first residence after leaving Mora; and during this residence Martin Luther was born, November 10, 1483.

The story to which Seckendorf gave currency, on the authority of a writer too late by a century to be a witness, namely, that Luther was born while his parents, yet residents of Mora, were attending a fair at Eisleben, is not only improbable in itself, as D'Aubigné well remarks, but has been proved to be untrue from the fact, that fairs were never held at Eisleben in the month of November. Melancthon, the best authority on this subject, says: "The parents of Luther first dwelt in the town of Eisleben, where Luther was born, and afterwards they went to Mansfeld." This view is confirmed by Ratzeberger's Manuscript, which says: "Forasmuch as the mining business had for many years been in a prosperous state in the county of Mansfeld, Hans Luther, with his wife Margaret, betook himself to that place, and gave himself, according to his best ability, to mining, till he became owner of a share in the mines and of a foundry. There, in the town of Eisleben, in the year 1483, was his son Martin Luther born, ... but the elder Luther, Hans, removed with his household to Mansfeld and was, on account of his knowledge and industry in mining, much beloved of the old Count Gunther."

The report that Luther's father fled to Eisleben in consequence of having killed a person at Mora, was undoubtedly got up at a later period by the Papists, in order to throw discredit upon the Reformation. Eisleben, which has now a population of about seven thousand, was, at that time, the largest town of the territory of the Counts of Mansfeld.*

As Luther passed only about half a year of his earliest infancy in Eisleben, it was only the associations of his mind and subsequent connections with this place that could have any influence upon him. Indeed, it may be said that Eisleben owes more to Luther, than Luther to Eisleben. He always cherished an affection for the place, and had warm and intimate friends there ; and the very last act of his life was, to make arrangements for establishing a Latin high-school in Eisleben, which soon numbered seven hundred pupils, and has not only existed, but flourished from that time to the present.

After about six months' residence at Eisleben from the time of Luther's birth, his parents removed to Mansfeld, six miles to the north-west, of which the present population is about twelve hundred and fifty. Though this was a much smaller place than the former, it was the residence of the various branches of the family of the Counts of Mansfeld. The castle, now in ruins, stood upon a rocky eminence on the south, and overlooked the vale in which the town was situated. The scenery, in and around the place where Luther spent the first thirteen years of his life, was rather wild and romantic. The country, though not mountainous, is elevated and hilly ; partly cultivated, partly covered with pine forests, and partly a bald and sterile rock. The pits and slag lying on the

---

* The independent county of Mansfeld was a small irregular tract, lying between Halle and Nordhausen, not extending forty miles in any direction; and yet D'Aubigné says Mora was in it, whereas it was more than sixty miles from its nearest boundary.

surface indicate at once that it is a mining district. To the south-east, towards Eisleben, an extensive, varied and smiling landscape meets the eye. In the time of Luther's childhood, Mansfeld was a place of active business. Money, in considerable quantities, was coined from the silver ore; and the copper worked in those mines led to commercial intercourse with the larger places of trade in the south of Germany, and with Venice. It was undoubtedly the prospect of doing better in his business that induced the miner, Hans Luther, to leave Eisleben, and settle at Mansfeld; and the result justified his expectation. For we find him at a later period rising, if not to affluence, to a state of comfort and respectability. He became the owner of a house and two furnaces, and left, at his death, besides these, about one thousand dollars in money. He was so much esteemed, that he was made a member of the town council.

SECTION II.—*Character of Luther's Parents, and their Condition during his Boyhood.*

LUTHER always spoke of himself and of his ancestors as belonging to the peasantry. "I am a peasant's son. My father, my grandfather, and my forefathers were all true peasants. Afterwards my father went to Mansfeld, and became an ore-digger." As it has been already intimated, Luther's father, after he became a miner, rose by industry and effort from the condition of a peasant to that of a burgher or free citizen. He commenced his career at Mansfeld in penury, but with a force of character that could not leave him in that state. "My parents," says

Luther, "were, in the beginning, right poor. My father was a poor mine-digger,* and my mother did carry her wood on her shoulders; and after this sort did they support us, their children. They had a sharp, bitter experience of it; no one would do likewise now."

It was not till about seventeen years afterwards, when Luther was a member of the university, that his father had the means of paying the expenses of his education.† His honesty, good sense, energy and decision of character won for him the respect of his fellow-citizens. He was open-hearted and frank, and was wont to follow the convictions of his understanding, fearless of consequences. His firmness was characterized by severity, sometimes approaching to obstinacy. In his actions which are known to us, he appears clear-headed and decided, going right forward to his object. His son's bold and unwavering course after committing himself to the work of reform, was just to his mind. In the very

---

* *Hauer*, a word which has often been misunderstood as meaning a *wood-cutter*. It is time this mistake was corrected in the English and American writers on Luther.

† Michelet is evidently in an error when he speaks of the parents being "in the enjoyment of a small property, for which they were no doubt *indebted to their son*." The position of the father in society at Mansfeld, long before Luther's celebrity, the liberal support which he is known to have given his son while at the university, his appearance with an attendance of twenty horsemen at the time of Martin's consecration as priest, the present of thirty guldens then made, and Luther's own poverty up to the time of the father's death. all forbid such a conjecture. Besides, the early biographers of Luther, who were his intimate friends, testify directly to the contrary.

midst of the Peasants' War, which the enemies of Luther said was caused by him, his father advised him to take the bold, and, at that time, even hazardous step of trampling on the vow of celibacy, and, in that way, bearing his most decided testimony against the pretended sanctity of a monastic life.

Hans Luther was strictly religious in his character, but, at the same time, had the good sense, (so rare in that age,) to distinguish religion from monasticism, upon which he looked with suspicion and aversion. Hence he was highly displeased when his son became a monk, and it was two years before a reconciliation was effected, and even then his opinion remained unchanged. When Martin left the monastic life, as he afterward says, "My father was heartily glad, for that he well knew the wicked cunning of the monks." Melancthon describes him as being "a magistrate at Mansfeld, beloved of all for the honesty of his character." Mathesius, who had lived in the family of Luther, represents the father as "patterning the widow of Sarepta, and training up his son in the fear of the Lord."

Of the history of Luther's mother less is known. Her maiden name was Margaret Lindemann. She was born at Neustadt, a small town directly south of Eisenach, and west of Gotha. Her father, who had been a burgher there, had removed from that place to Eisenach. It was, no doubt, here that Luther's father formed an acquaintance with her. The circumstance that three of her brothers were liberally educated would seem to indicate that she belonged to an intelligent family. Melancthon says, "She had many virtues agreeing to her sex; and was especially notable for her chaste conversation, godly fear, and diligent prayer, insomuch that other honourable women looked upon her as a model of virtue and honesty." That her piety was strongly tinged with the superstitions of the times and had a monastic severity, is proved by a variety of incidental remarks found in the writings of Luther. On one occasion he says, " My mother's strait and rigorous carriage toward me served afterward to make me fly to a cloister and become a monk."

As one of the most important objects aimed at in this biography is to trace out the causes that operated in the formation of Luther's character; and as the incidents of his early life have been very sparingly handed down to us, it will be requisite to direct attention successively to the character of the various influences that acted upon him; and then to collect from the scenes of common life, in the time and places of his education, and from his own frequent allusion to them in his later writings, as many collateral rays of light as possible, and concentrate them on the points in question. In this way, we can, in no small degree, fill up the chasm which has so long existed in respect to his early history.

SECTION III. —*Luther's Domestic Education.*

LUTHER'S parents bestowed great care upon his early training. In the strictest sense, he was brought up in the fear of God, and with reverence for the then existing institutions of religion. The intentions of his parents were of the most laudable character; the faults of their discipline were those of the age in which they lived. They were highly conscientious, earnest and zealous in the discharge of

their parental duties.   But the age was one of rude-
ness and severity, and they themselves had more
talent than culture, more force and sternness of character than skill in awakening and fostering the
generous impulses of childhood.   Their discipline
was, almost exclusively, one of law and authority.
The consequence was, that Martin, instead of feeling
at ease and gamboling joyfully in their presence,
became timid and shy, and was kept in a state of
alarm, which closed up the avenues of his warm and
naturally confiding heart.   "Once," says he, "did
my father beat me so sharply, that I fled away from
him, and was angry against him, till, by diligent endeavour, he gained me back."   "Once did my mother, for a small nut, beat me till the blood came
forth."   "Their intent and purpose were of the best
sort; but they knew not how to put a difference between dispositions, and to order their discipline accordingly; for that it should be exercised in a way
that the apple might be put with the rod."

To this rigid domestic discipline is to be traced, in
a measure, his being long subject to sudden alarms,
or being harsh and violent when he rose above them.
Though in later life he was fully aware that many
errors had been committed in his domestic training;
and though, as he himself says, he tried in vain to
remove all the effects of it upon his feelings and
habits, still he found in it much more to approve
than to condemn.   Alluding to his own case, and
that of others of his age, he says: "Children should
not be entreated too tenderly of their parents, but
should be forced to order and to submission, *as were
their parents before them.*"

The fact that, from three or four brothers, Martin
alone was designated for a liberal education, is suffi-

cient proof that he gave some early indications of
talent. It is also evident that the father took a religious view of this subject and desired for his son
something higher and better than mere worldly distinction. An early writer states, that he had heard
from the relations of Luther at Mansfeld, that the
father was often known to pray earnestly at the bed-
side of his son, that God would bless him and make
him useful. Mathesius says, that Luther's father,
not only for his own gratification, but especially for
the benefit of his son, frequently invited the clergy-
men and school-teachers of the place to his house.
Thus were domestic influences brought in aid, in
every suitable way, to form a taste for moral and intellectual culture. Well would it be for the world,
if others, in more eligible circumstances, and in more
enlightened times, would bestow similar care and
attention upon training up a son of special promise
in such a way that he may become a public bene-
factor. This is what Monica did for Augustine;
Arethusa for Chrysostom, and Basil's and Gregory
Nazianzen's parents for them, and, through them, for
the world.

Section IV.—*Luther in the School at Mansfeld.*

MANSFELD was situated in a narrow valley along
the brook Thalbach, skirted by hills on both sides.
From that part of the town where Luther's father
resided, it was some distance to the school-house,
which was situated on a hill. The house is still
standing, and the first story of it remains unaltered.
One writer says, (on what authority we do not
know,) that Luther commenced going to school at
the age of seven. Certainly he was so young that

he was carried thither by older persons. When forty-four years old, two years before his death, he wrote on the blank leaf in the Bible of Nicholas Oemler, who had married one of his sisters, the twenty-fourth verse of the fourteenth chapter of John, and under it : "To my good old friend, Nicholas Oemler, who more than once did carry me in his arms to school and back again, when I was a small lad, neither of us then knowing that one brother-in-law was carrying another in his arms." In this school, though its teachers were frequently guests at his father's house, he was brought under a much harsher discipline than he had been subject to at home. It was not without allusion to his own experience, that he afterwards speaks of a class of teachers, "who hurt noble minds by their vehement storming, beating and pounding, wherein they treat children as a jailer doth convicts." He somewhere says, that he was once flogged fifteen times in a single forenoon at school. Again, he says, "I have seen, when I was a boy, divers teachers who found their pleasure in beating their pupils." "The schools were purgatories, and the teachers were tyrants and task-masters."

The injurious manner in which such treatment acted upon his fears is illustrated by an anecdote related by Luther in his Commentary on Genesis. "When I was a lad, I was wont to go out with my companions begging food for our sustentation while we were at the school. At Christmas, during divine service, we went around among the small villages, singing from house to house, in four parts as we were wont, the hymn on the child Jesus born at Bethlehem. We came by chance before the hut of a peasant who lived apart at the end of the village; and when he heard us singing, he came out and, after the coarse and harsh manner of the peasants, said, 'Where are you, boys?' at the same time bringing us a few sausages in his hand. But we were so terrified at these words, that we all scampered off, though we knew no good reason why, save that from the daily threats and tyranny practised by the teachers toward their pupils at that time, we had learned to be timid." This incident, which has commonly been referred to the time when Luther was at Magdeburg, probably belongs to the period of his earlier childhood at Mansfeld. For it was when he was "a small boy," and was under severe teachers, which seems not to have been the case except at Mansfeld. The circumstance that Luther was then living at his father's house will be no objection, if we consider the customs of the times and the poverty of the family at that early period. We are elsewhere informed that Luther was then accustomed to attend funeral processions as a singer, for which he received a groschen, (about three cents,) each time.

The school at Mansfeld, at that time, was taught by one master, assisted by two members of the church choir, that is, two theological students, who, for a small stipend, attended on the daily services of the church. Here it becomes necessary to describe the character of the lower schools of Germany at the close of the fifteenth century. They were called "trivial schools," because originally the first three of the seven liberal arts, namely, grammar, rhetoric, and logic, were taught in them.

At this time, however, and particularly at Mansfeld, a little monkish Latin, the pieces of music commonly sung at church and the elements of arithmetic, constituted the studies of the lower schools. These schools were all taught by a master, assisted by theological students and candidates for some of the lower clerical offices. But as nearly all the offices of state at that time were in the hands of the clergy, there was a general rush to the schools on the part of all who were seeking to rise above the common walks of life. The great mass of the youth were wholly destitute of education. All the others, except a few from the sons of the rich, went through a clerical or ecclesiastical course of instruction. No matter to what offices they were aspiring, they must study under the direction of the church and under the tuition of monks and priests, or candidates for the priestly office. The *character*, however, both of pupils and of teachers in these schools, was as unclerical as could well be conceived. The schools were properly in the charge either of the bishop and the canons of his chapter, or of the monks; and hence they formed two classes, and were called cathedral and monastic schools. But these ecclesiastics and friars became indolent, and employed cheap substitutes as teachers, and lived in ease and in plenty. "The drones," says Luther, when speaking on this point, "drove the honey-bees out of the hive; and monk and canon divided the pay with the poor schoolmaster, as the beggar did, who promised to share equally with the church the half of what he received, and gave the outward half of nuts and the inner half of dates for pious uses, and consumed the residue himself."

The arrangements of the schools were these The teachers, and the pupils who were from abroad, occupied large buildings with gloomy cells. A sombre monastic dress distinguished them both from other persons. A large portion of the forenoon of each day was devoted to the church. At high mass all must be present. The boys were educated to perform church ceremonies, while but little attention was given to what is now commonly taught in schools. The assistant teachers, candidates for the clerical office, generally taught a few hours in the day, and performed, at the same time, some daily inferior church service, for both of which they received but a trifling reward.

Thus the schools were but a part and parcel of the church. The assistants were commonly taken from those strolling young men who infested the country, going from place to place either as advanced students, and changing their place at pleasure, or seeking some subordinate employment in the schools or in the church. When they failed to find employ, they resorted to begging and even to theft to provide for their subsistence. The older students would generally seek out each a young boy as his ward, and initiate him into the mysteries of this vagrant mode of life, receiving in turn his services in begging articles of food, and in performing other menial offices.

We have a living picture of the manners and habits which prevailed in these schools, in the autobiography of Thomas Platter, a contemporary of Luther and a native of Switzerland. "At that time," that is, in his tenth year, he says in his biography, "came a cousin of mine, who had been at the schools [to become a priest] in Ulm and Munich in Bavaria. My friends spake to him of me, and he promised to take me with him to the schools in Germany; for I had learned of the village priest to sing a few of the church hymns. When Paul (for that was my cousin's name) was ready to go on his way. my uncle gave me a gulden, [sixty-three cents,] which

I put into the hands of Paul. I must promise that I would do the begging, and give what I got to him, my bacchant, (protector,) for his disposal. We journeyed to Zurich, where Paul would wait till he should be joined by some companions. Then we determined to set out for Misnia, [in the present kingdom of Saxony.] Meanwhile I went a-begging, and thus furnished the sustentation of Paul. After tarrying eight or nine weeks, we left Zurich and went on our way to Misnia, in a company of eight, whereof three of us were young schütze, [wards;] the rest were large bacchantes, as they are called. Of all the wards I was the youngest. When I was so weary that I could hardly go, my cousin Paul would go behind me and scourge me on my bare legs, for I had no hose and only poor shoes. While on the way, I heard the bacchantes tell how that in Misnia and Silesia the scholars were wont to steal geese and ducks and other things for food, and that no other notice was taken thereof, if one could but only escape from the owners. Then said I to my companions, ' When shall we come to Misnia, where I may go out stealing geese ?' They replied, ' We are already there.' . . . . . We went to Halle in Saxony, and there we joined ourselves to the school of St. Ulrich. But as our bacchantes entreated us roughly, some of us communed on the matter with my cousin Paul, and we agreed together that we would run away from them, and depart to Dresden. Here we found no good school, and the houses, moreover, were infested with vermin. Wherefore we went from that place to Breslau. We suffered much in the way from hunger, having on certain days nothing to eat but raw onions with salt. We slept oftentimes in the open air, because we could not get an entrance into the houses, but were driven off, and sometimes the dogs were set upon us. When we came to Breslau we found abundant stores, and food was so cheap that some of our company surfeited themselves and fell sick. We went at the first into the school at the dome [cathedral] of the Holy Cross; but learning that there were some Switzer youth in the parish of St. Elizabeth, we removed thither. The city of Breslau hath seven parishes, with a school in each. No scholar is suffered to go around singing in another parish; and if any one taketh upon him to do so, he getteth a round beating. Sometimes, it is said, sundry thousands of scholars are found in Breslau, who get their living by begging. Some bacchantes abide in the schools twenty and even thirty years, having their sustentation from what their wards beg. I have oftentimes borne five or six loads home to the school the selfsame evening for my bacchantes; for being small, and a Switzer besides, I was kindly received by the people. . . . In the winter, the small boys were wont to sleep on the floor of the school-house, the bacchantes in the mean season sleeping in the cells, whereof there are not a few hundreds at the school of St. Elizabeth. In the warm parts of the year, we were wont to lie on the ground in the churchyard; and when it rained, to run into the school-house, and if it stormed vehemently to sing responses and other pieces the whole night long with the sub-chanter. Ofttimes after supper, in the summer evenings, did we go into the beer-houses to buy beer, and sometimes would drink so much that we could not find our way back. To be short, there was plenty of food, but not much studying here. At St. Elizabeth's, nine bachelors did teach every day, one hour each in the selfsame room. The Greek tongue was

not studied at all.   No printed books did the students
have of their own.   The preceptor alone had an imprinted Terence.   What should be read was at the
first dictated and copied, and then construed and ex-
plicated, so that the bacchantes bore away great heaps
of manuscripts."

It was from such strolling *bacchantes* as are here
portrayed to the life, by Platter, that the assistant
teachers were taken, who assumed the name of *locati* (located or settled) when they obtained a place.
Their education consisted of a knowledge of the church
service, of church music, of a little Latin, and of
writing and arithmetic.   Their character corre-
sponded to that of the church at large in that rude
and licentious age.   They were, for the most part,
mere adventurers and vagabonds, neither loving nor
understanding the art of teaching any better than
they did the nature of true religion, whose servants
they professed to be.   They remained but a short
time in a place, never pretended to study the character and disposition of their pupils, taught me-
chanically, and ruled not by affection but by brute
and brutal force.   The greater part of what they
taught was nearly useless.   Study was a mere exercise of the memory.

The school at Mansfeld was no exception to the
general character of the schools in the smaller towns
at that time.   We are not left to conjecture whether
Luther was familiar with such scenes as have been
alluded to.   Speaking, at a later period of life, on
the duty of maintaining good public schools, he
says, somewhat indignantly : " Such towns as will
not have good teachers, now that they can be
gotten, ought, as formerly, to have *locati* and *bacchantes,* stupid asses, who cost money enough and

yet teach their pupils nothing save to become asses like themselves." " Not a single branch of study," says he, in another place, " was at that time taught as it should be " Referring to their brutality, he says, " When they could not vent their spleen against the higher teachers, they would pour it out upon the poor boys."

In respect to the studies of Luther at Mansfeld, which continued up to his fourteenth year, Mathesius, his intimate friend, says he learned there " his Ten Commandments, the Apostles' Creed, the Lord's Prayer, Donatus, the Child's Grammar, Cisio Janus, and church music." Donatus was to the Latin grammar of the middle ages what Murray has been to English grammar. Cisio Janus are the first words of a church calendar in monkish Latin verse, made up of mutilated words, *cisio* standing for *circumcisio*, (circumcision.) Next to monastic works, Terence and Plautus, the two Roman comedians, were most studied, as they furnished the readiest means of learning the colloquial Latin, so important to the clergy at that time.

Luther laments that he had not, in those schools which he attended in his boyhood, " read the poets and historians, *which no one taught him*," instead of which he " learned with great labour what with equal labour he now had to unlearn." " Is it not plain," he somewhere says, " that one can now teach a boy in three years, by the time he is fifteen or eighteen years old, more than was aforetime learned in all the universities and cloisters ? Twenty, yea forty years have men studied, and yet known neither Latin nor German, not to mention the scandalous lives which the youth there learned to lead." " It was pitiful enough for a boy to spend many years only to learn bad Latin sufficient for becoming a priest and for saying mass, and then be pronounced happy, and happy, too, the mother who bore him." " And he is still a poor ignorant creature—can neither cluck nor lay eggs ; and yet such are the teachers which we have everywhere had."

It is impossible to read these and other similar passages of Luther, so full of reminiscences of his boyhood, and compare them with the account of Platter's boyhood about the same time, without a strong conviction that they both describe very similar scenes, and that the one writer serves but to illustrate the other.   What effort must it have cost Luther, under so great disadvantages, to learn what he did !   Without uncommon abilities and perseverance, it would have been impossible.

Section V.—*Luther's Religious Education.*

THIS is one of the most important and yet most difficult of all the inquiries to be instituted respecting the history of the great Reformer.   His character was formed under a variety of influences, each of which deserves particular notice.   He was educated in the bosom of the Catholic church—the church as it was in Germany—the church as it was in Thuringia.   He was furthermore influenced by the personal character of his parents, their social relations in Mansfeld, and the character of his teachers and associates at Mansfeld, Magdeburg, Eisenach, and Erfurt.   On most of these points some valuable information has, by the researches of Jürgens, been placed within our reach.

He was educated in the Papal church as it was about the close of the fifteenth century.   And what were its characteristic features at that time? The writings of Luther contain the answer. This is not the place to enter at large upon a description of the Papal church, partly because the subject is not novel, or unknown to the reader, and partly because it must necessarily be interwoven with all the narration of Luther's life. If, instead of bringing together what Luther and other writers of that age have left recorded on this point, we were to present an analysis of their testimony, we should find that nearly all their statements could be reduced to the following summary: The Papal religion is a religion of law rather than of gospel; a Pelagian system of works rather than of divine grace; a religion of forms more than of spiritual life; a religion of human rather than of divine mediation, priests and saints occupying the place belonging to our great High-priest and Saviour; a religion prescribed by the Papal hierarchy rather than by the Bible; a religion in which the sanctity of ceremonies and of the sacred orders prevailed over the sanctity of the heart and life; a religion of the senses and of a poetical imagination rather than of saving faith; and, in fine, a religion founded more on the ignorance and superstition of the middle ages than on the revelation of the truth by Jesus Christ and his apostles.

Luther was educated in the Papal church as it was in Germany. But what distinguished the church in Germany from that of the other nations of Europe, and particularly from that of Italy?

With the lower and middling classes in Germany, religion was, comparatively, though less than it should be, a matter of deep and sincere interest. With the Italian, it was a holiday amusement, merely sanctifying, by solemn ceremonies, a worldly and not unfrequently an unbelieving spirit. The German was superstitious, but was at the same time sincere and earnest. The piety of the Italian was frivolous and superficial; that of the German was serious and went to the heart. In the soul of the latter were deep fountains, but superstition and ignorance rendered their waters dark and turbid. That so many were found in Germany to embrace cordially the evangelical views of religion as soon as they were presented by Luther and his associates, proves that there was already, though smothered by the weight of rubbish that lay upon it, much of sincere devotional sentiment. We cannot reasonably suppose that all, or even the majority, of the early followers of Luther were converted to Christ by his preaching and writings. That which distinguished Germany from the rest of Christendom, therefore, was the amount of spiritual nourishment drawn from the teachings of the church, defective as they were. The flowers were no more plentiful here than in other countries, but the bees nevertheless gathered more honey. Of this we have an example in the mother of Luther; and she was but one of many.

Luther was educated under that peculiar type of religion which prevailed in Thuringia. Here it was that Boniface, the Apostle of Germany, in the eighth century, with other missionaries from the British islands, carried on their most important operations for evangelizing Germany, founding there the Papal church, and thus corrupting Christianity at its very introduction. Here was the great cloister of Fulda, the chief seminary of sacred learning, and the centre of religious influence for the surrounding country. It was in Thuringia that St. Elizabeth, the Thuringian landgravine, whose memory lived in popular legends till Luther's times, and who was a favourite saint with him, was the embodiment of the religious spirit of the people, a spirit of deep sincerity united with childish simplicity and superstition. The Thuringians are proverbially an honest and simple-hearted people. Luther's mother appears to have been of this character; possessing, perhaps, more earnestness in matters of religion, but not less superstition, than others. His father was also a genuine Thuringian of the better sort.

Either because Luther sympathized more readily with the warm and credulous piety of the mother than with the more sober and discriminating piety of the father, or because he was, in early life, more under the influence of the former and of priests and monks who strengthened her influence, he eagerly imbibed the popular religious sentiments of his neighbourhood. At Mansfeld, in particular, the religious views here described prevailed. As late as 1507, one of the Counts of Mansfeld made a pilgrimage to Jerusalem. Two countesses of the same family were in the nunnery at Eisleben during nearly all the period that Luther remained at home with his parents. The cloister of Mansfeld, about two miles east of the town, was supposed to be the scene of several miracles wrought by St. Elizabeth, with all of which Luther was necessarily very familiar in his boyhood.

The account of the Papal church in Thuringia, given by Myconius, who was preacher at Gotha, perfectly agrees with what has here been said on other authorities, as do also the many incidental notices of it by Luther in his writings. There can be no doubt, therefore, that we have before us a true description of the religious influence under which Luther spent his childhood. We also know that his

susceptible mind yielded itself like wax to receive
the impressions which his mother and his religious
teachers attempted to make.   The unsuspecting and
confiding simplicity of his character must be constantly borne in mind, if we would rightly interpret
his actions and understand his history.   He himself
was fully aware of it, and said it was the cause of
many blunders.   He was, even in 1517, simple-
hearted enough to believe that the church, and the
pope himself, would consent to reform.

To Albert of Mainz and other bishops he wrote
with confidence, not doubting that they would
readily correct the abuses of which he complained.
How long did he deceive himself with the vain hope
that a union with the Papal church might still be
effected?   Those who regard Luther as a sort of
Gregory VII., bringing about the greatest results by
a well-planned scheme, utterly mistake his character.
He was not a man of policy or calculation, but a
true-hearted, conscientious man, a man of principle,
whose great power consisted in doing right without
regard to consequences.   He himself says, "I once
thought all that came unto me, professing to have
a regard for the gospel, were godly men; but the
knaves have taught me to be wise.   A fish is never
more in his place than when in the water, nor a
knave than when on the gallows."   "I have become
a wise Rupert, as the proverb is."

Of a part of his religious education, he afterwards speaks with approbation; but of the rest, far
otherwise.   These are his words : " In the house or
church of the pope was I baptized; and there did I
learn the catechism and the Bible. . . . I will hold
my father's house in great honour, and fall prostrate
before it, if it will but leave me my Christ and my

conscience without a burden." "I cannot set forth
in a better or simpler way what one should believe, do,
leave undone, or know in religion, than hath been done
from the beginning in these three pieces, to wit, the ten
commandments, the creed, and the Lord's prayer. . . .
But these ought not to be taught *as they were in time
past*, by making them stick only in the memory."
"This only was taught and practised, to wit, the
invoking of the Virgin Mary and other saints, as
mediators and intercessors; much fasting and praying; making pilgrimages, or running into monasteries; the becoming a monk, or the establishing of
mass to be held at certain times. And while we
were doing such-like things, we dreamed we were
meriting heaven. Those were the times of darkness, when we knew nothing at all of God's word,
but, with our own mummery and dreamy cogitations, plunged ourselves and others into misery.
Whereof I was one, and was myself bathed in this
hot-bath of sweat and agony."

These expressions, referring to his own experience,
though they apply with chief force to his monastic life,
run back also to those earlier teachings and impressions which conducted him to the monastery. "From
my childhood up," he says still more explicitly, "I
was trained after such a sort as to turn pale with terror
when I heard so much as the name of Christ, for I
was not otherwise taught than to think of him as
a severe and angry judge, who would deal with me
according to my merits and works. Wherefore, I
was wont all the time to think how I might set forth
many good works, with which to pacify Christ, my
judge." In his commentary on the words—"Serve
the Lord with fear, and rejoice with trembling," in
the second Psalm, he remarks, "When I was a child

I was angry at these words, in that I did not then
know that joy and hope should be coupled with
fear." "We were scandalously led astray in the
papacy; for Christ was not painted out in so mild a
character as he is by the prophets and apostles."
"We were all taught that we must ourselves make
satisfaction for our sins, and that, at the judgment,
Christ would call us to an account in respect of our
penances, and the amount of our good works. . . .
And because we could never do penances and works
enough, and felt nothing else but terrors and fears
before his wrath, we were directed to the saints in
heaven, as them that should be mediators between
us and Christ. We were taught to call upon the
mother of Christ, that she would beseech him, by
the breasts wherewith she nursed him, to put away
his anger, and show mercy. If she were not sufficient, then the apostles and other saints were to
be invoked, till at last we came to saints whose
sanctity was unknown, nay, who for the greater part
never existed, as St. Anne, St. Barbara, St. Christopher, St. George, and such like." "I had none
other knowledge of Christ, than to form him in my
mind, as sitting on a rainbow, and to account him as
a rigorous judge. For that we had no true knowledge of Christ, we fell away from him, and cleaved
to the saints, and called on them to be our patrons
and mediators." "Especially had we recourse to
Mary, and prayed, saying, 'O, thou holy Virgin
Mary, show thy breasts to Jesus Christ, thy son, and
procure for me favour in his sight." Luther speaks
of himself as having a predisposition to an ascetic,
religious life. "I was so framed by nature, and so
trained up in the Papal church, that I *loved* to fast,
watch, pray, and accomplish pilgrimages and other

good works, to the end that I might make recompense for my sins." He says, that these ideas clung to him long after he had renounced the doctrine, for "this is an inbred corruption, whereunto is superadded education and custom, insomuch that we are not only born into superstition, but, in the papacy, are instructed and exercised in it."

Of the character of the preaching he heard he speaks thus : "The monks preached daily their new visions, dreams and fantasies, new wonders and tales, and that without measure. Not a monk, if he had preached two or three years, but he must needs make a new sermon book, which for a season would reign in the pulpit. Of such books the world was full, and yet was therein nothing of Christ and of faith, nothing else but our works, merits and worshippings, with abundance of false and scandalous tales. When therein they did their very best, it pertained to supplicating saints, those of their own Order not being forgotten, till they went so far as to portray before all the world the holy and excellent person, the Virgin Mary, as an intercessor for poor sinners even against her son, Christ. For we all know, and I as well as the rest, that we were taught to put Mary in the stead and in the office of Christ. . . No monk dreamed any thing, but it must needs come into the pulpit, and be made a matter of divine service. No falsehood so shameful which would not be received, if it was but brought into the pulpit. · · · Is it not true ? *Have we not, alas! all had trial and experience thereof ?*"

As children were ordinarily confirmed at the age of twelve, and brought at once to the confessional as preparatory to the supper, Luther's last two years at Mansfeld were undoubtedly imbittered with those superstitious fears and penances of which he afterward complained. While he was taught that baptism took away original sin, he was told that subsequent transgressions extinguished that grace, and that he must regain his former state by penances and satisfactions. He says, on this point, "As soon as we had laid aside our infantile socks, and were scarcely out of the laver of regeneration, they took it all away again by such teaching as this, to wit, 'Oh thou hast long since lost thy baptism, and polluted thy baptismal robe with sin. Now thou must consider how thou canst do penance and make satisfaction . . . till thou dost pacify God and come again to a state of grace.'" He adds that he had such experience before he was a monk, and that "by such thoughts he was driven to monasticism." From these and many other expressions of his, it appears that he was a faithful and submissive disciple in the school of superstition in which he was so diligently trained.

When Luther was a boy, the common belief in witches was at its height. Of the very celebrated work entitled "The Maul for Witches," (Malleus Maleficarum,) teaching priests and magistrates what rules to observe in their proceedings against witches, and circulated with both the papal and imperial sanction, three editions were printed while Luther was a boy, and was in his father's house at Mansfeld. He tells a story of a witch that lived near by, and used to trouble his mother very much; another, of an attempt of the devil, in human form, to separate husband and wife; and another still, of an instance where the devil actually entered the pulpit and preached for a minister. Some of these stories he seems to believe, others he ridicules. "I myself," he observes, "have seen monks, shameless and wicked fellows, who feigned to cast out the devil, and then to sport with him as with a child. Who can recount all their crafty tricks done in the name of Christ, of the Virgin Mary, of the holy cross, of St. Cyriac?"

Though Luther afterwards became much more enlightened on these subjects, still the superstitions in which he was educated in his childhood clung to him to the last. No one is ignorant of the story of his inkstand thrown at the devil in his cell in Erfurt. Though it may be an apocryphal story, it still is a true illustration of the character of Luther. We find him afterward holding such language as the following: "The devil is all about us, though he often putteth on a mask. I myself have seen that he sometimes appeareth as if he were a swine, and sometimes as a burning wisp of straw." "The devil often beguileth the outward senses, so that men think something taketh place before them which doth not, . . . as was the case in Hesse with the child that, when it was not dead, the devil so blinded the eyes of the people that they thought it to be dead. The devil held the child's breath, as he hath power to do." This is only some of the smut which adhered to Luther from the foul and smoky age in which he received his birth and education. If we are free from it, it is not owing to any individual superiority of our own, but to the noonday light, which never could have existed but for the dawn which preceded it. Luther and Bacon were among those from whom proceeded the rays of light which streaked the east, and ushered in the day, before which, the hobgoblins of false religion and false science have fled away.

That Luther, in his boyhood, was thoroughly initiated into the tastes, manners and habits of the miners, is certain. This might be inferred from the fact of his being a miner's son and living at Mansfeld; but we have statements in respect to his maturer life which can be explained on no other supposition. He always treated miners with particular attention. He was familiar with all their habits and even their amusements; he knew their songs and their plays, and could, through life, entertain them as few others could. Mathesius, in one of his discourses on Luther's life, says, "To-day let us hear about Luther's love and affection for mining and to miners." The council of Wittenberg had a festival which lasted several days. Luther was invited to attend. But as he had been the means of doing away several Catholic festivals on account of the excesses committed at them, he thought it imprudent to attend, and therefore declined the invitation. The young people, according to ancient custom, went about the streets in masks, and sought admittance to the houses of the citizens. "At one time," continues Mathesius, "some of them came to Luther's house or cloister. But, to avoid offence and scandal, he did not admit them into his house. Albeit, at length, a company, disguised as miners, came along, with their mining hammers, and a chess-board for their amusement. 'Let them come in,' said Luther, 'they are my countrymen, and the fellow-workmen of my father. Since they pass whole weeks under ground in a damp atmosphere and amid impure exhalations, we must allow them proper recreation.' They came, placed their chess-board upon his table, and he joined them. 'Now, miners,' said he, 'whosoever will go into this or other deep shafts and come out unharmed, or not close up the passage with refuse, must, as the saying is, not have his eyes in his pocket.' Luther easily won the game; and they all remained, and, under due restraint, indulged in merriment, singing and frolicking, as our doctor was inclined to be sportive at proper times, and was not displeased when he saw the young playful and merry, if it was but with propriety and moderation." This discourse of Mathesius is full of anecdotes about Luther's allusions to his father's employment, and his borrowing illustrations from it in his writings and conversations.

Luther was the son of a peasant, that is, of a poor miner who sprung from the peasantry. How did this circumstance affect his character? It had more effect upon his language, habits and associations than upon his sentiments and subsequent standing in society. For as his father became a burgher and magistrate, and as he himself was a man of education, he came to regard society from a higher point of view. But born and bred as he was, he was never adapted to court-life. He always appeared uneasy when speaking or writing to princes or nobles, not out of fear, but from a consciousness that he was not familiar with the modes of intercourse and of address customary among them. His language, though uncommonly rich and varied, and sparkling with sense and wit, was often homely. His illustrations were often drawn from common and low life. A vein of slight vulgarity, as well as drollery, pervades all his writings. His pungent wit, his creative genius and his sterling sense follow him everywhere. He was the man of the people, knowing all their thoughts and feelings, and employing all their words and expressions in his magnificent, but still rude eloquence.

But from the flower of his youth, through life, Luther was associated with burghers and attached to them, the middling class between the nobles and the peasants, the mercantile, enterprising, patriotic inhabitants of the larger towns and cities. To this class he was introduced, partly by his father's later connections and partly by his own cultivated practical sense and his hearty devotedness to the good of all the people. He was never fond of princes and nobles; nor, on the other hand, of the sottish, blind and disorderly peasantry. In all his writings, he treats both classes, a few individuals excepted, somewhat roughly. He did not depend on either for carrying forward the Reformation, but addressed himself more immediately to the magistrates and free denizens. He wished neither the authority of kings nor the violence of peasants to be brought to his aid, but preferred that these, no less than the middling classes, should be controlled by intelligence and virtue. He uniformly checked the two former, while he directed, stimulated and supported the latter.

His position as a man of education, always practical, led to the same results. Learning with him was not, as with so many others, a matter of profession, but a source of practical wisdom. He encouraged and sympathized with men of classical learning only so far as they aided in explaining the Scriptures and in enlightening the people. He wrote more and better in the language of the people than in the language of the learned. This circumstance strengthened his alliance with intelligent, active and patriotic men.

Thus, when he came to act the part of a reformer, he occupied the central ground of society, the point where extremes meet and opposite influences neutralize each other.

With this agreed his geographical position. Thuringia is the most German of all the German districts. The Saxon electorate was locally and politically what Virginia is in the United States, situated midway between the north and the south, having the advantage of position over either extreme. All Germany called Thuringia its own. It belonged to no section, but was the middle portion, often holding the balance of power. In the Middle Ages, it was neither the scholastic south, nor the barbarous north, but the enlightened, sober, practical district of Erfurt, and yet the chivalrous vicinity of the Wartburg, renowned in arms and in song.

In language, too, it was near the northern verge of the high German, and consequently not far south of the line beyond which the low German was spoken. Had Luther lived either north or south of Thuringia and Saxony, he could not have moulded the national language as he has done; nor have found the widespread sympathy which he did find; nor have acted from the heart of the nation out to all its extremities.

CHAPTER II.

LUTHER AT THE SCHOOLS OF MAGDEBURG AND EISENACH AND
AT THE UNIVERSITY OF ERFURT, FROM 1497 TO 1505.

SECTION I.--*Luther's Journey from Mansfeld to Magdeburg.*

UTHER had now reached his fourteenth year, when the ordinary or *trivial* school of Mansfeld no longer met his wants. Hard as his life had thus far been, a harder lot awaited him. He was to leave the paternal roof, and go forth, young and inexperienced, to try his fortune among strangers. Without money and without friends, he was to commit himself to the charities of mendicant monks and of the people of a great ecclesiastical metropolis. He did not, however, take his departure entirely alone. He was sent in company, or, as Mathesius intimates, under the care of John Reineck, a fellow-student of more experience, the son of a respectable citizen of Mansfeld. This friendship formed at the school, lasted through

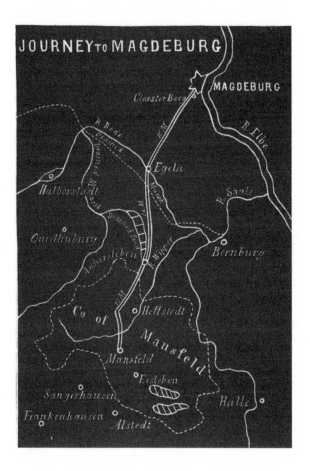

JOURNEY TO MAGDEBURG

MAGDEBURG

ClorsterBerg

R.Bode

R.Elbe

Oranird

Egeln

R.Saale

Halberstadt

Wipper

Quedlinburg

Aschersleben

R.Wipper

Bernburg

Co of

Hettstedt

Mansfeld

Mansfeld

Eisleben

Sangerhausen

Halle

Frankenhausen

Alstedi

life ; and it was this same person who accompanied Luther in his journey to the diet of Worms. Luther in his correspondence calls him "one of his best friends," and the letters of Melancthon to him and to his distinguished son, educated at Wittenberg, breathe the warmest friendship. Virtuous and choice friendships formed in early life are often of far greater importance than the young are apt to suppose.

Melancthon says, the "Latin schools of Saxony were then in good repute," and Mathesius says, "the school at Magdeburg was more celebrated than many others." Not far from the south gate of the city was the school of the Brethren of the Life in Common. Near this was the celebrated cathedral school, and in the north-west part of the town, the school of the Franciscan monks. It was to the Franciscan school that Luther and his friend are said to have resorted. As this is the only monastic school which he attended in his boyhood, we must suppose that he had this particularly in mind when he afterward wrote on the subject. In 1497, then, two boys, the one quite young and indigent, the other older and in better circumstances, left their home in a romantic town on the border of the Hartz Mountains, and journeyed on foot, north, about fifty miles, through a rich and level country to the large and fortified city of Magdeburg, then under the civil rule of the archbishop and the place of his residence. The direct road would lead them to the west of Hettstedt, (the last considerable town in the county of Mansfeld,) to Aschersleben, at which point the mountains and forests begin to disappear, to Egeln, beyond the territory of Halberstadt, and within that of Magdeburg, and thence to the place of their destination. The mode of travel was probably not very different from that described by Platter above.

What an impression must the scene now spread before our young traveller's eye have made upon him! For the first time in his life, he finds himself in a large and splendid capital, with a population of thirty or forty thousand. Eisleben was the largest town he had ever before seen. Magdeburg was the seat of the archbishop, at that time the sovereign of a large territory on both sides of the Elbe. Ernest, then archbishop, brother of Frederic the Wise, Elector of Saxony, was an excellent man, celebrated for the simplicity of his character, and yet no less than twelve trumpeters must entertain him with their music when he dined.* And yet of all the splendour of this city, Luther could enjoy little. He was to be shut up in the school-room of the gloomy Franciscan cloister. The spirit of the mendicant friars was to rule over him. In a city of great intelligence and high culture, he was to be under the guidance of ignorance and superstition, procuring his bread by choral and other services in the church, and by singing with his companions, in their dark clerical robes, in the streets, from door to door. This is the way in which boys were then accustomed to maintain themselves in the schools.

---

* The cathedral, the first finished specimen of Gothic architecture in the north of Germany, and the Closter Berg, had adorned the city for more than a century. When it was dedicated, there were present a papal legate, seven archbishops, six bishops, six abbots, three dukes of Saxony, two margraves of Misnia, three dukes of Brunswick, four princes of Anhalt, and many counts, lords, knights, nobles, deputies from the towns belonging to the see, ladies of rank, besides the people of the city and its suburbs. These and all the clergy were treated to a splendid repast, and then four days were spent in tournaments and other chivalrous entertainments!

The Franciscans wore a gray robe with black scapularies, and were especially employed in attending on the sick, and in the burial of the dead. The boy, in whose heart was a sealed fountain of fervent and joyous passion, found nothing under his new masters and in his new mode of life to satisfy his internal wants. The few incidents which he records, from his recollections of this period, are strikingly characteristic of the order, and indeed of the church at large. "I have seen," says he, "with these eyes, in my fourteenth year, when I was at school in Magdeburg, a Prince of Anhalt, brother of Adolphus, Bishop of Merseburg, going about the streets in a cowl, begging bread with a sack upon his shoulders, like a beast of burden, insomuch that he stooped to the ground. . . . He had fasted and watched and mortified his flesh till he appeared like to an image of death, with only skin and bones, and died soon after."

He speaks of a painting, symbolical of the sentiments entertained by the church, seen by him about this time, and leaving a deep impression upon his mind. "A great ship was painted, likening the church, wherein there was no layman, not even a king or prince. There were none but the pope with his cardinals and bishops in the prow, with the Holy Ghost hovering over them; the priests and monks with their oars at the side; and thus they were sailing on heavenward. The laymen were swimming along in the water around the ship. Some of them were drowning; some were drawing themselves up to the ship by means of ropes, which the monks, moved by pity, and making over their own good works, did cast out to them, to keep them from drowning, and to enable them to cleave to the vessel, and go with the others to heaven. There was no pope, nor cardinal, nor bishop, nor priest, nor monk in the water, but laymen only. This painting was an index and summary of their doctrine. . . . I was once one of them, and helped teach such things, believing them and knowing no better."

We know but little of this Franciscan school, and of Luther's residence there, except that in the mode of instruction there was no material improvement upon that which he had received at Mansfeld ; that the religious influence exerted upon him was of the same gloomy and superstitious character as before; and that his suffering from want became so extreme that it was no longer tolerable, and hence he left the school after one year's bitter trial, never to see the place again, till he should visit it in a very different capacity.

SECTION II.—*Luther's Removal from Magdeburg to Eisenach.*

So great were the privations and sufferings of young Luther at Magdeburg, that it was decided by his father that he should remove to Eisenach, where his maternal grandparents and other relatives resided, and where also there was a good Latin school. It was hoped that he would here be so far provided for as to be relieved from pressing want. But parents, who themselves were familiar with hardships, would expect that their son should be exposed to them also.

We can easily imagine with what different feelings the boy performed the journey home, from those with which he passed over the same ground when he first went abroad into the wide world. After indulging in the exquisite pleasures of home as they are felt by a boy on returning from his first absence— for Mansfeld was directly on the way to Eisenach—

he must have gone forth with moderated and yet pleasing expectations. Moderated, because he had taken one sad lesson in the knowledge of the world; and pleasing, because he was about to go, not among utter strangers, but among the kindred of his mother. What strange emotions would have filled the breast of the boy, had he then had a prophetic vision of the tragic events that should take place a quarter of a century after, in the places through which he was now to pass! About twenty miles on his way from Mansfeld, he might see Allstedt, where Muncer was to become the leader in the bloody Peasants' War. To the west is seen the river Helme, on whose beautiful banks is situated the Golden Meadow, (Goldene Aue,) extending more than thirty miles to the neighbourhood of Nordhausen.*

---

* This tract of enchanted land extends nearly the whole distance from Naumburg to Nordhausen. Memleben on the Unstrut, about ten miles south of Allstedt, was the favourite residence of the German emperors of the Saxon line. Here Matilda, royal consort of Henry the First, founded a nunnery. Here, probably, Henry the Fowler was busying himself with his falcons when it was announced to him that he was chosen emperor; and here, too, he breathed his last. Here his son, Otto the First, on his way to the diet of Merseburg, passed the season of Lent, and died immediately after the services. A little farther up the river, and on the opposite side, is Rossleben. Here was an ancient nunnery, afterward converted into an excellent cloister-school or gymnasium, in which Ernesti, Von Thümmel and other eminent men received their elementary education. Passing another cloister-school, we come to the junction of the Helme and Unstrut. South is to be seen the Palace of Heldrungen, and on the summit the ruins of Sachsenburg. Ascending the Helme, west of Alstedt, we come to Wallhausen, where Otto the Great built a palace and often resided, as did his son after him. In this vicinity the German emperors loved to pass their time. A

At a distance of about sixteen miles from Allstedt is Frankenhausen, where the decisive battle was fought, May 5, 1525, and Muncer and his party completely routed. Still farther on, toward Eisenach, lies Mühlhausen, which was the head-quarters of Muncer's army. Eisenach lies about twenty miles south of Mühlhausen. Between these two places is one of the largest of the five ranges of hills, which it is necessary to cross in taking this route. Just before reaching Eisenach we cross the most southerly range. As one enters the town from the north, he looks down upon it, and sees it lying before him in a valley, under the castle of Wartburg towering on the right.

Next to Wittenberg and Erfurt, this is the place richest in historical recollections in respect to Luther. Here he found the end of his sorrows arising from poverty. Here he first found sympathizing and skilful teachers, under whose influence he acquired a love of learning. Here his musical talent, his taste and imagination were first developed, throwing their cheerful serenity over his sorrowful and beclouded mind. Here, too, he subsequently lived in his Patmos, or desert, as he playfully termed the Castle of Wartburg, in the character of Squire George, and passed his time sometimes in the chase on the mountains, but mostly in translating the New Testament.

There were in Eisenach at this time three churches,

---

little farther on, beyond Tilleda, another royal residence, to the left of the Golden Meadow, rises Kyffhausen with Frederic's tower. There are many legends respecting Frederic Barbarossa and this castle. It was here that Henry the Sixth and Henry the Lion became reconciled to each other, and checked for a time the feuds between Guelf and Ghibiline. West of this is the peak of Rothenberg, with another tower, whose history runs back to pagan times.

to which were attached as many parochial schools.
Only one of these, however, was a Latin school; and
that was at the church of St. George, a little east of
the centre of the town.   The name of the head
master was Trebonius, the first skilful teacher under
whose care Luther came, and to whom he felt a personal attachment.   Though he did not belong to the
new school of classical scholars trained in Italy, his
Latin was much purer than that of the monks and
priests generally. His personal character, too, though
perhaps a little eccentric, was such as to win the
love of his pupils.   In coming before them, he used
to take off his hat and bow to them, and complained
that his assistants were disinclined to do likewise.
He said, with truth, and with a sense of responsi-
bility which showed that he understood the true
dignity of his office, "among these boys are burgo-
masters, chancellors, doctors and magistrates."
Though he is called a poet, that is, a writer of Latin
verses, we must remember that this was a *trivial*
school, and that but little more than Latin hymns and
prayers were read; and that it excelled other schools
only by having a better method, by employing in conversation a purer Latin, and by having exercises in
Latin verse.   It is a mistake to suppose that Luther
studied Greek here, or even such Latin authors as
Cicero, Virgil and Livy.   He commenced the study
of the latter in Erfurt, and the former at a much later
period in Wittenberg as professor.   The following
is Melancthon's account of Luther's studies at Eisenach: "After leaving Magdeburg, he attended in
the school at Eisenach four years on the instructions
of a teacher who taught him grammar (Latin) better
than it was elsewhere taught.   For I remember how
Luther commenced his talents.   He was sent thither

because his mother was descended from an honourable and ancient family of that town. Here he became master of grammar; and, because of his superior understanding and natural aptitude for eloquence, he made more proficiency, and easily excelled his fellow-pupils, both in his powers of speech and in writing prose and verse." Here is the first intimation we have of the manifestation of those remarkable powers which distinguished him in after-life. His teacher undoubtedly knew how to draw out of him what had hitherto been suffered to lie dormant. Perhaps, too, this was the time in life when his mind came, by the course of nature, to develope itself. At such a crisis, the value of a wise and genial instructor is inestimable. It is precisely when the corn is shooting most rapidly from the earth that the weeds should be subdued, so that all the strength of the soil may be given to the growth of the future harvest.

Luther, who had been driven from Magdeburg by poverty, removed to Eisenach in hopes of sympathy and support from his relatives in that place. In this his hopes were disappointed. He was still compelled to beg his bread, singing in a choir from door to door. His sufferings appear to have been even greater here than in Magdeburg. No doubt, the early indigence of Luther, and the fact of his feeling that he was thrown back upon his own resources, contributed to the strength of his character. He probably had his own case in view when he said, "The young should learn especially to endure suffering and want; for such suffering doth them no harm. It doth more harm for one to prosper without toil than it doth to endure suffering." "It is God's way, of beggars to make men of power, just as he made the world out of nothing. Look upon the courts of kings and princes, upon cities and parishes. You will there find jurists, doctors, counsellors, secretaries and preachers, who were commonly poor, and alway such as have been students, and have risen and flown so high through the quill, that they are become lords." "I have been a beggar of crumbs, and have taken my bread at the door, especially in Eisenach, my favourite town, although afterwards my dear father with all love and fidelity sustained me at school in Erfurt, and by his sweat and hard labour helped me to that whereunto I have attained. Nevertheless I have been a beggar of bread, and have prospered so far forth with the pen, that I would not exchange my art for all the wealth of the Turkish empire. Nay, I would not exchange it for all the wealth of the world many times over. And yet I should not have attained thereunto, had I not gone to school, and given myself to the business of writing. Therefore doubt not to put your boy to study ; and if he must needs beg his bread, you nevertheless give unto God a noble piece of timber whereof he will carve a great man. So it must always be; your son and mine, that is, the children of the common people, must govern the world both in the church and in the commonwealth."

The pressure of poverty, on the other hand, may be too great, so as to depress the spirit instead of invigorating it. Luther is represented as having verged, while at Eisenach, to the very brink of despondency, and to have contemplated relinquishing study altogether, and returning to the occupation of his father.

It is difficult for us to suppress speculation as to

what would have been the probable results of such a determination,—what his influence upon the destinies of mankind, and his place in the records of history. But Providence had other counsels than those the disheartened youth was almost ready to adopt, and an event, in itself trifling, decided a point on which were suspended interests of inconceivable magnitude.

One day, as he and his companions were passing through St. George street, not far from the school, their carols were unheeded, and, at three successive houses, the customary charity was withheld. With heavy hearts they passed on to Conrad Cotta's house, where they often received tokens of friendly regard. Madam Cotta had conceived an affection for young Luther, from the musical talents which he had displayed, and from the earnestness of his devotions at church. She invited him in, gave to him liberally, and afterwards received him into her house. Though probably not a relative of his, as some writers would have us believe,—he constantly called her his hostess,—she treated him as a son, and gave him support till he went to the university. It is pleasant to know that, though Madam Ursula Cotta herself died in 1511, Luther, after arriving at an eminence hardly second to that of any man of the age, remembered the debt of gratitude, and in the years 1541 and 1542, only a few years before his death, received Henry Cotta, Ursula's son, into his house in turn, and this act of kindness towards him as a student at Wittenberg is mentioned in Cotta's epitaph at Eisenach, where he died as burgomaster.

The influence of this connection upon Luther's mind could hardly be otherwise than favourable.

Both his heart and his intellect were rendered dark and gloomy by the exclusively monastic character of his training. The path of his life thus far had been cheerless. Even the music which he loved, and in which he indulged, was mostly pensive. Domestic life he had been taught to regard as impure and sinful; and to the pleasures of a cheerful home of his own he was forbidden, by his monastic super stition, to look. "When I was a boy," he afterwards said, "I imagined I could not think of the married state without sin." In the family of Cotta, he acquired other and more correct views of life. Here he became sensible to the charms of refined society. Not only were the generous affections strengthened by exercise, but the taste was cultivated in that family circle. The perversions of the monastic morality were somewhat checked, though not fully exposed and corrected. Madam Cotta vindicated the dignity and sanctity of married life, and taught Luther that his preconceived notions on this subject were false. "My hostess at Eisenach," he remarked, "said truly, when I was there at school, 'There is not on earth any thing more lovely than an affection for females (conjugal affection) when it is in the fear of God.'"

It was here that Luther learned to play on the flute. Some affirm that he at this time also learned to compose music and to touch the lute. Though he speaks of his voice as "slender and indistinct," he had in reality a fine alto voice, and Melancthon says " it could be heard at a great distance."

Beneficial as were these gentle and bland influences, and winning and inspiring as were the instructions of the head-master of the school, Eisenach itself was a priestly town, or, as the writers of that age call it, " a nest of priests," and all the religious associations of the place were adapted to nourish and strengthen the convictions with which Luther had grown up. There were nine monasteries and nunneries in and about the town, and an abundance of churches, priests and chaplains. There, too, lay the remains of the landgrave, Henry Raspe, at whose tomb the visiters on St. Julian's day could obtain two years' indulgence. Here St. Elizabeth, that most benevolent and religious of the Thuringian landgravines, had lived and laboured for the good of the poor, and monuments of her zealous but superstitious piety were everywhere to be seen.

SECTION III.— *Luther in the University of Erfurt.*

ARLY on the 17th of July, in 1501, at the opening of a new and great century, our student left the place " where," in his own language, " he had learned and enjoyed so much," and directed his steps toward the celebrated city and university which towered high above all the rest in influence in that part of Germany. Fifteen miles distant was Gotha, then, as it is now, the beautiful capital of the duchy of the

same name.   Here lived Mutianus, the centre of the
poetical club to which many of Luther's subsequent
Erfurt friends (as Lange, Spalatin, Crotus and others)
belonged.   Here Luther preached in 1521, on his
way to the diet of Worms, and his doctrines were
received ; and here Myconius, the historian of the
Lutheran Reformation, was afterward the principal
Lutheran ecclesiastic.   Proceeding as much farther,
through a country appearing, as one advances, more
and more like the Saxon plains, he came to Erfurt,
formerly the great mart of interior Germany.   This
city, though in the very heart of Thuringia, was
never subject to the landgrave.   It was once the
place of an episcopal see, and when this was transferred to Mainz, the archbishop of which was made
primate of Germany, Erfurt was retained under his
jurisdiction, and regarded as the second capital of
his electoral territory.   Meanwhile the citizens of
Erfurt were aiming to make it a free imperial city,
and the emperor favoured the project.   The result
was, that in the disorders of that feudal age, when
rights were settled less by law than by physical
power, the three contending parties, the Archbishop
of Mainz, the citizens of Erfurt, and the emperor,
each had a share in the government of the city.   In
general, however, in the course of the struggle, the
citizens acquired more and more power, and the city
became more and more free.   It was the citizens,
and not the archbishop nor emperor, who founded
the university, and consequently it had a practical
and liberal character which distinguished it very
widely from that of Cologne.   The university of Erfurt had more than a thousand students, and Luther
said that "it was so celebrated a seat of learning
that others were but as grammar schools compared

with it." At the time Luther entered there, it had thirteen regular professors, besides the younger licentiates, or tutors, and there were several richly endowed *colleges*, or religious foundations, where the professors and students lived together as distinct corporations. Theology and the canonical or ecclesiastical law took the highest rank among the studies pursued there. In the two other learned professions, law and medicine, the old Roman civilians and the Greek medical writers were chiefly studied. In the wide department of philosophy, a sort of encyclopædia of the sciences, as contained in the writings of Aristotle, constituted the course of instruction. The Bible was not studied, and none of the Greek authors above named were read in the original. Neither languages, except the Latin, nor history were taught after the manner which afterward prevailed in the universities. Every thing still wore the garb of the Middle Ages. There were no experiments or observations in natural philosophy, no accurate criticism in language or history. Learning was either a matter of memory, or it was a sort of gladiatorial exercise in the art of disputation. In one of the foundations at Erfurt, the beneficiaries were obligated to observe daily the seven canonical hours, as they are termed, or appointed seasons of saying prayers, to read the *miserere*, or supplication for the dead, and to hear a eulogy on the character of the Virgin Mary. The laws were very oppressive, from the minuteness of their details and the solemn oaths by which men bound themselves to obey them. This is what Luther called "an accursed method." "Every thing," said he, "is secured by oaths and vows, and the wretched youth are cruelly and without necessity entangled as in a net."

The **university life** of Luther at Erfurt forms a striking contrast with his abject and suffering condition while begging his bread at the doors of the charitable, and also with his monastic life immediately after leaving the university. He now cherished, though with great moderation, that more cheering view of human life with which he had been made familiar in the house of Madam Cotta. He was furthermore stimulated by a natural love of acquisition in useful knowledge, now for the first time awakened into full activity. The study of classical literature, which had been revived in Italy and France, was beginning to be cultivated with enthusiasm in Germany. Of the young men who prosecuted these studies with zeal, there was a brilliant circle then at Erfurt. Without formally uniting himself with this classical and poetical club, he took up the study of the best Latin writers in prose and verse, with an earnestness that fully equalled theirs, and imprinted indelibly upon his memory those passages which were most striking whether for the sentiment or the expression. Thus he was the friend, and in many respects the rival, of the poetical geniuses who sparkled at Erfurt, though the more earnest and practical character of his mind gave him a decided preference for solid and practical learning. Besides the Roman classics, the scholastic philosophy engaged much of his attention. This must not, as has often been the case with the biographers of Luther, be confounded with the scholastic theology. It embraced logic, intellectual philosophy, and such a course of physical science as is found in the writings of Aristotle. Indeed, compends from Aristotle and comments upon his writings constituted the sum and substance of the philosophy taught in the universities at this time.

Luther was now in comparatively independent circumstances. His father had been so far prosperous in his business as to be able to support him at Erfurt. Could we have seen Luther at this time. from the age of eighteen to that of twenty-two, full of vigour and activity, exulting in the consciousness of superior intellectual power, winning golden opinions by the rapid progress made in his studies, appearing, according to the usages of the age, with a sword at his side, now eagerly devouring the contents of Virgil and Cicero, now poring over the subtleties of the Aristotelian logic,—at one time overcoming his opponents with surpassing power in debate; at another, teaching the Aristotelian philosophy, while preparing for the legal profession,—we can easily imagine the sensation it created in Erfurt, and the chagrin it gave his father, when it was announced that Luther had entered the Augustinian convent!

During the first two years which he spent at Erfurt, (from 1501 to 1503,) he was chiefly engaged in the study of Roman literature and of philosophy, at the end of which period he took his first degree. The year in which he received this honour is supposed also to be the one in which the following occurrence took place. Early in the spring, he set out in company with a friend, equipped as usual with a sword, to visit his parents. Within an hour after leaving Erfurt, he, by some accident, ran his sword into his foot and opened a main artery. A physician was called from the city, who succeeded, not without difficulty, in closing up the wound. An unusual swelling arising from the forced stoppage of the blood, and a rupture taking place during the following night,

Luther feared the accident would prove fatal, and, in immediate prospect of death, commended himself to the Virgin Mary. " Had I then died," he afterward said, " I should have died in the faith of the Virgin."

It was during the same year that Luther had his second severe illness. His first was while he was at Magdeburg. In his extremity, and while despairing of life, he was visited by an aged priest, who spoke those memorable words which were afterward regarded by some as prophetic : " Be of good comfort, my brother ; you will not die at this time. God will yet make a great man of you, who shall comfort many others. Whom God loveth and purposeth to make a blessing, upon him he early layeth the cross, and in that school those who patiently endure, learn much."

Of two of Luther's principal teachers, Usingen and Jodocus of Eisenach, and of the subject-matter and manner of their teaching, we have the means of knowing more than is common in such cases. The works which they published between 1501 and 1514, containing undoubtedly the substance of the very lectures which Luther heard, suggest to the curious reader interesting trains of thought. A comparison of their teachings in the physical sciences with what Luther, long after, interwove in his commentary on the beginning of Genesis, proves not only that these books are but little more than the printed lectures of their authors, but also that Luther faithfully stored those instructions away in his capacious and retentive memory for future use. Here we cannot suppress the general remark, that the mass of the opinions which Luther afterward expresses, on these and other kindred subjects, are to be regarded, not as originating with himself, but as coming to him through the lectures which he heard and the books which he read. Though the two teachers just named were more simple in their method and more just in their thoughts than most of their contemporaries, they are sufficiently prolix and dry to satisfy even a scholastic taste. Usingen belonged to the Augustinian monastery in Erfurt, and was, no doubt, Luther's teacher there in the scholastic theology, as he had been before in philosophy or dialectics. Jodocus of Eisenach, often called Trutvetter, was more eminent than Usingen. He was afterward associated with Luther at Wittenberg as professor of theology, and was one of those early friends of Luther who were grieved at his bold and decided measures as a Reformer. Süsse, a very pious young man, who, later in life, openly espoused the evangelical cause, is by some represented as Luther's room-mate at the university. Others suppose he only occupied the same cell with him in the convent. The intimate friendship which subsisted through life between Luther and Spalatin and Lange, was commenced when they were all students in Erfurt.

It was in 1505, two years after taking his first degree, that he was made master of arts, which entitled him to teach in the university. He actually entered upon the duties of this office, and taught the physics and logic of Aristotle. It was the wish of his father that he should qualify himself for some civil office by studying law; and, at the same time that he was teacher, he actually commenced the study, which, though soon broken off by the events which led him to the cloister, was important to him, as enabling him to discuss those points in the canon law which were urged against the Reformation by his opponents.

SECTION IV.—*The Bible first seen by Luther in the Library of the University.*

WE learn from Mathesius, what we might, indeed, infer from Luther's subsequent character, that he was a young man of buoyant and cheerful feelings; and, at the same time, that he began every day with prayer, and went daily to church service. Furthermore, "he neglected no university exercise, was wont to propound questions to his teachers, did often review his studies with his fellow students, and whenever there were no appointed exercises, he was in the library."

"Upon a time," continues the same writer, "when he was carefully viewing the books one after another, to the end that he might know them that were good, he fell upon a Latin Bible, which he had never before seen in all his life. He marvelled greatly as he noted that more text, or more epistles and gospels, were therein contained than were set forth and explained in the common postils* and sermons preached in the churches. In turning over the leaves of the Old Testament, he fell upon the history of Samuel and of his mother Hannah. This did he quickly read through with hearty delight and joy; and because this was all new to him, he began to wish from the bottom of his heart that our faithful God would one day bestow upon him such a book for his own."

Luther, who often alludes to this incident, once says that it occurred "when he was a young man and a bachelor of arts." At another time he says, "when I was twenty years old, I had never seen a Bible."

---

* Collections of Homilies.

In another place, he intimates that he saw the Bible only once while he was in the university, and that an interval of about two years intervened before he saw another copy in the cloister. " I was reading," he says, " a place in Samuel; but it was time to go to lecture. I would fain have read the whole book through, but there was not opportunity then. I asked for a Bible as soon as I had entered the cloister." He became owner of a postil, which pleased him much, because it contained more of the Gospels than were commonly read during the year. The study of the Scriptures, therefore, seems, in the case of Luther, to have commenced rather in the cloister than in the university. It is natural, however, and almost necessary to suppose that the history of Samuel, who led a consecrated life in the temple, and in whom Luther became providentially so deeply interested, was not without its influence in leading the mind of the latter to contemplate a monastic life.

CHAPTER III.

THE origin of the Reformation, as a religious movement and as connected with the efforts of Luther, is to be traced chiefly to what he himself experienced in the convent at Erfurt. There he first made thorough trial of that outward and legal system of religion which had nearly banished the gospel of Christ from the church. There he groped his way through the mazes of papal error, and found the path that led to Christ as the simple object of his faith and love. He went through all the process of overcoming the elements of a ceremonial, and of appropriating those of an evangelical religion, by the force of his individual character, and by the power of the word and the Spirit of God. He found himself standing almost solitary on the ground of justification by faith alone, and private judgment in interpreting the Scriptures. From the time of his going to Wittenberg to the year 1517, he was chiefly employed in working out these two ideas, reconciling his experience with well-established truths, and trying upon the minds of others, namely, of his pupils and some of the younger professors, the same experiment which he had unconsciously made upon himself. When he came to feel the full strength of his foundation, and, with the Bible and the sober use of reason as his weapons, prostrated the scholastic theology, and professor and student confessed their power, his conscience impelled him to seize upon the first and upon every public opportunity to propagate these principles, that others might share with him so unspeakable a blessing.

The study of Luther's religious experience has a two-fold interest, first, in itself as one of the most striking on record, and then as a key to the religious character of the Reformation. Until recently, the subject has been wrapt in such obscurity and confusion that it has appeared more as a romance than as a reality. To Jürgens belongs the honour of having first collected and arranged all the known facts of the case in such a way as to furnish a pretty clear history of what was before both imperfect and chaotic.

Section I.—*Luther becomes a Monk.*

THE whole course of Luther's training tended to impress upon his mind the sanctity of the monastic life. This, in his view, was the surest way of pleasing God, and of escaping the terrors of the world to come. Educated as he was to a legal view of religion, and conscious, at the same time, that he had not fulfilled the law, nothing remained to him but to continue as he was, at the risk of his salvation, or to seek for a higher kind of piety by which the law of God might be satisfied. His prevailing feeling was to continue in his former course of life, but any sudden terror would revive the alarms of his conscience, and suggest the thought of putting his anxious mind for ever at rest by fleeing to a cloister as a refuge for his soul. In this way was his mind finally determined. In 1505, Alexius, a friend of Luther in the university, was assassinated.

Soon after, about the first of July, as Luther was walking in a retired road between Erfurt and Stotterheim, probably on his way home to escape the epidemic then prevailing at Erfurt, he was overtaken by a violent thunder storm, and the lightning struck with terrific force near his feet. He was stunned, and exclaimed in his terror, "Help, beloved St. Anne, and I will straightway become a monk."*

Besides the above-mentioned occurrences, there was an epidemic raging in the university, many of the teachers and pupils had fled, and it was very natural that Luther's mind should be in a very gloomy state. St. Anne was the reigning saint in Saxony at this time, having recently become an object of religious regard, to whose honour the Saxon town Annaberg was built, and who, for a time, was the successful rival even of the Virgin Mary. Hence, the invocation of this saint by Luther.

Referring to this event, in a dedication of a work on Monastic Vows to his father, Luther says : "I did not become a monk joyfully and willingly, much less for the sake of obtaining a livelihood, but being miserable and encompassed with the terrors and anguish of death, I made a constrained and forced vow." He again says, "It was not done from the heart, nor willingly" These statements, taken in connection with several others where it is

---

* Such is the view in which the testimony of Luther, Melancthon, Mathesius and other early witnesses is best united. The representation of later writers that Alexius was killed by lightning is now abandoned by most historians.

said that certain views of religion drove him to the monastery, make it plain that it required the force of excited fears to induce him to enter upon a life which he had always regarded as the most sacred, and as most surely leading to heaven. How much he then needed the instruction which Staupitz at a later period gave him!

Before executing his purpose, he took two weeks for reflection. It has been said, that during this interval he regretted his rash vow. No doubt he had to pass through severe mental struggles, that in his calmer moments opposite considerations would present themselves to his mind, and none with more power than that of having gone counter to the known wishes of his father, by whose toils he had been sustained at the university. In his Commentary on Genesis xlix. 13, he says, "When I had made a beginning in the study of the liberal arts and in philosophy, and comprehended and learned so much therein that I was made master, I might, after the example of others, have become teacher and instructor in turn, or have prosecuted my studies and made greater advancement therein. But I forsook my parents and kindred, and betook myself, contrary to their will, to the cloister, and put on the cowl. For I had suffered myself to be persuaded that by entering into a religious order, and taking upon me such hard and rigorous labour, I should do God great service."

Here may properly be introduced a few other sayings of Luther in respect to the motives which led him to take this step. In a manuscript preserved at Gotha, he is represented as saying, "I went into the cloister and forsook the world because I despaired of myself." "I made a vow for the salvation of my soul. For no other cause did I betake myself to a life in the cloister than that I might serve God and please him forevermore." "I thought God did not concern himself about me," he says in one of his sermons; "if I get to heaven and be happy, it will depend mostly on myself. I knew no better than to think that by my own works I must rid myself of sin and death. For this cause I became a monk, and had a most bitter experience withal. Oh! thought I, if I only go into a cloister and serve God in a cowl and with a shorn crown, he will reward me and bid me welcome."

During the interval of two weeks, while he kept his design from his parents and from his fellow-students, the Gotha manuscript says that he communicated it to Andrew Staffelstein, as the head of the university, and to a few pious females. Staffelstein advised him to join the Franciscan order, whose monastery had just been rebuilt in Erfurt, and went immediately with him to the cloister, lest a change should take place in Luther's mind. The teacher resorted also to flattery, no doubt with a good conscience, saying that of none of his pupils did he entertain higher hopes in respect to piety and goodness. When they arrived at the cloister, the monks urged his connecting himself immediately with the order. Luther replied that he must first make known his intention to his parents. But Staffelstein and the friars rejoined that he must forsake father and mother, and steal away to the cross of Christ. Whosoever putteth his hand to the plough and looketh back is not worthy of the kingdom of God. In this "monstrous inhumanity," as Luther calls it, "savouring more of the wolf and the tyrant than of the Christian and the man," the monks were only carry-

ing out the principle which Jerome had taught them,
and which was the more weighty, being sanctioned
by his great name. As quoted by Luther, in his
Commentary on Gen. xliii. 30, the words of that
ancient Father run thus : " Though thy father should
lie before thy door weeping and lamenting, and thy
mother should show the body that bore thee and the
breasts that nursed thee, see that thou trample them
under foot, and go onward straightway to Christ."
By such perversion of Scripture and reason did the
monks deprive many a parent of the society of his
children. " That," says Luther again, "is the teaching of antichrist, and you may boldly tell him, he
lieth. Next to obedience to himself, before all things
and above all things, God requireth obedience to
parents. . . . A son or a daughter runneth away from
his father, and goeth into a cloister against his will.
The pope with his party of Herodians approveth the
act, and thus compelleth the people to tear in pieces
a command of God in order to worship God." "Hadst
thou known," it is said in the above-mentioned dedicatory epistle of Luther to his father, " that I
was then in thy power, wouldst thou not, from thine
authority as a father, have plucked me out of my
cowl? Had I known it, I would not have essayed
such a thing against thy will and knowledge, though
I must suffer a thousand deaths." It seems, therefore, that Luther's mind was in a conflict between a
sense of duty to his parents and a false persuasion
of duty to his own soul and to God. Even the
father was somewhat puzzled by the speciousness of
the monastic logic. But the son made the former
consideration yield to the latter, which the father
always maintained was an error. We must not be
surprised that such scruples were entertained in re-

spect to the filial obligation of one who was about
twenty-two years of age; for, not to mention that by
law a son did not reach the age of majority till he
was twenty-five years of age, filial obedience was, as
in the patriarchal age, considered as due to an indefinite period of life.

Luther, however, did not enter into the cloister of
the Franciscans, but preferred that of the Augustinian eremites. Undoubtedly a regard for the literary
and more elevated character of that order decided
his choice. This took place, as Luther himself once
said, on the 17th of July, 1505. On the evening
preceding, he invited his university friends to a social party. The hours passed away in lively conversation and song. Until near the close of that evening, according to Melancthon, the guests had no
intimation of what was to follow. When Luther
announced his purpose to them, they endeavoured to
dissuade him from it. But it was all in vain. "To-
day," said he, "you see me; after this, you will see
me no more."

The very same night, or early the following morning, he presented himself at the door of the convent, according to previous arrangement, and was
admitted. His scholastic, classical and law books
he gave to the booksellers; his master's ring,
given when he took that degree, and his secular
attire, he sent to his parents. The only books which
he retained were the two Roman poets, Virgil and
Plautus, a circumstance that throws light upon the
peculiarly susceptible and almost romantic character
of his mind, no less than does the festive hour with
which he had the resolution to close his secular
career. He informed his other friends and his parents, by letter, of the important step he had taken.

The former, lamenting that such a man should be buried alive, as it were, almost besieged the cloister, seeking for two successive days an interview with their friend. But the cloister door was bolted against them, and he was not to be seen by them for a month. Luther's father probably did not come immediately to the cloister, (as some writers have asserted, confounding this occasion with that of his ordination as priest,) but replied to his son's letter in a manner which showed the highest displeasure, and withheld the respectful form of address (*Ihr*) which, from the time the degree of master of arts was conferred, he had ever given him, and employed one (*du*) which was ordinarily given to children and servants.

To human view, the course of Luther, in leaving the university and the study of the law and in entering a cloister, seems a most unfortunate one. The best years of his life, one would think, were thrown away upon solemn trifles. But, if we consider that, after a public education, a secluded life often contributes most to true greatness, by holding a man long at the very fountain-head of thought and reflection, (as was the case with Chrysostom, Augustine and many others,) and if, moreover, we consider that the false foundations of a system of error are often best understood by him who has made the most perfect trial of them, we shall conclude with Luther, " God ordered that I should become monk not without good reason that, being taught by experience, I might take up my pen against the pope."

Section II.—*The Novitiate*—1505

THE first act was that of assuming the vestments
of the novitiate. The solemn ceremonies of that
occasion were settled by the rules of the order. The
transaction was to take place in the presence of the
whole assembly. The prior proposed to the candidate
the question, whether he thought his strength was sufficient to bear the burdens about to be imposed upon
him; at the same time reminding him of the strict-
ness of their discipline, and the renunciation which
one must make of his own will, subjecting it to that
of the order. He referred to the plain living and clothing, the nightly vigils and daily toils, the mortifications of the flesh, the reproach attached to a state
of poverty and mendicancy, the languor produced by
fasting, and the tedium of solitude, and other similar
things which awaited him. The candidate replied,
that with the help of God he would make trial thereof. The prior said, "We receive you then on probation for one year; and may God, who hath begun a
good work in you, carry it on unto perfection." The
whole assembly then cried "Amen," and struck up
the Magne pater Augustine, (Great Father Augustine.) Meanwhile the head was shorn, the secular
robes laid aside, and the spiritual robes put on. The
prior intimated to the individual that with these last
he was also to put on the new man. He now kneeled
down before the prior, antiphonies were sung, and
the divine blessing invoked, thus: "May God, who
hath converted this young man from the world and
prepared for him a mansion in heaven, grant that his
daily walk may be as becometh his calling, and that
he may have cause to be thankful for this day's doings," &c. Then the procession moved on, singing

responses again, till they reached the choir, where they all prostrated themselves in prayer. The candidate was next conducted to the common hall of the cloister, where he received from the prior and all the brethren the fraternal kiss. He then bowed the knee again before the prior, who, after reminding him that he who persevereth to the end shall be saved, gave him over to the preceptor, whose duty it was to instruct him during his novitiate.

The order of Augustinian eremites, which originated about the middle of the thirteenth century, was said to have nearly two thousand cloisters, besides three hundred nunneries, and more than thirty thousand monks. It was reformed and organized anew at the Council of Basle, in the fifteenth century. The celebrated Proles, who was at Magdeburg when Luther was there at school, was the second vicar after the re-organization, and in 1503 Staupitz was the fourth, who, in the following year, that is, the year before Luther entered the cloister at Erfurt, gave to the order a new constitution. The abler and better men of this order, such as Proles and Staupitz, were led, by the study of the writings of Augustine, to entertain his views of the doctrine of divine grace and of justification by faith. The Augustinian friars were generally more retiring, studious and contemplative than the ambitious, gross and bigoted Dominicans and Franciscans. Hence Luther's preference of the order.

According to the new rules laid down by Staupitz, the prior was to give to each novice a preceptor and guide, who should be learned, experienced and zealous for the interests of the order. It was the duty of this preceptor to initiate the novice into a knowledge of all the rules and regulations that had been established; to explain to him the system of worship

to be observed, and the signs by which directions
were silently given; to see that he was awakened by
night to attend to all the vigils; that he observed,
at their proper times and places, the prescribed in-
clinations, genuflections and prostrations; that he
did not neglect the silent prayers and private confessions; and that he made a proper use of the books.
sacred utensils and garments. The novice was to
converse with no one except in the presence of the
preceptor or prior; never to dispute respecting the
regulations; to take no notice of visitors; to drink
only in a sitting posture and holding the cup with
both hands; to walk with downcast eye; to bow low
in receiving every gift, and to say, "The Lord be
praised in his gifts;" to love poverty, avoid pleasure
and subdue his own will; to read the Scriptures
diligently, and to listen to others eagerly and learn
with avidity. Luther was so thoroughly drilled in
all these practices that he retained some of them, as
a matter of habit, through life. "The young monks,"
says he, in referring to one of these practices, "were
taught, when they received any gift, if it were but a
feather, to bow low and say, 'God be praised for
every gift he bestoweth.'"

Trespasses were classified under the heads of small,
great, greater, greatest. To the smaller belong the
failing to go to church as soon as the sign is given,
or forgetting to touch the ground instantly with the
hand and to smite the breast, if in reading in the
choir or in singing the least error is committed;
looking about the house in time of service; making any
disturbance in the dormitory or in the cell; desiring
to sing or read otherwise than in the prescribed
order; omitting prostration when giving thanks at
the Annunciation or Christmas; forgetting the bene-

diction in going out or coming in; neglecting to
return books or garments to their proper places;
dropping one's food, or spilling one's drink, or eating
without saying grace, &c. &c. To great trespasses
were reckoned contending with any one, reminding
one of a former fault, breaking the prescribed silence
or fasts, looking at women, or talking with them,
except at the confessional or in brief replies, &c.

Luther was at once put into subjection to all these
trivial and often senseless laws. The good monks
seemed to delight in teaching lessons of humility.
With his studies, in which he was already too much
distinguished for them, they were not at all pleased.
He himself says, "As I came into the cloister, they
said to me, 'It shall be with you as it was with us—
sack on the neck.'" Again he says, "In Italy there
is an order of *Ignorants*, who vow sacred ignorance.
All orders might lay claim to that title, for that they
give heed only to the words, but not to the sense, of
what they read or repeat. They say, if thou under-
standest not the meaning of the Scriptures and the
prayers, Satan doeth and fleeth. The alpha and
omega of the monks is to hate knowledge and study.
If a brother is given to study, they straightway sur-
mise that he wishes to bear rule over them."

The Erfurt monks were not all of the most spiritual character. Luther says of the monks in general, that "For one fast they had three feasts. At
the evening collation two cans of good beer and a
little can of wine were given to each monk, besides
spiced cakes and salted bread to quicken their thirst.
The poor brethren appeared like fiery angels." That
Luther had in mind the monks at Erfurt is pretty
evident, from his saying that he had, in the papacy,
never seen a proper fast; that "abstinence from

meat" signified only to have the best of fish, with
the nicest seasoning and good wine; besides, "They
taught," says he, "that we should despise riches,
vineyards and fields; and yet they seek after them,
most of all, and eat and drink the very best.   One
brother in the cloister could consume five biscuits,
when one was enough for me."   One doctor, in the
cloister, had omitted the canonical hours for three
months, so that he could not now make them all up.
He therefore gave a few guldens to two brethren to
help him pray, that he might get through the sooner.

Of the treatment which Luther received after entering upon his novitiate, it is not easy to judge.
Was it according to the spirit of the order, and consequently a mode of treatment to which all without
distinction were at first subject? or was the deportment of the monks toward Luther particularly harsh
and severe?   Some considerations may be urged in
favour of the former view.   Luther himself represents it as the vice of the system.   "True obedience,
that alone of which they boast, the monks seek to
prove by requiring unreasonable, childish and foolish
things, all which were to be cheerfully submitted to."
He never complains of faring worse than others : but
he does complain that *no* distinctions were made according to the physical constitution and mental state
of individuals; that "every man's shoes were made
on one and the same last, and that all were governed
by one inflexible rule."   "Augustine," he says,
"acted more wisely, teaching that all men were not
to be measured by the same rule."   So much, however, seems to be true in regard to the members of
the cloister of Erfurt, that they looked with jealousy upon the distinguished and learned novitiate,
and felt a satisfaction in seeing him performing the

menial offices of doorkeeper, sweep, and street-beg-
gar in the very city where he had so many literary
acquaintances to witness his humiliation.

With what patience and acquiescence he submitted
to all the duties and tasks imposed upon him by his
order, we learn from his own declarations. These
are his words: " I was a monk without ever complaining; of that I can justly boast." " When I
first became a monk, I stormed the very heavens."
He speaks of having exposed himself in watchings,
" till he nearly perished in the cold ;" of having
afflicted and tortured his body, " so that he could
not have endured it long ;" and of having prayed,
fasted, watched, and inflicted bodily pains, and so
seriously " injured his head, that he had not recovered, and never should so long as he lived."

For the sake of the connection, we will introduce
here a passage that probably relates, in part at least, to
a somewhat later period : " I verily kept the rules of
my order with great diligence and zeal. I often
fasted till I was sick and well-nigh dead. Not only
did I observe the rules straitly, but I took upon myself other tasks, and had a peculiar way by myself.
My seniors strove against this my singularity, and
with good reason. I was a shameful persecutor
and destroyer of my own body; for I fasted, prayed,
watched, and made myself weary and languid beyond
what I could endure."

Connected with such a state of mind and such
religious severities, we should naturally expect to
see the greatest reverence for the papal hierarchy.
It cannot be surprising, therefore, to hear him say,
"I can with truth affirm, if there ever was one who
held the papal laws and the traditions of the fathers
in reverence, I was such." " I had an unfeigned

veneration for the pope, not seeking after livings, or places, and such like, but whatsoever I did, I did with singleness of heart, with upright zeal and for the glory of God." "So great was the pope in my esteem that I accounted the least deviation from him a sin, deserving damnation; and this ungodly opinion made me to hold Huss as an accursed heretic, so much so that I esteemed it a sin only to think of him; and, to defend the pope's authority, I would have kindled the flames to burn the heretic, and should have believed that I was thereby showing the truest obedience to God."

We have learned that Luther was driven to the cloister by a disquieted conscience and superstitious fears and hopes. It is natural to inquire how far his conscience was quieted, his fears allayed, and his hopes realized. Let him answer for himself: "When I was a monk, I was outwardly much holier than now. I kept the vow I had taken with the greatest zeal and diligence by day and by night, and yet I found no rest, for all the consolations which I drew from my own righteousness and works were ineffectual." "Doubts all the while cleaved to my conscience, and I thought within myself, Who knoweth whether this is pleasing and acceptable to God, or not." "Even when I was the most devout, I went as a doubter to the altar, and as a doubter I came away again. If I had made my confession, I was still in doubt; if, upon that, I left off prayer, I was again in doubt; for we were wrapt in the conceit that we could not pray and should not be heard, unless we were wholly pure and without sin, like the saints in heaven." It is difficult for us to conceive of the anguish which a tender and delicate conscience would feel under the influence of the doctrines which were then taught in

respect to confession.   Who could be certain that he
knew the nature and extent of all the sins he had
committed ?   What infallible rule had he by which
he could judge rightly of all the acts and circumstances connected with sin ?   Of his motives and intentions he might have a tolerably accurate know
ledge, but how was it with acts in themselves considered, which were the main thing in the ethics of
the confessional?   Even of those sins which were
defined and measured by the rules of the order, since
they related to a thousand trifling acts recurring almost every moment, few persons could retain a distinct consciousness or recollection so as to be perfectly sure at each confession that nothing was omitted
or forgotten ; and yet one such omission vitiated
the whole confession and rendered prayer useless.
This was the scorpion-sting which Luther so keenly
felt.   He always doubted the completeness of his
confession.   If he prayed, it might be of no use;
if he neglected prayer, his doubts were increased.
"The confession was an intolerable burden laid upon
the church.   For there was no sorer trouble, as we
all know by experience, than that every one should
be compelled to make confession, or be guilty of a
mortal sin.   Moreover, confession was beset with so
many difficulties, and the conscience distressed with
the reckoning up of so many different classes of sins,
that no one could make his confession complete
enough."   "If the confession was not perfect, and
done with exceeding particularity, the absolution was
of none effect, nor were the sins forgiven.   There-
with were the people so hard pressed, that there was
no one but must despair of confessing so perfectly,
(it was in very deed impossible ;) and no conscience

could abide the trial, nor have confidence in the absolution."

"When I was a monk, I used oft-times to be very contrite for my sins, and to confess them all as much as was possible; and I performed the penance that was enjoined unto me as straitly and as rigorously as I could. Yet for all this, my conscience could never be tranquil and assured, but I was always in doubt, and said to myself, This or that hast thou not done rightly; thou wast not sorrowful enough for thy sins; this and that sin thou didst forget in thy confession." Though he "confessed every day, it was all in vain." "The smart and anguish of conscience," he elsewhere says, "were as great in the cowl as they were before out of it." These declarations may easily be reconciled with others which represent him as feeling happy when he could say, "To-day I have done no wrong; I have been obedient to my prior, have fasted and prayed, and God is gracious toward me." These occasions were of rare occurrence, and were the results of that superficial feeling which the strongest and profoundest minds are liable to have in those passive moments when they surrender themselves to the influence of popular belief. But the chief current of Luther's feelings, in spite of all the violence he did to himself to prevent it, ran counter to that belief, so that in after-life, when reverting to these scenes, he could speak of the predominant state of his mind as though there had been no other. The effect of such a view of religion as he then entertained, and of such an experience as he had of a daily deviation from its precepts, is truthfully described in the following words, undoubtedly the utterance of his own heart: "He who thinketh that a Christian ought to be without any fault, and yet

seeth many faults in himself, must needs be consumed at length with melancholy and despair."

Not only did Luther suffer from the unexpected
discovery of the real sinfulness of his heart, but he
was scarcely less tormented with imaginary sins and
false scruples of conscience. "The devil," says he,
"seizeth upon some trifling sin, and by that casteth
into the shade all the good works which thou hast
thy life long done, so that thou dost see nothing but
this one sin." "I speak from experience; I know
his wiles and subtleties, how of one little mote he
maketh many great beams, that is to say, of that
which is the least sin, or no sin at all, he maketh a
very hell, so that the wide world is too strait for
one."

The fiery imagination of Luther, which solitude
served but to kindle into an intenser flame, the
strength and depth of his religious passions, which
found no such vent as they needed, and the bewil-
dered state of his mind in respect to the elementary
principles of Christianity, all conspired to give him
an air of peculiarity which the monks could not comprehend. Too much of original character lay concealed beneath that demure yet singular deportment
to be controlled even by the iron forms which the
order laid upon all alike. Luther's mind had an in-
dividuality which separated him from the mass and
heightened his solitude. In the mental processes
through which he passed, he was alone and without
sympathy. He was driven, at last, almost to
phrensy. Often was his bodily frame overpowered
by the intensity of his excited feelings, and there was
no skilful physician of the soul at hand to prescribe
for his case. Speaking on this point, he observes,
"In my huge temptations, which consumed my body

so that I well-nigh lost my breath, and hardly knew whether I had still any brain left or not, there was no one to comfort me." If he opened his heart to any one, the only reply he received was, "I know nothing about such temptations," and he was left to the gloomy conclusion, that he "was to be alone in this disconsolate state." But as the melancholy mood here described only commenced during his novitiate and extended through the second year of his life in the cloister, we must break off the narration for the present, and direct our attention to his other employments during the first year.

"When I was received into the cloister," he said once to his friends, according to the Gotha manuscript, "I called for a Bible, and the brethren gave me one. It was bound in red morocco. I made myself so familiar with it that I knew on what page and in what place every passage stood. Had I kept it, I should have been an excellent textual theologian. No other study than that of the Holy Scriptures pleased me. I read therein zealously, and imprinted them on my memory. Many a time a single pregnant passage would abide the whole day long in my mind. On weighty words of the prophets, which even now I remember well, I cogitated again and again, although I could not apprehend the meaning thereof; as, for example, we read in Ezekiel, 'I desire not the death of the sinner.'" Again he says, "Not till after I had made myself acquainted with the Bible, did I study the writers." By "the writers," he must mean the scholastic theologians. For he himself says, in a preface to Bugenhagen's edition of Athanasius, that he "read the colloquy between Athanasius and Arius with great interest, in the first year of his monastic life, at Erfurt." No doubt he also read at that time the legends of the saints, the Lives of the Fathers, (a favourite book with him,) and other works of a similar tendency. The new rules of the order prescribed, however, the diligent study of the Scriptures, and the probationary year appears to have been designated for biblical study. But we must guard against being misled by the fact that there was such a rule, and by the name that was given to the study. Neither the sentiments nor the practice of the Erfurt monks coincided with the rule. Though they could not refuse to give a Bible to the novice who requested it, they discouraged the study of it. Besides, Luther's time was so much occupied with other useless and menial services that his progress in the study of the Scriptures must have been much impeded. He was, furthermore, destitute of suitable helps for studying them critically. He did not see the Bible in the original, nor had he then any knowledge of the Greek or Hebrew. He had only the Latin Vulgate, with a most miserable commentary, called the *Glossa Ordinaria*, or Common Gloss. And, what is more than all, he brought to the study of the Bible a mind overborne with monastic and papal prejudices. The method of what was called biblical studies, as then pursued in the monasteries and universities, was entirely different from that to which we, in the present age, are accustomed. The Bible was not studied as a whole, nor any of the sacred writers in a connected manner, so as to learn the scope and general design of the book. Of course, the author was not made his own interpreter, nor were any sound rules of interpretation observed. A text was, in the first place, taken out of its connection, and interpreted metaphysically, as if it were a scholastic maxim, and forced at once into an unnatural connection with dialectics, or used as a secondary and subsidiary support of a doctrine which rested mainly on a metaphysical basis. In the next place, the literal sense was deserted at pleasure, and an allegorical one introduced to suit the object of the interpreter. The absurd conceits of Origen, Jerome, and other early fathers of the church, were handed down by tradition, and the study of such traditionary interpretation, collected in compends, was called biblical study. The false interpretations to be found in the papal bulls and decretals, and in the approved works of the scholastic writers, would furnish a large chapter in the book of human follies. Luther was not only under these influences, but yielded to them. In a letter to Spalatin, June 29, 1518, he says, " I myself followed the doctrines and rules of the scholastic theology, and according to them did I desire to handle the Scriptures." In his Commentary on Genesis ix. he says, "I have often told you of what sort theology was when I first began the study thereof. The letter, said they, killeth. For this cause I was especially opposed to Lyra more than to all other teachers, because he cleaved so diligently to the text and abode by it. But now, for this selfsame reason, I prefer him before all other interpreters of Scripture." Again, he says, "When I was young, I loved allegories to such a degree that I thought every thing must be turned into allegories. To this Origen and Jerome gave occasion, whom I esteemed as being the greatest theologians." Well, indeed, might he afterwards say, "I did not learn all my theology at once." The beginning with him was feeble, and, the sincerity of his heart excepted, was of a very unpromising character.

SECTION III.—*Taking the Vow—Second year in the Cloister,*
1506.

SUCH was Luther's year of probation, a year in
which he experienced some gratification in the study,
however defective, of the Scriptures which he loved;
but, on the other hand, was disappointed in respect
to what was of the highest concern to him, namely,
obtaining peace within himself.   If it excite our
wonder that he did not, at this time, while it was in
his power, and before taking the irrevocable vow,
determine to abandon the monastic life, and return
to the university or seek some other occupation,
there are other considerations which may remove
our surprise.   Luther's mind was of too determined
a character to be turned from its course by any slight
considerations.   He had been trained in the school
of adversity, and could courageously bear the privations and sufferings attendant on his present mode
of life.   The subject of religion interested him more
than all others, and to this he could give his undi-
vided attention here more easily than elsewhere.
Here, too, he found a few friends, such as Usingen,
his former teacher, Lange, whom he assisted in study,
and the excellent Susse, who is said to have been
his room-mate.   If his mind had as yet found no
rest, possibly a longer trial, after actually taking
the vow, might prove more effectual.   Certainly a
return to the world would imply a want of firmness,
and would, besides, promise no better results.   Even
if there had been no disgrace attached to leaving the
cloister at the close of the novitiate, this would probably have made no difference with Luther, who
seems to have made up his mind from the beginning.

Speaking of the unsuccessful attempt of the friends who endeavoured to keep him from entering the monastery, he says, "Thus did I abide by my purpose, thinking never again to come out of the cloister."

The rules of the order prescribed that the prior should, at the close of the year of probation, examine the novice as to his being worthy of admission. If the result was favourable, the bell was to be rung and the monks to assemble, and the prior to take his place before the steps at the altar and to address the kneeling novice in the following words: "You have become acquainted with the severe life of our order, and must now decide whether you will return to the world, or be consecrated to the order." If the answer was in favour of the latter, the individual was directed to put off the garb of the novice, and the part of the service beginning with the words, "Our help is in the name of the Lord," was repeated, whereupon the prior laid the monk's apparel upon him, and then the ceremonies were very similar to those of entering the novitiate, described above. The vow was taken, in connection with the imposition of the hands of the prior, in these words, as reported by Cochlæus: "I, brother Martin, do make profession and promise obedience unto Almighty God, unto Mary always a virgin, and unto thee, my brother, the prior of this cloister in the name and in the stead of the general prior of the order of the Eremites of St. Augustine, the bishop and of his regular successors, to live in poverty and chastity, after the rule of the said St. Augustine, until death." Then a burning taper was put into his hand, prayer was offered for him by the prior, and the brethren sung the hymn, *Veni Sancte Spi-*

ritus, "Come, Holy Spirit," after which the new
brother was conducted by them to the choir of the
church, and received of them the fraternal kiss.

The most extravagant ideas were entertained of the
effect of such a formal consecration to a monastic life.
As baptism was supposed to take away all sin, so this
monastic baptism, (as the initiation was called,) was
said to be equally efficacious, and to have even a
greater sanctity.   Hence Luther was congratulated
on the present occasion as being, by his own act,
freed from sin and introduced into a state of prim-
eval innocence.   With this he felt flattered and
pleased for the moment, but upon experiencing its
utter futility, he came at length to regard it as
"a pill of infernal poison, sugared over on the outside."   In his brief reply to George, Duke of Saxony, he said : "That the monks likened their monastic life to Christian baptism, they cannot deny ;
for thus have they taught and practised, throughout,
in all the world.   When I made my profession, I
was congratulated by the prior, the convent and the
confessor, that I was now innocent as a child which
had just come forth pure from its baptism.   And
verily I could heartily rejoice over such a glorious
deed,—that I was such an excellent one, who could,
by his own works, without the blood of Christ, make
himself so good and holy, and that too so easily and
so quickly.   But though I could hear with satisfaction such sweet praise and shining words concerning
my own doings, and let myself pass for a wonder-
worker, who could, in such a wanton manner, make
himself holy and devour both death and the devil,
yet would it fail when it came to the trial.   For
when only a small temptation of death or of sin
came upon me, I fell away, and found no succour

either in baptism or in the monastic state. Then
was I the most miserable man on earth; day and
night there was nothing but lamentation and despair, from which no one could deliver me. So I
was bathed and baptized in my monasticism, and
verily had the sweating sickness."

Luther was three years in the cloister at Erfurt.
Of his employments and of his state of mind during
the first year, or the year of his novitiate, we have
already had an account. During the second year,
with which we are now concerned, he was devoted
to the study of the scholastic theology and to his
preparation for the priesthood. His religious feelings continued of the same character substantially
as in the first year, except that his anxieties and his
sorrows increased. It was not till the third year,
the year of his priesthood, that new views on the
subject of works and of justification shed light upon
his mind and joy upon his path, and not till after
that change did he take up the study of the early
Christian fathers. Here then we have the means
of deciding, in most cases, to which of these three
periods his numerous allusions to his monastic life
in Erfurt refer. If, in any passage, there be a reference to the duties of the priestly office, saying
mass, for example, or to the study of Augustine and
other church fathers, or to more cheerful and confiding feelings in respect to God, as a loving father
rather than as a stern revenger, and to Christ, as a
compassionate Saviour rather than as a dreaded
judge, we may safely apply the passage to the last
year of Luther's residence in Erfurt. If a state
of bodily and mental suffering be alone referred to,
it is doubtful whether Luther had the first or second
year in mind. But if harsh treatment or the regu-

lar study of the Scriptures be mentioned in the same connection, the first year is thereby indicated; whereas if occupation with the scholastic theologians and with works which treat of the duties of the priesthood be alluded to, the second year only can be meant.

Of the personal appearance of Luther about the time of this second year, probably near its close, (this being the time of his most intense mental anguish,) we have a representation in a portrait taken in 1572, preserved in a church at Weimar, when the artist had the means of ascertaining how Luther appeared at the time referred to. This is furthermore supported by a letter of Luther's, in which he describes his features as they then were. The youthful flush had disappeared from his countenance. His black, piercing and fiery eye was now sunken. His small and plump face had become thin and spare. With all his sadness and dejection there was a solemn earnestness in his mien, and his look bespoke a mind in conflict and yet determined.

It was, no doubt, either during the latter part of the preceding year, or near the beginning of this, that Staupitz, general vicar or provincial of the order in Germany, on one of his visitations to examine into the state of the several cloisters under his care, first had his attention attracted to Luther. By the rules of the order, drawn up by himself, it was made his duty, as general vicar, to visit the convents for the purpose of seeing that a paternal discipline was maintained, and particularly to inquire in respect to the care taken of the sick, the instruction given to novices, and the observance of the fasts and other prescribed duties. Staupitz was a model which all provincials might well imitate. He made it his con-

cern to promote the study of the Bible, though his
efforts were not always seconded by others, and to
seek out and encourage young men of talent and
of elevated religious character, and to inspire them,
as far as possible, with a sincere love of God and
of man.   Such a person as Luther,—learned, able,
ardent, perplexed, abused, and sinking both in health
and in spirits,—could not escape his notice.   His
singular attachment to the Bible was no less gratify-
ing than it was surprising to Staupitz. "The monks,"
says Luther, " did not study the Scriptures, save here
and there one, who like myself took singular delight
therein.   Often did I read them in the cloister, to
the great astonishment of Doctor Staupitz."

Here commenced the most important acquaintance
which Luther ever formed.   Staupitz, at once, after
knowing the character of the young monk, directed
the prior to have more regard to his standing and
previous habits, and to release him from those humi-
liating and onerous tasks which had been imposed
upon him.   He, at the same time, encouraged Luther
to prosecute the study of the Scriptures with unabated
zeal, till he should be able to turn readily to any
passage that should be named.   Luther now, for the
first time, found a spiritual guide who was, in every
essential respect, qualified to treat such critical cases
as his,—one who, in his comprehensive view, recognised as well the laws of the physical and the
mental constitution as the fundamental principles
of the gospel.   A varied order of living and new
trains of thought, originating in suggestions respecting the true nature of Christianity, which were
then as strange as those which were once made to
the two disciples on the way to Emmaus, were the
beginnings of a healthful process, which ultimately

wrought a complete religious revolution in Luther's mind, and laid, in his personal experience, the foundation for the Reformation. In a letter to Staupitz in 1523, he says, " I ought not to be unmindful or forgetful of you, through whom the light of the gospel first began to shine out of darkness into our hearts."

John von Staupitz was descended from an ancient noble family of Meissen or Misnia in the kingdom of Saxony. In order to gratify his love of study and pious meditation, he became an Augustinian monk, and in various universities went through an extended course of scholastic philosophy and theology. In 1497, he was made master of arts, lector or public reader of his order, and connected himself with the university of Tübingen, in the south of Germany. He rose rapidly to distinction ; for in the following year he was appointed prior of the convent of Tübingen ; in the next, he took the degree of biblical bachelor, or the first degree in theology, that of sententiary, or the second degree, and in 1500, that of doctor of divinity

Early disgusted with the dry and unprofitable speculations of the scholastic theologians, he turned his attention to what are called the mystical theologians, or the spiritual and experimental Christians of that age. Bernard and Gerson were his favourite authors, men in whom a spirit not unlike that of the pious Thomas à Kempis prevailed. The influence of some of the professors at Tübingen, especially of Sommerhard, united to that of the writers above named, led him to appreciate the Bible more highly than any other book, and to look to that as his only safe guide in religion and the only sure foundation of Christian theology. " It is needful for us," says Staupitz, " to study the Holy Scriptures with the

greatest diligence and with all humility, and earnestly to pray that we fail not of the truth of the gospel." He regarded that principle of love which
the Holy Spirit originates in us, and which produces
a union with Christ by faith, as constituting the es-
sence of religion. This is not produced by any
good works of ours, but is itself the producer of all
good works. Our piety, therefore, does not depend
on the performance of rites and ceremonies prescribed
by the church, nor can it be estimated by such a
standard; but it depends on the state of the heart
and on the exercise of the spiritual affections. Our
union with the church is not the cause of our union
with Christ, but *vice versa*. "First, God giveth
unto all the faithful one heart and one soul in him,
and on this wise uniteth them together, and of this
cometh the unity of the church."

These are some of the characteristic features of
the piety and faith of Staupitz; and in them we
cannot fail to recognise the undeveloped germs of
salvation by grace and justification by faith in Christ,
as afterward maintained by his greater disciple.
Such a spirit was the very opposite of that which
animated Tetzel in the sale of indulgences.

When, in 1502, the Elector Frederic of Saxony
founded the university of Wittenberg, he employed
Staupitz first as a counsellor and negotiator, and then
as a dean or superintendent of the theological faculty.
In the next year, the chapter of the order chose
him general vicar; and it was in this capacity that
he was brought into connection with Luther. His
influence upon the cloisters under his charge was of
the happiest kind; and his efforts to promote biblical
studies, and to revive the spirituality of his brethren,
no doubt prepared, in part, the way for multitudes

of them to embrace the doctrines of Luther. The testimony of the latter to his worth may properly have place here: " He was an estimable man; not only worthy to be listened to with reverence, as a scholar, in seats of learning and in the church, but also at the court of princes and in the society of the great, he was held in much estimation for his knowledge of the world."

From the nature of the case, we could not suppose that the first interview of Staupitz with Luther could produce any great and sudden change in the latter. At that time, they were attached to opposite systems of theology, the mystic and the scholastic; and Luther's views were so interwoven with his entire character and previous training, that they could not be surrendered without many an inward struggle Now we are expressly informed by Melancthon that Luther's mind did not find relief till after he commenced the study of the Christian fathers; and we learn elsewhere that this did not take place till the third year of his residence in the cloister of Erfurt. Consequently, there was an interval of nearly a year at least, and, according to the common view, (namely, that Staupitz saw Luther during his novitiate,) an interval of nearly two years between their first acquaintance and the conversion of Luther to the evangelical faith.

From all the circumstances of the case, we are not allowed to suppose that Staupitz, at the first interview, did more than to gain some general information in respect to Luther's character and condition, and to make a few suggestions and leave them to their effect. But though the general vicar was well grounded in the truth, and the young monk almost equally fortified in error, there was one point of strong sympathy between them, and that was, the love of the Bible. But at this time, the Bible was to Luther a very dark book. It came to him in his spiritual ignorance, almost buried under the rubbish of the papal glosses. The gospel itself was turned into law; Christ was but a second Moses, a stern legislator and judge, from whom the oppressed sinner fled in terror, because he had not a sufficient righteousness of his own, and knew nothing of the justifying righteousness of Christ. Such was the state in which Staupitz found Luther.

Instead of proceeding from a consciousness of the necessity of redemption and gratuitous justification to the ascertainment of its reality and availableness, the benighted though learned young monk went back, in a contrary direction, to speculate upon the origin and nature of evil, and upon the mysteries of Providence, over which lay a pall of still denser darkness. Thus he was sometimes subject to the keenest despair, and sometimes to the most distressing thoughts. "Why," said Staupitz to him, "do you vex yourself with these speculations and high thoughts? Look upon the wounds of Christ and upon the blood which he shed for you. From these will the counsels of God shine forth." That is, in the cross of Christ is the best solution of the mysteries of Providence in respect to the eternal destinies of men. This undoubtedly took place at the first confession which Luther made to Staupitz as the general vicar. The scene, according to Luther, was equally surprising to both parties. Such a confession, going so deeply into the nature of sin as consisting not so much in single acts as in a moral state, a confession of the doubts and daring speculations of a great mind abused in its religious training, and consequently in a perfectly chaotic state, Staupitz had never before heard. Luther knew no better what to make of the unexpected and strange directions given him by Staupitz. No name was more terrific to him than that of Christ, an avenger and a judge, to whom he did not dare to approach without first preparing the way by engaging in his behalf the more tender sympathies of the virgin mother, to soften the severities of her Divine Son. In a sermon of his, first published in 1847, Luther says, "Under the papacy I fled from Christ, and trembled at his name; . . . for I looked upon him as a judge only; and in this grievously erred. St. Bernard, otherwise a godly man, said: 'Behold, in all the gospel, how sharply Christ often rebuketh, upbraideth and condemneth the Pharisees, and flieth at them, while the virgin Mary is ever gentle and kind, and never spoke or uttered one hard word.' From hence arose the opinion that Christ reproacheth and rebuketh, while Mary is all sweetness and love."

The first confession only created mutual surprise, and Luther was still left in his sadness. This we learn from an occurrence that seems to have taken place soon after. At table, Staupitz, seeing Luther still downcast and clouded with gloom, said to him, "Why are you in such heaviness, brother Martin?" "Alas!" replied Luther, "what then am I to do?" Staupitz rejoined, "I have never had knowledge nor experience of such temptations; but so far forth as I can perceive, they are more needful for you than your food and drink. You know not how salutary and necessary they are for you. God bringeth them not upon you without a purpose. Without them, nothing good would come of you. You will yet see that God hath great things

to accomplish through you." Numerous passages
in Luther's later writings were evidently suggested
by his own experience as here described. One will
here suffice as a specimen. "When the heart of
man is in great anguish, either the Spirit of God
must needs give him gracious assurance, or there
must be a godly friend to comfort him and take from
him his doubts by the word of God." But as we
afterward find Luther in his former state of mind,
and devoting himself with more zeal than ever to
the study of the scholastic writers, we must conclude
that no great and permanent change was effected in
his religious views during Staupitz's first visit.

SECTION IV.—*Luther studies the Scholastic Theology.*

THE effect of Staupitz's influence was delayed by
the fact that, according to the usages of the order,
which he could not think of setting aside, the monk
who had finished his biblical studies, as they were
improperly called, was to direct his chief attention
next to the scholastic theology. Staupitz was not
the man for energetic or violent reform; and Usingen, whose influence in the Erfurt convent was now
great and who was probably Luther's preceptor at
this time, was a zealous scholastic. Luther himself
says, "When I had taken the vow, they took the
Bible from me again and gave me the sophistical
books. But as often as I could, I would hide myself in the library, and give my mind to the Bible."

Luther, who never shrank from a task because it
was hard or disagreeable, but, on the contrary, with
a consciousness of his power, took pleasure in its
full exercise, now studied with iron diligence the
sentences of the Fathers, as collected into digests by

the schoolmen.   Biel and D'Ailly he is said to
have learned by heart.   With the writings of
Occam, Aquinas and Scotus, he made himself very
familiar.

Here we find Luther in a new conflict—his own
inclination and religious wants, together with the
influence of Staupitz, leading him to the Bible; the
influence of the convent and his occupation with the
scholastic writers, on the other hand, strengthening
the false impressions under which he had grown up.
Both of these contending elements were having
their effect upon Luther, and he was to be prepared
for his great work by feeling the full power and
coming to a complete knowledge of each.

SECTION V.—*Luther's Preparation for the Priesthood.*

THIS also constituted a part of Luther's occupation during his second year in the monastery. Biel,
the last of the scholastics, his favourite author, was
the writer most studied on this subject.   In what
follows, it will be made to appear that such employment, no less than the study of the scholastic writers
in general, was adapted to carry him further and
further from the Bible and the spiritualism of Staupitz, and to involve him more deeply than ever in
the labyrinth of papal error.   We find here a striking analogy to the mazes of error through which the
great Augustine passed, when, half in despair and
half in docile submission, he was conducted step by
step through the hollow and deceitful system of the
Manicheans.   The church service with which the
priest was concerned, was a complicated system of
symbolical acts, at the same time exercising the ingenuity and furnishing ample materials for exciting

the imagination of the students. The central point in the system was the service of mass. To this the selected passages of Scripture, their arrangement, the prayers and the hymns all referred. The antiphonies and the priestly ornaments both relate to the sacrificial offering in the mass. The rites themselves were sacred mysteries, and the officiating priest a sacred person. Luther never lost the impression which these imposing and solemn, though false, forms of worship made upon him. Christ was considered as daily repeating the offering up of himself.

Biel had written an extended work on the mass-service, which was adopted as a text-book in the monasteries. He there teaches, that men must repair to the saints, through whose intercessions we are to be saved; that the Father has given over one-half of his kingdom to the Virgin, the queen of heaven; that of the two attributes of justice and mercy, he has surrendered the latter to her, while he retains the former. The priest is intercessor between God and man. He offers the sacrifice of Christ in the supper, and can extend its efficacy to others. This neither the Virgin Mary nor the angels can do.

In another part of the work, Biel has several nice disquisitions on such questions as, whether the bread must always be made of wheat; how much ought to be consecrated at a time; what would be the effect of a grammatical blunder on the part of the priest in repeating the words. Thus Luther was trained by daily study to a system of practical religion which subsequently, when he was more enlightened, became abhorrent to all the feelings of his heart. "Let any one," he says, "read Biel on the

Canonical Constitutions concerning the mass, which
is nevertheless the best book of the Papists on that
matter, and see what execrable things are therein
contained.   That was once my book."   Again;
"Gabriel Biel wrote a book on the Canonical Constitutions which was looked upon as the best in
these times; . . . when I read it, my heart did
bleed," that is, was in anguish from the scruples
which it caused in respect to the duties of the priesthood.

The rules laid down were carried to an astonishing minuteness of detail, and the least deviation
from them was represented as highly sinful.   Luther was so conscious of his sinfulness that he often
despaired of ever being able to officiate worthily
as a priest.   We, in this age, cannot appreciate his
feelings in this respect, unless we place ourselves, in
imagination, precisely in his circumstances, and learn
with him to feel a creeping horror at the ghostly
superstitions of the times.   His own language will
best transport us to the gloomy cell and its spiritual
terrors, and to the chapel with its over-awing mysteries.   "Those priests," he remarks, "who were
right earnest in religion, were so terrified in pronouncing the words of Christ, delivered at the institution of the supper, that they trembled and quaked
when they came to the clause, 'This is my body;'
for they must repeat every word without the least
error.   He who stammered, or omitted a word, was
guilty of a great sin.   He was, moreover, to pronounce the words without any wandering thoughts."
Again he says, "It was declared a mortal sin to
leave out the word *enim*, (for,) or *aeterni*, (eternal.)
If one had forgotten whether he had pronounced a
certain word or not, he could not make the matter

sure by repetition. . . . Here was distress and anguish. . . . How sorely were we vexed with the
mass, especially with the signs of the cross!" About
fifty of these and some hundreds of other prescribed
motions of the body were to be punctiliously observed in the mass-service. Special rules were given
as to what was to be done if a little of the wine were
spilled. Nothing can give us a better impression of
the awe which the idea of Christ's real presence inspired than an incident which occurred but four
years before Luther's death. In the year 1542,
during the celebration of the Eucharist, some drops
of the wine were accidentally spilled. Luther, Bugenhagen and the officiating minister sprang instantly and licked it up with their tongues! If such
were the feelings with which the reformer noticed
any little irregularity in this service in his old age,
what must they have been when he was timidly
preparing himself to become a Catholic priest?

In the mass itself, every thing is Jewish and legal.
Christ's original sacrifice is regarded as atoning only
for original sin; all other sins were to be atoned for
in the mass. Through the intercession of the saints,
the sacrament effects an ablution from all actual sin,
a defence against all dangers, against all the evils
incident to the body or the mind, against the assaults
of Satan, and a remission of the sins of the dead as
well as of the living. How strangely is Christ here
thrown into the back-ground, and saints and priests
raised to an impious eminence! How is the cross
of Christ obscured, and an empty rite, a human in
vention, covered with the halo of a divine glory!

THE day appointed for his ordination as priest, the 2d of May, 1507, at length arrived. Such a day was of too solemn interest, as it was observed at that time, to be allowed to pass without the presence of Luther's father, who had continued during nearly the whole period of two years to be alienated from the son in consequence of his entering the monastery. It is a mistake committed by several biographers of Luther, to represent the reconciliation, and even the visit of John Luther at the convent, as having taken place in 1505, a short time after Luther entered his novitiate. Martin was his father's favourite son. He had been sent to the university and supported there by the father's hard earnings, in order that he might become a learned jurist and rise to distinction. His brilliant career as a student, and then as a teacher, and his entrance, under favourable circumstances, upon the study of the law, served only to give poignancy to a father's grief, when he saw that all his high hopes were to be disappointed. He was so chagrined that he refused to see his son. On the death of two other sons, who were carried off by the plague, and on the intelligence that Martin had also died of the same, his heart began to relent. His friends took that opportunity to reason with him, and to convince him that he ought to be willing to make an offering to the Lord of whatever was dearest to him, even though it were his favourite child. To this reasoning he never assented, entertaining, as he always did, unfavourable views of monastic life; but he became so far reconciled as to accept the invitation to be present at the ordination. He came in the pomp required by the occasion, mounted on horseback with attendants, twenty in all, and honoured his son with a present of twenty guldens. It was "with a sad, reluctant will," as Luther says, that his father finally consented to his permanent connection with a religious order. "Well, be it so," was his language, "God grant that it may turn out for good." When they were all seated at table, at the time of the ordination, Luther, trusting to the favourable impressions produced by the occasion, and to the influence of the company around him, ventured to touch upon the delicate subject with his father, in the following language : "Dear father, what was the reason of thy objecting to my desire to become a monk? Why wast thou then so displeased; and perhaps not reconciled yet? It is such a peaceful and godly life to live." He went on to recount the alarming events which he construed as indications of the divine will, and was warmly supported in all he said by the monks at his side. The plain-spoken and honest miner, notwithstanding the place and the occasion, boldly and tersely replied, "Didst thou never hear that a son must be obedient to his parents? And you learned men, Did you never read in the Scriptures, 'Thou shalt honour thy father and thy mother?' . . . God grant that those signs may not prove to be lying wonders of Satan." "Never," said Luther afterward, "did words sink deeper into a man's heart than did these of my father into mine."

The sentiments of the age, in respect to the ordination of a priest, must be kept in view, if we would understand Luther's history at this period. He himself informs us that "a consecrated priest was as much above an ordinary Christian as the morning star was above a smoking taper." "It was a glorious thing to be a new priest, and to hold the first mass. Blessed the mother who had borne a priest. Father and mother and friends were filled with joy." "The first mass was thought much of, and brought no little money, for the gifts and offerings came like drops of rain. The canonical hours were then observed with torch-lights. The young priest danced with his mother, if she was still living, and the bystanders, who looked on, wept for joy. If she was dead, he delivered her from purgatory."

We learn from Luther, that the bishop at his ordination gave him the cup, and said to him, "Receive power to offer sacrifice for the living and the dead," and Luther adds, "it is a wonder that the ground did not open and swallow us both up." The words which Luther was then to employ in the mass service, which immediately followed, were, "Accept, holy Father, this unblemished sacrifice, which I, thine unworthy servant, offer unto thee, the true and living God, for my innumerable sins, offences and omissions, and for all who are here present, and for all believers living, and also for the dead, that it may be for our salvation." Luther was filled with trepidation and fear, and faltered in the service, and would have left the altar, which would have occasioned his excommunication, if his preceptor, who was standing by, had not stopped him. It was the idea of "standing before God without a mediator," as he had been taught to interpret the act, and other superstitious fears with which Biel's book had filled his head,—it was this that made him pause in terror when he came to the words, "the sacrifice which I offer unto thee." "From that time forth," says Luther, "I read mass with great fear."

Still he became a very zealous and fanatical priest, as the following passages from his writings clearly show. We now find him going from village to village "begging cheese," and "saying mass" for the peasants, and sometimes "with difficulty refraining from laughter" at the blunders of the awkward country organists, who, as he says, would introduce the wrong piece in the midst of the service. How false the principles were upon which he then acted he himself afterward strongly testifies. "I was an unblushing Pharisee. When I had read mass and said my prayers, I put my trust and rested therein. I did not behold the sinner that lay hidden under that cloak, in my not trusting in the righteousness of God, but in my own; in not giving God thanks for the sacrament, but in thinking he must be thankful and well pleased that I offered up his Son to him, that is, reproached and blasphemed him. When we were about to hold mass, we were wont to say, 'Now I will go and be midwife to the Virgin.' Did we not know that the worst of abuses can be practised without remorse when false principles in religion are adopted, we could scarcely believe that such representations as the following could be made in sober earnest by Luther. "Some had mass in order to become rich, and to be prosperous in their worldly business. Some, because they thought if they heard mass in the morning, then would they be secure through all the day against every suffering and peril. Some, by reason of sickness, and some for yet more foolish and sinful causes; and they could find abject priests, who, for money, would let them have their way. Furthermore, they have put a difference in the mass, making one better for this, another better for that occasion, by inventing the seven-gulden mass.* The mass of the holy cross has a different virtue from the mass of the virgin. And everybody keeps still and lets the people go on, for the sake of the accursed lucre, flowing abundantly through the mass which has so many names and virtues." "Here, you yourselves know, my dear sirs," says Luther to his opponents in 1520, "what a scandalous trafficking and marketing you have made with your sacrament. This hath been the regular and every-day business of you all, buying and selling throughout all the world so many thousands of masses for money, some for a groschen, (three cents,) some for eight pfennigs, (two cents,) and some for six. There is no excusing nor denying it." "I also, when I was a monk, was wont daily to confess, to fast, to read, to pray, and to offer sacrifice, to the end that, from the vigils, mass and other works, I could impart and sell something (merit) to the laity. The monks bartered their merits away for corn and wine, as well as for money, and gave formal receipts, as is shown by many copies still extant, which ran thus: 'In consideration of one bushel of wheat, we by this writing and contract make over to you the benefit of our fastings, watchings, mortifications, mass-services and such like.' I, an arrant Papist, and much fiercer mass-monger than all the rest, could not distinguish between the mass and the sacrament any more than the common people. To me the mass and the sacrament upon the altar were one and the same thing, as they were to all of us at that time. . . . I have lain sick in the infirmary, and viewed Christ in no other light than that of a severe judge, whom I must appease with my monastic works. . . . Therefore,

---

* A Saxon *gulden*, in the 16th century, was about sixty-two and a half cents.

my way and custom was, when I had finished my
prayers or mass, always to conclude with such words
as these: 'My dear Jesus, I come unto thee and
entreat thee to be pleased with whatsoever I do and
suffer in my order, and to accept it as a composition
for my sins? Twenty years ago, if any one desired
mass, he should have come and purchased it of me;
I cleaved to it with all my heart and worshipped it.
. . . I held mass every day, and knew not but that
I was going straight to heaven. . . . I chose for myself twenty-one saints, read mass every day, calling
on three of them each day, so as to complete the
circuit every week. Especially did I invoke the
holy Virgin, as her womanly heart was more easily
touched, that she might appease her Son." Again,
he says, " I verily thought that by invoking three
saints daily, and by letting my body waste away with
fasting and watchings, I should satisfy the law, and
shield my conscience against the goad of the driver.
But it all availed me nothing. The further I went
on in this way, the more was I terrified, so that I
should have given over in despair, had not Christ
graciously regarded me, and enlightened me with the
light of his gospel."

Need we any further proof that a long period intervened between his first conversations with Staupitz
and the time that the true light of the gospel broke
in upon his soul? Here he represents himself as in
the grossest darkness and in the most wretched condition, long after he had entered upon the duties
of the priesthood; and yet he was not ordained till
May 2, 1507. So much is certain; Staupitz was only
occasionally at Erfurt, probably not more than twice
or three times during Luther's residence in the cloister there. His first visit brought him in contact with

Luther, but had not the effect to extricate the latter from the scholastic errors in which he was completely entangled. It was at a later period, and probably after the second visit of Staupitz at Erfurt, that Luther wrote to him frequently on the subject of his wretchedness. "When I was a monk," said Luther once to his friends, "I wrote oft-times to Dr. Staupitz; and once I wrote to him, exclaiming, 'Oh, my sins, my sins!' Then Staupitz gave me this reply: 'You would be without sin, and yet you have no proper sins. Christ forgives true sins, such as parricide, blasphemy, contempt of God, adultery, and such like. These are sins indeed. You must have a register, in which stand veritable sins, if Christ is to help you.'" This paradoxical language is explained in a letter of Luther to Spalatin, written in 1544. "Staupitz once comforted me in my sorrow, on this wise: You would be a painted sinner and have a painted Christ as a Saviour. You must make up your mind that Christ is a very Saviour, and you a very sinner." The importance of these words to Luther, and their influence upon the character of Luther's subsequent religious views, as seen in all his writings, it will not be easy for the casual reader to apprehend. Luther was in serious error, and had great and incessant anguish on two points. He looked upon unintentional negligence or forgetfulness of the arbitrary rules of his order, which were as countless as they were foolish, as being a heinous sin against God; and then he supposed great sinfulness was a bar to forgiveness. On the former point, Staupitz used a little raillery; and on the latter, he furnished Luther the cardinal doctrine of the Reformation, that forgiveness did not depend at all upon the number or magnitude of one's sins, but

simply and solely on penitence for them. This is
what Luther means, where, hundreds of times in
his sermons and other writings, he says that the
Papists did not preach the gospel, which is the forgiveness of sins; but the law, which is only the
knowledge of sin, without a Saviour. We might fill
the remainder of this chapter with passages from
his works, which do nothing but re-echo the sentiment which he learned first from the lips of his
spiritual counsellor, and then by an uncommonly
deep and protracted experience. We must, therefore, not fail to notice, that in these very suggestions
of Staupitz lie the true seeds of the Reformation.
In proof of the above assertion, we will adduce but
one passage. We will take it from the same letter
to Spalatin just mentioned. "You have thus far
been but a slender sinner; you reproach yourself
with very trifling sins. Come and join yourself to
us, real, great and daring sinners, that you may not
make Christ of no account to us, who is a deliverer
not from pretending and trifling sins, but from true,
great, nay the greatest of sins. Let me put you in
mind of my own case, when I was tempted and tried
like as you now are, albeit I am now strong in Christ.
Believe the Scripture, that Christ is come to destroy
the works of the devil, of which this despondency is
one." This joyful and confident view of the infinite
fulness of a Saviour's love, instead of that terrifying
conception of him as a merciless judge and executioner, which he had hitherto entertained, constitutes
the radical difference between the Catholic and the
Protestant religion as a matter of experience. In
the one, good works are sought as a recommendation
to Christ, and these, though imperfect, are graciously
accepted and rewarded, so that faith itself is nothing

but a work of righteousness, beginning in the intellect and the outward act, and gradually becoming spiritual; in the other, Christ meets the sinner as a sinner, and takes the load himself, shows his adaptedness to just such cases; gives, of his own accord, a penitent and believing heart, and forgives gratuitously, and unites the soul to himself by faith, which is justifying only by virtue of this union.

It was a long time before Luther's mind was clear on this subject. The theory of the scholastic divines and the practice of the church had grown up with him. The new tendency, which began to make its appearance, was suppressed and hemmed in on every side. No expression in the Bible was more terrific to him than that of "the righteousness of God." The Fathers had explained it as that attribute of justice by which God executes judgment. "This interpretation," says Luther, "caused me distress and terror when I was a young theologian. For when I heard God called righteous, I ran back in my thoughts to that interpretation which had become fixed and rooted in me by long habit. . . . So powerful and pestilent a thing is false and corrupt doctrine, when the heart has been polluted with it from youth up." Staupitz and an aged confessor, whose name is not given, taught him that "the righteousness of God," in Paul's epistles, had a very different meaning, namely, that righteousness which becomes the sinner's the moment he believes in Christ Referring to this new explanation, he said: "Then I came to understand the matter, and learned to distinguish between the righteousness of the law and the righteousness of the gospel." "When I began," says he again, "to meditate more diligently upon the words 'righteous,' and 'righteousness of God,'

which once made me fear when I heard them: and
when I considered the passage in the second chapter
of Habakkuk, 'The just shall live by faith,' and
began to learn that the righteousness which is acceptable to God is revealed without the deeds of the
law, from that very time how my feelings were
changed! and I said to myself, If we are made
righteous by faith; if the righteousness which availeth before God is saving to all who believe therein,
then such declarations ought not to alarm the poor
sinner and his timid conscience, but rather be to
them a consolation." In another place he says, "I
had the greatest longing to understand rightly the
Epistle of Paul to the Romans, but was always
stopped by the word 'righteousness,' in the 1st
chapter and 19th verse, where Paul says, 'the righteousness of God is revealed in the gospel.' I felt
very angry at the term, 'the righteousness of God;'
for, after the manner of all the teachers, I was taught
to understand it, in a philosophic sense, of that righteousness by which God is just and punisheth the
guilty. Though I had lived without reproach, I
felt myself a great sinner before God, and was of a
very quick conscience, and had not confidence in a
reconciliation with God, to be produced by any work
of satisfaction or merit of my own. For this cause
I had in me no love of a righteous and angry God,
but secretly hated him, and thought within myself,
Is it not enough that God hath condemned us to
everlasting death by Adam's sin, and that we must
suffer so much trouble and misery in this life? Over
and above the terror and threatening of the law, must
he needs increase, by the gospel, our misery and
anguish; and, by the preaching of the same, thunder
against us his justice and fierce wrath? My con-

fused conscience oft-times did cast me into fits of anger, and I sought, day and night, to make out the meaning of Paul ; and, at last, I came to apprehend it thus : Through the gospel is revealed the righteousness which availeth with God, a righteousness by which God, in his mercy and compassion, justifieth us, as it is written, 'The just shall live by faith.' Straightway I felt as if I were born anew ; it was as if I had found the door of Paradise thrown wide open. Now I saw the Scriptures in altogether a new light, ran through their whole contents, as far as my memory would serve, and compared them, and found that the righteousness was the more surely that by which he makes us righteous, because everything agreed thereunto so well. . . . The expression, "the righteousness of God," which I so much hated before, became now dear and precious, my darling and most comforting word ; and that passage of Paul was, to me, the true door of Paradise."

This long passage is one of the most interesting to be found in all Luther's writings. Though we are rarely able to state positively the moment of one's conversion, we may confidently affirm that this paragraph refers us distinctly to the time when the scales fell from Luther's eyes, and when he broke through that complicated and strong net-work of papal error which had hitherto held him captive. From this time Luther is a new man. He had a footing of his own, and felt the strength of his foundation. Although he had almost every thing to learn in respect to this new land of promise, he knew that he was in it.

Again, we learn to a certainty here, that Luther's own mind laboured long and hard upon this point. Nothing can be more erroneous than the impression received by many from the meagre accounts commonly given of this struggle, that a few short and simple words of Staupitz speedily set him right. The process was very protracted and complicated, and the fierce contention between two opposite elements was carried on long and extended through all the domain of monasticism, its habits and usages, its Scripture interpretations, its dialectics, and the whole mass of its cumbrous theology. A gigantic effort of intellect was requisite in order that Luther should feel his way out, in opposition to all the scholastic and monastic influences, not only without the aid of the original Scriptures, but with a version (the Vulgate) in which the key word to this doctrine of justification was rendered by *justitia*, justice, which, with its false glosses, greatly increased the difficulty.

But we should err, if we were to dilute this great change down to a mere intellectual process. Luther himself viewed it very differently, and always represented it as a spiritual transformation, effected by the grace of God. He remarks on this subject, "Staupitz assisted me, or rather God through him. . . . I lay wretchedly entangled in the papal net. . . I must have perished in the den of murderers, if God had not delivered me. . . . His grace transformed me, and kept me from going with the enemies of the gospel, and from joining them now in shedding innocent blood." Who can doubt that he spoke from his own experience, when he said, "As soon as you receive the knowledge of Christ with sure faith, all anger, fear and trembling vanish in the twinkling of an eye, and nothing but pure compassion is seen in God! Such knowledge quickeneth the heart and maketh it joyful, and assured that God is not angry with us, but tenderly loveth us."

The remainder of the time that Luther spent in Erfurt, was employed in the study of the Christian Fathers, and especially the writings of Augustine, in connection with the Scriptures and the doctrine of justification.   That it is a mistake to place the study of Augustine and others of the church Fathers, except the casual reading of them, at an earlier period, is evident from the account given by Melancthon, who says it took place after he had ascertained the doctrine of justification by faith.   With the works of Augustine he became very familiar, and afterward he edited one of his treatises.   In the preface, he remarks, "I can safely affirm, from my own experience, that next to the Holy Scriptures there is no writer of the church who can be compared with Augustine in Christian learning."   Another favourite author with Luther at this time was Gerson, with whose moral writings he was particularly pleased, "because he alone, of all the writers of the church, treated of spiritual trials and temptations"

CHAPTER IV.

**LUTHER AS PROFESSOR IN WITTENBERG, TILL THE BEGIN-
NING OF THE REFORMATION IN 1517.**

SECTION I.—*Luther's Removal to Wittenberg.*

E now come to the close of an important period of Luther's life. During a residence of a little more than seven years in Erfurt, from July 17, 1501, to the autumn of 1508, in which he had passed from youth to the state of manhood, both his intellectual and religious character underwent a great transformation. Four years of time, devoted with signal success to secular learning in the university; and nearly three and a half to experimental religion and to theology in the monastery, changed the boy, who knew nothing of learning beyond the catechism and Latin grammar, and nothing of religion beyond a gloomy apprehension of it, and a crude mass of superstitions, into a mature scholar and theologian, to whom the young university of Wittenberg looked as to one likely to increase its usefulness and its fame. The appointment was very peculiar. Such was his modesty and his reluctance to appearing abroad in any public capacity, that Staupitz, as provincial of the order, peremptorily required him to repair to the monastery at Wittenberg, and to lecture there on philosophy. The conscientious monk, who had learned nothing more perfectly than he had the duty of obedience, and who, no doubt, would have resisted any entreaty and declined any appointment, hastened to comply with the order, not waiting even to take leave of his friends, and hardly providing himself with a change of apparel. Inasmuch as this event opens a new period in his life, in which an extraordinary development of character was wrought, and a transition made from the passive submission of the monk to the activity and control of one born to rule, it becomes necessary, at this point, to pause and take a survey of the new theatre of action upon which he was now entering, and of the widely different relations which he was henceforth to sustain.

WITTENBERG.

Probably Luther never saw this place till he went to take his station there for life. And what a station was that! and how did he fill it! Passing beyond Weimar, Naumburg and Leipsic, and directing his course toward Düben, which is about midway between Leipsic and Wittenberg, he would see spread out before him a rich arable tract of country, dotted with countless small villages. Only Eilenburg on the right, and Delitsch on the left, several miles distant, rise to the dignity of towns. Near Düben, pleasant woodlands and fine meadows begin to appear, and extend far in both directions along the banks of the Mulde. A mile beyond that town, Luther, of course, entered the Düben Heath, a desolate, sandy region, seven or eight miles in extent, covered with stunted trees, where an equally stunted race of wood-cutters, colliers and manufacturers of wooden-ware, led a boorish life. Near the entrance of the heath is a rock, called Dr. Luther's Rock, with the letters D. M. L. inscribed upon it, because he is said to have made a pause here once when on a journey, and to have taken a repast upon it. To the right of the heath, near the Elbe, is Schmiedeberg, whither the university was sometimes temporarily removed in seasons of peril. Beyond the river is the castle of Lichtenburg, where Luther held an anxious interview with Spalatin, in 1518, to determine whether he should retire from Wittenberg or not. North of this are Annaburg, the occasional residence of the electors, and the Cloister Lochau, so often mentioned by Luther. Directly on his route, lay Kemberg, which was also connected variously with the university. The last place he passed through was Prata, whose distance from Wittenberg, he once said, would give an idea of the width of the Po. To the left lay Sagrena, Carlstadt's resort, when he retired from the university, and lived as a peasant. Beyond this were seen the Elbe and the white sand hills, which gave to Wittenberg its name. The town itself, containing then three hundred and fifty-six houses, and about two thousand inhabitants, lay before him on the north side of the Elbe, and two hundred rods distant from it, in a long oval form, with the electoral church and palace at the western extremity, the city church in the centre, and the Augusteum or university toward the Elster gate, at the eastern extremity.

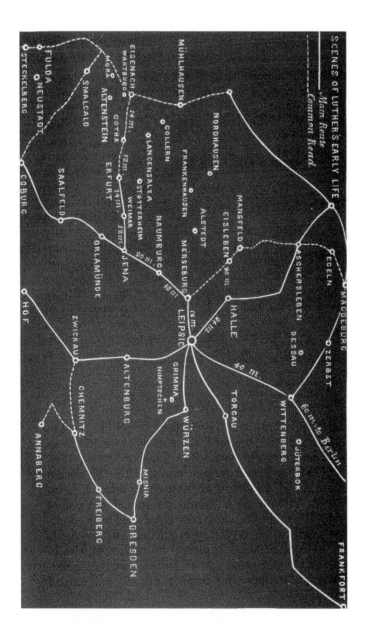

SCENES OF LUTHER'S EARLY LIFE

— Main Route
--- Common Roads

STECKELBERG
FULDA
NEUSTADT
SMALCALD
MORA
ALTENSTEIN
WARTBURG
EISENACH
GOTHA
14 m.
12 m.
COLLERN
NORDHAUSEN
MÜHLHAUSEN
ERFURT
14 m.
LANGENSALZA
STOTTERNHEIM
FRANKENHAUSEN
WEIMAR
NAUMBURG
COBURG
SAALFELD
12 m.
JENA
ORLAMÜNDE
20 m.
MERSEBURG
ALSTEDT
MANSFELD
EISLEBEN
30 m.
ASCHERSLEBEN
EGELN
MAGDEBURG
18 m.
12 m.
HALLE
DESSAU
ZERBST
24 m.
60 m. to Berlin
HOF
ZWICKAU
LEIPSIC
GRIMMA
NIMPTSCHEN
40 m.
TORGAU
WITTENBERG
JÜTERBOK
ALTENBURG
CHEMNITZ
WÜRZEN
ANNABERG
MISNIA
FREIBERG
DRESDEN
FRANKFORT

Though Wittenberg was the capital of the old electorate, its appearance was far from being splendid
On the north side are seen plains broken by sand
hills and copses of wood ; on the south, a low flat
heath, behind which flowed the broad Elbe, fringed
here and there with willow and oak shrubs. Many
wretched hamlets were seen in the distance, and the
city itself, if we except the public buildings, was but
little more than a cluster of mean dwellings. The
people were warlike, but so sensual that it was
thought necessary to limit their convivialities by
law. At betrothals, for example, nothing was allowed to be given to the guests, except cakes, bread,
cheese, fruit and beer. The last article so abounded
at Wittenberg, that it was said, "The cuckoo could
be heard there in winter evenings;" speaking, of
course, through the throats of the bottles. There
were one hundred and seventy-two breweries in the
city in 1513. Among the expenditures of the city,
recorded in the treasurer's books, for the ten years
preceding Luther's arrival, are moneys paid for fire-
arms ; for race-grounds, where oxen were the prize
won in the race; for paintings and masks used in
plays; for garments, masks, rings, scaffolding, linen,
dresses for Satan and his companions ; for Judas and
the two thieves, all to be used in the amusements of
Passion-week. Luther rarely speaks in praise of the
inhabitants in and about Wittenberg. At one time,
he says, "The Saxons are neither agreeable nor
civil;" at another time, "The Wittenbergers trouble
themselves neither about honour, courtesy, nor religion; they do not send their sons to school, though
so many come here from abroad." There seems to
have been an almost entire destitution of lower
schools here, at that time, and there was no Latin

school till 1519. The first press at Wittenberg, for printing learned works, that is, in the Latin language with the Roman type, was established in the Augustinian cloister, the year after Luther became an inmate there; and a German press had existed there only five years before his arrival.

What has just been said will find a sufficient explanation in the fact that Wittenberg was situated on the north-eastern verge of German civilization, being a border-town, between the Wends on the east and the Saxons on the west, and being as yet but feebly influenced by the refinements of learning, which came from the south and the west, from Italy and France. Cologne, Heidelberg and Erfurt were the principal seats of learning, until Wittenberg, ten years from this time, came to eclipse them all, and to fix the source and centre of illumination far to the north.

THE UNIVERSITY.

WITTENBERG UNIVERSITY had been in existence six years when Luther was appointed professor. Until 1507, it was supported chiefly from the funds of the Elector Frederic, who now incorporated with it the collegiate church, with all its sources of income, and the provostships of Kemberg and Clöden, the parish of Orlamünde, &c., the canons of the former becoming lecturers without cost or trouble, and the incumbents of the latter providing vicars in their churches, and removing to the university, where they lived upon their incomes. The university was organized after the model of Tübingen, and bore resemblance to the university of Erfurt. All these were less under ecclesiastical control than the universities of Louvain, Cologne, Ingoldstadt and Leipsic.

The rector —who must be unmarried, and maintain his dignity by studied seclusion, and appear in public only in great pomp,—assisted by three *reformers*, whose duty it was to superintend the instruction, and the deans of the four faculties, constituted the Academic Senate. The university, contrary to the usual custom, was under the protection of the elector, and not of the pope, or a cardinal, or an archbishop, a circumstance which greatly favoured the Reformation. None, therefore, but the elector could control the university from without, and none but the rector and his assistants, the *reformers*, could do it from within. These, however, had enough to do. In the very year that Luther came there, the students had so insulted some of the court of the Bishop of Brandenburg, that he put the whole city under the interdict, which was removed only on the payment of two thousand gulden. The year before, when Scheurl, a very energetic man, was rector, he checked the prevailing vice of intoxication among the students, and prohibited the practice of going armed with gun, sword and knife. Still, in 1512, another rector was assassinated by an expelled student; and Melancthon once barely escaped with his life.

Paul and Augustine were the patron saints of the theological faculty, a clear intimation on the part of Staupitz, the organizer and first dean of this faculty, that the theological system which he had always taught was to be favoured here. Thus a place was from the beginning prepared for Luther, who had studied Paul most of all the sacred writers, and Augustine most of all the ecclesiastical. The whole university was to observe the festivals of the saints of each faculty. The faculties were the theological, in which there were four professors : the law, in which there were five : the medical, in which there were three : and the philosophical, including science and literature, in which there were ten. In the theological faculty were Staupitz, Pollich, (one of the founders of the university,) Truttvetter, Luther's teacher in Erfurt, and Henning. Amsdorf and Carlstadt were teachers of the scholastic philosophy. There was as yet no teacher in Greek, Hebrew, or mathematics. The number of students who entered that year (1508) was one hundred and seventy-nine, and the whole number in the university could not have been more than four or five hundred, though it amounted in a few years to two thousand. As Luther passed rapidly through all the degrees conferred in theology, it becomes necessary to explain their nature. The first was that of *biblicus*, though the candidate ordinarily knew little of the Bible beyond a few papal glosses on favourite proof-texts : the second was that of *sententiarius*, who could lecture on the first two books of the Sentences of Peter Lombardus : the third was that of *formatus*, who could lecture on the last two books of the same author : the fourth was that of *licentiatus*, one licensed to teach theology in general : the fifth was that of doctor of divinity.

THE CHURCHES AND ECCLESIASTICAL RELATIONS OF WITTENBERG.

WITTENBERG belonged to the diocese of Brandenburg, of which Scultet was bishop, subject to the Archbishop of Magdeburg, who at that time and til 1513 was Ernest, brother of the Elector Frederic He was succeeded by Albert, of the Brandenburg family, who retained the see of Magdeburg after he became Archbishop of Mainz, and, of course, primate of Germany.   These, next after Staupitz, were Luther's ecclesiastical superiors.

The Electoral Church (called also the Church of Ursula and her eleven thousand virgins, or All Saints') gave, on account of its innumerable relics and unprecedented indulgences, a very superstitious air to the religious character of Wittenberg.   In 1353, the elector, who had been rewarded for his faithful services to the King of France by a thorn from the crown worn by Christ, erected a chapel for the relic, and appointed seven chaplains.   This grew by degrees into an important collegiate church, being exempted from the bishop's jurisdiction, and exercising the right of patronage over the other churches of the city.   When vacancies occurred in the chapter, the canons, the number of whom were increased to eighty, were presented by the elector.   All who worshipped here had forty days' indulgence. Every week occurred the anniversary of some saint, which was announced every Sunday, together with the relics to be shown.   The electoral church, which occupied the place of that old chapel, was erected by the Elector Frederic, and finished nine years previous to Luther's removal to this place. Relics were now, at great expense, collected from every quarter, the pope and foreign ecclesiastics aiding those who were engaged in the work.   They were divided into eight classes, and shown in as many courses to superstitious worshippers.   The number of the relics amounted to five thousand and five, which were enclosed in cases of wood, stone, glass, silver and gold, embossed with pearls.   Most of them belonged to holy virgins, widows, confessors, martyrs, apostles and prophets ; but the eighth class, containing three hundred and thirty-one, re-

lated to Christ, such as garments, teeth, hair in
abundance, relics of the children slain by Herod,
milk from the holy Virgin, thread spun by her
straw from the manger in Bethlehem, and fragments
from the cross, and from Mount Sinai. Every person, to whom all these, and another collection of
seventeen hundred relics should be shown, was entitled to fourteen hundred and forty-three years of
indulgence! equalled by no other place in Christendom except Assisi, the native place of St. Franciscus.
In this single church, 9901 masses were said, and
35,570 pounds of wax consumed every year! One
of the first books printed at Wittenberg after Luther
arrived there, was a " Description of the Venerable
Relics," with one hundred and nineteen wood-cuts.
This was the church where Luther sometimes preached,
where the higher degrees were conferred, and on
whose doors the ninety-five theses were posted up.
The city or parish church where most of Luther's
sermons were delivered, and of which Pontanus and
Bugenhagen were successive pastors, was in another
part of the town.

FREDERIC THE WISE—BORN 1463—DIED 1525.

THE reigning Saxon family was divided into two
branches, the Albertine and the Ernestine. From
Albert, (whose ordinary residence was Dresden,) descended Duke George, Luther's bitter enemy, and to
him succeeded first Henry and then Maurice. To
Ernest, who resided sometimes at Torgau and sometimes at Wittenberg, were born four distinguished
sons, the Elector Frederic the Wise, who in his
birth preceded Luther twenty years, and in his death
twenty-one; Albert, who at the age of eighteen was
Archbishop of Mainz, in 1482, but died in the same

year; Ernest, who, after being Administrator of
Magdeburg for several years, was archbishop from
1489 to 1513; and John the Constant, now associated with Frederic in the government, and in 1525
his successor.

If we bear in mind that the Archbishops of
Magdeburg and Mainz had large territories under
their civil government, and actually had more of
the character of princes than of ecclesiastics, we shall
not fail to perceive the great extent of the Saxon
dominion at the time that the family occupied all
the places above-named.   Hence the jealousy between that house and the house of Brandenburg,
when Albert, belonging to the latter, was at the same
time Archbishop both in Magdeburg and in Mainz.
This explains the circumstance that Tetzel, Albert's
agent in selling indulgences, was coolly received in
Saxony, but was favourably received in all the territories of the Brandenburg family.

Frederic, like all his brothers, was well educated,
and could write and speak the Latin and French, besides the German.   In the absence of the Emperor
Maximilian, in 1507, he administered the affairs of
the empire in the character of vicar.   He had done
the same before, and was called to do it once again at
the important crisis in respect to the Reformation,
during the interval between the death of Maximilian
and the election of Charles V., in 1519.   He attended thirty diets in all, in which he took frequently
the most important, and never a subordinate part.
He was, for those times, an admirable ruler in his own
territories; increasing steadily the power of the electorate, and commanding universal respect at home
and abroad.

Though surnamed the Wise, he was rather virtuous

and prudent than great. If he did not regard the
interests of Saxony too much, he regarded those of
Germany too little. He undoubtedly contributed his
share towards weakening and dividing the empire, by
uniting with other electors and princes in raising the
states to sovereignty and independence. His patriotism was narrower than that of Ulrich von Hutten,
Francis von Sickingen, or even Philip of Hesse.

As he was a liberal patron of letters, those who
have written his history were so much indebted to
him that their praises are to be received with some
little caution. He was a great lover of peace ; and it is
said, that during his reign blood never flowed in his
dominions. His private virtue was not quite spot-
less. Luther complains that intoxication was too
much indulged in at his court ; that taxes were sometimes oppressive ; and that the administration of
justice and of other public affairs was often too long
delayed. But he was remarkably upright and firm.
When the imperial throne became vacant, he refused
all presents offered him as elector by the competitors ;
declined the imperial crown when offered to him ;
and though he favoured the election of Charles, he
was active in limiting his authority by a capitulation
to be previously signed.

His cautious and hesitating course towards Luther
and the Reformation was undoubtedly favourable ;
inasmuch as it left the work to depend on spiritual
resources, and thereby kept it from assuming the
character of a political revolution. He was originally a superstitious but not bigoted papist. He
expended no less than two hundred thousand gulden
on his favourite collegiate church and its relics He
made a pilgrimage to Jerusalem, accompanied by the
painter Cranach and others. Of course there could,

at first, be but little sympathy between him and
Luther.

SECTION II.—*Luther's early Labours in Wittenberg.*

WE are now prepared to follow Luther in the new
scene of his labours.   The precise time of his journey thither is not known, but as we find his name
entered as teacher in the winter semester, or half-
year term, of 1508-1509, we may infer that he was
probably on the ground by November, to commence
the term.   Luther, who had so long resided in the
large and beautiful city of Erfurt, and, before that,
in Eisenach and Magdeburg, sensibly felt the change
when he came to a little, unattractive town, consisting mostly of a cluster of low houses, with mud walls
and thatched roofs.   " I wondered," said he, " that
a university should be placed here."   As monk, he
found his new home in the Augustinian cloister, which
the elector was then rebuilding.   How little did
Frederic, while preparing that apartment, which is
still preserved, or brother Martin, when taking up his
residence there, which he never afterwards changed
think that in this obscure place should be forged
the weapons, and from it the missiles be showered
forth which, in connection with other agencies, should
put to flight the ranks of the enemy, and change the
destinies of nearly all the north of Europe !   Parts
of the building it was necessary to take down during
Luther's lifetime, at which it was natural that he
should feel sad.   "If I should live another year,"
he remarked with emotion, " I must behold the removal of my poor little room, from whence I have
stormed the pope, for which cause it deserves to stand
for ever."

He commenced his labours by lecturing on the dialectics and physics of Aristotle, without salary or tuition fees. It is remarkable that he never received any thing from students for his labours, nor from booksellers for his writings.* After he laid aside the cowl, the elector gave him an allowance of two hundred gulden a year.

From the change through which Luther's mind had recently passed, and from the fresh interest he now took in the study of the Bible and of theology, we might infer that the Aristotelian philosophy would have few attractions for him. It was indeed with reluctance that he turned away from his favourite studies, and laid out all his strength in preparing for his philosophical lectures. So entirely was he obliged to surrender himself to his new occupation that he could not find time to write to his most intimate friends. A letter which he wrote to his old acquaintance, Braun, in Eisenach, a week after he was transferred to the department of theology, unbossoms to us his feelings during the first few months of his residence at Wittenberg. "That I came off," he writes, March 17, 1509, "without saying a word unto you, you must not marvel. For so sudden was my departure that my closest friends there hardly knew it. I would fain have written unto you, but could not then for lack of time, and could only but grieve that I was constrained to fly away in such haste, without bidding you farewell. But now, at God's command, or by his permission, I am here in

---

* The publishers of his works offered him four hundred florins a year, if he would give them his manuscripts; but he refused "to make merchandise of the gifts with which God had endowed him."

Wittenberg. Would you know my state and condition, I would say it is, by God's favour, very good, saving that I must force myself unto my studies, especially philosophy, before which I preferred theology from the beginning. I mean that theology which seeketh for the inside of the nut, for the kernel of the wheat beneath the husk, for the marrow within the bone. But God is God, and man often, nay, always, erreth in his judgment. This is our God, and he shall guide us in his loving-kindness for ever."

The circumstance that within about four months he became lecturer, or elementary teacher, in theology, renders it highly probable that Staupitz, and perhaps himself, considered his first appointment as merely preparatory to the second. At any rate, the ninth of March was a joyful day to him. In the university book, where his name is registered, we find the amusing remark : "On the ninth of March, master (*i. e.*, A. M.) Martin was admitted to the Bible, (*i. e.*, made *biblicus*,) but being called away to Erfurt hath not unto this time paid his fee." In the margin is added, in Luther's own hand, "And never will. I was then poor, and under the rule of monastic obedience, and had nothing to give. Let Erfurt pay."

The biblical bachelors knew nothing of the original languages of the Bible, nor did they in any respect resemble the modern professors of biblical literature. They merely studied the interpretations, or select passages of Scripture, given by the fathers, the popes and the councils. The study was but a superficial and hasty preparation for reading the books of sentences. According to the laws of the Wittenberg university, the biblical teacher must promise to teach the Scriptures one year, or, if he was a monk, half a-year. In the programme of lectures for the year 1507, the only one extant of that period, no lecturer of this kind is mentioned, and but little account was generally made of that office. Though Luther could not now read the Scriptures in the original languages, nor the Greek fathers except through Latin translations, his present views of theology, and his love of the Bible led him to enter upon his official duties with an unprecedented earnestness and zeal. To this and the following period he refers in a work published in 1539, in which, speaking of the assurance and yet the ignorance of his opponents, he says, "I have also read the Fathers, and that, too, before I set myself in such stiff opposition to the pope. I read them, too, with much more diligence than they have done who now bring them arrogantly and vauntingly against me. For I know that not one of them hath ever undertaken to lecture in the schools on a single book of the Bible, and make use of the writings of the Fathers as helps, as I have done. Let them take up a book of the Bible, and look for the glosses to be found in the Fathers, and it then will be with them as it was with me when I took up the epistle to the Hebrews, with the aid of Chrysostom's commentary; Titus and Galatians, with the aid of Jerome; Genesis, with the help of Ambrose and Augustine; and the Psalms with all the helps that could be found, and so of other books."

The impression, therefore, which his biblical lectures at first made, must have depended more on his having thrown his heart into it, and exhibited boldly and clearly some long forgotten doctrinal truths than upon his mastery of biblical studies.

THE monastic shyness and timidity which he had
before manifested adhered to him still.   Being
called upon about this time, probably in the summer of 1509, by Staupitz to preach, he manifested
extreme reluctance.   "It is no little matter," said
he, "to appear in place of God before the people,
and to preach to them."   As they were one day sitting in the cloister-garden, refreshing themselves in
the shade of a certain pear-tree, which was a place
of frequent resort, the case was long argued between
them, and Luther at length yielded.   His own account of the interview is thus given in the Table-
Talk.   "I had fifteen arguments with which I purposed, under this pear-tree, to refuse my vocation;
but they could nothing avail.   At the last I said,
Dr. Staupitz, you will be the death of me, for I cannot live under it three months.   Very well, in God's
name, go on !   Our Lord God hath many great things
to do : he hath need of wise folks in heaven, too."
He was, at the time he made this remark, sitting
in the same place with his friend Antony Lauterbach,
who was telling how much difficulty, trial and weakness, he experienced in preaching.   "My dear sir,"
said Luther, "it hath gone even so with me.   I had
as great a dread and terror of the pulpit as you
have; yet was I compelled to go right onward.   I
was constrained to preach, and to make a beginning
in the refectory with the brethren.   Oh, what a
horror I had of the pulpit !"   The spot where Luther first preached, is thus described by Myconius.
"In the new Augustinian cloister at Wittenberg, the
foundations of a chapel had indeed been laid, but
the walls were raised no higher than to a level with

the ground. Within them was yet standing a little old wooden chapel, about thirty feet long and twenty wide, the timbers thereof being laid in mortar, very much leaning, and propped up on all sides. By the wall on the south side was to be seen a pulpit of old rough-hewn planks, raised about an ell and a half from the floor. . . . In this poor little chapel did God cause his holy gospel, and his dear child Jesus to be born anew. It was no minster or great cathedral, though there were many thousands of them, that God chose for this purpose. But soon this chapel was too strait, and Luther was called to preach in the parish church."

How Luther overcame his timidity in preaching, he himself informs us. " When a preacher for the first time goeth into the pulpit, no one would believe how fearful he is, he seeth so many heads before him. When I go up into the pulpit, I do not look upon any one. I think them to be only so many blocks before me, and I speak out the words of my God."

Creuziger once said to Melancthon, "I do not like to see you at my lectures." "Nor do I," said Luther, " at mine, or at my pulpit discourses; but I bring the cross right before me, think Melancthon, Jonas, Pomeranus, &c., are not present, and count no one to be wiser in the pulpit than myself."

SECTION III.—*Journey to Rome.*

LUTHER's visit to Rome was of such consequence to him, that it demands our special attention. He travelled on foot with a brother, whose name is not mentioned, and, according to general usage, passed the nights in the various convents of his order that lay in his route. Travelling as a pilgrim to the holy apostolical see, with little intercourse, except with sequestered monks, he would not be likely to make all the observations upon the countries through which he passed, and their inhabitants, which would be expected of the curious traveller.

The first resting-place, of which any account is preserved on this journey, was at Heidelberg, whither he was accompanied by Staupitz. The chronicle of that city speaks of his visiting it "in 1510, when he was sent by the convent of the Augustinians to Rome." While there, he preached and engaged, as was usual, with the learned monks, in public disputations. His journey now took a south-easterly direction through Suabia into Bavaria. Tradition mentions Munich as one of the places at which he called as he proceeded on his way. The last point mentioned in Germany is Füssen, at the Tyrol pass, and the first in Italy is Milan. He consequently took a south-westerly direction in crossing the Alps, and passed near to Lake Como.

Some of his remarks on the character of the people, and of the countries, which fell under his observation, are not a little amusing. We will quote his own words. "Were I to travel much, I would go nowhere of a readier will than into Suabia and Bavaria; for there the people are kind

hearted and hospitable, and are forward to treat
strangers and pilgrims charitably, and give them full
their money's worth."   "When, in 1510, I was
journeying to Rome through Milan, I perceived that
a different mass-service was used there, and was told
I could not join in the celebration, because they
were Ambrosians." He speaks of Lombardy, as
" a goodly and pleasant country," as " a valley a hundred miles wide, on both sides of the Po, (which is
as wide as from Wittenberg to Prata,) extending
from the Alps to the Apennines." He adds, " In
Lombardy, on the Po, is a very rich Benedictine
cloister, with a yearly income of thirty-six thousand
florins. Of eating and feasting, there is no lack,
for that twelve thousand florins are consumed upon
guests, and as large a sum upon building. The residue goeth to the convent and the brethren. I was
in that cloister, and was received and treated with
honour." The air of Italy was so pestilential that
it was necessary to exclude it entirely during the
night by closing the windows. "That," said he,
" did I and my brother experience. When we were
in Italy, (near Padua,) on our way to Rome, we
slept at one time till six in the morning, with our
windows open, and when we awoke, we found our
heads so stopped with catarrh, and so heavy and
void of sense, that we could travel that day but
only five miles." At Bologna, he was taken so ill
that he despaired of recovery. His mind reverted
in its anxiety to the cardinal doctrine of his newly
adopted creed, the only point on which a clear light
had begun to shine, and he drew consolation from
those words, which three years before gave new life
to his soul, " The just shall live by faith." During
all his journey, this memorable passage would ever

and anon occur to his memory. He speaks with admiration of the foundling and other excellent hospitals which he saw at Florence, and gives evident signs of satisfaction at the honourable mention of the name of the Emperor Frederic, of Germany, whose sayings were still preserved among the people. At length he came in sight of Rome, whereupon, with the feelings of a pilgrim who has reached the hallowed spot of his most earnest longings, he fell prostrate to the ground, and raised his hands, and said, "Hail, sacred Rome, thrice sacred for the blood of the martyrs here shed!"

LUTHER IN ROME.

CICERO and Julius Cæsar would hardly have recognised the ecclesiastical city which Luther has just greeted, and with scarcely less difficulty would he recognise the Rome of the present day. Its hills, indeed, are the same, and the same Tiber flows there still. But Alaric, Genseric, Ricimer, and Totila had been there, and desolation reigned on many of the seven hills. Another priesthood, and a people of another faith were there; and instead of the temples of Jupiter Capitolinus, of Esculapius and of Apollo, were to be seen St. Peter's, the Lateran and Santa Maria Maggiore. Modern Rome was not yet in full existence. The residences of the great were still chiefly within the angle made by the curve of the Tiber, in the vicinity of the Campus Martius and the Circus.

Luther entered the Porta del Popolo, its northern gate. Near it was the Augustinian monastery, where he is said to have taken his lodgings and to have held mass as soon as he entered the city. On his right, across the river, and beyond the castle of St. Angelo, was seen the half finished St. Peter's, which had been begun and was now carried on by Pope Julius, that lover of war and of architecture. It was finished at a later period by Leo, who was equally fond of splendour, and who in the arts of peace was as heathenish as his predecessor was in the arts of war. As one enters the gate above mentioned, he finds himself in a square, from which diverge three long streets, in nearly direct lines, the one on the right running to the Campus Martius and near to the Pantheon; the one in front passing directly to the old Capitol and Forum ; the one on the left passing in a south-easterly direction across the Quirinal and Viminal hills, leaving the Diocletian Baths to the left, and extending to the Santa Maria Maggiore, which, with the Lateran, are next in splendour to St. Peter's. The Lateran, the proper parish church of the pope, and "the mother and head of all the churches of the world," is about half as much farther, and near the walls of the city. Directly south of this, and two miles beyond the walls is St. Sebastian's church, built directly over the catacombs. West from the latter, near the bank of the Tiber and a mile below the city, is St. Paul's, next in magnitude to St. Peter's.

This introductory view will enable us to follow Luther in his frequent visits to the sacred places in Rome, and to perceive the full import of his casual observations. Fortunately, a guide-book for pilgrims, —*Mirabilia Romœ*, the Wonders of Rome—had been prepared and was reprinted the very year of Luther's pilgrimage. Of the general appearance of the city, he remarks, "Rome, as it now appeareth, is but a dead carcase compared with its ancient splendour.

The houses now rest on ground as high as the roofs
once stood, so deep are the ruins.   This do we perceive at the banks of the Tiber, where the ruins
reach perpendicularly to the length of two spears,
such as are used by our troops."   "Rome, where the
most magnificent buildings once stood was razed to the
ground by the Goths.   On the hill, and the Capitol,
stands a Franciscan convent."   "Rome, as I saw it,
is full five miles in circumference.   The vestiges
where ancient Rome stood can scarcely be traced.
The theatre and the Baths of Diocletian are still to
be seen. . . . The erection of St. Peter's has lasted
more than thirteen hundred years, (including the
old building,) and upon it a huge sum of money has
been expended."   "In the Pantheon at Rome, now
converted into a church, are representations in paintings of all the gods. . . . When I was there, I saw
this church.   It had no windows, but was one high
vault, with an opening above to admit the light.   It
had large marble pillars, which could hardly be com-
passed by two men with their arms extended."

Luther visited Rome as a pilgrim.   Twice while
in Erfurt had he vowed to make a pilgrimage to
Rome; and he himself affirms that he made the
journey in consequence of his vows.   This statement does not, however, stand in the way of his
having other objects to accomplish at the same time.
Rome was then regarded as second only to Jerusalem
in sacredness.   The soil was supposed to be hallowed, not only by the graves of thousands of martyrs,
and many Roman bishops, but of the apostles Peter
and Paul.   Pilgrims came in multitudes, sometimes
two hundred thousand at a time, to visit this sacred
city.

"The Wonders of Rome," the guide-book already mentioned, describes the stations, the relics, and the indulgences, especially those connected with the seven principal churches. The Lateran church had power to give as many days of indulgence as the drops of rain which would fall in three days and nights. Each chapel belonging to the group of the Lateran buildings, each altar and relic, had, moreover, its particular number of indulgences. Instructions are given how to deliver souls from purgatory by means of *Pater nosters* and *Ave Marias*. When Luther was there paying his devotions, with frantic zeal like the rest of the infatuated multitude, he regretted, as he says, that his father and mother were both living, so desirous was he to release their souls from purgatory. He afterwards alludes to this insane passion with bitter scorn and contempt, saying, "How gladly would I then have made my mother happy, but was denied the opportunity, and must content myself with a good dried herring!" "Such a foolish saint was I, running to all the churches and sepulchres, and believing all the pitiable stories that were told me."

According to the same book, one may obtain every day at the high altar of St. Peter's eighteen years indulgence and eighteen *carenas*, each carena being equal to seven years and forty days' fasting. All the past sins of every visitor who comes with good intention can be forgiven. He who devoutly goes up and down the stair-way to St. Peter's, has a thousand years' indulgence in respect to penance imposed; and seven times as much if he look at the handkerchief of St. Veronica containing the likeness of the Saviour. Luther went up those stairs on his knees to obtain the large indulgence promised; but while he was so doing a voice like thunder seemed to say to him, "The just shall live by faith." No wonder that his former experience should come up like a spectre before him, and rebuke his idolatrous worship. His mind was then like a field overgrown with briars and thorns, in which, however, one good germ had taken root, that was soon to produce a great fruit-bearing tree—one which should overshadow all the rest and take up the strength of the soil.

In regard to the pretended handkerchief which St. Veronica is said to have given to Christ in his agony to wipe off his sweat, and upon which, when applied to his face, his likeness was miraculously impressed, Luther remarks, evidently from personal observation: "It is nothing but a black square board, with a cloth hung before it, and before that another which is raised when the Veronica is shown. The poor besotted pilgrim can see nothing but a cloth before a black tablet. That is what they call seeing the Veronica; and with such low falsehoods are connected great devotion and large indulgences." There was never such a person as Veronica; and the name was unknown till the Middle Ages. It is the corruption, as Mabillon and others have shown, of the two words *vera* and *icon*, a true image, which were inscribed beneath paintings of Christ's countenance upon cloth.

Luther, while credulously gazing at such sacred relics in St. Peter's church, saw also the heads of the apostles Peter and Paul in the court before the church. "They boast at Rome of having the heads of Peter and Paul, and show them as sacred relics, though they are nothing but wooden heads, made by a bungling artist. I can boldly affirm, according to what I myself have seen and heard at Rome, that

no one there knows where the bodies of St. Paul
and Peter lie. . . The popes show every year (on
St. Peter and Paul's day) to the blind and silly
populace two heads of Peter and Paul, carved in
wood, and would fain make them believe that these
are the veritable skulls of Peter and Paul; and on
the altar where these heads are preserved, the pal-
liums of the bishops are consecrated."

Of the catacombs of Rome, which extended all
along the eastern part of the city and the adjacent
country, from the church of St. Sebastian or St. Calixtus to that of St. Agnes without the walls, Luther speaks more than once. They evidently filled
his imagination, as well they might, more completely
than any thing else he saw at Rome. In early
times, great excavations were made under the city
to furnish stone and sand for building. In this
complete net-work of subterranean passages, the
Christians secreted themselves during the persecutions, buried all their dead there for two or three
centuries, placing them in niches at the sides of the
passages; and built small chapels near the bodies of
the martyrs, where they resorted for prayer and
the communion service.

Thus, while pagan Rome was in the light of
day above, living in splendour and luxury, and
putting the Christians to death, or driving them
from the abodes of men, Christian Rome, beneath
the surface of the earth, "the church in the catacombs" as Maitland calls it, was preparing to
come forth from her caverns and take possession
of the city above. "At Rome," says Luther, "by
the church of St. Calixtus (or St. Sebastian) lie
in one vault, as is said, more than eight thousand
martyrs and that is a most sacred spot. Under the

church, enclosed in sarcophagi, lie one hundred and
seventy-six thousand holy bodies, and forty-five popes
who were martyrs. The place is called the *Crypt.*
For full three hundred years did the persecutions
rage; and they rose to such a pitch of fury that, as
we learn from history, seventy thousand martyrs
were slain in the empire in one day. There is still
to be seen at Rome a burial-place, where, as it is said,
eighty thousand martyrs and forty-six bishops lie."
The exaggeration in these accounts which were given
to Luther, consists not so much in the numbers of
the dead, as in pronouncing them, on fallacious
grounds, martyrs. These catacombs, which were
closed in Luther's time, as they had been during
all the Middle Ages, have since been opened, and
their contents, containing a wonderful history in
the inscriptions, placed in the Vatican.

But Luther saw other things which shocked his
feelings, though they did not then shake his faith.
Afterwards, when he came to understand the true
character of the papacy, the recollections of what he
had seen at Rome were constantly springing up in
his mind as illustrations of the most shocking corruption of the church. "The pope," he observes,
"moves as if making a triumphal entry, with beautiful and richly caparisoned horses before him, and
he himself bears the sacrament upon a splendid
white palfrey." "At Rome, when they pronounce
the ban of excommunication, about twenty cardinals
sit and throw from them burning torches, extinguishing them by the cast, thereby showing that the well-
being and salvation of the persons so excommunicated
will be extinguished in like manner. And (as a little
bell was rung at the same time) this ceremony was
called lighting and tinkling a man." Little did

Luther think while learning such things at Rome that he was one day to be thus "lighted and tinkled." In another place he says, "I have been in Rome, have held many mass-services there, and have seen others hold many in a way that filleth me with horror when I think thereupon." In the following, he seems to speak as one who had been an eye-witness. "What Christian can, without pain, observe that the pope, when he is to partake of the communion, sitteth still like a gracious lord, and maketh a cardinal, with bended knee, reach to him the sacrament in a golden tube!" He speaks of the revolting licentiousness which prevailed even among the cardinals whom he saw, and pronounces the Roman court a brothel. He adds, "I myself have heard people say openly, in the streets of Rome, if there be a hell, Rome is built upon it." He once said he would not take one hundred thousand florins for what he had seen at Rome; "we speak of what we have seen." Still all these abominations did not alienate Luther from the Roman church. He revered her, in spite of the sins of pope and cardinal, monk and priest. As late as 1519, he could say, "The Roman church is honoured of God above all others. . . There St. Peter and St. Paul, and forty-six popes and many thousand martyrs did shed their blood. . . Though, alas! it is not as it should be at Rome, notwithstanding there is, and can be, no reason for separating from it."

SECTION IV.—*Luther at Wittenberg again.*

OF his return from Rome, and of his studies and
occupations for the next succeeding year or two but
little is known. The first important event after that
period is his promotion in theology, in 1512. He
had taken the second degree, or that of sententiarius,
during the interval, probably in 1511, both at Wittenberg and at Erfurt. Of the singular dispute
which afterwards arose between him and the monks
of Erfurt on this subject, mention will be made
elsewhere.

Staupitz, who had interested himself so deeply in
Luther's welfare ever since his first acquaintance
with him, and who, for the benefit of the church,
had undertaken to guide his steps, was not disappointed in the hopes he had entertained of his young
friend. He had already made him reader at table
in the monastery, substituting the Scriptures in the
place of Augustine's writings, which had hitherto
been read to the monks during meal times. He
was raised to the rank of licentiate in theology, (the
next degree above sententiarius,) the 4th of October,
1512, and finally to the degree of doctor of divinity,
on the 19th of the same month. His reluctance to
receive this honour, (or rather office as it then was,)
appears to have been not less than that which he
felt when it was proposed to make him preacher.
It was manifested in a similar way, and overcome
by similar arguments. In his letter of invitation to
the Erfurt convent to attend the ceremony, he says,
he is to receive the degree "out of obedience to the
fathers and the vicar." In a dedicatory epistle to
the Elector Frederic, written several years after he

says, "At your expense was the doctor's hat placed upon my witless head, an honour at which I blush, but which I am constrained to bear, because those whom it is my duty to obey would have it so." Among the letters of Luther is found the receipt which he signed for the fifty florins furnished him by the elector for paying the costs of the degree. A doctor's ring of massive gold was presented to him by the elector at the same time, which is still to be seen in the library of Wolfenbüttel. On the 19th of October the ceremony was performed with great pomp, with solemn procession and the ringing of the great bell. This appointment—for it was not a mere honour—given him by the united voice of his religious superiors, his sovereign, and the university, he construed, and ever after regarded, as a Divine call to teach religion in the most public manner. "I was called," says he, "and forced to the office, and was obliged, from the duty of obedience, to be doctor contrary to my will, . . . and to promise with an oath to teach purely and sincerely according to the Scriptures." Tübingen and Wittenberg were the only universities where such an oath was required. Under this oath, administered to him by Carlstadt, Luther claimed the right to appeal to the Bible as the only ultimate authority, and thus formally did he plant himself upon the fundamental principle of Protestantism.

At the time, both he and the highest authorities, secular and ecclesiastical, supposed there was a substantial agreement between the teachings of the church and those of the Bible. When he became thoroughly convinced of the contrary, he adhered to the letter of the oath, and turned it against the very power that had exacted it. He even burnt the papal bull, as he says, "because his title, office, station and oath required him to overthrow or ward off false, dangerous, and unchristian doctrines!" Thus when his enemies assailed him as a disobedient son of the church, he availed himself of this defence. When Satan sorely pressed him with doubts and temptations in respect to the great commotion which he was the means of exciting in the Christian world, his heart found assurance and his conscience relief, in recurring to his public and formal call. In reference to this matter he remarks: "At the command of the pope and of the emperor, (both of whom had given to the university authority to confer degrees,) and in a regular and free university, (its freedom, too, had been conceded to the elector,) I began, as became a doctor who had taken an oath to that effect, to explain the Scriptures before all the world, . . and having begun thus to do, I had cause to continue, and cannot now with a good conscience go back or break off, even though pope and emperor should put me under the ban." Whether all his reasoning on the subject was strictly correct or not, he was evidently very conscientious about it. He affirms that he had times of distress in relation to this point, when he felt the perspiration start all over him.

The period of about two years immediately following the date above-mentioned, appears to have been chiefly taken up in preparing for his lectures, and in acquiring the original languages of the Bible. The only events mentioned in connection with him during that time, are a disputation, in 1512, by a candidate for the first degree in theology, and another in 1513, for the second degree, at both of which he was the presiding officer. Such things were of frequent occurrence with him at a later period. Inasmuch as it is evident that Luther knew little of Greek or Hebrew before the year 1513, whereas we find him making use of both with some facility the next year, the inference is plain, that he must have studied them zealously about this time. Mathesius represents Luther as "spelling out the words of the Bible" after he commenced lecturing upon it. The first books on which he lectured were the Epistle to the Romans and the Psalms, which the same biographer informs us, took place immediately after he was made doctor. How admirably would lecturing on that epistle agree with the long and hard struggle through which his mind had passed on the subject of justification; and how well was such an exercise adapted to prepare him for his great work as Reformer! In the Psalms, too, so peculiarly a book of the heart, how much would a man of Luther's ardent, devout, and poetical mind, discover to be just what his religious necessities called for! Here we find in part the secret of his great success as a university lecturer. He not only brought to light treasures of spiritual knowledge from an almost forgotten book, but treated of those subjects in which his whole soul felt a vital interest, and that, too, in the ardour of acquisition both as a scholar and as a Christian.

"These writings," (the Epistle to the Romans and the Psalms,) says Melancthon, "he explained after such a sort that, in the estimation of all pious and intelligent persons, a new day, succeeding a long night of darkness, was dawning upon the Christian doctrines." His earnest discussions, in which he clearly distinguished between law and gospel, justification by works and justification by faith, opened a new world of ideas to the student. Still his interpretations, judged by a modern standard, must often appear imperfect.

Let us here pause a moment and contemplate the position he now held. He had fully adopted the two great Protestant principles of justification by faith in Christ, and the right of private judgment in interpreting the Scriptures; but he was by no means aware that these were the germs of a new order of things which could not be developed without separating him from the church. Meantime he was becoming a bold, strong, and independent thinker, and beginning already, without directly intending it, to wield a commanding and renovating influence over his pupils and friends. Others, who had opposed the church, had fixed their eye primarily on certain evils, and begun, of set purpose, to operate against them, using religion as a means only to that end, and thereby became but negative reformers. Such were the promoters of classical learning, who were offended at the ignorance and stupidity of the clergy, and many of the actors at the councils of Constance and Basle, who were more anxious to crush the power of the pope and correct public abuses than to revive a spirit of primitive piety. But Luther first fed, for a long time, the flame of experimental religion in his own heart, and then spread the fire by his conversations and lectures, and thus became the instrument of a regenerating movement by merely unfolding and expounding the religious elements which he brought with him from the convent of Erfurt.

In the Wolfenbüttel library is preserved Luther's copy of the Psalms in Hebrew, printed on a quarto-page, in the centre of which stands the Hebrew text, with wide spaces between the lines. On the broad margin and between the lines are to be seen the notes, in Latin, of his first lectures on this book, delivered probably in 1513. It is believed that he caused copies to be printed in this form for the greater convenience of the students in taking notes and connecting them with the words of the text. The great value of this singular book consists in the record it contains of Luther's religious and theological views at that period. Jürgens, who has carefully examined this earliest of Luther's Scripture expositions which have been preserved—it exists only in manuscript, and in Luther's hand-writing—remarks: "It contains the clearest indications how little Luther had advanced in biblical interpretation; and yet it occasionally points to the way in which he afterwards became so eminent as an expositor of Scripture. We refer particularly to his disposition to go back to the original sources. But he appears still to be without a competent knowledge of the Hebrew. He makes use of a defective Latin translation, agreeing with the Vulgate, and adheres closely to it, though he knows the Hebrew text, and constantly refers to it as well as to the Greek version." We find him, as he is represented by these notes, still a perfect monk, filled with all the monastic notions and superstitions; in his interpretation, given to allegory and conceits, except on two or three points where he becomes luminous, which circumstance gives to the whole the appearance of a morning twilight with its attendant indications of approaching day. We must constantly keep this in mind; for with him, the dawning light approached slowly, and for ten years it was dark in the west after the east was streaked with red.

It is now time to notice more particularly his misunderstanding with the university at Erfurt. It seems that after he had taken his second degree in theology in Wittenberg, complaints were made from Erfurt, where he had received his education, and that he consequently postponed lecturing on those subjects for which that degree was regarded as a license, and went to Erfurt, and with some difficulty obtained the degree there. Three or four years afterwards, some monks of that city, who envied his growing reputation, attempted to humble him by circulating reports unfavourable to his integrity, and by going back to that old difficulty to rake up evidence against him.

As the correspondence contains some of the earliest indications of the slumbering lion that was in him, it will be a matter of interest to glance at its character. The affair itself remains in great obscurity. Only two letters of Luther's are extant to give us any light on the subject; and of these but one is published. The new complaint was, that Luther, in taking the degree of doctor in divinity at Wittenberg instead of Erfurt, had violated an oath he had taken when he received the degree of master in theology, or sententiarius at the latter place. The accusation was made by a certain master Nathin, who was both inmate of the convent and teacher in the university.

Luther's first letter on the subject is dated June 16, 1514, and is directed to the prior and seniors of the Erfurt convent. In this he refers to two preceding letters, now lost, in which he had refuted the charges falsely brought against him. There was, indeed, a law in the Erfurt university requiring that he who should receive the first degree in theology there, should take an oath to receive the second there also; and he who received the second was to do the same in regard to the degree of doctor of divinity. He exculpated himself by saying that he never took the first degree at Erfurt, but at Wittenberg; and that, in taking the second, nothing was said or done about the oath. The irregularity, therefore, was on the part of his accusers, and not on his. But let us hear his own words:

"Although I have heard and read sundry evil reports spread by some of your convent which make against you, and more particularly against myself; yet, by the late letters of master John Nathin, written in the name of you all, by his falsehoods, his biting words, his bitter provocations and reproaches, I was so disturbed that I came near pouring out, after the example of master Paltz, both upon him and upon the whole convent, the full vials of my wrath and indignation. For this cause I wrote unto you two foolish letters. I know not whether they came into your hands, and should soon have sent you the hidden mystery thereof, had not that slanderous tongue been silenced by your convocation. I am, therefore, constrained to excuse many of you, nay, most of you. If, then, you were in any degree offended, or if some of you find yourselves mentioned by name in those letters, take in good part what I have done, and reckon it all to the account of the bitter things which master Nathin did write. For my vehement indignation was just. But now do I hear what is yet worse, that this same man everywhere proclaimeth, I know not on what grounds, that I am a perjured and infamous person. I request you, since I fear you cannot stop his mouth, to avoid him, and warn others not to regard his speeches. I have violated no oath, for I was promoted in another place. Both the universities and you all know that I did not receive my biblical degree, wherein the oath is taken, at Erfurt. Nor am I conscious of ever having taken any oath in my whole course. My degree of sententiarius I did, in truth, take at Erfurt; but no one, I trow, will affirm that I took any oath. But what master Nathin hath yet to hear from me, concerning the authority given unto me to teach and to govern, (when the degree was conferred,) will perhaps be seen at the proper time. I write these things, most excellent fathers, to the end that the Erfurt theologians may not look upon me as a despiser of their university; to which, as to a mother, I attribute all that I have. I have not contemned them, nor will I ever, although my abode and promotion elsewhere have separated me from them. The convent could then, with a word, have prevented both of these events, if it had desired. But what it could then do, but would not, it cannot now do, if it would. Thus, it hath pleased God to bring to nought the dissensions and threatenings of them that were asking for vengeance. But let them go on. I am at peace and reconciled unto you all, though I was offended. God hath singularly blessed me, unworthy as I am, so that I have cause only to rejoice, to love, and to do good to them that deserve the contrary of me, just as I receive of the Lord the contrary of what I deserve. I therefore pray you to be resigned, and lay aside bitterness, if any remains, and no to be disturbed by my connection with another university, for so God would have it, and we cannot resist him."

The other letter was written in January of 1515, and directed to the theological faculty of the university. It enters more into particulars. which we must pass over with the single remark that it states the fact of his having been called to Erfurt to be examined in respect to the degree of *sententiarius*, which he had received at Wittenberg, and which, after much difficulty, was confirmed at Erfurt. Nathin, of course, had continued his opposition, till the university was so far affected by his representations that it was necessary for Luther to exculpate himself before them.

In the tone of these letters, we look in vain for the spirit of the once timid and submissive monk. He comes forward, single-handed, against a host, with a sense of his rights; and a consciousness not only of his innocence, but of his power. With a desire for peace, and the olive leaf in his hand, he, at the same time, gives no doubtful indications that he is prepared for war. Here we see the same Luther that could stand up alone at the diet of Worms, and speak without fear, before emperor and princes and cardinals.

Something more than the mere habit of lecturing had contributed to this result, in respect to his present boldness of character. His biographers state that he had held frequent public disputations with his colleagues, and that in these he always came off triumphant. The reason of his meeting so much opposition was, that he advocated new and strange views; and the reason of his being victorious was, as well that he was in the right, as that he knew how to maintain his ground. He openly assailed the authority of Aristotle in theology, on whom the sententiarists mainly relied. Carlstadt and Truttvetter, in particular, disputed him.

The point in debate was fundamental. It related, as Luther says, to first principles, namely, whether the doctrines of the schoolmen, who followed Aristotle, were to be received on the assumption that they were true, and argument to proceed from them as from well-settled principles; or, whether these doctrines were themselves to be called in question, and examined anew in the light of Scripture and of reason. Both parties were well aware that on this hinge turned all the questions between the old and the new, the scholastic and the biblical views of theology. Luther fought out the battle with gigantic strength. He completely converted Carlstadt and the other young theologians to his biblical doctrines. Truttvetter, his old teacher, not being able to maintain his position, and not being willing to succumb to his own pupil, retired from the conflict, and went back to Erfurt in 1513. Luther afterwards supposed he was the innocent cause of hastening the death of that sturdy old scholastic divine.

In all this, it is easy to find an explanation of the perfectly independent and decided tone with which Luther stood up and declared that he could but just refrain from "pouring out the full vials of his wrath against the whole convent;" and, perhaps, the return of Truttvetter, under such circumstances, to the university of Erfurt, will suggest at least one reason why the calumny of Nathin should be listened to there, after it had been put down at the convent.

The little information we have respecting Luther from the beginning of 1515, to the beginning of 1516, may be regarded as indirect evidence that he was going steadily and prosperously on in the course he had begun, constantly accumulating that power and influence which was so soon to be put in requisition. The interest he felt in the controversy which was then raging between Reuchlin and the stupid Dominicans at Cologne, in respect to the utility of the study of the Hebrew and Greek languages, and

the advancement which he himself made in the
knowledge of these languages about this time, put
it beyond doubt that the lectures which he delivered
on the various books of the Bible were founded,
more and more, on the original Hebrew and Greek
Scriptures. He also continued earnestly engaged in
academic disputations, for, from some of the older
professors, he still met with opposition. During this
year, he was made dean of the theological faculty,
and under him, according to the university records,
a large number of Augustinian eremites received
their degrees in theology. Odelkop, who heard his
lectures, particularly those on the Epistle to the
Romans, at this time, says Luther diligently prosecuted his studies and preached, and delivered lectures and held debates. In this year were preached
the first three discourses of his which have been preserved. In these he manifests decided progress in
the clearness and solidity of his religious views. In
the first of those discourses, he strongly urges the
doctrine, that piety consists not in outward works,
but in an inward principle; that an act, in itself good,
becomes even sinful if the motive be sinful. Nothing could more clearly indicate that Luther was
outgrowing the discipline and tuition of that church,
whose religion consisted chiefly in outward forms
and ceremonies, and whose theology was as void of
vitality as was its piety.

1516.

Not only is this an important year in the life of
Luther, as a period of transition from a condition
of comparative retirement to one of great publicity,
as forming the boundary line between Luther the
learned and somewhat disputatious monk, and Lu-

ther the Reformer; but here, for the first time, the mist of obscurity which has hitherto mantled his personal history is cleared away, and, from this period on, all the principal events of his life are so fully chronicled that we can follow his course with comparative ease. Of his published letters, only seven precede this date : one in 1507, inviting his friend Brown to his ordination as priest; one in 1509, to the same, excusing himself for having come away from Erfurt without taking leave of him; one in 1510, to Spalatin, expressing a favourable opinion of Reuchlin, and censuring his opponents; two in 1512, the former being an invitation to the convent at Erfurt to be present at his promotion to the rank of doctor of divinity, the latter being his receipt for fifty florins to defray the expenses of the ceremony; and two in 1514, the one, the bold letter already mentioned, relating to his difficulties with Erfurt the other a second letter to Spalatin, condemning the course of Ortuin, one of Reuchlin's opponents at Cologne. In this last, we perceive that vein of drollery and sarcasm with which his subsequent writings abound. He speaks of that "poetaster," as he calls him, in terms of derision and scorn, and allows himself to use language always objectionable, but less noticed then than at the present day. After applying to him several opprobrious epithets, he adds: "I think that he himself, instructed by our Reuchlin, did feel his asinity, so to express myself, to such a degree that he meditated laying aside the ass and putting on the majesty of the lion, but unluckily, undertaking a metamorphosis beyond his strength, he took too short a leap, and fell into a wolf or crocodile."

Though up to this period we have in all only

seven or eight of his letters preserved, in the single
year 1516 we have twenty, in the following year
twenty-three, in 1518, fifty-six, and so on, to the
amount of five large octavo volumes. From these
letters alone a tolerably full biography of Luther
might be written.

February 2, 1516, he writes to his intimate friend,
John Lange, prior of the cloister at Erfurt, a letter
which strikingly illustrates the state of his mind in
respect to the Aristotelian philosophy, and the scholastic theology founded upon it; and also the relations of his old teachers, Truttvetter, or Jodocus
of Eisenach, as he generally calls him, and Usingen,
both to scholasticism and to himself. He writes:
" I send the accompanying letter, reverend father,
to the excellent Jodocus of Eisenach, full of positions against [the Aristotelian] logic, philosophy
and theology, that is, full of blasphemies and male-
dictions against Aristotle, Porphyry, and the sententiarists, the pernicious study of this our age. . . .
See that these be put into his hands, and take pains
to find out what he and all the rest think of me in
this matter, and let me know. I have no other
more eager desire than to make known to many,
and, if I have time, to show to all, how ignomini-
ously that old actor, under his Greek mask, playeth
and maketh pastime with the church. . . . My
greatest sorrow is, that I am constrained to see
brethren of good parts and of gifts qualifying them
for study, spend their time and waste their lives in
such vain pursuits, while the universities cease not
to burn and to condemn good books, and then make,
or rather dream out new ones in their room. I wish
Usingen as well as Truttvetter would leave off these
studies, or at least be more moderate therein. My

shelves are stored with weapons against their writings, which I perceive to be utterly useless; and all others would see the same, were they not bound to a more than Pythagorean silence."

Thus we see Luther hating Aristotle, because the scholastic theologians perversely put him in the place of the prophets and apostles; entertaining a feeling of respect for his two principal university teachers, and yet doubtful whether what he wrote to them would not rather offend than enlighten them; impatient to expose the monstrous abuse, pitying the hapless youth who must be perplexed with these tedious studies only to be misled; indignant at those birds of night at Cologne, who scream out, "Heresy!" at what they have not sense enough to comprehend; confident that he possesses the means of exploding the whole system; but sighing over the timidity of those who would easily be convinced but for their fear of giving offence. Nothing but time and circumstances were wanting to call him out, even at this early period.

But there was another element of character combined with this, that gave depth and a regenerating power to Luther's influence. In a letter dated April, 1516, we learn that his mind was, in reference to that particular feature, undergoing a most favourable development.

Our meaning will be apparent by the language of the letter itself. After a few words relating to a certain economical transaction, he writes to Spenlein, a monk of Memmingen, a little south of Ulm: "But I desire to know how it is with your soul; whether, weary of your own righteousness, you have learned to refresh yourself with, and put your trust in, the righteousness of Christ. For in our times presuming of ourselves is the chief temptation, especially in them that are striving with all their might to be righteous and good. Being ignorant of the righteousness of God, which is abundantly and freely given to us in Christ, they seek continually to perform good works of themselves until they can have confidence to stand before God, adorned in their own good works and merits, which is impossible. When you were with us [in the cloister at Erfurt?] you were of this opinion, or rather in this error, and so was I. I still have to fight against this error in myself, and have not yet altogether overcome it. Therefore, my dear brother, acquaint yourself with Christ and him crucified; learn to praise him; despairing of yourself, say to him, 'Lord Jesus, thou art my righteousness, and I am thy sin: thou hast taken to thyself what is mine, and given me what is thine: thou hast assumed what thou wast not, and given to me what I was not.' Beware of aspiring to such purity as to be unwilling to appear, and also to be in very deed, a sinner. For Christ dwelleth only in sinners. For this cause Christ descended from heaven, where he dwelleth in the righteous, to the end that he might dwell also in sinners. Meditate upon this love of his, and you will find therein his most sweet consolations. For if by our toils and conflicts we could obtain peace of conscience, why should he die? Therefore you will not find peace save in him, by utterly despairing of yourself and of your own works. Learn then of him, as he received you and made your sins his own, so to make his righteousness yours.

"If you steadfastly believe this as you ought, (and cursed is he who believeth it not,) then receive your brethren, who have been refractory and gone astray, and patiently carry them along and make their sins yours; and if you have any thing good, let it be theirs, as the apostle saith, 'Receive one another even as Christ hath received you to the glory of God;' and again, 'Let the same mind be in you which was in Christ Jesus, who when he was in the form of God, emptied himself,' &c. So you, if you seem to yourself to be better, do not look upon it as a plunder, as if it were yours alone; but empty yourself, and forget what you are, and be as one of them, and bear them in your arms. His is an unhappy righteousness which maketh him unwilling to support others who appear worse in comparison, and maketh him flee and retreat when he ought to be present and succour them by his patience and prayers and example. This is burying the Lord's talent, and not giving to his fellow-servants what is their due. If then you will be a lily and a rose of Christ, know that you must be among thorns. Only be careful that by impatience, hasty judgment, or secret pride, you do not yourself become a thorn. The kingdom of Christ is in the midst of his enemies, as the Psalm saith. Why then do you think of it as in the midst of his friends? In whatsoever therefore you are deficient, seek the supply, prostrate before the Lord Jesus. He will teach you all things. Only consider what he hath done for you and for all, that you may learn what you ought to do for others. If he had wished to live only among the good and to die for his friends alone, for whom, I ask, would he have died, or with whom would he ever have lived? Thus do, my brother, and pray for me, and the Lord be with you."

We have presented the whole of this letter, ex-

cept the introductory paragraph, in order that the
reader may see into the heart of Luther as he was
at this period, and form some conception of the
power of his religious influence, as exerted upon
numerous brethren by a mass of letters of similar
import, which have not been preserved. Mathesius
informs us that he wrote many such during the
first four years of his doctorate.

One other letter of similar tendency, and written
in the same month, is still extant. A brother Leiffer
in Erfurt "was agitated by the tempests and billows of temptation." After affirming, "from his
own experience as well as that of his brother, nay,
from the experience of all, that our worldly wisdom
is the cause of all our disquiet," and that his own
exceedingly depraved reason, or "vicious eye," as
he terms it, had vexed him with extreme wretchedness, and continued to do so still, he proceeds:
"The cross of Christ is distributed throughout all the
world, and to each one is always given his portion.
Do not you, therefore, cast it away, but rather receive it as a most sacred relic, and place it away,
not in a gold or silver casket, but in a golden heart,
that is, a heart imbued with gentle charity. For
if the wood of the cross was consecrated by contact
with the flesh and blood of Christ, so that fragments
of it should be treasured up as the choicest relics,
how much more should the injuries, persecutions,
passions and hatred of men, whether of the righteous or of the wicked, be regarded as most sacred
relics, which, not indeed by contact with Christ's
flesh, but by the love of his most anguished heart
and of his Divine will, have been embraced, kissed
and blessed, and more than consecrated, inasmuch
as cursing is turned into blessing, injury into equity,

suffering into glory, and the cross into rejoicing. Farewell, dear father and brother, and pray for me." How characteristic! Written in the very midst of the sumptuous collection of sacred relics in the Electoral church, which to his spiritual mind served no other purpose than to furnish imagery for deeper truths, this letter leads us back to Erfurt, to those scenes where Luther first found the true cross of Christ, and then along the path of his subsequent experience, where, like Bunyan's pilgrim, he is seen as a sort of religious mirror reflecting the whole interior of the Christian life.

In both these letters we see the intensity and fervour of his religious feeling, showing a depth and maturity of character as great as in those vigorous assaults made by him upon the scholastic theology—spiritual health within, and a bold activity without.

Not far from the date of the foregoing letters, Staupitz was sent into the Netherlands to collect relics for the Elector Frederic. What strange incongruities meet us just at the moment that the night of superstition is passing away! In consequence of this singular embassy, Luther was made vicar of the order in Saxony and Thuringia, in place of Staupitz, for about a year and a half, or from April, 1516, to about November of 1517. "This," as Jürgens well remarks, "was a sign of great confidence on the part of Staupitz,—a sign of Luther's high standing already in the order. Staupitz could not have committed his own office to so young a man, unless the intellectual superiority of the latter was universally acknowledged, or at least felt. Otherwise, how could Luther venture to appear as overseer of the very cloister where not many years before he had been misused in his novitiate, where his singularities had been witnessed, but hardly approved, and where until very recently an unfriendly feeling had been cherished against him in respect to his degree, or whatever else was the cause of the misunderstanding? There were distinguished and celebrated men there, such as Lange, Link and Usingen."

It is remarkable that, in his accepting this office, we find no traces of that shrinking timidity which he manifested in 1509, when he was appointed preacher, and in 1512, when he was made doctor of divinity. In a religious point of view, he had passed to a joyful and confident state of mind. In his theology, he had come to feel strong in the Bible, and anxious to open to others, as widely as possible, those living fountains of truth by which he himself had been so refreshed. In practical life, he had, as lecturer and debater and principal professor, acquired great skill and power, and seemed to feel like a young hero panting to engage in some worthy enterprise. He entered upon his duties with eagerness, and with a firm hand. To the decorous but unhesitating tone of authority which he assumed, the cloister of Erfurt never uttered a murmur. On the contrary, his correspondence with Lange, the prior, implies the highest degree of confidence and cordiality.

Luther, immediately after his appointment, set out upon a journey of visitation, and passed the last of April, all of May and the beginning of June in going from cloister to cloister in his province, regulating discipline, encouraging education and the study of the Bible in particular, dismissing unskilful priors and appointing others in their place.

The faithful discharge of the duties of this office made him intimately acquainted with the moral condition of the monks of his order, and the knowledge thus acquired was invaluable to him at a future period.

The first monastery he visited was that of Grimma, near Leipsic, and still nearer the nunnery of Nimptschen, where Catharine von Bora, Luther's future wife, then a girl of sixteen, was nun. As Staupitz and Link accompanied Luther to this place, and as the former performed in this instance the duties of visitation, it would seem that Luther was here practically initiated into his new calling. While they were thus engaged at Grimma, Tetzel made his appearance in the adjacent town of Wurtzen, and practised his arts in selling indulgences so shamelessly as to arouse the indignation of both Luther and Staupitz. This is the time when the former resolved to expose the traffic, and threatened "to make a hole in Tetzel's drum."

We next find him in Dresden, examining the state of the monastery of the Augustinians in that place. Here he writes a letter, May 1, to the prior in Mainz, requesting him to send back to Dresden a runaway monk, "For," says he, "that lost sheep belongeth to me. It is my duty to find him and bring him back from his wanderings, if so it please the Lord Jesus. I entreat you therefore, reverend father, by our common faith in Christ, and by our profession, to send him unto me, if in your kindness you can, either at Dresden or Wittenberg, or rather persuade him, and affectionately and kindly move him to come of his own accord. I will meet him with open arms, if he will but return. He need not fear that he has offended me. I know full well that offences must come; nor is it strange that a man should fall. It is rather strange that he should rise again and stand. Peter fell, that he might know he was but a man. At the present day also, the cedars of Lebanon, whose summits reach the skies, fall. The angels fell in heaven, and Adam in paradise. Is it then strange that a reed should quiver in the breeze, and the smoking lamp be put out?" This is the first letter in which he signs his name as "Vicar of the Augustinian Eremites in Misnia and Thuringia."

His next letter, (and we give all in their order which are written in 1516,) is dated May 29, after he had nearly finished his tour. He had been in Erfurt and was then in Gotha, which he was unwilling to leave without paying his respects in some way to Mutianus, a great classical and belles-lettres scholar, who, as long ago as when Luther was a student at Erfurt, was at the head of a literary club, to which many of the university friends of Luther belonged. Luther addresses him thus: "That I have not visited you, most learned and accomplished Mutianus, nor invited you to visit me, is owing first to my haste and the stress of my business, and secondly, to my high opinion and true veneration of you. Our friendship is of too short a standing to justify me in humbling your excellence so far as to request you to visit me. I must now go where my duty calleth me, but not without first saluting you, though, from a sense of my ignorance and uncouth style, I shrink from it. But my affection for you overcometh my modesty; and that rustic Corydon, Martin, barbarous and accustomed only to cackle among the geese, saluteth you, the scholar, the man of the most polished erudition.

Yet I am sure, or certainly presume that Mutianus valueth the heart above tongue or pen; and my heart is sufficiently erudite, for it is sufficiently devoted to you. Farewell, most excellent father in the Lord Jesus, and be not forgetful of me." Postscript. "One thing I wish you to know: father John Lange, whom you have known as a Greek and Latin scholar, and what is more, as a man of a pure heart, hath now lately been made prior of the Erfurt convent by me. Unto man commend him by a friendly word, and unto God by your prayers."

The same day he wrote another letter from Langensalza, a little north of Gotha, to Lange himself, instructing him how to proceed in his official station. He says at the close: "I have not found in this district any convents in so good a state as here and in Gottern," [between Langensalza and Mühlhausen.] "I have despatched my business here in one hour, and think I shall do the same there in two. By the blessing of God, I hope to proceed toward Nordhausen to-morrow, trusting that in these two places God will work without me both in spiritual and temporal things, though the devil is unwilling."

On the 8th of June, he is again in Wittenberg, and writes to Spalatin, Frederic's secretary, dissuading the elector from his purpose of making Staupitz bishop. "These are not times to be happy, or even comfortable in ruling as bishop, i. e. in being given up to carousals, sodomy and Roman corruption." Though he is "free from such vices," he ought not to be involved "in the whirlpools and violent tempests of the bishops' courts."

On the 22d, he writes to Dressel, prior of the

monastery at Neustadt, a little south of Jena, who
had some difficulty with the monks, endeavouring
to comfort him in his afflictions. He was obliged
afterward to depose him, for want of skill rather
than of good intention, and to permit the convent
to choose another.   In the former letter, he says :
"You seek and strive for peace, but in a wrong
way. You seek it as the world giveth it, not as
Christ giveth. . . . You cry with Israel, 'Peace,
peace,' and yet there is no peace. Cry rather with
Christ, 'The cross, the cross,' and yet there is no
cross. The cross ceaseth to be such as soon as you
can say, 'Blessed cross; among all the kinds of
wood, there is nothing like unto it.' Behold, then,
how kindly the Lord inviteth you unto true peace,
when he besetteth you all around with such crosses."
In the latter, he addresses Dressel and the chapter
thus: "I hear with grief, as I well deserve, excellent fathers and brethren, that you are living void
of peace and unity, and though you are in one house,
you are not of one way; neither are you, according
to the rule, of one heart and one mind. This miserable and unprofitable kind of life cometh either from
your lack of humility—for where humility is there
is peace—or from my negligence, or at least from
your fault and mine, in not beseeching the Lord
that made us, and praying that he would direct our
way in his sight, and lead us in his righteousness.
He erreth, he erreth, he erreth, who presumeth to
direct himself, not to say others, by his own counsel." He then lays the blame chiefly on the brethren
for not submitting to the prior, but, with kind
words, requires the prior to resign, at the same time
pronouncing him a well-meaning, upright man. But
there must be peace and concord. The brethren

are to choose their own prior, and then pray and strive for union.

The remaining letters of this year are those written to his particular friends Lange and Spalatin. They give an interesting view of his occupations and cares. To the former, under date of June 30, he says : " I wrote to you from Sangerhausen, [north of Erfurt and near Eisleben,] most excellent father, that if you had any insubordinate brother, you might send him thither by way of correction. I now write unto you again from Wittenberg, not only desiring, but beseeching you, to send George of Schleusingen or William Fischer to the brethren at Eisleben, or at least allow them to go, till the reverend father [Staupitz] shall return. Rigorous necessity requireth it. Say to that brother, and to all, that this is done by me not from violence, but because we are all bound, and I especially, to maintain the honour of the vicariate everywhere and particularly that of our reverend vicar. These same fathers [at Eisleben] sent me a brother who came near introducing the plague into that young conventual house. Brother Caspar, a senior there, lieth dead. Reader Antony is dead. Father Bacalaureus is in Leipsic. Two others are abroad, as you know, begging money for the building. The brother before-mentioned is now here with me. You yourself see how we need succour. Neither you nor others need be afraid, the plague doth not prevail there. Farewell, and say farewell to the fathers, masters, the reader and others, not in my name, but the Lord's." The reader here mentioned is his friend George Leiffer, to whom the letter of April 15th was addressed. The next letter, written August 30th, to Lange, is accompanied with Luther's oration delivered to the convent at Gottern wishing him to show it or send it to Braun of Eisenach, Wigand of Walthershausen, and reader George Leiffer, or any who should wish to see it. The remainder of the letter relates to difficulties experienced in maintaining study in the cloisters. "You need not send brethren who are students to me, first for that we have too many [in the cloister] already; and secondly because the plague hath broken out vehemently here." October 5th, he writes again to the same; "Just as if we [at Wittenberg] were in such abundance here, that those which you [at Erfurt,] who are rich, cannot maintain, we in our poverty could. We shall have [in the cloister] thirty-six here this winter, unless the plague prevent, and forty, if all whose names are entered should come. You seem to have drunken in the Erfurt spirit of distrust, as though God could not feed even the ungrateful, and preserve even those that do not desire it. Then you make this monastery so much your own, that you call other monks strangers, and ask me to come to the aid of my mother [the Erfurt monastery.] Take care that you continue to walk according to your Tauler, and remain free [from all particular interests,] and common for all things, as becometh the son of a common God and of a common church. Brother John Metzel I will send you as soon as I learn that he can be spared from Eisleben.

"Touching my theses, or rather Bartholomew Feldkirk's, there is no cause why your Gabrielists [followers of Gabriel Biel] should marvel, albeit ours here continually do the same. The theses were not written by me, but were gotten up by Feldkirk, because of the cackling of my enemies against my lectures. This he did, to the end that these things might be publicly debated, under my presiding, in order to stop the mouths of the garrulous, or to learn the opinions of others.* . . . . I will keep a few days the brethren which you sent unto me, and see what I can do, or how it shall turn out with the plague, which has begun. I should be sorry to send them back again, for they are apt for study. And yet I am urged by want; but the Lord liveth and reigneth." The large number of these inmates of the Augustinian cloisters who were sent to Wittenberg to study in the university and live in the monastery, without expense, will account for the fact that so many of the students who took their degrees in theology at Wittenberg about this time, and of those monks who first embraced the doctrines of the Reformation, were Augustinians. How admirably was Luther, all this time, sowing the seed for a future harvest; as well by directing the studies of nearly all the promising young men of his order, as by securing, through his diligence and energy an entire ascendency in the monasteries of his province!

During the month of August he made several journeys on business connected with the duties of his office. After a letter on matters of local interest, written from Kemberg, whither the professors and students often fled in the time of the plague, we find another, in which there is an amusing account of Luther's accumulated labours. "I have need, almost," he writes again to Lange, "of

---

* It is these theses on the freedom of the will, written and defended by Feldkirk, but in reality emanating from Luther, that were the occasion of the sparring between Carlstadt and Eck, which terminated in the Leipsic disputation.

two scribes or secretaries. I do hardly any thing
through the whole day, but write letters. I therefore cannot tell whether I do always write the same
things or no. See for yourself. I am the preacher
of the cloister; I am reader at the table; I am required every day to be parish-preacher; I am direc-
tor of the studies of the brethren; I am vicar, that
is, eleven times prior; I am inspector of the fish-
ponds in Litzkau; I am advocate for the Hertze-
bergers in Torgau; I am lecturer on Paul; I am
commentator on the Psalms; and, as I have said,
the greater part of my time is occupied in writing
letters. I seldom have time for the canonical hours
and for the mass, to say nothing of the temptations
of the flesh, the world and the devil. You see what
a man of leisure I am. Concerning brother John
Metzel, I think my opinion and reply have already
reached you. Nevertheless, I will see what I can
do. How do you suppose I can find a place for all
your Sardanapaluses and sybarites [easy monks]?
If you have trained them up wrong, you must support them after thus training them. I have useless
brethren enough everywhere, if any can be useless
to a patient mind. I am satisfied that the useless
can be made of more use than the most useful. Support them, therefore, for the present. In respect of
the brethren you sent to me, I think, (but I am not
sure,) I lately wrote unto you. The convert,* with
the young men, I sent to master Spangenberg, as
they desired, to the end that they might escape
from breathing this pestilential air. Two I have
kept here, with two others from Cologne, in whose
good parts I felt so deep a concern that I chose

---

* One who becomes monk late in life.

rather to keep them, at no little cost, than send them away. There are now twenty-two priests and twelve youths, forty-one persons in all, who live upon our more than most scanty stores. But the Lord will provide. You say you began yesterday [to lecture] upon the second part of Lombard's Sentences. To-morrow, I shall begin on the Epistle to the Galatians. Albeit, I fear the plague will not suffer me to go on. It taketh away two or three each several day. A son of our neighbour, Faber, opposite, who was well yesterday, is carried to his burial to-day. An-other son lieth infected. What shall I say? It is already here, and hath begun to rage suddenly and vehemently—especially with the young. You ask me and Bartholomew [Feldkirk] to flee with you. Whither shall I flee? I hope the world will not fall to pieces, if brother Martin do fall. The brethren I shall disperse throughout all the country, if the pesti-lence should prevail. But I am placed here, and my duty of obedience will not allow me to flee, until the authority which commanded me hither shall command me away."

Who can fail in this letter, to see Luther with almost every trait of his character? How frank and agreeable his manner with Lange, and how sportive his rebukes! Yet how sensible and earnest in respect to useless monks; and how ready to turn the evil to a spiritual account! How strong his sympathy with young students of enter-prise, and how prompt to aid them! What fidelity in maintaining his post in time of danger, and in securing all but himself! Death was a trifle to him, compared with unfaithfulness. So we see him here, just one year and five days before the ninety-five theses or indulgences were published, like

a stream, broad and deep, and ever growing broader
and deeper as it advances. No character was ever
more steadily progressive than his, from 1507 to
1517.

The only remaining letter to Lange, during the
year 1516, is but a note, in which he commands
that the three obstreperous monks, of whom repeated
complaints had been made, should be sent to Sangerhausen; which seems to have been frequently
honoured in this way. The letters to Spalatin
speak with disapprobation of the way in which
Erasmus explains "the righteousness of the law;"
returns thanks to the Elector Frederic, "for the
present of a garment of too fine cloth for a monk's
habit, did it not come from a prince;" gives an account of the success of Staupitz in collecting relics
along the cities of the Rhine; and explains why
Luther is not yet prepared to publish his notes on
the Psalms.

We have now reached the year 1517, so celebrated
as the one from which the great Reformation of the
sixteenth century takes its date. But there are yet ten
months to the 31st of October, the day on which Luther
posted up his theses against Tetzel. We cannot do
better than follow him through this brief period in
his correspondence. January 27th, he writes to his
old acquaintance and colleague Scheurl, a jurist, then
at Nüremberg, acknowledging the receipt of his letter, which is "to me," he says, "most pleasant and
yet most sad. But why do you wrinkle your brow?
For what could you write more pleasant than the
merited eulogy of our reverend father, the vicar, or,
rather, Christ in him? Nothing more grateful to
me could be said than that the word of Christ
[through Staupitz] is preached, heard, received; nay,

rather lived and felt and understood.   On the other
side, you could write nothing more bitter than the
courting of my friendship and the honouring me with
so many vain titles." And in this strain of unaf-
fected modesty the whole letter is written.

In a letter to Lange, dated March 1, after mentioning that he sends Didymus, "who is still ignorant of the usages of the order," to Erfurt, and that
he is about to publish his translation and exposition
of the Penitential Psalms, he proceeds to say: "I
am reading our Erasmus, and my esteem for him
groweth less every day. . . . . . With him, what
is of man prevaileth over what is of God.   Though
I am loth to judge him, I must admonish you not
to read his works; or rather, not to receive all he
saith without examination.   These are dangerous
times, and I perceive that a man is not to be esteemed
truly wise because he understandeth Greek and
Hebrew; seeing that St. Jerome, with his five languages, did not match Augustine with one—though
to Erasmus it may seem otherwise. . . . . . This
opinion of him I keep hid, lest I should strengthen
the opposition of his enemies [the monks and priests].
Perhaps the Lord, in due time, will give him understanding.   Farewell.   Salute the fathers, the masters and the reader; and inquire whether Dr. Jodocus [Truttvetter] will reply to me."

In two notes to Spalatin, (April 3d and 9th,) Luther begs a stipend for a poor student; and, in reply
to a previous request, recommends the reading of
certain works of Augustine, Ambrose and Cyprian.
On the 6th of May, he writes again to Scheurl, as
follows: "First, I thank you, most excellent man,
for the present of the treatises of Staupitz, but lament
that my trifles should be spread among you by the

reverend father.   They were not written for your
delicate and polite Nürembergers, but for the rude
Saxons. . . . . Upon your requesting me to write
familiarly to Eck, I wrote as carefully as I could.
. . . . The propositions hereunto joined, I send to
you, and through you to master Wenceslaus [Link],
and to any others who are entertained with such
things.   They are not the paradoxes of Cicero, [who
wrote a book under this title,] but of our Carlstadt,
or rather of St. Augustine.   These paradoxes will
expose the carelessness or ignorance of all those that
looked upon them as more *paradox* than orthodox."*

The next succeeding letter, giving a provost instructions how to treat a fallen monk, may be passed
over.   May 15, Luther sends a few lines to Lange,
in which he says, "The reverend vicar writeth that
he shall soon return to us.   Our theology and St.
Augustine go on prosperously by God's help, and
reign in our university.   Aristotle is sinking by
little and little, and verging towards a fall from
which he will never more rise.   The scholastic lectures have wonderfully lost their savour; and no
one can expect to have hearers, unless he consent to
lecture on the Bible, or on St. Augustine, or some
writer which has church authority."   Thus completely had Luther revolutionized the university,
and given a new direction to its studies.

Omitting two unimportant letters to Lange, we
come to the one bearing date September 4, in
which he says, " I send you, by master Otto, my
propositions, [against the scholastic theology,] and

---

* These propositions, in connection with those of Feldkirk, mentioned above, led to the disputation which, in
the following year, ensued at Leipsic between Eck and
the Wittenberg theologians.

my exposition of the ten commandments.　. . . . .
I wait with much, with very great, with stupendous
anxiety, to learn what you think of these paradoxes
of mine.　I suppose that to your theologians these
paradoxes will appear heterodox; though to us they
cannot be otherwise than orthodox.　Let me know
as quick as you can; and say, in my name, to my
masters and reverend fathers of the theological
faculty and others, that I am fully prepared to
come and discuss these subjects with them; either
in the university or in the monastery.　Let them
not suppose that I wish to whisper these things in
a corner; if our university is still so insignificant as
to seem to be a corner."　How evidently are things
tending to a crisis!

On the 11th of the same month, he wrote a letter to
Scheurl, the last from which we shall quote, the three
which remain being but casual notes.　It well illustrates, what is indeed everywhere obvious, how perfectly Luther adapted himself in tone and manner to
the various characters of his correspondents.　He
writes thus: " Although, my dearest Christopher, I
have no occasion to write to you sufficient to justify
me in writing to such a man, yet this is a sufficient
one for me, namely, the desire to write to a friend,
(setting aside all the titles and dignities with which
you are adorned,) to a friend who is pure and most
upright and urbane, and—what is most to the point—
lately known and acquired.　If silence is ever to
be esteemed a fault, the silence of friend toward
friend is particularly so, since playfulness and trifles,
not less than weighty matters, strengthen, not to
say perfect friendship.　St. Jerome exacted this
of his friend, that he should write and inform him
that he had nothing to write.　Thus, I determined

to write trifles rather than to be silent toward a friend. But what will that brother Martin, falsely called the theologian, ever write besides trifles?—who, amid the creaking and pell-mell of syllogisms, hath made no proficiency in polite literature; or, if he ever had any taste of learning and eloquence, it hath been kept back in a state of stammering infancy by long practice and use in that other style of writing. But my preface is long enough, and too long, if I am not to write a volume, instead of a letter, that is, doubly to unbend in trifles and foolishness, when to do it once, is more than enough for a theologian. The aim of my letter is to let you know how high an opinion I have formed of you, and of your fidelity. . . . But it cometh to mind, that you sent by Ulrich Pindar, the small treatises of our reverend father, the vicar, about two florins' worth, a part whereof I have sold, and a part given away to good friends of the reverend father. The money received, I have given to the poor, as you required, that is, to myself and the brethren, for I could find no one poorer than myself. . . . I send you my propositions, or paradoxes, or heterodoxies, as many regard them. You can show them to our learned and ingenious Eck, that I may know what he thinketh of them."

We have now concluded what has generally been treated as an almost unknown period of Luther's life, and what most biographers have despatched in a few pages. Henceforth, the career of the great Reformer is of the most public character, attracting the attention of the religious world more than that of any other individual in Christendom.

PART II.

CHAPTER I.

THE OPENING OF THE REFORMATION IN 1517, TILL THE
TIME OF THE LEIPSIC DISPUTATION IN 1518.

SECTION I.—*Indulgences.*

THOUGH much yet remained for Luther to learn, and many and great changes in his opinions were yet to take place, we may consider the ground-work of his character as having been already firmly laid. In tracing his internal history, and searching out all the influences which the social and religious institutions of his times exerted upon him in the formation of his character, we have incidentally brought before us many scenes which strikingly illustrate the fallen and corrupt state of the church. To this, in its contrariety to the religious character and aspirations of Luther, as represented in the foregoing statements, it is now necessary to direct particular attention. The Reformer stands before us in all his leading peculiarities. It would be well as distinctly to see the church in all those deformities, which called so loudly for a reformation. The limits of this work, however, make it necessary to confine our attention to that class of abuses which the preceding account has not exhibited,—the abuses practised under the name of INDULGENCES.

The tendency of the Catholic church to degrade religion from its high spiritual character to a mere round of outward forms and ceremonies, reached its height in the practical workings of the system of confessions, penances and indulgences. As the most marked peculiarities of Luther's reform consisted in making every thing in religion depend on Christ, rather than on human mediators, whether on earth or in heaven, and our connection with Christ to depend on the spiritual affections of each individual's heart, rather than on outward rites and ecclesiastical relations, it was perfectly natural that a collision should take place just where it did, namely, at those points of the two opposite systems which related to the removal of sin. In the one system, the agent was the church: in the other it was Christ. In the one, the sinner was to be reformed by penances, from which he might purchase release; in the other, he was to exercise godly sorrow for sin and faith in Christ. The one was external and sacramental; the other was internal and spiritual.

How could such a perversion of the New Testament doctrine of repentance and remission of sin ever make its way into a nominally Christian community? To this inquiry there is a decisive historical reply; but the process is long and the answer complicated. Like the formation of a coral island, the perversion was one of gradual accumulation. It had small beginnings, and went on for fifteen centuries, keeping even pace with the intellectual and moral character of the age.

First, outward mortifications were injudiciously, but with good intentions, imposed by the church upon members under ecclesiastical censure, as signs of repentance. Next, the priest enjoined similar things privately, upon those members who, in consequence of certain sins, were supposed to be unprepared for the communion. Then the priest, who had already assumed a false position in the church, as mediator between God and his people, became lord of the individual conscience, examined every one before the communion, decided, as an infallible judge, upon the exact amount of each one's sin, and affixed a corresponding penance. Repentance itself, instead of being regarded as a duty always to be performed, was made a part of an ordinance of only periodical recurrence. At those stated times, the individual was to feel contrition, to confess to the priest, and to make satisfaction by submitting to the penances imposed. The first of these three parts of the ordinance, namely, contrition, was lightly passed over. The second, the confession, was accepted on condition of its being full and complete. The third, satisfaction, was to be attended to afterward; and with reference to this, too, absolution was conditionally pronounced by the priest, and the penitent was then admitted to the communion. In theory, those three successive acts must be faithfully performed by the penitent, or the absolution was of no efficacy.

But how was one to know that his penitence was sufficient? How would he be sure that no individual sin was omitted in the confession? Why should absolution be pronounced before the conditions were all fulfilled, before satisfaction was known to be made?

These were the questions which tortured the mind of Luther, when he was a conscientious monk. The theological objections to the whole system are, that the third part is without foundation, a mere human invention; that the second is in no sense necessary, and arose from a false interpretation of two or three passages of Scripture; is founded on an absurd view of the nature of sin, as a measurable quantity, and is, moreover, utterly impracticable, as no mortal has the means of searching the heart and ascertaining the precise amount of a man's sins. The first part is the only one which has any value or authority, and this is perverted by being so far limited to a particular time and place. But the worst of all is, that the practice fell far short of the theory, miserable as that was: and contrition, the only shadow of a virtue that remained, was just the part which the poor ignorant people least regarded. Luther attacked the *practice;* his opponents defended the *theory,* and there the matter stands to this day.

The theory of the treasure of the church, consisting of the superabundant merits of Christ and of his followers, especially the martyrs, on which the Bishop of Rome could make drafts at pleasure, was a mere scholastic invention, made at a late period, for the purpose of propping up a system which had long existed in practice. On this there was no agreement among the scholastic theologians; Alexander of Hales maintaining one view, Albert the Great another, and Thomas Aquinas a third.

Luther did not fail to take advantage of this circumstance, and triumphantly maintained, that in
attacking these modern individual opinions, he by
no means attacked the doctrines of the ancient universal church.

Indulgences relate only to the third part of the
sacrament of penitence, and consist in substituting,
in the place of satisfaction, or the endurance of the
penance imposed by the priest, pilgrimages to sacred places, crusades against the infidels, or pecuniary contributions for certain religious purposes
The last were, in theory, a substitute for the others,
or for ecclesiastical penalties : but in practice, a tax
for sins. Indeed, it is said, that the modern system
of taxation is borrowed from the church practice.

Plenary indulgence could proceed only from the
pope, and was granted to those who went on a pilgrimage to the holy sepulchre at Jerusalem. The
indulgences given by archbishops and bishops were
restricted to their own dioceses, and could not extend beyond forty days. When the crusades had
lost their novelty, pilgrimages to Rome were accepted as a substitute. There, at certain sacred
places, were stations for prayer, which were resorted
to by pilgrims. Most of all were indulgences given
at St. Peter's, on Christmas eve. As Boniface VIII.
happened to be elected on such an occasion, he appointed a jubilee in 1300, after the manner of the
old Roman secular games, and promised plenary indulgence to all who should daily visit St. Peter's
and St. Paul's for thirty successive days. Strangers
who came to Rome as pilgrims were required to spend
but half that length of time in visiting those places.
The income of that single jubilee has been estimated at fifteen millions of florins. Hence, Luther

said, it was "truly a golden year" Because men could not live long enough to see the close of another century, Clement VI. appointed another jubilee, to take place at the end of fifty years, and added the Lateran church, as a third station or place of sacred resort. Even this period, one has observed, seemed an eternity to Urban VI. He, therefore, caused the next to be held after thirty-three years, the period of the Saviour's life, and appointed St. Mary Maggiore as a fourth place of pilgrimage. These four churches had each a golden door, opened only on the year of jubilee. The money, which the pilgrims must not forget, was received by priests at these four churches, and afterward at three others also. Just before the year of jubilee, preachers of jubilee and of indulgence were sent into various countries, calling the attention of the people to the approaching year of grace. In 1400, the King of France prohibited his subjects from visiting Rome at the jubilee. In 1450, the Duke of Bavaria did the same, the council of Basle having passed a decree against the practice. This last year of jubilee seems not to have been so profitable to the successor of St. Peter as the preceding had been, for after it had passed, he sent a legate, Nicholas of Cusa, into all the dioceses of Germany, to receive the change from those who had not found it convenient to visit Rome!

But it was found that money for building and repairing churches and bridges could be most conveniently raised by selling indulgences. Thomas Aquinas had taught that indulgences could be given in consideration of any act performed for the glory of God and the good of the church, "such as building of churches and bridges, performing pilgrimages and giving alms." In 1319, John XXII. granted forty days' indulgence to those who should aid in building a bridge across the Elbe at Dresden. In 1484, the papal legate promised the same to all who should contribute towards rebuilding a church destroyed by fire at Freiberg, in Saxony, and a hundred days to those who should do so for another church in the same city. In 1491, Innocent VIII. granted to the inhabitants of Saxony, a dispensation from the quarterly fasts for a period of twenty years, on condition that each person would pay the twentieth part of a Romish florin annually toward building a bridge and chapel at Torgau, and the collegiate church at Freiberg. One-fourth, however, of the whole sum was to go to Rome, for building St. Peter's. This ordinance was resisted by the faculty of law in Leipsic, and the Bishop of Meissen refused to publish the bull in his see.

In 1496, Alexander VI. endeavoured to allay the opposition, by promising that when the twenty years were expired, this kind of indulgences should not be repeated in Saxony. But his successor, Julius II., paid no regard to that promise, for in 1509, the year before Luther went to Rome, he revived the indulgences for twenty years thereafter. In 1512, the year of Luther's doctorate, when he took the oath by which he felt himself authorized to oppose Tetzel's doctrines, Julius enlarged and extended the system of indulgences in an unheard-of manner, in order to prosecute the enterprise in which he had been engaged six years, of erecting the magnificent structure of St. Peter's. Leo X. followed in his steps, and in 1514, 1515, and, most of all, in 1516, sent his agents into Germany, to sell indulgences for this purpose.

At this point, an extraordinary character presents himself, to whom we have before alluded and whose name is, for all time, so fatally connected with Luther's that it cannot be passed over in silence. It is Tetzel, the notorious preacher and vender of indulgences. Born in Leipsic, not far from 1460, he studied in the gymnasium of his native city, and then entered the university in 1482, one year before Luther was born. After a protracted course of study, particularly under the celebrated Professor Wimpina, he took his degree in 1487, and ranked as the sixth student in a class of fifty-five. As he excelled in oratory, his friends were surprised at his entering, two years afterward, the Dominican monastery, then called the Paulinum, and now known as a university building under that name. He was soon made priest, and was sent to Zwickau, where, by his ready and showy eloquence, he acquired considerable popularity as a preacher. But here, also, he furnished the first proof of his worthless character.

On a certain day, he proposed to be the sexton's guest, who excused himself, saying, he was too poor to furnish suitable entertainment for so distinguished a man. "No matter," was the ready reply, "we will easily provide ourselves with the money. Look at the calendar, and see what saint's-day it is to-morrow."

It happened to be the day of Juvenal, and the sexton regretted that the saint was so little known. "We will make him known," said Tetzel. "To-morrow, ring the church-bell as at all high festivals, and we will hold high mass." His orders were obeyed, and the mass was accordingly held.

When the ceremony was ended, Tetzel ascended the pulpit, and said, "Dear people, I have some thing to say unto you. If I should withhold it, your salvation would be in peril. You know, we have long prayed to one saint and another, but they have become old, and are tired of attending to us and aiding us. To-day is the festival of Juvenal, and though he hath not yet been known to you, it is all the better. He is a new saint, and will hear us the more patiently. Juvenal was a holy martyr, who shed his innocent blood for the truth. If you would enjoy the benefit of his innocence, lay something, each one of you, upon the altar, on this day of high mass. You, that are noble and rich, go forward and give to the rest a good example." He received the collection, placed a part of it upon the altar, and took the remainder himself, and said, with a smile to the sexton, "Now, we have enough for our evening cups." Such is the account of the old Zwickau Chronicle, and it can hardly be supposed to be a pure fiction.

In 1502, he was selected as papal agent and preacher, offering indulgences for the jubilee that had just passed, to the multitudes in Nurenberg, Leipsic, Magdeburg, and other German cities who did not visit Rome. Next, we find him on the Vistula, similarly employed, and raising money for a crusade by the Teutonic Knights, against the Russians and Tartars. From 1507 to 1513, he was itinerating again in the cities and towns of Saxony. For two years he made Annaberg, a new mining town considerably to the south of Leipsic, his headquarters. "The surrounding mountains," said he, "would be turned into silver, if the people would only purchase indulgences."

In the summer of 1510, while in Annaberg, at St Anne's, with the red-cross raised, as usual, be-

fore the altar, he said : "Three days more, and the
cross will be taken down and the door of heaven
closed." Never again would the time return when
eternal life and forgiveness of sins would be had so
cheap, nor would the liberality of the pope to Germany ever be so great again! "Now," said he, "is
the accepted time, now is the day of salvation."

At Görlitz, where the city council wished to raise
money for indulgences to put a copper-roof upon
the principal church, Tetzel was employed, and was
aided by the parish preacher, the penitentiary priests,
the confessors, the rector of the school and his assistants, and the Franciscan monks, and they succeeded in collecting forty-five thousand rix dollars!
Of the many anecdotes recorded of him, only one
more can find a place here. Whether true or not, it
is perfectly characteristic. Wishing, on a certain
occasion, to quicken the devotions of the people, he
promised to show them, the next day, a feather which
the devil plucked from the wing of the archangel
Michael. But, during the night, some rogues made
their way into his room, found the box of relics,
took out the feather and put some coals in its place.
Next morning he proceeded to the church with his
box, without having opened it, and spoke at large
of the virtues of this celestial feather, and opening
the box, behold, there was nothing but some black
coals! Not at all disconcerted, he exclaimed, "No
marvel that with such a treasure of relics, I have
chanced to take the wrong box," and went right on
to explain the value of these coals, which were the
remains of the burnt body of St. Laurentius! Nothing better illustrates the childish character and
spirit of those times than such original anecdotes,
whether true or false.

Tetzel afterward went to Innspruck, where he was detected in the grossest immorality and lewdness, and at the intercession of powerful friends, instead of being enclosed in a sack, and cast into the river, according to the sentence passed against him, was only imprisoned.

Before we proceed farther with our narrative, we must introduce another new personage, though of a very different order, Albert, the accomplished, but worldly and ambitious Archbishop of Mainz, a young prince now twenty-eight years old. He was the youngest brother of Joachim I., Elector of Brandenburg, (Prussia.) He had been carefully educated under Eitelwolf von Stein, an ardent lover of classical literature, and one of the founders of the Frankfurt University on the Oder. The young prince attached himself to the liberal party, and favoured the cause of Reuchlin, Erasmus and Von Hutten. Being destined for the church, he was, while a boy, made canon at Magdeburg, Mainz and Treves. At the age of twenty-four, he was made Archbishop of Magdeburg, and, ten days later, Administrator of Halberstadt, and in five months from that time, Archbishop and Elector of Mainz, thus holding, at the same time, three of the large and wealthy sees of Germany. For the see of Magdeburg, he had obtained from Rome the pallium, (the archbishop's badge of office,) at great expense. He was not sufficiently in funds to procure at his own expense another for the see of Mainz, and yet, at his election, it was expressly stipulated that he, and not the people, should be at that expense. Albert being the third archbishop elected at Mainz, within a period of eight years, the see, if it paid for his pallium thirty thousand florins, the usual

sum given, would, during that short period, be at
the enormous expense of ninety thousand florins
for that white strip of cloth.*   Albert was obliged
to borrow the money of Jacob Fugger, the rich
broker, the Rothschild of Augsburg.   To get out
of his pecuniary embarrassments, he applied to the
pope for the appointment of commissary for indulgences in his own three dioceses and in the Mark of
Brandenburg, for a period of three years.   The appointment was given him, on the condition that he
was to retain half of all the money that should be
collected, and pay the remainder to the pope, as
usual, for building St. Peter's.   The appointment
was afterward confirmed and extended.

Meanwhile Tetzel had got released from prison,
with the understanding that he should proceed to
Rome and obtain absolution from the pope.   He
went by way of Mainz, and desired Albert to
use his good offices in recommending him to the
papal favour, promising his services in turn, if successful, in raising the thirty thousand florins.
With a letter of recommendation from the archbishop he went to Rome and applied to Leo, who was
not very nice in matters of morality, and not only
obtained absolution, but was made sub-commissary
for disposing of indulgences under Arcimboldi, general commissary for Germany.   In April, 1516,
Tetzel was in Wurzen practising his old art, to
which most of his public life was devoted, and this
was the time that Luther and Staupitz came in near
contact with him, when they were at Grimma.   Ar-

---

* It was made of lamb's wool, spun and woven by nuns,
and consecrated at the graves of the apostles Peter and
Paul.

cimboldi resigning his office near the end of the same year, Albert was raised to the post of nuncio and general commissary; and Tetzel went immediately to Halle, the favourite residence of Albert, and entered into his service. Of this last connection, Luther was ignorant; and very innocently wrote to Albert, as his ecclesiastical superior, requesting him to put a stop to the shameful traffic!

In the Archbishop Albert, and in Pope Leo, Luther found himself disappointed even more than in Erasmus. They were all enlightened and liberal men, but their interest overruled their better judgment, and they all became the personal enemies of the reformer, whom they respected and feared; and whom, in the main points in question, they knew to be in the right.

It was about the beginning of the year 1517 that Tetzel entered the service of Albert, and well did he redeem the pledge given when on his way to Rome; for, during the year, he succeeded in collecting one hundred thousand florins, in nominal value sixty-two thousand five hundred dollars, but in real value vastly more. In the Saxon territories, Tetzel was not very popular. The Saxon house was, moreover, jealous of the house of Brandenburg and did not care to have their lands drained to fill Albert's coffers. Tetzel, therefore, found the best reception either in Albert's territories, the sees of Magdeburg and Halberstadt, or in those of his brother, Joachim of Brandenburg. From February to June, we find him at Halle, which belonged to the diocese of Magdeburg, at Annaberg, and once at Leipsic. In September, he went north to Berlin, was a short time at Zerbst, and finally came to Jüterboch, in a detached district of Magdeburg, about eighteen miles to the

Mrs. Spenser gave him a pocket Bible.

north-east of Wittenberg, and there he was the means of calling out Luther. The house of a certain Teupitz, in which Tetzel then lodged, is still shown to visitors.

It was reported to Luther that Tetzel made the following declarations in his sermons, viz.: That he had such grace and power from the pope, that though one had corrupted the Holy Virgin Mary, the mother of God, he could grant forgiveness—provided the individual should put into the box the proper amount of money; that the red cross of indulgence, with the papal coat of arms, when erected in the church, had as much efficacy as the cross of Christ; that, if St. Peter were present, he could not have greater grace and power than he himself had; that he would not divide with St. Peter in heaven, for he had redeemed more souls with his indulgences than Peter had with his preaching; that when one puts money into the box for a soul in purgatory, such soul escaped to heaven as soon as the money tinkled in the box; that the grace of indulgences was the very grace by which a man was reconciled to God; and that if one obtained indulgences, or a certificate of indulgence, there was no need of contrition, nor sorrow, nor repentance.

Some of these statements, particularly those more offensive to Papal than to Protestant ears, may be exaggerated. At any rate, Tetzel procured two certificates from the clergy and authorities in Halle, where the first statement was said to have been made, testifying to the contrary. Those certificates were first discovered and published in 1844. But that the reports were for the most part true, is evident, not only from what Luther says, but from Tetzel's own words. In his published instructions to the priests, he said, " Let the people consider that Rome is here. God and St. Peter call you. Give your mind, then, to the obtaining of such great grace, both for the salvation of your own souls and those of your deceased friends. They that impede this work are thereby excommunicated by the pope, and are under the indignation of Almighty God, and of St. Peter and Paul." In his printed sermons he said, " Let your sheep [an ominous word] know that on these letters are imprinted and inscribed all the ministries of the suffering of Christ. For every mortal sin a man must needs endure seven years penance, either in this life or in purgatory. But with these letters of pardon, you can at one time, and for all cases, have plenary indulgence from all penalties due unto that time; and, afterwards, throughout all your lives, whensoever you shall wish to confess, you can have a like remission; and, last of all, in the article of death, plenary indulgence from all penalties and sins."

In order to be prepared to estimate rightly the work of Luther, one must understand not only what his character and views were and what the corruptions and abuses of the church were, but also what others before his time had thought and said on the same subject. But not every kind of opposition which was made to the papal hierarchy can claim to be a reformation. A reformation, in the proper sense of the term, is not merely the reaction of reason and philosophy against stupidity and folly, as some modern rationalists would have it; nor of classical education and refinement against ignorance and barbarism, such as was manifested by many in Italy, France and Germany at the revival of learning; nor of civil liberty and national independence against

the tyranny of a foreign ecclesiastic, for in this many
German emperors, princes and statesmen were far
from being deficient; but it is the reaction of a pure
and spiritual Christianity, resting solely on the Bible,
against the degeneracy, corruption, false authority
and traditions of the Church of Rome; a sort of
Christianized Boodism, which had subjugated the
masses of the people to an almost unheard-of superstition and spiritual despotism.

To this monstrous system of abuses, men of profound piety and of great hearts had offered resistance
in the form of religious and theological objections,
long before the time of Luther. To say nothing of
such men as Wicklif and Huss, out of Germany, or of
the many in Germany who had uttered their unavailing
lamentations and transient murmurs, we may mention
three men, whose theatre of action was along the
middle and lower Rhine, who were, theoretically, far
in advance of Luther at the time of publishing his
well-known theses, namely, John of Goch, whose public life covered the interval from 1450 to 1475; John
of Wesel, professor of theology at Erfurt from the
year 1440 to 1460, and then for about twenty years
preacher at Mainz and Worms; and John Wessel,
a disciple of Thomas à Kempis, and, from 1452 to
1479, professor in Cologne, Paris and Heidelberg.
What these men did, for about the last quarter of a
century before Luther's birth, in undermining the
foundations of the papal hierarchy, was certainly not
without its effect upon the community; preparing it
for Luther's influence, though he himself was formed
for his great enterprise independently of them.

The first of the three theologians here named, who
regarded the Bible as the only authority in matters

of religion, and Christ as the only mediator and helper, treated, in his writings, largely of grace and works, and is even an abler and clearer writer on this subject than Luther. Of the last of the three, Luther himself says, "If I had formerly read his works, Luther might have appeared to his enemies as having derived every thing from Wessel, so perfectly is the spirit of both the same. This coincidence giveth me new joy and strength."

The second, John of Wesel, took up the subject of indulgences in particular, and was more mature and more decided than Luther was at the commencement. The very title of his book, which was not "On Indulgences," but "*Against* Indulgences," is indicative of his position. Among other things, he says: "We read the discourses of Christ, containing, perhaps, all that is necessary to salvation, but we find in them nothing touching indulgences. Afterwards the Apostles wrote epistles and preached, but in them there is no mention made of indulgences. Finally, the distinguished teachers Gregory of Nazianzum, Basil, Athanasius, Chrysostom, Ambrose, Jerome, and Augustine wrote many works, approved by the church, and yet they contain nothing about indulgences." "That any priest, or even the pope, can give indulgences by which a man may be released from all the punishments imposed by God, is not taught in the Scriptures." "Some say, and this is the common opinion, that Christ gave to the church the keys of *jurisdiction*, and that indulgences rest on this power. They *say* so, but do not prove it Neither the Old Testament nor the New saith any thing about the keys of jurisdiction. Jurisdiction, as it now is in the church, was brought in by men."

" One may affirm that indulgences are a pious deception of believers, and so many priests have said.
They are a pious deception, because believers are
thereby moved to make pilgrimages to holy places;
to give alms for pious uses; to build churches;
and to raise armies against the infidels. They believe they shall thereby be delivered from the punishment due to their sins, and from suffering in purgatory. In this they are deceived."

Enough, perhaps, has been said to indicate what
is important in the circumstances under which Luther entered publicly upon what may, without af-
fectation, be called his "mission."

SECTION II.—*Luther's Collision with Tetzel, and the Publication of the Ninety-five Theses.*

FOR a year and a half before the controversy broke
out between Luther and Tetzel, the former had
directed his attention to the abuses practised in the
sale of indulgences. His exposition of the decalogue,
delivered as lectures, as early as 1516, and afterwards
published, may be referred to as evidence. A sermon
against indulgences, as then dispensed, delivered July
17, 1517, in the presence of the elector, who had,
but little more than a year before, procured the right
of granting indulgences in the very same church
where the preacher now stood, was not much relished
by the prince. When Luther perceived that half
of the population of Wittenberg were resorting to
Jüterbock and Zerbst, where Tetzel and his colleague.
Rauch, were practising their arts upon the ignorant
populace, he warned his hearers, in a discourse held
in the little old cloister-chapel, against the deception.
" It would be better," said he, " *to give alms to the
poor* according to the command of Christ, than to

buy with money *such uncertain grace.* He that repenteth during all his life, and turneth to God with all his heart, receiveth *heavenly grace, and the forgiveness of all his sins;* which Christ, by his sacrifice and blood hath obtained for us, and offereth us without money, from pure grace." Meanwhile, Luther perceived that some of his congregation, who had purchased indulgences, relied upon their certificates, and consequently did not come to the confessional, nor seek absolution before the communion. He, therefore, refused to administer to them the supper, unless they would first make to him confession of their sins, and submit to the penances he should impose. This they refused to do, and referred to their certificates of indulgence, in which they were pronounced absolved from the grossest crimes—not only past, but those yet to be committed; and that without penitence or satisfaction. Luther adhered to his resolution; and said, to the great surprise and consternation of the individuals concerned, "Except ye repent, ye shall all likewise perish." Some of them went back to Tetzel, complained that Luther would not receive the certificates, and demanded their money again, but to no purpose. Tetzel, who was also inquisitor, was thrown into a rage of passion; and, in his sermons, poured out curses upon the heretics; and, to give emphasis to his denunciations, he caused, at different times, piles of fagots to be kindled in the public square, as signals of what awaited the heretic who should dare utter a word against the papal indulgences.

There are three stages of the doctrine of indulgences which, in the case of Luther, must be distinguished from each other. The first is that of the ancient church, in which indulgence is the mere relaxation or removal of ecclesiastical, that is, human penalties, in respect to penitents who confess their faults and feel contrition. The second is that which prevailed in the twelfth and thirteenth centuries, when penance had become a sacrament; and the indulgence was a spiritual grace, securing the forgiveness of sin; but true repentance was a condition of pardon. The third was the same system, except that the condition of repentance was but little regarded; and in some cases declared not to be necessary; as in some of the later papal bulls, and in the instructions and public declarations of Tetzel. In the first of these, Luther was still a sincere believer. The third he openly assailed, without knowing that either Leo or Albert were implicated. In respect to the second, he spoke doubtfully, and, by way of discussion, ready to adopt whatever should be proved.

Luther, in these circumstances, felt it his duty to write to Albert, his metropolitan, as Archbishop of Magdeburg, and Jerome Scultet, Bishop of Brandenburg, to whose see Wittenberg belonged, informing them of the disorders and abuses against which he had already preached; and calling upon them to interpose their episcopal and metropolitan authority, and put a stop to the evil. But Albert had good reasons for paying no regard to the request. Scultet replied, indeed, but timidly and unsatisfactorily. Luther then wrote to the Bishops of Meissen and of Merseburg and of Naumburg, but with what effect is not known. None of the above-mentioned letters have been preserved.

Perceiving that nothing was to result from the application he had made to his ecclesiastical superiors, he felt bound in conscience to perform his duty as preacher in the city parish, where he was assistant of Pontanus, and accordingly preached anew on the

subject there. Nor was he content with his efforts
to check the evil in a practical way before the common people, where it began, but he resolved to bring
forward the subject of indulgences as a matter of
public debate before the learned, and before the
theologians as such. The Electoral Church, on account of its many sacred relics, and the indulgences
which could be procured there on certain days, attracted many pilgrims there; particularly on the
first of November, the anniversary of the dedication,
and All Saints' day. Luther took the occasion of
that solemn celebration for a disputation; and, on
the day before, viz. Saturday, October 31, at twelve
o'clock, posted up on the doors of that church his
ninety-five propositions respecting the power of papal
indulgences, inviting any and all persons to discuss
the subject with him.

These theses have a very remarkable character
and history. They show that the mind of their
author was drifting on a current in a direction of
which he himself was hardly aware. An expression of abject submission to the authority of the
church and of the pope,—still a part of his religion,—and then a startling declaration, or a sarcasm
that shocked the servile sons of the church and
servants of the pope; and to finish the medley,
some doubts, thrown out to elicit discussion—these
are the three ingredients of propositions, which
acted with the velocity of lightning, and threw all
the centre of Europe into a ferment.

Though designed only for the learned, and proposed
only as a sketch of the topics for debate, they were
translated and circulated by thousands among all
classes. Luther, perceiving that an unexpected and
unextinguishable fire was kindled in the popular

mind, and that the propositions, by their abstruse, scholastic and querying rather than affirmatory character, were ill adapted for the common people, published a sermon in the vernacular tongue, the substance of discourses previously delivered to the people, in which he first struck upon that popular tone of plain and energetic eloquence for which he was ever afterwards distinguished. From the latter part of this sermon, as better adapted than the theses to give a plain and simple view of Luther's opinions at that time, we shall here make a few extracts. After laying down eleven propositions, he proceeds to say:

"12. We are told, indeed, that for the residue of the punishment, the sinner should be referred to purgatory, or to indulgences. But many other things are also said without reason or evidence.

"13. It is a great error for one to think to make satisfaction for his sins, in that God always forgiveth gratuitously and from his boundless grace, requiring therefor nothing but honest living. The church doth indeed require somewhat, [penance, as a sign of sorrow,] but it may and should mitigate its demands, and ought, moreover, never to lay upon men any thing too grievous or intolerable.

"14. Indulgence is granted unto weak and slothful Christians, that will not manfully exercise themselves in good works, or endure mortifications. For indulgences carry no one forward in godliness, but rather bear with and wink at his backwardness. For this cause no one ought to speak against indulgences, nor ought any one to be persuaded to them.

"15. One would act much more safely, and do far better, to give purely for God's sake unto the building of St. Peter, or unto any other object, than to take indulgences for it. For it is not safe to give, in such matters, moved by indulgences rather than by the love of God.

" 16. Far better is a deed of charity done to the poor than a tribute for building churches, or than indulgences granted for the same. For, as before said, one good deed performed is better than many omitted. Indulgence is a relaxing of the requirement of many good works; otherwise no indulgence would be given. . . . My will, desire, entreaty and counsel are, that no one obtain indulgences. Let loitering and drowsy Christians do after this manner; but do thou go thine own way.

" 17. Indulgences are not things required, or even recommended; but pertain to those things which are only permitted, or allowed. Therefore it is not a work of obedience, nor meritorious, but a drawing away from obedience. Therefore, though we may not forbid men to obtain indulgence, we ought to dissuade all Christians therefrom, and exhort and move them to do those works and suffer those pains which are remitted in indulgence.

" 18. Whether souls be delivered from purgatory by indulgency or no, is more than I can tell; but I do not hold to that opinion yet. Certain modern teachers hold and maintain it, but they cannot prove it; neither hath the church established it as true. It is therefore much safer that thou thyself shouldst pray and act for them. For this is more sure and certain.

" 19. On these questions I make no doubt. They are sufficiently settled in the Scriptures. You, therefore, should not doubt, but let the scholastic teachers be scholastic teachers. All of them together cannot give authority to a doctrine with their opinions.

" 20. If some, to whose coffers such truth is not of advantage, shall cry out and call me a heretic, I shall little heed their clamour, inasmuch as it will be made only by those cloudy heads that have had no taste of the Bible, that have never studied the Christian doctrines, that have never understood their own teachers, but in their ragged and tattered opinions have gone well-nigh to decay. For had they understood them, they had known that no man is to be condemned until he has been heard and confuted."

At a later period, Luther, looking back upon his first efforts at reform, speaks thus: "By these theses [then published anew] will be publicly set forth my shame, that is, my great weakness and ignorance, which, at first, made me begin the work with great fear and trembling. I was alone; and plunged myself into the business without foresight; and now that I could not go back, I not only gave place to many weighty articles of the pope, but sincerely and earnestly reverenced him. . . . What and how my heart endured and suffered the first and second year; into what humility, not false and feigned, but real, nay into what despondency I sunk, the unmolested actors of these peaceful times know little. . . . I, who braved the danger alone, was not so easy, confident and sure of my cause. I was then ignorant of much that I now, thank God, know. I only debated the matter, and was ready to be instructed. . . . With great earnestness and veneration I held the church of the pope to be the true church."

No one had appeared at the time appointed to debate with Luther on the subjects embraced in his theses. On the festival day, he had preached before the multitude, though with great moderation, on the subject of indulgences. A few days after, probably within a week, he published the sermon above mentioned. As there had been no free and extended discussion of these topics, and as his brief intimations in the theses were liable to be misunderstood, especially by the common people, for whom they were not designed, he wished to publish an extended explanation of his views, and for this purpose wrote his work entitled " Proofs or Solutions of the Theses." But his bishop objected to their publication, as we learn from the following letter to Spalatin, dated Nov. 1517 : " Yesterday the Abbot of Lenin [a rich abbey situated nearly midway between Wittenberg and Brandenburg] was here. In the name and in behalf of the Bishop of Brandenburg did he come, bringing a letter from him, and likewise saying to me, by our bishop's order, that he, the bishop, desired and entreated me to put off the publishing of my Proofs and other similar writings. He was sorely grieved that I had put forth the sermon on Indulgences, and desired that it should not be published again or sold any further. Overcome with modesty that so high a prelate should humble himself to send unto me such an abbot, I said on this behalf alone, ' Very well, I would rather obey than do miracles.' . . . Although, in his esteem, nothing heretical was to be found in those writings, but every thing was orthodox, and though he himself did condemn those indiscreet declarations (as they are called) on the power of indulgences, yet, to avoid offence, he thought it best to remain silent for a season and delay publishing." To J. Lange of Erfurt, he wrote under date of Nov. 11, 1517, sending at the same time a copy of his theses : "If your theologians should be offended at these, and say (as all the world doth of me) that I declare my opinions and impugn other men's rashly and arrogantly, . . . say to them in my name, that I commend their ripe modesty and grave moderation, so that they reduce their principles to practice. . . . But why do they not use moderation in their judgment of me? Why do they not modestly wait for the issue of the controversy?" He signs himself, "Martinus Eleutherias, (freeman,) or rather servant and captive at Wittenberg."

In a letter of the same date to Spalatin, he acknowledges the receipt of a piece of cloth, and thanks the prince for the present.

In another letter of but five lines, written in November, to the same, he says, "To be short, I will do all that you ask in your letter. The bishop has made answer and released me from my promise. Only I do not know whether I can preach these three following days. Nevertheless I will see; if not, Amsdorf can come to my aid."

In these few words we see the busy and business-like man, who was beginning to attract that universal attention which was never afterward withdrawn from him. His relations to the elector at this period are also apparent from his familiar letters. "My theses," he writes in the same month again to Spalatin, "I did not wish to have fallen into the hands of our illustrious prince or any of his court, till after they had seen them that may find themselves touched therein, lest these persons should think that I, by the command or will of the elector, had sent them forth against the Bishop of Magdeburg, (Albert,) as I hear say many already imagine. But we can now swear that they were brought to the light without

the knowledge of the Elector Frederic.   More at
another time, for I am now very busy." In a postscript he says: "You said in your letter that the
prince had promised me a garment. I would fain
know to whose charge he has committed the business." This is not the same present mentioned in
a previous letter. Luther recurs to the subject in
another letter, addressed a few days after to the
elector himself, in such a manner as to give us a
peep into court life, as well as a view of the
character of both the elector and of the Reformer.
"Most gracious lord and prince," he writes, "inasmuch as your grace formerly promised through
Hirsfeld to give me a new garment, I now beg
leave to put you in mind of the same. But I must
ask, as I did before, that if Pfeffinger is to fulfil
the promise, he do it by deed, and not by soft
words. He knoweth how to spice up fine discourse,
but that never maketh good cloth."

After endeavouring to reconcile him to Staupitz,
who had been misrepresented and maligned, Luther proceeds to say, "To give proof of my fidelity,
and to render myself worthy of my court garment,
I will say, that I have heard your grace intendeth
after the present taxing to lay another and perhaps
heavier one upon his subjects. If your grace will
not despise a poor beggar's petition, I entreat you
in God's name not to let that be done, for it
grieveth me, as it doth many of your grace's
friends, to learn that this last taxation hath dero-
gated much from your good name."

It is time to notice the various annoyances which
Luther experienced in consequence of the publication of his theses, and the many petty strifes in
which his enemies engaged with him. Here we

shall see the Reformer appearing in all the qualities of his mind and heart, profoundly sincere and honest, entirely religious and conscientious, though still held in bondage to many errors and superstitions; more and more deeply convinced of the justness and importance of his biblical views of theology and religion, and of the corruption of the church, of the ignorance and stupidity that reigned in the monasteries and the schools, and finally undeceived in respect to the character of Pope Leo, the Archbishop Albert, and other high dignitaries of the church. Sometimes we shall see him sighing over these evils; sometimes reasoning with Herculean strength in order to convince the wise and the good; sometimes, when assailed by malignant foes with the vilest arts, either indignant and blasting them as by a thunderbolt, or comical, and making them appear superlatively ridiculous.

Before the close of the year 1517, Tetzel sought to elevate himself to an equality with Luther by taking, at the University of Frankfort on the Oder, the degree of doctor of divinity, and, on that occasion, he brought forward and defended a set of theses directed against those of Luther. Not only was he obliged to resort to Professor Wimpina, a distinguished man, formerly of Leipsic, but now of Frankfort, who was jealous of the fame of the Wittenberg theologians, to draw up those theses in tolerable Latin, but he had the mortification to be beaten in the argument by a young student, by the name of Knipstrov. Though the latter, for so daring a crime, was confined in a monastic prison, he was afterward professor of theology and vice-chancellor of the University of Greifswald.

At the close of the following spring, Tetzel published a reply to Luther's sermon on Indulgences, pointing out in it twenty alleged heretical doctrines. Luther did not let this ridiculous cry of heresy and menace of the flames pass unanswered He said it would be more in keeping with the character and habits of Tetzel, if, instead of appealing to "water and fire," he had appealed to "the juice of the grape and the flames over which fowls were roasted." After rebuking the levity with which a man, guilty of almost every crime named in the Decalogue, himself not fearing the fires of hell and eternal death, attempted to frighten Christian teachers, as though they were children, by means of fire and sword, he goes on to say, comically enough: "Inasmuch as this matter doth not pertain to faith and to salvation, nor is one of necessity or of command, and since these persons are so very godly and abundant in charity that they are eager to burn Christians for things indifferent and devoid of heresy, may my gracious God and Father forgive me, that, setting aside all honour, as a thing alien from you, I should bid defiance to my Baalites. Here am I at Wittenberg, Dr. Martin Luther, and if there be any inquisitor who thinketh he can eat iron and rend rocks, I hereby give him to understand that he shall have safe conduct, open doors, free lodgings and living to boot, at the expense of our excellent prince, Duke Frederic, the Elector of Saxony."

Silvester Prierias, a monk of the same order with Tetzel, and master of the sacred palace or chief censor of books at Rome, replied to Luther's theses as early as January, 1518, and consequently was the first writer who published a work against the doctrines of Luther. It was a dialogue, in which the positions of Luther constituted one part, and the replies of Prierias the other. The sole aim of this weak and supercilious production was to exalt the church of Rome, and to maintain the supremacy of the pope.

The discussion which Luther had with the theologians, at the general meeting of his order at Heidelberg, in which he developed his views on the great questions of the day, was attended with the happiest consequences. While his arguments were such that the aged men, who disliked them, could not answer them, he made converts to his doctrine among young men of the highest promise. To these belonged Bucer, afterward the Reformer in Strassburg and in England, Brentz and Schnepf, the reformers of Suabia.

With Eck also, with whom he had lived on terms of friendship, he was led into a controversy which ended in the Leipsic disputation. And, finally, he was obliged to defend himself against the Bishop of Rome. These remarks will enable the reader to understand without difficulty most of the letters of Luther, written during the period immediately following the publication of the theses.

To Spalatin he writes this hasty note, under date of January 7, 1518 : "The schedule, which you demand, my dear Spalatin, is not with me. I will see whether it be in Wittenberg or no, and, if it be, will send it unto you. But I send you the late phantoms of Silvester [Prierias] from the city [of Rome,] which have just come to hand through Nüremberg. When you shall have read them, do your diligence to send them back to Wittenberg, that I may commune with my friends whether to answer them, or let them go unanswered. I have no other but this one copy." On the 14th of the same month, he wrote to him another long letter, from which we take the following: "Do not think it strange, my dear Spalatin, that certain persons should declare that I was overcome while at a supper in Dresden. They say, and have long been used to say, whatsoever they please. I was verily at the house of Jerome Emser with Lange and the Dresden prior, having been not so much invited as forced to a supper. Though I thought myself among friends, speedily I found a snare was laid for me. There was a paltry master there, who had dipped a little into Aquinas, and thought himself wondrous wise. He, burning with anger at me, first entreated me kindly, but when a discussion arose, he inveighed against me bitterly and clamorously. In the mean season there was standing without the door a certain mendicant friar, who listened unto all I said, (as I afterward learned,) and who declared he was in anguish of spirit, and could hardly keep from coming forth and spitting in my face, and calling me by every evil name; so vexing was it to the poor man that I should confute that little master, the Thomist. This is the man that everywhere boasteth, even until now, that I was so beaten that I could not say a word either in Latin or in German. Because we spoke in Latin and German commingled, he gave out that I did not know a word of Latin."

In another letter to the same, he gives his friend advice and instruction, as to the best way of prosecuting the study of the Bible; and in a third, dated February 15, 1518, he replies to inquiries in respect to good works and indulgences. "As touching indulgences," he remarks, "the matter is still in dispute, and my propositions are drifting along in the waves of calumny. Two things, however, I dare say; the first unto you alone and my other friends, until the matter shall be known and come to the light, namely, that indulgences look to me to be nothing but a delusion, and of no profit, save to such as are drowsy and sluggish in the way of Christ. Albeit Carlstadt doth not hold the same opinion, I make no doubt he esteemeth them lightly. To pluck away this delusion, I, for the love of the truth, have cast myself into a dangerous labyrinth of disputation, and have stirred up against me a thousand centaurs. Secondly, ... I counsel you to buy no indulgences, till you can no longer find a poor neighbour to give the money to. I doubt he will bring upon himself wrath, who neglecteth the poor and buyeth indulgences. But, God willing, you shall see more on this matter when the Proofs of my Propositions come out. To this measure am I forced by men more ferocious than ferocity itself, who, in all their discourses, pronounce me a heretic; and their wrath goeth to such a length that, for my sake, they arraign the University of Wittenberg, and stigmatize it as heretical. They are so ignorant of things, both divine and human, that it is a reproach to have a controversy with them; and yet their ignorance giveth them incredible audacity, and a front of more than brass. . . . They clamorously give out that what I have in hand took its rise with our illustrious prince, out of enmity to the Archbishop of Magdeburg (and Mainz.) I pray you, therefore, to consider what must be done, whether the matter should be laid before the prince or no. I cannot abide that he should be brought under suspicion for my sake; and I shudder with fear and horror at the thought of being the cause of dissension between such princes."

To Dr. Scheurl, advocate in Nüremberg, he writes, March 5: "I have received from you, most excellent and learned Christopher, two letters at the same time, one in Latin, the other in German, together with a gift from the famous Albert Dürer, (the painter,) and also my theses in Latin and in German. You marvel that I did not send you a copy. I make answer, that it was not my purpose nor will that they should be published, but that they should be examined by some persons in our own neighbourhood, and afterward, according to their opinion, be condemned and abolished, or be approved and published. But they have been printed and spread abroad beyond all expectation, so that I repent of having sent forth this foetus, not because I am unwilling the common people should know the truth, for that is what I most desire, but the manner and form of it is ill adapted for the instruction of the people. Some things therein contained are to myself doubtful; others I would have declared after a different and more positive sort, or left out, had I seen the end from the beginning. Though, from this manner and degree of their dispersion, I know what men think in respect of indulgences, nevertheless they do it secretly, for 'fear of the Jews.' I am, therefore, constrained to prepare proofs and explanations of the theses, though the Bishop of Brandenburg, with whom I have taken counsel, being much troubled in this matter, hath caused me so long to delay the publishing of them. Nay, if the Lord give me opportunity, I desire to bring out in German, a treatise on the power of indulgences, and thus to suppress those theses which are so dispersed."

March 21, 1518, he writes to Lange, in Erfurt: "Wonderfully do the indulgence-mongers fulminate against me from the pulpit. Not content with the portentous names they have given unto me, they add threats, some prophesying that within two weeks, others that within one month, I shall assuredly be burned by the people. Against my theses they now set forth others, so that I fear they may burst for the greatness and vehemence of their anger. Finally, I am besought by everybody not to go to Heidelberg, lest I be despatched by fraud, if I cannot be by violence. But I shall fulfil my duty of obedience, [as a monk to attend the general meeting,] and shall journey on foot, and pass through Erfurt, if God permit. Albeit do not tarry for me, for I shall not set out till the 13th of April. Our prince, moved by great zeal for solid learning, hath, without our asking, undertaken earnestly to defend me and Carlstadt, and will not suffer me to be dragged to Rome, which torments my enemies here, who are not ignorant of his will toward me.

"To the end that you may know the truth, if the report of the burning of Tetzel's theses should come to your ears, and that nothing, as is wont to be the case, may be added to the tale, I will certify you of the matter. The students, holding in odium the old sophistical studies, and being inclined to the Scriptures, and perhaps to me, when they had learned that a man, sent by Tetzel the author, had come hither, went forthwith to him to terrify him for having the audacity to bring such things hither. Some of them did buy a few copies, but others plucked away the eight hundred which remained

and burnt them, having already given notice that,
if any desired to see the funeral pile of Tetzel's
theses burned, to be at the place at two o'clock.
This was done without the knowledge of the elector,
of the academical senate, of the rector, or of any
of us."

In a letter to Egran, preacher at Zwickau, written March 24th, he says, "Some obelisks have of
late been written against my theses by a man of
true learning and of excellent parts, and what
grieveth me more, by one for whom I had not long
ago conceived a warm friendship, Dr. John Eck,
vice-chancellor of the University of Ingolstadt, already a noted man and well known by his published
works. Did I not know the devices of Satan, I
should wonder what fury influenced him to break
those new and pleasant bonds of friendship, without
giving me any warning, or taking leave of me. . . .
As for myself, I desired to swallow patiently this
cake, worthy of Cerberus. But my friends compel
me to reply, though I shall do it privately. Blessed
be the Lord Jesus! to him alone be glory. Confusion may deservedly cover us. Rejoice, my brother,
rejoice, and be not terrified by those flying sheets,
nor cease to teach as you have begun, but, like the
palm in Cadiz, rise under the weight that is laid
upon you. The more they rage, the more I go on.
I leave former things behind for them to bark at,
and go on to those that are before, that they may
have more to bark at."

On the 31st of March, he writes to Staupitz:
"Being very busy, my father in the Lord, I can
write unto you but little. First, I firmly believe
that with many my name is in ill odour. So much
do the good men lay to my charge because I have

condemned rosaries, crowns, psalteries, and other prayers, and indeed all good works. So St. Paul was accused of saying 'Let us do evil that good may come.' But I have followed the theology of Tauler and of that work [the German Theology] which you have lately caused to be printed by Aurifaber, and teach that men must put their trust in nothing else but Jesus Christ alone, neither in their prayers and merits, nor in their good works. For, not by our running, but by God showing mercy, are we saved. From such teachings do those men draw forth the poison which you see them scatter abroad. But as I did not begin, so neither will I give over either for glory or for infamy."

Several of the letters next succeeding relate to his journey to Heidelberg, where the monks of his order were to meet in convention. The story of the incidents connected with that occasion is best told by himself. From Coburg, nearly two-thirds of the distance, he wrote to Spalatin, April 15th: "From Pfeffinger I suppose you have learned all that we talked about, when I met him at the village of Judenbach, [a few miles before reaching Coburg.] Among other things, I rejoiced at this, that an opportunity was given unto me to make that rich man poorer by some shillings. For he paid not only for my dinner, but for that of two other companions. And now, if I could, I would make our prince's officer here at Coburg pay for us. But if he is not willing, still we shall live at the elector's cost. . . All things go well with us, except that I sinned, I confess, in setting out on my journey on foot. But for this sin, as the contrition is perfect, and a full penance hath been imposed and borne, there is no need of indulgence. I was very much wearied, [the distance was more than one hundred and forty miles,] and could not get conveyed, and so there was abundance, enough and more than enough of contrition, penance and satisfaction. I was unknown to all, except as the presence of Pfeffinger made me known. But at Weissenfels, the parish priest, though a stranger to me, knew me and treated me with great kindness. He was a Wittenberg master."

His next letter to the same is dated Wurzburg, April 19. "We at length arrived at Wurzburg on the 17th, and, on the evening of the same day, presented our letters to the illustrious prince [Bibra, the excellent Bishop of Wurzburg.] . . . The reverend bishop, on receiving them, called for me, communed with me, and desired to give me at his own charges another messenger to accompany me all the way to Heidelberg. But as I found here many of my order, and especially Lange, the Erfurt prior, I thanked the kind-hearted prince, saying it was not necessary to provide me with a messenger. I wished, moreover, to ride with them, being exhausted with fatigue. Only one thing did I ask of him, and that was a safe-conduct, which I have just received. . . . If something more can be paid to my messenger Urban, I think he deserveth it; for he was delayed in the journey on my account. I would bring this to pass if I could see our Hirsfeld. The man is worthy of it for his fidelity and honesty. Do you also plead his cause. I am poor, as I am bound to be, and therefore could give him but little."

On his return to Wittenberg he gave an account of the remainder of his journey to Spalatin, May 18th: "At length, by the favour of Christ, I have returned to my home, dear Spalatin, and arrived at Wittenberg the Sabbath after Ascension-day. Though 1 went on foot, I returned in a carriage. For I was compelled by my superiors to ride with the Nürembergers to Wurzburg; thence with the Erfurt brethren to that place ; and from Erfurt with the brethren from Eisleben, who, at their own charges, and with their own horses, conveyed me to Wittenberg. I was quite well all the way, my food agreeing with me marvellously, so that some think I have grown more fat and corpulent.

"The Count Palatine (at Heidelberg) and Simler, and Hase, masters of the palace, received me with great honour. The count invited us, that is, Staupitz, Lange, now provincial vicar, and myself, to his palace, where we rejoiced and were made merry in each other's company, eating and drinking and seeing all the adornments and weapons of war which beautify that regal and truly noble castle. Simler could not enough extol the letter of our prince given for me, saying, 'Those are most precious credentials which you have.' Indeed, nothing of humanity was wanting.

"The learned doctors willingly suffered my disputation, and disputed with me so courteously as to make themselves very dear to me. Although my theology seemed strange to them, they argued against it honourably and acutely; save one young doctor, who made the whole audience shout with laughter when he said, 'If the peasantry should hear that, they would stone thee to death.'

"To the Erfurt doctors my theology was a bitter pill, especially to Jodocus of Eisenach. . . . I had a conference with him, and made him to understand at least as much as this, that he could never establish his own positions, nor confute mine. With doctor Usingen, as I rode with him, I laboured more than with all the rest, in order to convince him, but know not whether it had any effect. I left him cogitating and wondering."

These two men, it will be recollected, were Luther's principal teachers at the university. In a previous letter to Lange, he sent a friendly salutation not only to father Usingen, but to father Nathin, his former enemy, and the chief agent in producing the misunderstanding between Luther and the University of Erfurt. This magnanimity and love of brotherly concord are noble traits in the character of the bold and stern reformer.

In the midst of all these cares and tumults, Luther was active in raising the literary character of the university. He at first introduced the study of the Bible; next he endeavoured to banish the scholastic philosophy. Now he was active in introducing the study of Hebrew and Greek, and promoting the Latin. He looked out new professors, laid new plans of study before the elector through Spalatin, and counteracted the parsimonious views of Pfeffinger, the financial minister of state. Leipsic, espousing warmly the cause of Tetzel and of the pope, was more than ever the jealous rival of Wittenberg. "Our studies," says Luther, March 21, "are advanced so much that we expect soon to have lectures in both languages, [Latin and Greek,] or rather in three, [by adding the Hebrew,] in Pliny, in mathematics, in Quintilian and some others of the best sort, giving up the puerile lectures on Peter of Spain, Tartaretus [of France] and Aristotle. The elector hath already signified his approval, and the council have the subject under consideration."

On the 18th of May, he writes to Spalatin, "I hope and pray you will not be unmindful of our university, that is, that you will be zealous in establishing a Greek and a Hebrew professorship. I suppose you have seen the programme of lectures at Leipsic, our rival as ever. Many are there pompously announced which I do not believe will ever be delivered." The measures here referred to led first to a negotiation with Mosellanus, and then, that failing, to the appointment of young Melancthon, as professor of Greek.

On the 30th of May, 1518, Luther wrote two letters of great historical value, the one to Staupitz, the other to Leo X.; the former giving an account of the gradual change his mind underwent on the subject of indulgences; the other stating the rise, character and progress of the outward controversy. In the letter to Staupitz, he says: "I remember, reverend father, that among those most delightful and profitable conversations of yours wherewith the Lord Jesus used wonderfully to comfort me, mention once happened to be made of the word *repentance*. Being distressed for the consciences of many, by reason of the manner wherein those murderers of the conscience taught the duty of confession, by countless and intolerable precepts, I heard from you, as if by a voice from heaven, the declaration that 'there is no true repentance, save that which beginneth with the love of righteousness and of God; that what these men make the end and completion of repentance is rather the beginning thereof.' Those words of yours stuck to me like a sharp arrow of a strong archer. I afterward compared them with those passages of Scripture which teach repentance, and how sweetly did they all play in and agree with this opinion. Formerly there was in all the Bible scarcely a word more bitter to me; now none sounds more sweetly or agreeably to my ears than the word repentance. At a later time, I learned, by the help of those scholars who made us acquainted with Greek and Hebrew, that the Greek word for repentance, signified 'thinking of a fault after it was done,' . . . and, as I proceeded farther in the knowledge of the Greek tongue, I perceived that it also signified 'a change of mind.' . . . Being confirmed in these opinions, I made bold to consider those as false teachers who imputed so much of repentance to [outward] works, making it of little account beyond certain satisfactions and scrupulous confessions. . . . When my mind was kindling into a blaze with these meditations, behold, all of a sudden. a new trumpet of indulgences and of pardons was sounded, or rather rung with a loud clangour in our ears, whereby we were not summoned to war, but . . . . these heralds proclaimed, with great pomp and in a manner unheard of before, not repentance, nor even the weakest part thereof, satisfactions, but the *remission* of this weakest part. Moreover did they teach ungodly, false and heretical doctrines with such authority, (I should say, audacity,) that if any one muttered a word against it, he was straightway a heretic, devoted to the flames, and worthy of eternal malediction. Not able to sustain their fury, I determined to dissent from them modestly, and to call into doubt their opinions, standing upon the doctrine of all the teachers of the whole church, viz. that it is better that the satisfactions be performed than that they be remitted, that is, released by indulgence. Nor did any one ever teach otherwise. Thus I took up

the disputation, that is, stirred up against my unlucky head every thing, top, bottom and midst, so
far as it was in the power of these persons, who are
so zealous for money, or as they will have it, for
souls. These gentle creatures, resorting to base
sleights, inasmuch as they could not dispute what I
had said, set up the pretence that the power of the
pope was impugned in my disputations. This, reverend father, is the cause of my now coming un-
happily before the people. I always wished rather
to be in a corner, and would now much sooner look
at the august spectacle of the great men of our age
than become myself an object of the public gaze.
But I see it is needful for the chick-weed to be with
the pot-herbs, and the dark colour with the light,
to set off the charm by contraries. I pray you,
therefore, receive these trifles of mine, and send
them forward as speedily as may be to Leo X., that
they may appear there as my defence against my malignant foes. Not that I wish to draw you into my
perils. I desire that the perils be mine alone. Christ
will know whether these things which I have said
are his or mine. . . . As to those threats, I have nothing to reply to my friends but the words of Reuchlin, ' He that is poor hath nothing to fear, for he hath
nothing to lose.' I have nothing, and I desire nothing.
If I enjoyed any good name or honour, this they are
now fast destroying. But one thing remains, that is,
my frail body, already weak and decayed by constant
sufferings. If, by the will of God, they should destroy
this by violence or fraud, why, they will only make me
poorer by a few hours of my life. Enough for me
is my sweet Redeemer and Saviour, the Lord Jesus
Christ, and his praises will I sing as long as I live.
If any one will not sing with me, what is that to

me? Let him bark, if he please, by himself. The
Lord Jesus Christ preserve you evermore, my dearest father."

The letter addressed to Leo, at the same time
with the above, accompanying the Proofs and Explanations of the Theses, is important as determining
Luther's views of the papacy and of Leo at this
period, views which he soon had occasion to change.
"I have heard," says he, "the worst account, most
blessed father, touching myself, namely, that certain friends have made my name most odious to you
and yours, as of one who was labouring to diminish
the authority and power of the keys and of the
supreme pontiff; and that I am called a heretic, an
apostate, a traitor, and a thousand other ignominious
names. These things shock and amaze me; one
thing only sustains me, a sense of innocence. But
this is nothing new. Even here in my own country I am honoured with such tokens by these men
of honour and truth, I mean these conscience-smitten
men, who strive to heap their monstrous crimes upon
me, and, by my ignominy, to cover their own. But,
most blessed father, condescend to hear the whole
matter from me, a child and rude though I be.
The jubilee of apostolic indulgences began to be
proclaimed here not long ago, and was carried on
in such a sort, that the preachers thereof, employing
the terror of your name, thought there were no
bounds to their license, and presumed to teach
openly things the most blasphemous and heretical,
to the great scandal and contempt of ecclesiastical
authority, as if the decretals touching the abuses
practised by preachers of indulgences had nothing
to do with them. Not satisfied with scattering their
poison by their licentious tongues, they published

tracts and dispersed them among the people, in which, to say nothing of the insatiable and unexampled avarice flowing forth at every letter and point, they repeated those blasphemous and heretical declarations, and bound the confessors with an oath to enjoin the same most faithfully and earnestly upon the people. I speak nothing but the pure truth, which cannot be concealed from the light. The books themselves are extant, and they cannot deny these things. They have carried on their business with great effect, and with their false promises they have drained the purses of the people, and, as the prophet saith, 'plucked the flesh from their bones,' themselves the meanwhile faring most sumptuously.

"To stay the public scandal, they have resorted to the terror of your name, to the menace of the flames, and to the ignominy of heresy. It is incredible how bent they are on using these weapons, wheresoever their opinions, even in the very least matters, are called in question. This, however, is not so much quenching public scandal as it is stirring up schisms and seditions by deeds of tyranny. At the same time, tales concerning the avarice of the priests, and detraction in respect of the power of the keys and of the supreme pontiff, were going from mouth to mouth in the taverns, as the voice of the whole land giveth witness. I burned, I confess, with zeal for Christ, as it seemed to me, or with youthful heat, if any one please; but perceived that it did not belong to me to do or decide any thing in this matter. Accordingly, I admonished privately a few of the dignitaries of our church. Some received what I said, some did ridicule; some one thing, and some another; for they were terrified by

the use made of your name, and by the threat of
the inquisition. At length, when I saw I could do
nothing else, I thought it best to arraign them
gently, that is, to make their dogmas a matter of
doubt and of debate. Therefore, did I publish a
disputation, inviting only the learned to discuss the
subject with me, if they chose. This my enemies
may know, as it standeth in the prefatory words at the
head of the propositions.

"Behold, this is the conflagration whereof the
whole world complain, indignant, perhaps, that I, a
master of theology by your authority, should, after
the custom of all the universities and of the whole
church, have the right to dispute in a public school,
not only on indulgences, but . . . . on incomparably greater things. . . . . By what unlucky chance
it is, that these particular propositions of mine, more
than all others, either of my own or of any teacher,
should go forth into nearly all the earth, I am at a
loss to know. They were set forth here for our
use alone, and how they should come to everybody's
knowledge is incredible to me. They are not doctrines or dogmas, but matters of debate, stated,
according to custom, obscurely and enigmatically.
Could I have foreseen the result, I would assuredly
have taken care to make them more plain and clear.
But what shall I do? Recall them I cannot; and
yet I see that their notoriety bringeth upon me
great odium. . . . In order, then, to soften my adversaries, and to gratify many friends, I send forth
these trifles, [Proofs, &c.] to explain my theses.
For the greater safety, I let them go forth, most
blessed father, under your name, and under the
shadow of your protection. Here, all who will
may see how sincerely I honour the ecclesiastical

power and reverence the keys; and also how basely I am reproached and belied by my enemies. If I were such as they would make me to be, if those things were not all proposed for the sake of debate, it would be impossible that the illustrious elector should allow such a pestilent thing in his university,—being, as he is, a vehement lover of the catholic and apostolical doctrine,—or that I should be borne with, by the acute and zealous teachers in our university. But I speak to no purpose; for these gentle spirits do not stick at covering with the like infamy the elector and the university. Wherefore, most blessed father, I cast myself, with all I am and have, prostrate at your feet. Save or slay, call or recall, approve or disapprove, as it shall best please you; I will acknowledge your voice as the voice of Christ presiding and speaking in you. If I am worthy of death, I refuse not to die; for the earth is the Lord's, and the fulness thereof; blessed be his name, and may he keep you evermore. Amen."

A course of events was rapidly hastening on which was destined to shake Luther's confidence, both in the bishop and in the church of Rome. Eck had circulated extensively, though privately, his manuscript comments, or "Obelisks," on Luther's theses. The latter sent his "Asterisks," also privately, as a reply. Carlstadt, in the mean time, made a public answer. Eck professed to regret the course things were taking, and Scheurl, a friend of both, undertook to mediate between him and Luther. The following is Luther's reply: "What you desire in behalf of our Eck, my dearest Christopher, would not have needed the mediation of such a friend, if the matter were still open, and he had been beforehand with you in writing of his letters. My suspicion that Eck's heart was turned away from me, is much increased for the reason, that, after all the opprobrious words heaped upon me by him, though privately, he never communicated with me on the subject, either in writing or by word of mouth. Now, as Carlstadt's Positions are already published, though without my consent or knowledge, I know not what can be done by either of them. Sure I am, that I hold the man's good parts in great esteem, and his learning in admiration; and what has taken place, I testify to you, moves me to grief, rather than to anger. On my part, I have written him the kind and friendly letter which you will herewith receive and can read. Not only for your sake am I reconciled, but on account of the confession made by him, though not to me, that his notes have been sent forth by the fraud or malice of others. Therefore, both you and he have me in your power in this matter. Only see that he do not answer our Carlstadt too sharply. Let him remember that it was his fault that these evils should spring up among friends. As my Asterisks were given out only privately, there is no need of his answering them if he do not choose. But if he desires to rejoin, I stand ready for either event, though I should choose peace."

Before advancing to the correspondence relating to Luther's citation to appear for trial at Rome, and his actual appearance at Augsburg for that purpose, it will be convenient to advert to some other particulars connected with his present situation and occupations, equally illustrative of his character and of his feelings at the present juncture.

June 4, he wrote to Spalatin : " I pray you, my dear Spalatin, to take it patiently, that I am so slack and negligent in writing to you. I am not able to perform half the business which is unexpectedly and fast increasing upon my hands. Peter Mosellanus was here not long ago, and is content to accept the conditions and begin his duties [at Wittenberg] as professor of Greek; and he desired me to write unto you to that effect. I promised to write, which I now do, not knowing whether there had been any negotiating between you. It will remain for you to do in this matter as God shall give you knowledge and ability. . . . John Tetzel hath written against my German discourse a treatise in German, a singular witness and herald of his ignorance. I will hold the light to it, so that all may see what it is."

For reasons not known, the negotiations with Mosellanus were broken off, and Reuchlin was consulted, who recommended Melancthon as professor of Greek; and in August he was on the ground, thenceforward the second great pillar of the Reformation.

June 29, he writes again to the same : " I am not angry, most excellent Spalatin, that those men say the worst things of me, or that they give out that the Proofs and Conclusions owe their origin to the elector. I only fear that this will be the occasion of stirring up enmity between such princes, especially, if the Elector of Brandenburg should allow, by way of requital, any thing to take place like unto what we lately heard of him.

" You ask me, how far I think dialectics useful to a theologian. I see not how they can be otherwise but hurtful. In the training and exercising the minds of the young, they may have their use; but in sacred learning, where faith and heavenly illumination alone are sought after, they ought to be left behind, as Abraham, about to offer sacrifice, left the servants and asses behind."

To his most intimate friend, Link, now in Nürem berg, who, together with Scheurl, kept Luther informed of all that was going on in the south of Germany for or against the Reformation, Luther writes, July 10 : " I should have sent you, reverend father,* the Proofs of my Theses, but for the slackness of our printer, who himself feels ashamed of it. Eighteen of the conclusions [about one third of the book] were already printed, which I have endeavoured to have sent to you immediately. . . . Our vicar, John Lange, [chosen at the late meeting at Heidelberg,] who is here to-day, saith, he hath been warned by a letter from Count Albert of Mansfeld, to suffer me by no means to go from Wittenberg, [to Augsburg,] because some nameless persons of power are lying in wait to hang me or drown me. I am plainly that man of contention and discord mentioned in Jeremiah, and do daily vex the Pharisees with new doctrines, as they are called, though I am conscious of teaching nothing but the purest theology. I have all along known that I should present an offence to the sanctimonious Jews, and folly to the most wise Greeks. But I hope that I am a debtor to Jesus Christ, who saith to me also, I will show him how great things he must suffer for my name's sake. For, if he doth not say this, why hath he made me invincible in the ministry of this word? Why hath he not taught otherwise than I preach? Such was his holy will. The more men are enraged, the more confidence will I have. My wife and children are provided for, [he was then un-

---

* Title as monk and theologian.

married.] My lands, houses, and goods are all set in order, [he was still a monk, and owned nothing.] My reputation and name are already torn and mangled, and only a frail body remaineth. . . . I know that the word of Christ from the beginning of the world hath been of such a sort, that he who would maintain it must, with the apostles, forsake and renounce all things, and stand in waiting for death every hour. If it were not so, it would not be the word of Christ. It was purchased with death; it was promulgated with death; it hath been maintained with death, and must be hereafter. Thus, our enlisting was to us an enlisting to blood. Pray that the Lord Jesus may increase and preserve this spirit in his faithful poor sinner."

"I have lately preached before the people on the power of excommunication, wherein I have taken occasion to chastise the tyranny and ignorance of that most sordid horde of officials, commissaries and vicars. All cry out with wonder that they never heard such-like things. We are all aware what ills this will bring upon me; a new fire will be kindled. But so the word of truth is made a sign everywhere spoken against. I had desired to debate these matters in a public disputation, but behold public rumour prevented, and stirred up so many of the great, that my Brandenburg bishop desired, through a noted messenger, that I would put off the disputation, which I have done, especially as my friends also advised it. Behold, what a monster I am, whose every endeavour is intolerable! Doctor Jodocus of Eisenach hath sent me a letter, running over with the greatest zeal, (for so must I mention with honour the most impassioned passion of this man,) far more bitter than that which you heard read before the chapter.

He said the same things openly to me in Erfurt
It excruciates even to madness these men that they
must become fools in Christ; that our most eminent
masters in all the world must be considered as having erred for so long a time."

On the 7th of August, 1518, Luther received a
formal citation to appear within sixty days at Rome
for trial.   Prierias, his opponent and bitter enemy,
was appointed one of the judges by whom he was to
be tried.   All Luther's friends readily perceived that
this was but a Romish trick to secure his destruction   At that time the German diet was in session
at Augsburg; the one at which Ulrich von Hutten
published his attack upon Rome; the last which the
Emperor Maximilian ever attended.   The Elector
Frederic, with his secretary and counsellors, was there.

On the following day, August 8th, Luther wrote
thus, to Spalatin: "Now, my dear Spalatin, I
greatly need your succour; or, rather, the honour
of almost the entire university requireth it with me.
What is wanted is, that you should use your power
with the illustrious prince (the elector) and Pfeffinger, that he, the prince, and his majesty the emperor,
procure a release for me, or permission to have my
cause tried in Germany, as I have written to the
elector.   For I see how craftily and maliciously those
murderous preachers are plotting my destruction.   I
would fain have written to Pfeffinger that he
might, by his good offices and those of his friends,
seek the same favour for me from the emperor and
the elector.   But this must be done without delay,
for only a short time is allowed me, as you will see
in this monster of a summons.   Read it, with its
hydra heads and portents.   If you love me and hate
iniquity, obtain the counsel and succour of the elec-

tor as speedily as possible; and when you have done so, signify it to me, or rather to our reverend father Staupitz, who is either already with you at Augsburg, or will be there soon. . . . I beg you not to be anxious or cast down on my account. The Lord will, with the temptation, make a way of escape. To the dialogue of Silvester [Prierias,] which is indeed *silvan* and rustic, I am now making a reply. You shall have it entire, as soon as it is ready. This same sweet creature, my adversary, is also to be my judge; as you will see in the summons."

On the 20th, he writes again: "The messenger whom I sent to our illustrious Prince Frederic hath not yet returned. I am, therefore, still waiting to learn what the Lord intendeth through you to do in my case. I have heard that the reverend Cardinal Cajetan is specially charged by the pope to use his endeavours to imbitter the emperor and the elector against me. [Happily the effort did not succeed.] So timid is the conscience of great pontiffs; or rather such is the insufferable power of truth over deeds done in darkness. And yet I, as you know, my dear Spalatin, have no fear in all these things. Even if their flatteries or their authority should have the effect to render me odious unto all, I have this left in my heart and conscience, that I know and confess that whatsoever I hold and they impugn, I have from God, to whom I cheerfully refer all and offer all. If he take them away, let them be taken away; if he preserve them, let them be preserved; and let his name be hallowed and blessed for ever, Amen. I do not yet well see how I can escape that ecclesiastical censure which is purposed, unless the prince shall come to my aid. And, on the other hand, I would much rather be under perpetual censure, than have the prince suffer in his

good name on my account. As I have before offered
myself, so believe and be assured I still hold myself
ready for any thing you should wish, or think best
A heretic I will never be; err I may in disputation.
But I wish to decide no doctrine; *only, I am not
willing to be the slave of the opinions of men.* It
seemeth best to our learned and prudent friends
here that I should ask our prince, Frederic, for a
safe-conduct through his dominions, and that he
should refuse it, as I know he would, and that this
should be urged as my reason and excuse for my not
appearing in Rome."

It was in the very midst of these transactions, and
before any thing was agreed upon between the elector, the emperor, the cardinal and the pope, in respect
to Luther's trial, that the latter was cheered by the
accession of a brilliant young man to the university
and to the circle of his particular friends; who, from
that time, enjoyed his confidence and supported
him in his great work more than any other individual.
Nothing could have been more advantageous or more
opportune than this event. At the time when the
timidity of Staupitz was beginning to cause him to
withdraw from Luther, and when the mature and
learned Carlstadt began to betray a want of tact in
the management of affairs, Melancthon was sent by
Providence, with his winning and amiable character;
with his varied, elegant and profound learning; with
his clear, philosophic views, his sincere piety and
warm friendship, to take his stand by the side of
Luther, and join him as his truest and ablest associate
in fighting out the battle of truth.

When the negotiations with Mosellanus, in respect
to the Greek professorship, were broken off, in July,
1518, the elector applied to Reuchlin, then residing

at Stuttgard, to recommend two professors, one for the Greek and one for the Hebrew language. Reuchlin recommended Melancthon for the former, and Œcolampadius for the latter. Melancthon was at that time twenty-one years of age, and was temporarily occupying the chair of rhetoric at the University of Tübingen, but a few miles from Reuchlin's house. Being the grandson of Reuchlin's sister, the young Melancthon had been carefully educated under his direction. He distinguished himself by his rapid acquisitions in the Latin school of Simler at Pforzheim. At Heidelberg, where he entered the university at the age of twelve, he acquired the reputation of being the best Greek scholar. At Tübingen, to which, at the end of two years after having taken his first degree, he resorted, and where he spent six years in laborious study, he made such extensive and various acquisitions in learning as to stand prominent above all the youths of the university. Destined, as he was, to be the "preceptor of Germany," it was well that his range of study at Tübingen was very wide. Proceeding from the Latin and Greek, as from a common centre, he extended his studies to history, rhetoric, logic, mathematics, philosophy, theology, law, and even to the leading medical writers, and attended lectures on all these subjects. He not only warmly espoused the cause of Reuchlin, as the representative of Greek and Hebrew literature, and its persecuted but victorious defender against the ignorant Dominican monks of Cologne, but he made himself familiar, even from boyhood, with the New Testament, in the original—a copy of which, received as a present from Reuchlin, he always carried about his person. Reuchlin, in his reply to the elector, said he knew of no German who was Melancthon's superior, except it be Erasmus of Rotterdam. July 24, 1518, Reuchlin wrote to his young kinsman : "I have received a letter from the elector, offering you a place and a salary; and I will apply to you the promise of God made to Abraham : 'Get thee out of thy country, &c.; and I will make thee a great nation ; and I will bless thee, and make thee a great name, and thou shalt be blessed.' So I prophesy of thee, my dear Philip, who art my care and my comfort."

He went by way of Augsburg, in order to see the elector there before he should leave the diet, then in session. On leaving Augsburg, Melancthon proceeded to Nüremberg, where he made the acquaintance of Pirkheimer and Scheurl, and then pursued his way to Leipsic, where he saw the young Greek professor Mosellanus, and on the 25th of August, 1518, reached Wittenberg. Luther's joy, on learning what an acquisition was made to Wittenberg in this remarkable young man, was great; and never had he occasion to abate his admiration. In the very next letter after the one last quoted from him, under date of August 31, he writes to Spalatin, still in Augsburg with the elector: "As touching our Philip Melancthon, be assured all is done, or shall be, which you desire in your letter. He pronounced an [inaugural] oration on the fourth day after his arrival here, [in which he set forth the new method of study in contrast with the old scholastic method,] full of learning and force, meeting with such favour and admiration in all, that you may now leave off all anxiety in commending him unto us. We soon lost the feeling produced by his [small] stature and [his weak bodily] frame; and now we do wonder and rejoice at that which we find in him, and thank the illustrious prince and yourself for what you have done. You have need, rather, to inquire in what study he may render himself most acceptable to our prince. With his consent and approval, I would choose that Philip be made Greek professor. I only have fears that his feeble health will not abide the severity of our climate. I hear, furthermore, that he receiveth too small a stipend, so that the men at Leipsic are hoping to get him away from us. He was beset by them on his way to this place."

September 2, he writes to the same, informing him that the students, now eagerly pursuing the new studies and hearing, by way of preference, lectures on the Bible and the ancient languages, complain that, before receiving their degrees, they are required to attend useless courses of lectures on scholastic theology. Luther and his friends desired that those studies be made optional, and that persons be admitted to the degrees in theology on passing a regular examination on the new branches of study introduced by him, Melancthon and others. He closes by saying, "I commend unto you heartily the most Attic, the most erudite, the most elegant Melancthon. His lecture-room is full, and more than full. He inflameth all our theologians, highest, lowest and midst, with a love of Greek."

On the 9th of the same month, he writes to Lange: "The very learned and most Grecian Philip Melancthon is professor of Greek here, a mere boy or stripling, if you regard his age, but one of us if you consider the abundance of his learning and his knowledge of almost all books. He is not only skilled in both languages, [Latin and Greek, then a rare thing,] but is learned in each. Nor is he wholly ignorant of Hebrew." After going to Augsburg, whither he

resorted for reasons soon to be given, he wrote to
Melancthon himself, under date of Oct. 11 : "There
is nothing new or strange here, saving that the
whole city is filled with the rumour of my name,
and everybody is eager to see the new Herostratus
that has kindled such a conflagration.   Concerning
yourself, go on in your manly course, as you have
begun.   Teach the youth right things.   I give myself up to be sacrificed for them and for you, if it
be the will of God.   I will sooner perish, and,
what is most grievous, for ever lose your delightful
converse, than recall what hath been rightly said, and
become the occasion of extinguishing good learning.
Italy is covered with Egyptian darkness, together
with those sottish and yet savage enemies of letters
and of study.   They neither know Christ nor the
things of Christ; and yet they are our lords and
masters both in matters of faith and of morals."

WE must now resume our narrative in respect to
Luther's summons and trial.   So far was Luther
from being terrified at the threatening aspect things
were beginning to wear at Rome, that he published
a bold reply to Prierias.   At the close, he says,
"Behold the answer I make you, hastily and within
the space of two days, because what you have brought
forward against me appeared so trifling. . . . If you
wish to rejoin, see that you bring your Thomas upon
the arena a little better equipped; otherwise you
will not get off so easy as you have this time.   I
have put myself in check, lest I should render evil
for evil."   Such language did he venture to hold to
an adversary now his judge!   The nature and extent of his Christian courage are well portrayed in a
letter to Staupitz, Sept. 1.   "Do not doubt," he
writes, " my reverend father, that I shall maintain

my freedom in examining and expounding the Scriptures. Neither the summons nor the threats given out shall move me. I suffer, as you know, incomparably worse things, [spiritual conflicts,] which make me regard those temporal and momentary thunderings as trifles. Still, I sincerely regard ecclesiastical authority. . . . If Silvester [Prierias,] that *silvan* sophist, shall go on, and provoke me further with his scribblings, I shall not play with him again, but giving loose reins to my mind and pen, will show him that there are in Germany men who understand his Roman arts. . . . I see that attempts are made at Rome that the kingdom of truth, i. e. of Christ, be no longer the kingdom of truth. They continually ply their rage to hinder truth from being heard and entertained in its own proper kingdom. But I desire to belong to this kingdom, if not truly, as I should, in life, truly at least with my tongue and heart, renewed, albeit, and making true confession. I learn from experience that the people are sighing for the voice of their Shepherd, Christ, and the youth are burning with wonderful zeal for the sacred oracles. A beginning is made with us in reading of Greek. We are all giving ourselves to the Greek for the better understanding of the Bible. We are expecting a Hebrew teacher, and the elector hath the business in hand."

Meanwhile the elector, still at Augsburg, was using his influence with the emperor and with the papal legate, that Luther might receive his trial in Germany. Sept. 9, Luther writes to Lange: "The illustrious prince hath written unto me, that he hath persuaded the legate, Cajetan, to write to Rome, asking that my cause may be tried within the country; and that I must wait for the answer. I have hopes,

therefore, that the ecclesiastical censure will be with-
holden. But I am offensive to many, more, most."
Nevertheless the cardinal, without waiting for any
new instructions from Rome, agreed that Luther
should appear before him at Augsburg, at the close
of the diet. Of the character and conditions of that
trial, however, nothing was decided. The elector
and many other members of the diet had left the
place before Luther's arrival. The latter, happy to
learn that he was released from the obligation to
appear at Rome, readily complied with the request
to present himself before the papal legate at Augsburg. He set out on foot, availing himself of the
hospitality of the cloisters that lay in his route.
He reached Weimar, Sept. 28, and on the following
day, which was a great festival, he preached in the
chapel attached to the palace, and touched upon the
character of the bishops, who, instead of appearing
in the form of servants of the church, acted the part
of lords and tyrants. The treasurer of the monks
at Weimar, by the name of John Kestner, approached Luther, and expressed great solicitude in
respect to the result of the step he was about to
take. "Oh, my dear doctor," said he, "the Italians
are very learned people. I fear you will not be able
to gain your cause with them, and they will put you
to the flames." Luther replied, "With nettles I
could bear; but with fire it would be rather too hot.
Dear friend, pray to our Lord God in heaven with
a paternoster for me and for his dear Son, whose is
my cause, that he would show mercy. If he will
maintain my cause, let it be maintained; if he has
not a mind to maintain it, then I will not maintain
it; I will let him see to that." From this place he
was sent forward by the elector, who furnished him

with many important letters to those who were to
be his counsellors and protectors at Augsburg. A
few miles before reaching the place, he was so exhausted that he was obliged to take a carriage. He
had also borrowed a robe of his Nüremberg friend
Link, that he might appear the more respectably
before the great men at Augsburg.

Three days after his arrival, he wrote to Spalatin:
"I arrived, my dear Spalatin, at Augsburg on St.
Mark's day, Oct. 7. We were very much wearied; I
especially was almost consumed by the journey, being
exhausted from a disordered stomach. But I have recovered. This is the third day since my arrival, and
I have not yet seen the most reverend legate. I sent
to him, on the first day, Doctor Link and another to
announce my arrival. In the mean while, my good
friends here have been diligent in procuring for me
a safe-conduct from the emperor and the senate [of
Augsburg.] By the authority of our illustrious
prince, they are all very kind unto me and careful
of my wants. Although the reverend cardinal
legate promiseth to use all lenity, [he had made
such a promise to the elector,] yet my friends are
not willing that I should put any trust in him.
They take upon themselves to exercise their own
prudence and diligence in this matter. For they
know that, whatsoever he pretendeth outwardly, he
is inwardly very bitter against me. I have had the
same thing hinted, in no obscure manner, from other
quarters. To-day I shall go unto him, and seek my
first audience, and see him face to face. What will
be the issue, I know not. Some think it a good
omen for my cause that the Cardinal Gurk is absent;
others, that the emperor himself is absent, though
the latter is not far away, [engaged in the chase,]

and his return is daily expected. The Bishop of Augsburg is also absent from the city. Yesterday I dined with Dr. Conrad Peutinger, and a better citizen and man I have never seen. He is most of all engaged in my interest, and other senators are scarcely less so. Whether the reverend legate is afraid of me, or is cherishing a monster,* I do not know. Yesterday he sent unto me the orator of Montferrat, who told me not to visit the legate without first having a conference with himself. It is thought by all, that he came by the legate's order. With many words, and, as he saith. 'judicious counsels,' he endeavoured to persuade me to submit forthwith to the legate, and to return to the church by recanting my hard speeches, at the same time proposing to me the example of Joachim, Abbot of Florence, who, by such means, though he had said heretical things, escaped from being a heretic. Then the sweet creature wished me to abstain from giving the reasons for what I had said. 'Dost thou wish to break a lance?' said he. To be short, he is an Italian, and will always be an Italian. . . . He went on to make the most absurd declarations, and acknowledged openly that it was right to preach what was false for the sake of a good profit, as he called it, and filling the purse. . . . But I dismissed this Sinon, [who deceived the Trojans in regard to the wooden horse,] who had so little of the Grecian cunning, and he went his ways. Thus I am in suspense between hope and fear; for this unapt mediator hath inspired me with no little confidence.''

Luther goes on to mention that he had engaged Rossenstein, of Ingolstadt, as professor of Hebrew,

---

* Secretly favouring a bad cause.

and provided for his travelling expenses to Wittenberg; that Staupitz had written that he would be at Augsburg as soon as he should know that Luther was there; that the orator of France had left Augsburg, but not without leaving a signal proof of his regard for him; that the golden rose was sent to the elector by the pope, and "salutes all his Wittenberg friends, and wishes them prosperity, whether he returns to them or not." The letter to Melancthon, written about the same time, has been already given above.

October 15, he wrote again to Spalatin: "I am not minded, my dear Spalatin, to write to our illustrious prince. You, therefore, who are familiar with him, receive my communication, and signify it to him. The legate hath treated with me, or rather against me, now for the space of four days; having before promised our illustrious prince that he would act a kind and fatherly part, but, in truth, doing every thing by inflexible power alone. He was loth to have me debate the matters in dispute with him publicly; nor was he willing to discuss them with me privately. His replies were all of this one tenor: 'Recant; acknowledge your error; the pope will have it so, and not otherwise, whether you will or not,' and such like. . . . At length, overcome by the entreaties of many, he consented that I should give my reasons in writing; which I have done this day, in the presence of the elector's minister, Felitzsch, who brought to mind the prince's request. At length the paper was rejected with disdain, and my revocation loudly demanded; and with a long rehearsal from the fables of Aquinas, he seemed to conquer and silence me. I essayed a dozen times to say a word, and he chopped in upon me as many

times with thundering tones, and reigned alone."
Luther finally said to him, " If you will prove your
point even from those papal decrees you have been
reading, I will revoke as you desire." " And now
such airs and such laughter! He suddenly seized
the book, read eagerly and out of breath," till he
came to a certain passage, when Luther stopped him,
and said, " This expression teacheth just the contrary
of what you assert. My conclusion is, therefore,
right." " He being confused, and yet not wishing to
appear so, prudently dashed off upon another matter.
But I eagerly and not very reverently interrupted
him, and said: ' Let not your reverence suppose
that the Germans are ignorant of grammar, too.'
. . . His confidence deserted him ; and as he cried
out, ' Recant,' I left him, he meanwhile saying ,' Go,
and return not to me, till thou art willing to recant.'"
What is here thrown together took place at different times, as will appear from the following.

Luther had received the imperial safe-conduct on
Monday, the 11th of October. On Tuesday, in company with Frosch, prior of the Carmelite convent,
with whom he lodged, two other brethren of the
same order, and Link, and another Augustinian monk,
he had proceeded to the legate, with whom he found
the apostolical nuncio and the orator Urban, above
mentioned. According to instructions previously
received, Luther prostrated himself upon his face
before the legate. When the latter bade him rise,
he rose first upon his knees, and afterward upon his
feet. Meanwhile, a throng of curious Italians had
crowded into the room, in order to see the fearless
monk. After acknowledging that he was the author
of the theses, and saying, that he was willing to be
instructed if he had erred, the legate required him

to confess his errors, and promise to drop them, and
no more trouble the church. The errors were chiefly
two, the denial that the merits and sufferings of
Christ are the treasure of the church, and the assertion that faith was necessary in order to partake of
the holy communion. Here ensued the discussion
mentioned in the foregoing letter. On returning to
his lodgings at night, he found Staupitz there, having just arrived from Salzburg, his present residence.
On Wednesday, Luther proceeded again to the cardinal's house, accompanied by Staupitz, the three
imperial counsellors, Auerbach, Peutinger and Langenmantel, and by Felitzsch, and desired permission to reply, in writing, to any errors which might
be imputed to him; and this, after a long discussion, in which Staupitz took part, was granted. On
Thursday, he came again with Felitzsch, the elector's minister, and Dr. Rühel, and presented a full
reply in writing, in which he resolutely maintained
the two positions complained of, and showed the
heresy of the contrary view. This was the paper
which the legate threw aside in contempt; and then
it was that he was reduced to silence by Luther, who
turned against him the very passage the legate was
reading to prove his point. In the afternoon, the
legate sent for Staupitz, and requested him to undertake the work of persuading Luther to renounce his
heresy. But Staupitz replied, that he could not do
it, as Luther was too strong for him in the Scriptures. He finally made the attempt, but when Luther brought forward his passages of Scripture, and
asked Staupitz to give any other interpretation of
them, he confessed he could not, and concluded by
saying to Luther: "Remember, dear brother, that
thou hast taken this matter up in the name of

Jesus." The cardinal then agreed with Staupitz that he would point out the particular articles which Luther should retract. But the articles did not come, and Luther sent his friend Link to request that the points in dispute might be adjusted. The legate appeared friendly, said he did not regard Luther as a heretic, and that he would not excommunicate him, unless he should receive further command so to do from Rome, whither he had just sent a special messenger with Luther's reply. If Luther would but admit the single article on indulgences, he continued, the case might easily be disposed of, for the article on faith might admit of some explanation. "A clear proof this," said Staupitz, on hearing it, " that Rome hath more care for money than for faith and salvation."

It was the opinion of the various friends of Luther, that Staupitz and Link should leave Augsburg, and put no further confidence in these wily Italians; and consequently they both went, though by different routes, to Nüremberg the same day. Luther remained all day, Saturday, without hearing from the legate; also the following Sunday, when he sent a very humble communication to Cajetan, saying, he had, in his excitement, been too violent and disrespectful toward the pope; that it would have been better to have been more temperate, and not to have answered a fool according to his folly; that he would be silent in respect to indulgences, if the other party should be made to do the same. He would furthermore gladly renounce whatever his conscience would allow; but at no one's command, nor to please any one, could he violate his conscience. Having received no word in reply, he wrote again on Monday, saying, he was not conscious of neglect·

ing any thing which belonged to him as a faithful son of the church; he could not waste his time, nor be longer burdensome to the Carmelite monastery. Besides, the legate had forbidden him to appear again without a revocation. His friends had advised him to appeal from the pope misinformed to the pope better to be informed. Ecclesiastical censure he had not deserved; neither did he stand in fear of it. By the grace of God he had reached to that point, that he feared excommunication less than he feared error. The legate, he hoped, would, before the pope, put a kind construction upon his departure and upon his appeal. Luther remained Monday and Tuesday, and, as he heard nothing from the cardinal, his friends thought such silence no good omen, and, according to their advice, Luther left Augsburg, Wednesday, the 20th, on a horse which Staupitz had provided for him, and with a guide furnished him by the council. Langenmantel let him out of the city by a small gate by night. Luther, without suitable garments, that is, in a monk's robe, without boots, rode about forty miles the first day, and when he alighted from his horse at the stable at night, he was unable to stand, and fell down on the straw. In Gräfenthal, half-way between Coburg and Jena, Count Albert of Mansfeld found him, and laughed heartily at the barefooted and bare-legged rider, and made him his guest.

Luther felt thankful for his safe return, respecting which he had been apprehensive. To Carlstadt he had written: "But whether I come back to you without injury or separation, or be banished to some other place, may you prosper and adhere to Christ, and exalt him without dismay or discouragement."

Still, with a single word, (*revoco*, I revoke,) he might, he assures us, have rendered himself most acceptable and beloved. "But," says he, "sooner than renounce that doctrine which has made me a Christian, will I die, be burned, banished and cursed."

The very day he reached Wittenberg, Oct. 31, precisely twelve months from the time he came out with his theses, he wrote to Spalatin: "To-day, my dear Spalatin, have I come, by the grace of God, safely to Wittenberg, not knowing, however, how long I shall abide here, for I am in a state of uncertainty between hope and fear." After saying that if his first appeal is without effect, he will make another to a general council, he adds, "I am full of joy and peace, so much so as to marvel that this my trial should appear a great matter to many notable men." At Nüremberg, on his way home, he saw, for the first time, the papal brief and other instructions given to Cajetan, by which it appeared he was already condemned, unless he renounced his errors. He was greatly incensed at this "apostolical, or rather diabolical brief." "It is incredible that a thing so monstrous should come from the chief pontiff, especially from Leo X. . . . If, in truth, it did come forth from the Roman court," he continues, "then I will show them their most licentious temerity and their most ungodly ignorance." He did, indeed, afterward publish that brief, with a cutting running commentary, in which, among other things, he says, "The best of all is, that the brief is dated August 23, and my citation was given August 7, leaving a space of but sixteen days. . . . . . What, then, becometh of the sixty days spoken of in my summons?—[within which he was to appear for trial.]

Is this the fashion and custom of the Roman court, to cite, warn, accuse, judge, condemn and give sentence all on one and the same day; and that, too, when the person indicted is so far from Rome as to know nothing thereof? What answer will they make to this? Peradventure they forgot to clear their brain with hellebore before entering upon these acts of deception and fraud."

In the same letter, quoted from above, Luther mentions that Frosch, prior of the Carmelite monastery at Augsburg, who had treated him "with incredible liberality and kindness" during his stay there, was about to apply for the degree of doctor of divinity at Wittenberg. "He is worthy on sundry accounts," says Luther, "to be requited with a favour from us. By promise of the elector, as he saith, he expecteth a public dinner to be given unto him on occasion of that solemnity. I may rest well assured it will be so, if the elector hath promised it. All needful preparations will, without doubt, be made. See to it, then, that his expectation be fulfilled on our part with due honour." The elector seems either not to have had a distinct recollection of the promise, or to have found some difficulty in fulfilling it. Luther observes, not without chagrin, in a subsequent letter: "Lest a man so worthy of being honoured be dismissed without honour, we have had recourse to our own monastery, and shall provide the dinner at our own trouble. . . . But we are very poor, and there is already a multitude of us, so that we cannot, without difficulty, be at that expense. I pray you, therefore, to see that the prince furnish us with the wild fowl and venison." On the 18th of November, Luther, as dean of the theological faculty, conferred the degree. But Melancthon, the young Greek professor, whom the heroic reformer had as yet seen but a few times, did not come to the dinner. Luther wrote him the same day the following facetious note, inviting him to supper: "To-day, you have despised me and the new doctor, which may the muses and Apollo forgive you. And I, though the affair was not altogether mine, myself forgive you. But unless you appear this time to meet Dr. Carlstadt, licentiate Amsdorf, and especially the rector, neither your Greek learning, nor little brother Martin, as Cajetan calleth me, will excuse you. The new doctor jocosely saith he supposeth he, as a barbarian, is lightly esteemed by the Greek. Be careful what you do, for I have promised that you will assuredly be present this time."

As early as the 25th of October, Cajetan wrote to the Elector Frederic, complaining of Luther, and affirming that his teachings were contrary to those of the Roman see, and deserving to be condemned. "Your grace," he continues, "may believe me, for I speak the truth, from what I certainly know, and not from mere opinion." He then begs and exhorts the elector either to send Luther to Rome, or to banish him from the country. This letter was put into the hands of Luther, with the request that he would indicate what reply ought to be given. Luther took this opportunity to rehearse the whole course of the transactions with Cajetan; to expose the unfairness of them, and to open the eyes of the prince more fully in respect to the chicanery practised by the Roman court. In this letter he says to the elector: "In order that no evil may accrue to your grace on my account, a thing which I least of all desire, I purpose to forsake your dominions, and go wheresoever my gracious God will have me, and submit myself to his divine will, whatsoever may come." He wrote to Spalatin that he should regret to be arrested in his course at Wittenberg, not so much on his own account as on that of the university and the many excellent young men who were there, burning with zeal for a knowledge of the Holy Scriptures. If he should be silenced, the turn would next come to Carlstadt and to the whole theological faculty. The university wrote to the elector, entreating him to interest himself especially in the cause of Luther To his congregation Luther said, "I am, in these times, as you well know, an irregular preacher, having often gone away without taking leave of you Should that ever take place again, I will now say farewell, in case I should not return."

As Frederic was very reserved in regard to his opinion of Luther's course, and as the latter was desirous not only not to involve his prince in the controversy, but to enjoy more freedom for discussion than he supposed could be allowed him in Saxony, he seriously purposed retiring from his post, and seeking some other place of abode. Paris seemed to be the place of his choice, as he vainly imagined the defenders of the liberties of the Gallican church would sympathize with him. There was much consultation with Spalatin and other friends about the place and manner of retirement, and all things were arranged by Luther for a speedy departure, when suddenly, on the 1st of December, a letter came to him from the secretary Spalatin, which prevented the execution of the plan.

December 2, he writes: "Had your letter not been received yesterday, my dear Spalatin, I had taken measures for my departure, and I still hold myself ready either to go or to remain. The concern my friends feel for me maketh me marvel, and is more than I can endure. Some have urged with great earnestness that I should give myself up as a captive to the elector, in order that he might take possession of me and keep me in custody, and then write to the legate that I was detained in safe keeping until I should render an account of my doings. What opinion ought to be entertained of this advice, I leave to be decided by your wisdom. I am in the hands of God and of my friends.

"It is certain that the elector is believed to be on my side. This I learn from a man who would assuredly not deceive me. At the court of the Bishop of Brandenburg, the question was lately moved what my confidence was, in whose support I trusted. One replied, 'In Erasmus, Capito, and other learned men.' 'No,' said the bishop, 'these would have no weight with the pope. It is the University of Wittenberg and the Duke of Saxony that uphold him.' Thus I clearly see that the elector is thought to be with me, and this displeaseth me. The suspicion he stands in as being joined with me will constrain me to withdraw, if any thing can have that effect, although the elector might say in his reply, that he is a layman, and doth not take upon him to judge in such matters; and the more so, because he seeth that the university, which hath the approval of the church, is not against me. But you have no need of these my cogitations. If I remain here, I shall be hindered from saying and writing many things; if I go away, I shall open my whole mind, and offer up my life unto Christ."

The pope resorted to another expedient in order to accomplish his purpose in respect to Luther. He appointed Miltitz, a Saxon by birth, now agent of the elector at Rome, as a nuncio to Germany, and fitted him out with a golden rose, a token of friendship given only to princes who were the pope's favourites. Miltitz was to unite with this flattering office that of making good what had been lost by Cajetan toward effecting a reconciliation. This undertaking of Miltitz, which from various causes was an entire failure, was a sort of interlude. The nuncio acted a shrewd part, and, but for Eck and other zealots, would probably have been successful. He avoided connection with Cajetan, who had become generally odious by his arrogance, and associated himself closely with Pfeffinger, the elector's minister. He demeaned himself as a subject of Frederic, admitted the justness of Luther's complaints against indulgences, and treated Luther with great consideration and tenderness. For a long time, he was received and treated with suspicion. Luther did not trust him. Still he induced Luther to make many important concessions, all that could possibly be made by him with a good conscience. When, in the beginning of the year 1519, the imperial throne became vacant, the pontiff was interested to exclude the house of Austria, already too powerful, from the succession, and secure the election of the King of France. Frederic's position, as one of the most influential of the electors and as vicar of the empire, now rendered it necessary for the Roman see to change its haughty tone toward him, and consequently Luther was left for several months comparatively free.

On the 9th of December, 1518, Luther wrote two letters to Spalatin, one in which he proposes a moderate reform in the university, by dropping one or two courses of lectures in the scholastic philosophy; the other in which he speaks thus: "That which you, my dear Spalatin, direct me not to do [the publishing of his account of the interview with Cajetan at Augsburg] hath been already done. My rehearsal of those doings have been published, and I have used great liberty therein, and yet have come short of the whole truth. Herein, as well as in all other matters, I perceive that I must act without any delay. Yesterday I was given to understand from Nüremberg that Charles von Miltitz was on his way hither with three papal briefs, as it is on good authority said, for apprehending me and delivering me up to the pope. The Eisleben doctor, who, with Felitzsch, was present when I stood before the legate, hath given me warning through our prior to be on my guard. . . . I have heard many such-like things which, whether they be true, or only given out in order to terrify me, must not, I think, go unheeded Therefore, to the end they may not come upon me unawares and despatch me, nor, on the other hand, cast me down and overcome me by means of judgments passed against me, I hold myself in readiness for any event, and so await the will of God. I have made my appeal to a future council. The more they rage and have recourse to violence, so much the less am I terrified. I will one day be yet more bold against those Roman hydras. That which you have heard, namely, that I have taken leave of the people of Wittenberg, is not so. I only said, . . . 'If I should ever again suddenly leave you, I wish now to say farewell, in case I should not return.'"

On the 11th of the same month, he wrote to his friend Link in Nüremberg: "The report touching the three apostolical briefs, given unto Miltitz against me, hath come to my ears. Casper, [Aquila,] who

had learned this from your letter, informed me of
the same by a special messenger, in his over-anxiety
for me. I send you my Transactions, written with
more sharpness than the legate would like to see
published. But my pen is already producing still
weightier things. I know not whence these cogitations arise. This matter hath in my esteem hardly
a beginning yet, so far is it from the end, which the
great ones of Rome are looking for. I will send
unto you my trifles, that you may see whether I
rightly interpret the words of Paul in respect of
antichrist, as referring to the court of Rome. I
think I can plainly show that the Romans are even
now worse than the Turks. . . . I live in expectation of the attempts of my murderers, whether from
Rome or from any other quarter. I marvel that
the excommunication tarries so long. . . . Our studies are going actively on, and we are as busy as
bees. Farewell. Greet all my friends, especially
the preacher Sebaldinus, and the other master, but
most of all Pirkheimer, Albert Dürer, and Christopher Scheurl, [the most influential men in Nüremberg.] Eck writeth that he is not altogether pleased
nor altogether displeased with my reply to Prierias ;
but he addeth a very sagacious and true clause,
namely, that he well knoweth his opinion will not
weigh much with me."

Two days later, he wrote to Staupitz then in
Salzburg, mentioning his safe return from Augsburg,
and then proceeding to say : "The elector dissuaded
me altogether from bringing out my account of the
Augsburg Transactions; but at length he hath given
his consent, and they are now in course of printing.
In the mean season, the legate wrote [to him,] bitterly accusing me and you and my associates, as he

calleth them, complaining that I departed secretly
from Augsburg, and that it was done in guile.　He
then counselleth the elector to send me bound to
Rome, or to banish me from his dominions, in order
that he bring not a foul spot upon his name for the
sake of one little monk.　He saith the cause will be
sustained and prosecuted at Rome; that he himself
hath written to the city, giving an account of my
fraud, and that he hath washed his hands of the
fault.　The elector desired me to reply to that
letter, in order that he might put my answer with
his own, and send both to the legate.　This have I
done, and, as I think, in a satisfactory manner.　The
elector manifests much concern for me, but would
choose I were somewhere else.　He ordered Spalatin
to call me to Lichtenburg, and to confer fully with
me on the matter there.　I told him, that if the excommunication should come I would not continue
here.　He entreated me not to think of going to
France.　I am still waiting to learn his final decision.　As for you, my beloved father, farewell.　Commend to Christ my soul alone.　I see that these men
have determined on my death; but Christ deter-
mineth not to yield in me.　Let, yea, let his holy
and blessed will be done.　Pray for me. . . . Our
studies prosper well, save that there is a lack of time
for our best lectures."

To Reuchlin, the very next day, December 14th,
Luther wrote the following spirited and magnificent
letter.　"The Lord be with you, most courageous
man: I rejoice in the goodness of God which is
manifested in you, most erudite and most excellent
sir, in that you have been able to stop the mouths
of evil-speakers.　Surely you were an instrument of
the Divine will, though not knowing it yourself, yet

longed for by all the lovers of a pure theology. Quite other things are accomplished by God than that which seemeth outwardly to be done through you. Of those who desired to be joined with you I was one; but I had no opportunity. Yet was I always most present with you in my prayers and wishes. But now, that which was denied me when I would fain have been your fellow-labourer, is abundantly granted me as your successor. The teeth of that behemoth are now gnashing upon me, to repair, if possible, the dishonour received through you. I meet these men with much less of ability and learning, but not with less confidence than that wherewith you met and overcame them. They abstain from contending with me. They refuse to reply unto me, and have recourse to nothing else but force and violence. But Christ liveth, and I can lose nothing, because I possess nothing. By your firmness the horns of those bulls are not a little broken. This doth the Lord accomplish through you to the end that the sophistical tyrants may learn to be a little more tardy and moderate in resisting the truth; that Germany may draw breath again, and the teaching of the Scriptures be revived, which, alas! have for so many centuries been not only kept down, but extinguished." He excused himself for writing so familiarly, by saying that his affection for him, and his knowledge of him both through common fame and through his books, together with Melancthon's assurance that it would be kindly received, emboldened him thus to write. Reuchlin's dispute with the Dominican monks of Cologne was at first personal, and related to the value of Hebrew and Greek literature; but it ended in dividing Germany into two great parties, henceforth to be represented by Luther and his opponents.

In a letter to Spalatin, December 20, on the subject of the elector's letter to Cajetan, Luther, among other things, says: "I have seen the excellent letter of our illustrious prince to the reverend legate. With what joy did I read that letter over and over again, which so aboundeth in Christian confidence, and is yet so wonderfully meek. I do only but fear that the Italians will not understand how much is meant under that humble attitude and form. They are a people, whose custom and use it is, both in their doings and in their writings, to set every thing forth with great ostentation and show. But they will, at least, see so much as this, that nothing which they have put their hands to seemeth to prosper. It cannot be otherwise but that they will be greatly displeased. Wherefore, I entreat you in the Lord, to thank the prince on my behalf, and show unto him how joyful and grateful I am. It hath all turned out well that he, [Cajetan,] who, a little while before, was but a poor monk like myself, did not fear to draw near to great potentates, [such as Frederic,] without showing them any honour or reverence, and to threaten them, to command them, and to treat them as haughtily as he pleased. He may now know, though late, that the civil power is of God, and that the honours thereof may not be trodden in the dust, especially by one who hath received his own authority from only a man, [the pope.] It pleaseth me much, that in this matter the prince hath shown an impatience so *patient* and prudent. The Lord own and acknowledge all this, whatsoever it be, as his."

On the 27th of December, Miltitz reached Alten-

burg, his head-quarters while in Saxony. Having
learned the vile practices of Tetzel, and especially
his squandering habits, he wrote to Leipsic, only
twenty-seven miles distant, where that monk passed
the remaining few months of his life, ordering him
to appear at Altenburg, to give an account of his doings. We have the reply of Tetzel, preserved in
full. Under date of December 31, 1518, he begins
his letter thus : " Your excellency hath given me
notice, that I am required to come to Altenburg, to
hear somewhat in particular from you. Now, I
would willingly undertake the labour of such journey, if I could, without peril of life, go out of Leipsic For the Augustinian monk, Martin Luther,
hath stirred up not only all the German estates, but
even the kingdoms of Bohemia, Hungary, and Po-
land against me, so that I am nowhere in safety."

He complains of Luther's hostility and false accu-
sations, particularly as made in the account which
the latter had recently given of the transactions at
Augsburg, "in which all the blame was cast upon
Tetzel and his abettors ; and closes by saying, that
he has already suffered very much for his fidelity to
the pope, but will nevertheless continue to be faithful until death. He died not long after, in such
wretchedness as to excite Luther's compassion, and
draw forth from him a letter of Christian consolation. His death occurred during the Leipsic disputation, on the 4th of July, the very day that Luther,
but a few rods distant from Tetzel's retreat, began
his debate with Eck.

Meanwhile, Luther had an interview with Miltitz,
at Altenburg, the first week in January, 1519. On
the second day, he writes without date to the elector:
·· It is quite too much that your electoral and princely

grace should be so entangled in my affairs and troubles; but as it is a thing of necessity, which God hath so ordered, I pray you accept it graciously. Yesterday, Charles von Miltitz set forth very earnestly the discredit and dishonour done through me to the Roman see, and I promised to do, with all humility, what I could to make reparation. . . . First, I agreed to drop the matter, and let it die of itself, on condition that my adversaries do the same. For I think if they had let my writings pass, all should have been still, and the song ended, and the people weary of it long ago. Furthermore, I fear, if this course be not taken, but the strife go on either by violence or by disputation, something ill will come of it, and the play will turn out to be too much in earnest. Therefore, I think it best to let the matter end where it is. Secondly, I have promised to write to his holiness the pope, submitting myself humbly to him, and acknowledging that I have been too heated and violent, though I did not intend thereby to harm the holy Roman church, but rather, as a true son of the church, to set myself against blasphemous preaching, which brought the Roman church into contempt and reproach among the people. Thirdly, I consented to put forth an address, exhorting all to follow, obey and honour the Roman church, and to interpret my writings, not to the discredit, but to the honour of that church; and I promised to confess in the same, that I have been too warm, and, perchance, out of season, in what I have said. . . . Fourthly, Master Spalatin, at the instance of Fabian, proposed to lay the matter in dispute before the most reverend Archbishop of Salzburg, by whose decision, to be made after consultation with learned men, I must abide, unless I may choose to appeal from it to a future council. Perhaps, the jar may thus be stayed, and made quietly to pass away. But I fear the pope will not allow a judge, [to decide between him and me,] and I certainly will not allow the pope's authority. If, therefore, the first plan doth not work well, the play will be, that the pope will give the text, and I make the commentary. But that is not a thing to be wished. I have conferred with Miltitz thereon, who doubteth this will not be enough; and yet did he not demand a recantation from me, but will take the proposal into consideration. If your grace thinketh I can do more, condescend, for the Lord's sake, graciously to show it unto me; for all pains taken to draw from me a retractation will nothing avail."

To many it seems difficult to interpret these concessions in a manner that shall be honourable to Luther. His firmness seems almost to have deserted him. But we must remember that his case, at that time, appeared almost desperate. He was unwilling to stand in such relations of dependence to the elector, or to involve him in the controversy. The result was very uncertain. The papal nuncio treated him with great kindness, and conceded nearly all that he had asserted, so that Luther would come off quite as well as the pope would. Besides, the concessions of Luther related to the Roman church, *in the abstract*, apart from the abuses of unworthy functionaries; and for this church, so viewed, he never lost his reverence, nor did he ever adopt the theory of separation. Luther was always, and more particularly in the earlier and later parts of his life, a churchman, and therefore he could take the ground he did in this letter Finally,

be refused to retract, and would confess little, except
indiscretion in the manner he had written.   And,
after all, what if Luther was human, and was not
always equally the saint or the hero?   What if the
transactions with the nuncio betrayed a weak point in
the reformer in an hour of despondency and gloom?
Luther was not perfect, was not always consistent,
nor always right either in his opinions or in his feelings.   Far from it.

The interview on Luther's part was somewhat of
a diplomatic character.   He distrusted the Roman
courtier, though a Saxon by birth.   He doubted
whether the court of Rome would go so far as the
nuncio believed.   He wished to have it appear, in
case of failure, that the fault was not his.   And,
moreover, he all the while entertained views and
feelings which he thought it not best to betray either
to the nuncio or to the elector.   He was dealing with
men of the court.

In the freedom of confidential correspondence,
Luther, in letters to various friends, unbosoms all
his feelings and transient impressions.   But with
wonderful variety and adaptation to character, he
imparts to his several correspondents only what
their peculiarities would enable them to appreciate,
and what would meet with their sympathy.   To the
elector he writes with reserve, but in a way adapted
to win his confidence and affection, and speaks of
transactions as they would be likely to affect his
policy.   To Spalatin, he writes as to a friend and a
theologian more fully and freely, but with the evident expectation that it will, indirectly and on the
most fitting occasions, and with suitable accompani-
ments, reach the elector's ear.   To Scheurl, he writes
as to an intelligent statesman and warm friend,

whom he highly respects, and whose influence in Nüremberg is of great importance to him. Through him, he is virtually addressing the south of Germany, and he does not forget that in the tone of his letters. To Egran, an independent and bold innovator or reformer in Zwickau, he writes as to a kindred spirit, and speaks right out without reserve. To Staupitz, he writes with affection and a delicate regard to his character and position, as a timid friend, whom he wishes to draw forth from his papal connections and sympathies. All these things must be taken into the account, if we would rightly understand his letters.

To Scheurl he writes, January 13, 1519: "I have stolen from myself and from my labours this hour, and write, at last, to the intent that I may not seem unthankful for so many letters from you, or unwilling to reply. I, in all sincerity, thank you for the pure and true friendship whereby you lend me your counsels and show your solicitude for me. Gladly would I see the end of this turbulence, if my enemies were of the same mind. But they purpose, as I see, to compass their work, not by gentleness, but by power and violence. Hence, they daily stir up against themselves the more oppositions, and bring nothing to pass. That the upstir can never be put down by naked force, I well know. The trifles of Silvester [Prierias,] if they are indeed his, seem not to deserve a reply from me: they are puerile and womanly, nothing but the moanings of his grief. With Charles [Miltitz,] I have had a very friendly meeting, and it has been agreed, first, that utter silence on this subject shall be observed on both parts; and, secondly, that by order of the supreme pontiff, some German bishop shall point out

the errors which I shall retract. But, except God
interpose, nothing will be brought to pass, especially
if they shall take in hand to force me with that new
decretal, the which I have not yet seen. I have
heard that it asserts the plenitude of [the papal]
power, without bringing forward any support either
from the Scriptures or from the canons. But this I
would never grant to any decretal, even the most
ancient. Who can tell what God intends to raise
up through these monsters! As touching myself, I
am neither terrified nor desirous to hush the matter.
I have in store many things, which could touch the
Roman hydra, and which I would fain bring forth,
if suffered to do so. But if God will not that I
should have the liberty, the will of the Lord be
done." What, in the dubious state of things then
existing, could be said more adapted in any event
to secure the confidence and continued respect of the
friend who had evidently been advising him to a
peaceful course? How different the tone of his letter
to Egran, who had already broken, on his own account, with the Papists, or rather with the monks
who had assailed Luther. It was written February 2,
and begins thus: "Accept a brief notice, my dear
Egran, of the present state of my affairs. Charles
von Miltitz was sent unto our prince, armed with
more than seventy apostolical briefs, given to this
end, that he should bring me alive and bound to
Rome, that murderous Jerusalem. But being laid
prostrate by the Lord on the way, that is, being terrified by the multitude of those who favour me, after
he had most carefully noted the estimation in which
the people held me, he turned his violence into friendship, which was nothing but a pretence, and treated
with me a long while to persuade me, for the honour

of the church, to retract what I had said. To which I replied after this sort: 'Let the manner of retracting be determined, and the grounds of the error pointed out in such a manner that they would appear plain both to the common people and to the learned, lest a wrong retractation should stir up still greater hatred against Rome.' It was at length agreed by us, that the Bishops of Salzburg and Treves should be chosen, and that unto one of them the case should be referred for decision; and thus we parted as friends with a [Judas] kiss. For in his entreaties he shed tears. I, for my part, feigned not to understand those crocodile tears. Thus far hath the matter proceeded. What is now doing at Rome, I know not. Charles [Miltitz] said, there had not for a century been a cause which had given more trouble to that most odious herd of cardinals, and of Romanizing Romanists; that they would sooner give ten thousand ducats, than allow this matter to go on as it had begun." Here we perceive clearly, that Luther had no confidence in the nuncio's sincerity, but still thought it best to treat with him without appearing to comprehend his policy. In this way, Luther would either induce him to effect a relaxation of the severity of the pope, or make it appear to all the world that he himself was not in fault if the reconciliation was not effected.

The following letter to Staupitz, written February 20th, will serve not only to illustrate the foregoing, but to throw light upon Luther's present relations to Staupitz, and upon the view they took of the course of events. "Though you are far from me, [at Salzburg, near the western boundary of Austria,] reverend father, and keep silence, not writing to me as I had expected and desired, I nevertheless

will break the silence. I and all others are desirous
to see you here in these regions. I suppose you
have received my Transactions, that is, the ire and
indignation of Rome. God hurries and forces me
on instead of leading me. I am not master of my
self. While I desire to be quiet, I am driven into
the midst of tumults. Charles Miltitz has seen me
at Altenburg, and complained that I had drawn all
the world away from the pope unto myself; that he
had, on his journey, made observation and found that
scarcely two or three out of five held with the Roman party. He was armed with seventy apostolical
briefs for the purpose of carrying me captive to that
murderous Jerusalem, that Babylon in purple, as I
afterward learned from the court of the elector.
When that device was given up in despair, he undertook to persuade me to retract, and thus to restore
what I had taken away. On my asking to be instructed as to what I should retract, it was agreed
that the cause should be carried before certain
bishops. I made mention of the Archbishop of
Salzburg, Treves, and Freisingen. At evening I
complied with an invitation to sup with him, and
we had a pleasant season together, and when we
parted, he kissed me. I made as though I did not
understand this Italian dissimulation. He also
summoned and censured Tetzel. Afterward, at
Leipsic, he convicted him of receiving as wages
ninety florins a month, besides three horsemen and
a carriage, and all his charges to boot. Tetzel himself hath now disappeared, no one, save perhaps the
fathers of his order, knowing whither he hath gone.
Eck, a man of guile, draweth me, as you here see
[from his theses,] into new disputes. Thus the Lord
taketh care that I be not idle. But, by the will of

Christ, this [Leipsic] disputation shall turn out ill for those Roman laws and customs on which Eck leaneth for support. . . . The Leipsic professors have given their consent to have the disputation with Eck held in their university, and accuse me of rashness in saying that they refused, and ask me to take back what I said. But I learned with certainty from Duke George that they had refused him; and I have twice replied that their dean had refused me, as in truth he did, when I requested permission. Thus craftily do these men strive to stifle this disputation, but Duke George urgeth it forward."

By being "driven on and kept from idleness," Luther means that Eck's propositions and challenges frustrated the plans of Miltitz for effecting a reconciliation. For if the papal party should renew the discussion, Luther was, by the terms of the agreement, left free to reply. Tetzel did not leave Leipsic, as was supposed, but secluded himself there after his disgrace, and remained in the cloister, called the Paulinum, till his death, a few months after. Luther expresses his feelings, in respect to that humiliation and disgrace, in another letter thus: "I am sorry that Tetzel is reduced to such necessity in respect to his safety, and that his doings have been exposed to the light. I would much rather, if it were possible, that, by a reformation on his part, he should escape with honour. As I lost nothing by his glory, so I should gain nothing by his ignominy. I cannot sufficiently marvel that he should dare to take such a large amount of money from poor people for his own use, enough to support a bishop, nay, an apostle."

CHAPTER II.

THE LEIPSIC DISPUTATION.

SECTION I.—*Preliminary Correspondence.*

PUBLIC debate, held from June 27 to July 8, 1519, a Leipsic, between Eck on the one hand, and Carlstadt on the other, to which Luther was, with some difficulty, finally admitted, derives its interest partly from the topics discussed—chiefly the liberty of the will, the power of the pope and indulgences, and partly from the scene of the transactions, and the peculiar relations of Leipsic to Wittenberg. The Duchy of Saxony, with Duke George at its head, Dresden for its capital and Leipsic as its chief seat of theological learning, was strongly Papal, and continued to be so for twenty years from this time, or till 1539. The Electorate of Saxony, belonging to the other line of Saxon princes, with Frederic, cousin of George, for its reigning sovereign, and Wittenberg for its capital, and its centre of theological influence, was the headquarters of the Reformation.

Eck chose Leipsic as the place for holding the disputation, both for the favour which he expected there from the sympathies of the people and of the judges, and for the glory he hoped to acquire from the university and the court of George, by a victory over the two champions of reform. Eck was perhaps the most learned, certainly the most celebrated Catholic theologian of Germany. He was then Vice-chancellor of the University of Ingolstadt. He owed his great reputation principally to his shrewdness and practised art as a debater. It was neither greatness of mind, nor depth and solidity of learning, but varied knowledge, self-possession, and skill in studying the passions and prejudices of men and turning them effectively to his account,—it was this that made him a formidable antagonist. And in this he succeeded at Leipsic, though those who could estimate arguments by their intrinsic worth gave the victory to the other party.

Eck, as it appears in the accounts already given of him, had been, for some little time, an acquaintance and personal friend of Luther, having been introduced to him by Scheurl of Augsburg. A little sparring between them had occurred in the Obelisks, or notes of the former, on the ninety-five Theses, and in the Asterisks, or reply of the latter. But at Augsburg, in 1518, they had met on friendly terms; and the proposal of Luther that a disputation should be held between Eck and Carlstadt on the subjects embraced in certain propositions which the latter had recently published, was agreed to, and Eck was allowed to choose between Leipsic and Erfurt as the place for the discussion. But when Eck came to publish his counter-propositions, setting forth the points which he was to maintain, he not only put himself in opposition to Carlstadt's propositions, but also to Luther's theses and other writings, thereby covertly drawing Luther also into the debate. It was this disingenuous act which discharged Luther from the obligations he had entered into with Miltitz, according to which he was to remain silent, provided his opponents should do the same. . The breach of the truce came, therefore, from the papal side; and Eck's intemperate zeal was far more wounding to the feelings of Miltitz than to those of Luther.

In the letter of Feb. 2, to Egran, quoted above in part, is the following paragraph : " Our Eck, who was besought by me, when at Augsburg, to meet Carlstaldt in debate at Leipsic, in order to bring the controversy to an end, hath at last accepted the advice. But behold the character of the man, of what sort it is. He hath [in his Propositions] fallen upon my theses, and vehemently assailed them, and hath passed by him [Carlstadt] with whom he is in controversy. You would think he was playing pranks at carnival. Therefore, in order to defend what I have said on indulgences, I am forced to enter the lists with him. He is a pitiable animalcula of fame." In a letter of congratulation to Lange, on the occasion of his receiving the degree of doctor of divinity, written Feb. 3, Luther observes : " Our Eck goeth about to stir up a new war against me; and the thing which I have long meditated will now, with the favour of Christ, be put in execution; that is, the bringing out before the public some work directed in good earnest against the hydras of Rome

Hitherto I have but sported and played in the case, though my adversaries grieve dolefully as over a serious and insufferable matter." To Spalatin he writes, under date of Feb. 7th, "Our Eck, an insect of fame, hath published his propositions against Carlstadt, to be debated at Leipsic, after Easter. This perverse man, after long making me the object of his hate, hath made an assault both upon me and my writings. While he nameth one antagonist, he aimeth his arrows at another. This stupid sycophancy of his doth ill please me, and therefore have I published counter-propositions, as you will see in the accompanying papers. Eck will, peradventure, be the mean of turning what hath been but play into serious work, which will do poor service to the Roman tyranny."

That the reader may understand what other subjects were, at this period, occupying Luther's thoughts, it may here be stated, by the way, that he wrote, according to promise, a very submissive letter, under date of March 3d, to Pope Leo X., in which he made great concessions,—greater than one would suppose possible under such circumstances. A few days previously, he had published an address to the common people, designed to conciliate them with the church of Rome. Referring to this address, in a letter to Spalatin, written March 5th, he says: " Twice, my dear Spalatin, have you requested me to speak of faith, of good works, and of obedience to the Roman church, in my Defence which was to appear in German. This I think I have already done; but it was published before your letter was written. Never was it my purpose to separate from the apostolical see of Rome. I am content that the Roman bishop should bear any title, even that of *lord*, if he please.

What doth that concern me, who know that the rule of the very Turks is to be honoured, and submitted to, because it is an existing and an established power? For sure I am that, as Peter saith, there is no power but by the will of God. But thus much do I at all times require, on the ground of my faith in Christ, namely, that they wrest not at their pleasure and corrupt the word of God. Let the Roman decretals but leave me the gospel pure and uncorrupt, and they may take away all else; I will not move a hair. What more than this should I, or can I do? I, then, will, on my part, strive for peace, as we have covenanted; and will go about no new thing. The disputation will, I hope, be nothing else but a disputation, and be listened to by the learned only [being held in Latin]; the common people may employ their own language." These statements serve to explain why Luther went so far—undoubtedly too far—in his concessions, and to confirm what is otherwise abundantly proved, namely, that he desired a reformation which should consist in spirit rather than in forms, in pious feeling rather than in social privileges and immunities. In respect to a rupture with Rome, there is an apparent inconsistency in Luther at this time, which finds its explanation in the fact, that he was in reality the subject of an inward struggle between two contending forces, drawing him alternately in opposite directions.

The preliminaries to the disputation were exceedingly complicated, consisting not only of the printed propositions and counter-propositions already mentioned, but of Eck's correspondence with Duke George and with the Leipsic professors; of that between these professors and Bishop Adolphus of Merseburg; between the bishop and Duke George;

between the latter and the Elector Frederic; between Frederic and Luther, and between Luther and the Leipsic professors.

In reply to a letter of Frederic's secretary, in which the terms of reconciliation, as proposed by Miltitz, were alluded to, Luther wrote to the elector himself, on the 13th of March, the following, among other things: "God knoweth that it was my solemn purpose, as it was also my hope and joy, that this game, so far as in me lay, should be played no farther; and so strict was I in keeping the agreement [made with Miltitz] that I gave no heed to the answer of Prierias, though I had good cause to reply. I let the contempt and contumely of my adversaries pass, and, contrary to the advice of my friends, kept silence. The agreement was, as Charles [Miltitz] well knoweth, that I was to hold my peace, if my adversaries should do the same. But now Dr. Eck, without giving me any warning, hath made such an assault upon me, that it is plain he seeketh to bring both me and the whole university into discredit and disrepute; and many honest-minded men think he hath been suborned to do the same. I looked upon it as wrong to give no heed to an assault so perfidious, and to allow the truth to be forsaken in such dishonour."

The elector consented that Luther should take part in the disputation, if Eck would really debate with him, and not with Carlstadt alone. The Leipsic professors and the Bishop of Merseburg made very extraordinary efforts to prevent the discussion. The letter of the former to Luther on the subject is still extant, and serves to throw a clear light upon their relation to the parties. It is dated Leipsic, February 19, 1519, and runs thus: "Not many days ago, dear doctor, while we were celebrating Christmas, the excellent John Eck, doctor of the Holy Scriptures, wrote to his illustrious highness Prince George, to this university and to the doctors of divinity, appointing the theological faculty to sit in judgment, and to decide on the dispute and controversy which is to ensue, and earnestly requesting that we would permit him to debate with Carlstadt in our celebrated university. . . . Because it seemeth to you that he hath [in his Propositions] made an assault upon you, and you are not minded to yield unto him, you have, in a printed document, challenged him in turn to a disputation. We greatly marvel that, contrary to our veritable decision, you have publicly said, that we refused his request in respect to the disputation, [they having granted it as a debate between Eck and Carlstadt, but refused it if Luther was to be a party.] Contrariwise, we marvel that you have given out that such a disputation, [in which Luther was to take part,] whereof we know nothing, would be held in our university, you having received no permission [to participate in the debate] either from us, or from our illustrious prince and gracious sovereign. Therefore, seeing this act of yours hath the appearance of lightness, upon which you are bound to look with abhorrence, we earnestly entreat you not to bring us, contrary to our will, into trouble, [i. e. to render them odious to the pope, by allowing his supremacy to be made a subject of debate in the university;] but, if it be agreeable to you, either to renounce your doctrines, or in a reply to us, which we earnestly desire, to sound a retreat, until you shall obtain leave from us." Duke George was indignant at this opposition to a disputation to which he had given his consent.

The professors said they were bound to the pope, and were moreover prohibited by their superior, the Bishop of Merseburg. The duke, therefore, addressed a letter of withering reproach to the bishop, which has been preserved. After expressing his "surprise that the bishop should set up an opposition to the custom handed down from the Fathers, of making free inquiry after the truth in matters of religion," and saying, that "the question newly started deserved to be earnestly considered, and the arguments on either side carefully weighed; whether, for example, as soon as the price dropped into the box, the souls of the dead were released from purgatory and ascended to heaven, by which imposition the silly people were robbed of their money," he adds, "it appears as though the bishop wished to show favour to useless, bladder-puffed persons, who, like cowardly soldiers, boast of their courage when out of the conflict, but flee as soon as the trumpet is blown." If those men, who glory in their titles, and claim the first place in assemblies and feasts, shall show themselves unwilling to earn their titles by defending and maintaining the truth, as their office requireth, "it would be cheaper and more useful to maintain old women and young children, who would do more good, and be more obedient than such theologians. Nay, the old women would be of some service by their spinning and sewing, or at least they could give pleasant pastime to the people by their voices." He closes by saying, that if the professors still persist in their refusal, he will issue a proclamation, from which it shall be known before God and all the world, that he desired the truth to be brought to light, but that the clergy, in their lack of knowledge and skill, could not abide a discussion, and therefore

opposed it. The Leipsic professors wrote also to
the bishop, saying, that the duke commanded them
to permit the disputation to be held, and that the
bishop's opposition would be of no avail. The
bishop replied to them, that he had not without
good reason prohibited them from allowing the debate ; but that he would, nevertheless, submit to the
will of the duke.

Eck was immediately informed both by the duke
and by the university of the result, and hastened to
write to Luther the following, dated Ingolstadt, February 19 : "That the learned men of the community
should refuse the burden of hearing our debate, was
very grievous to me, and I hardly knew what to do.
But at length, the most gracious prince, Duke George,
at my instance, hath prevailed on the university to
yield their assent, as I this day learn by letters from
him, from the university and the [theological] faculty. I have, therefore, appointed the 27th day of
June for the beginning of the disputation. We shall,
howbeit, meet the theological faculty on the 26th, to
determine who shall speak first in the discussion.
Since that Carlstadt is only an accessary of yours,
and you the principal, through whom those dogmas,
which, to my small and slender judgment, appear heretical and false, have been spread through Germany,
it is meet that you should be present, and stand by your
positions and impugn mine. But how earnestly do I
desire you to change your mind, and show yourself
obedient in all things to the apostolical see, and listen
to Leo X., vicar of Christ, not seeking for singularity,
but descending to the common opinions of the doctors
of the church, being well assured that Christ hath not
as you vainly imagine, left his church to their errors
for four centuries. You will see from my schedule of

articles for debate, that I have laid down propositions, not so much against Carlstadt as against your doctrines. Farewell, then, my Martin, and let us pray for each other that we may be enlightened."

Meanwhile, Luther was active as a negotiator, professor, commentator, student of Hebrew, and popular and controversial writer. A single letter of his, addressed to Lange, April 13, is all that can be presented on these various topics in this connection. In this we see the living, energetic and cheerful man, whose spirit was electrifying the whole continent of Europe.

" I rejoice and congratulate you, reverend father, that you also are one of those in whom the cross of Christ worketh. Be of good courage ; this is the way in which one goeth, or rather is carried to heaven. For your presents I give you my thanks. But the reason of my not coming to your public celebration, [when Lange was made doctor of divinity,] you already know ; my silence in respect to it is not a fault of mine so much as it is of the bad state of the roads, which hindereth persons from going, except now and then, to your place. That Hebrew teacher whom you recommend, I pray you send hither with all possible haste ; the more so, since that Bossenstein of ours, professedly a Christian, but in effect nothing else but a Jew, hath, to the reproach of our university, withdrawn himself. I add, as another reason, that you yourself are somewhat indebted to our studies. We will see that he be honourably supported in Christ, and received on proper terms, both because we all ought to encourage zealously a new convert, and because it is our duty to provide a suitable support for each. Eck hath determined upon the 27th of June for our future disputation. It will be between him and me, as you will see from this document. For Carlstadt will not debate those matters with him, partly because they were asserted by me, and not by him, and partly because that wily sophist [Eck] hath, with the design of entrapping him, started the question concerning the power of the pope, which a prebendary* cannot safely debate; and thus would, without combat or victory, terrify the latter into silence. . . . All are alarmed for me that I shall not come off well with my twelfth proposition, [in which the supremacy of the pope is declared to be a modern doctrine, founded on the miserable decretals of the popes themselves.] But though I do not expect to catch that slippery, clamorous and haughty sophist, I will, with the help of Christ, make good my own declarations. They were made in their present form, in order to give me occasion to bring out before the public the trivialness of those most senseless and ungodly decretals by which Christians are needlessly terrified; for they are full of falsehoods, supported only by the authority of the church of Rome. Christ will strip off the mask. . . . Meanwhile, the theologians lacerate me, especially that bull, ox [Professor Oxenfurth, of Leipsic] and ass, who knoweth not his owner, but eateth the straw. They cry out unto the people of Leipsic, not to join the new heretics, hoping that we may be avoided on account of the hatred of the people, and from fear of the pope. It is reported that Tetzel said, when he learned that the debate was to be held, 'The devil is in it.' . . . Cardinal Cajetan, who formerly wrote silly things about me to our

---

* Carlstadt was a canon, supported by the funds of the collegiate church at Wittenberg.

illustrious prince, hath now written like a madman.
I rejoice to see this Italian stolidity made known to
our laymen."

"Frobenius, [the celebrated printer and book-
seller,] of Bâle, hath written me, highly extolling my
freedom of speech, and saying, his Paris friends have
written to him, that my works are acceptable to
many persons there, and that they are read by the
doctors of the Sorbonne. Furthermore, he informeth
me that the copies [printed by him] are all distributed and spread throughout Italy, Spain, England,
France and the Netherlands. I rejoice that the
truth, though spoken in a barbarous and unlearned
manner, findeth such favour. I send you 'The
Wagon' by Carlstadt,* which showeth forth the folly
of the theologians. There is a tumultuous opposition to it in Leipsic. One preacher tore it in pieces
with his hands in the pulpit. Another examined
the young people when they came to the confessional
whether they indulged in laughter at the 'Wagon,'
or kept about them any of Martin's tracts. If they
pleaded guilty, they were punished with severe penalties. So Andrew Camitian writeth to me. Behold
what darkness, what madness! These are theologians! I think you have already received the beginning of my Commentary on the Psalms. I send
you another copy, whereby you can correct yours.
You see that our Emser [Luther's opponent at
Leipsic, but in this case printer or proof-reader] errs
even when printing the truth. I send you the [He-
brew] Grammar of Kimchi, until you can obtain

---

* A print of two vehicles, the one going the true and
straight way to heaven, the other, the false and tortuous
way of the scholastic theologians

another. I am also publishing a Commentary on the Galatians at Leipsic. If two sermons of mine have come into your hands, the one in Latin, on a Two-fold Righteousness; the other in German, on Matrimony, let justice be done me. They were taken surreptitiously and published without my knowledge. . . . I also send you the Lord's Prayer revised. . . . Have you seen my little works against Silvester [Prierias,] published at Bâle?—that in the title-page they have, rather by design than mistake, called him *magirum Palatii* [cook of the Palace] instead of *magistrum Palatii* [master of the Palace;] and that many other ludicrous typographical errors are made in the margin? It is reported that Cardinal Cajetan is put in prison at Mainz by the ministers of Charles [V.] of Spain, for using all his authority in favour of the faction of the French king. Philip [Melancthon] and I have written to Erasmus. Here you have every thing you asked for. The reverend vicar [Staupitz] hath quite forgotten me, so that he doth not write at all. Kindly salute Father Usingen, and also John Nathin, [formerly Luther's bitter enemy.] Finally, I put you in mind of that Hebrew teacher, that we may help those excellent young men who are prosperously studying theology, and burning with a love of good learning. Farewell, you and your cross, [some trouble of which Lange had complained,] if it be the will of Christ."

As, on the one hand, we must keep in mind the buoyancy of Luther's spirit, which gave a certain easy play to his great and varied activity, so, on the other hand, we must never forget the gravity and religious earnestness which lay beneath all this, as the deep ocean lies beneath the play of its waves; and the great fears and anxieties which never ceased to agitate the minds of his truest and firmest friends. Like every heroic man in the crisis of his affairs, he was left alone, to sustain his courage from his confidence in God, in truth and the right, and from his willingness to perish, if need be, and leave behind him a martyr's testimony for the benefit and instruction of coming generations. Nor this alone; he was obliged to sustain his friends and supporters by infusing into them his own spirit.

A letter of his, written some time in May to Spalatin, will illustrate these remarks. He writes thus: "I beseech you, my dear Spalatin, yield not unduly to fear, nor utterly slay your heart with human cogitations. Know that unless Christ moved me on and my affairs, I should have destroyed myself even in my first Disputation on Indulgences: then in my sermon on the subject in the vernacular tongue; later in my Proofs and Illustrations and in my Reply to Silvester; and last of all, in my Account of the Transactions at Augsburg, and especially in my journey thither. For what mortal did not either fear or hope that any one of these perils alone would prove my ruin? Finally, Olsnitzer hath lately written from the city to the chancellor of our Duke of Pomerania that I have so stirred up all Rome by my Proofs and my Dialogue [Reply to Prierias] that they know not how to restore quiet. Yet they have determined to assail me not by the way of the law, but by Italian practices, (these are his words.) By that I understand poisoning or assassinating.

"Many things which, if I were elsewhere, I should pour forth against Rome, or rather Babylon, that devastator of the Scriptures and of the church, I repress and restrain, for the sake of the elector and of the university. The truth of Holy Writ and of the church cannot, my dear Spalatin, be discussed without offending this wild beast. You must not, therefore, expect me to be unmolested or secure unless I renounce theology altogether. Let my friends then think I am beside myself. This matter, if it be of God, shall not have an end, except that, as the disciples and friends of Christ forsook him, so all my friends forsake me; and the truth too,—which saves with its own right hand, not mine, nor yours, nor that of any other man,—shall be left to itself alone; and that time I have been expecting from the beginning. That this twelfth proposition was extorted from me by Eck, and that the pope will have plenty of patrons in the approaching disputation, ought not, I think, to appear so evil, especially if we remember the license given to such disputations. In fine, if *I* perish, nothing will perish with me. By the grace of God, the Wittenbergers have made such proficiency that they do not need me any longer. But what shall I say? I am unhappy, because I fear I am not worthy to suffer and be put to death for such a cause. That felicity will be reserved for better men, not for such a vile sinner as I am. I have told you that I am at all times ready to withdraw, if my tarrying here seem to draw the illustrious prince into any danger. Death will certainly come at some time. Still, in the Apology already published in Germany, I have sufficiently flattered the Roman church and pontiff, if that can any thing avail."

To quiet Spalatin, he was obliged to lay before him the plan of his part of the discussion, and specify the particular arguments by which he should fortify him self in respect to the twelfth proposition on the supremacy of the pope. "I pray you," he says some what impatiently, "permit us to debate the matter, and be not of that class of men who, not understanding the counsels of God, immediately despair for that they do not see by their own counsels how a thing can be accomplished. . . . Do not ask that I reveal my whole plan, which would be but destroying it, but rather pray that Christ may make us seek his glory."

Before this disputation came on, Luther received, through the Bishop of Brandenburg, a condemnatory document, drawn up by the Franciscan monks of Saxony, at their late meeting in Jüterbok, in which they pointed out fifteen alleged errors of Luther. These Minorite brethren of the "stricter observance," as they were called, and who vowed ignorance as one of their virtues, Luther exposed in his brief but terrible reply, as having poorly observed the rules of Christ in not admonishing a brother privately before publicly condemning him, but as having given good proof that they had sacredly kept the vow of ignorance. "But not to return evil for evil," he adds, " I will give you your choice, either to retract your rash declarations and restore to me my good name, or let me go forward and publish your document with notes, setting forth your ignorance, which will not turn out for the honour of your order." After refuting their slanderous declarations, he closes by saying, "I await your speedy answer, that I may know whether you choose to incline your necks, or to hold them aloft and set yourselves against the truth. Be assured I will treat you nobly and show unto all men your wonderful ignorance. Fare ye well, and the Lord give you to be wise and to will what is right. If you wish to be friends, I will be friendly; but if not, do what you have to do, and, believe me, I will not be lacking to my name and to the word of Christ." The Franciscans wisely preferred peace, and kept silence.

On the 16th of May, Luther writes both to Spalatin and to Lange respecting Miltitz. In the letter to the latter he says: "Charles Miltitz hath cited me to Coblentz to appear before the Archbishop of Treves, in the presence of the legate Cajetan. Sweet creature! He confesseth that he hath not yet received any authority from Rome, and thinketh me stupid enough to come, though cited only by his rashness. You see that everywhere, and from every quarter and in every manner, they seek my life." To the former he says: "That ridiculous block of a Miltitz [notice the prudence with which he always speaks to Spalatin] confesseth that he hath not yet received any command from Rome, and yet he citeth me. *He* citeth me, not the archbishop; and then I must appear before the cardinal! Are not the men insane?" In this last letter he complains of the injustice and duplicity of the Duke of Saxony, saying: "Duke George hath twice replied to me, and will not admit me to the disputation, though I have given him assurance that Eck compelleth me, both in his private letters and in his published propositions, to reply to him. Why should he exact so much of me as to require that Eck should write in my behalf, when he did not refuse to yield to Eck, nor require any thing of Carlstadt? How monstrous! I send you both of his letters. I am now writing to him a third time. Tell me, I pray you, what you think it best to do."

In the midst of all this turmoil, the studies of the University of Wittenberg were moving briskly on, and the number of students rapidly increasing. Luther requests Spalatin, May 22d, before taking his

journey with the elector, to ascertain the views of
the latter in respect to the Hebrew professorship.
Cellarius, professor of Hebrew at Heidelberg, was at
Leipsic, waiting for an answer from Luther, ready to
accept the place, if the elector would give him a
suitable salary. "A great number of students," he
continues, "and notable ones, too, are flowing together
here. . . . Our town will scarcely hold them, for
lack of houses to serve them."

SECTION II.—*Course of the Debate.*

AT length the time for the debate drew near. The
duke ordered his palace, called the Pleissenburg, to
be prepared for the accommodation of the assembly.
In the great hall he caused two desks, facing each
other, to be erected for the disputants, the one
adorned with a picture of St. Martin, the other with
a picture of St. George. Seats for the audience and
tables for the clerks were also prepared and embel-
lished with tapestry. Eck arrived on the 22d of
June, the day before the festival of Corpus Christi,
and took part in the celebration, joining the procession, pompously arrayed in a mass vestment and
chasuble. Several monks and theologians from Ingolstadt and Erfurt accompanied him to Leipsic. He
was treated with great distinction by the theological
faculty and the city council, with whom he feasted
lustily. In a letter, he highly commended their
hospitality, as well as the beauty of the Leipsic ladies,
for whom Charles V. said he had too great a fond-
ness. On Friday, the 24th, the day after the festival,
the Wittenbergers arrived, a numerous company. In
the first carriage sat Carlstadt, as the chief disputant;
in the second, Prince Barnim of Pomerania, then a

student, and also, according to ancient usage, rector
of the university; in the third, Luther and Melancthon.   About two hundred students on foot, with
spears and halberds, according to Eck's statement,
accompanied their professors.   Lange, Amsdorf, and
several doctors of laws and masters, were in the company.   As they were near the Grimma gate of the
city of Leipsic, and opposite the Paulinum, where
Tetzel then was, Carlstadt had the misfortune to have
one of the wheels of his carriage break, and to be
thrown out, which some interpreted as an ill omen.
The duke from Dresden, and Emser, and the three
commissaries of the duke, Pflug, Rühel, and Wiede-
bach, were present as early as Saturday.   Emser
called on the masters in the university and urged
them to stand by Eck, and escort him to the palace
on Sunday, that a favourable impression might be
made upon the duke.   Here the commissaries and
the parties, after much discussion, came to an understanding in respect to the manner of procedure in the
debate.   Each of the parties was to choose a secretary.   Luther chose J. Agricola of Eisleben; Eck
chose J. Poliander, who, by the way, was converted
to Luther's views by the debate, and went directly
to Wittenberg.   More than thirty others also took
notes of the discussion.   From the decision, to be
made by certain universities, either party might appeal to a general council.

On Monday morning, (June 27th,) the time set
for the commencement of the disputation, a civic
guard was sent, with music and flags, to the palace
Pleissenburg to preserve order.   At seven o'clock
in the morning, the disputants met in the Princes'
college, where an address was made by Pistoris, of
the law faculty.   Thence the assembly moved in

procession, two by two, a Wittenberg and a Leipsic master together, quite across the city from north to south to St. Thomas's church, where the duke and two princes were awaiting them. Here mass was held, and the assembly proceeded to the palace, (a few rods to the east,) where Mosellanus, the professor of Greek, and the friend of Melancthon and Luther, delivered an oration in the name of the duke, admonishing the disputants to be gentle and courteous, and to seek for truth rather than victory. After singing the Veni Sancte Spiritus, (Come, Holy Spirit,) the meeting was adjourned for dinner. In the afternoon, after both parties had promised to debate with sincerity and love,—Luther meanwhile expressing his astonishment that of the Dominicans, with whom the whole affair of indulgences arose, none were present to take part,—Eck and Carlstadt commenced the debate on free-will, which lasted a week, or till July 4. Never was there a more unequal match; Carlstadt, learned, modest, slow, confined to notes, and opening books and giving his authorities with exactness; Eck, self-possessed, quick of memory, imposing, but loose, boisterous, and ostentatious. The former accused the latter of quoting falsely, the latter laughed at the poor memory and tediousness of the former. From the 4th of July, the day of Tetzel's death, to the 8th, Luther debated with Eck on the supremacy of the pope, and now the discussion grew animated, two practised debaters having come together, each of whom was accustomed always to bear off the palm. Luther proposed to close the discussion there, but the duke urged him to go on and debate on the subjects of indulgences, purgatory and the power of the keys, in which Eck hardly made a show of resistance. He wished to return to his first antagonist, and consequently resumed the discussion with Carlstadt on the 15th. But as the duke needed his palace, the disputation was closed, on the 16th, by an oration from a Dr. Lange, of Leipsic, in which he meted out to each disputant his share of praise, the most to Luther, not a little to Eck, and to Carlstadt what was his due. Eck and his Leipsic friends claimed the victory; and if popular favour is to be the standard of judgment, the claim must be admitted. But learned men decided otherwise. Let us now hear Luther's account of the matter, as related by him in a letter to Spalatin, dated July 20, 1519.

"Concerning that famous debate, I would have written you a long time ago, had I been able. The matter is thus: There are certain men at Leipsic, not over candid and upright, who triumph with Eck; and have, by their garrulity and vaunting, got a certain kind of glory. But the facts themselves will, in due time, speak and bring all things to light. The selfsame hour that we arrived in Leipsic, before we had alighted from our carriages, a prohibition of the proceedings by the Bishop of Merseburg was posted up, on the doors of the churches. But, by order of the senate, the individual who posted it up was sent to the dungeon, for doing it without their knowledge. Accomplishing nothing in this way, these men next resorted to another sleight, and, at Eck's request, laboured hard with Carlstadt privately to induce him to consent that the discussion proceed without any secretaries to record the arguments. For he hoped to succeed, as he had long been accustomed to do, by dint of voice and gesticulation. But Carlstadt would not consent. As that condition had been agreed upon, he said he should hold them to their stipulation. . . . At length, to make the matter sure, he was under the necessity of consenting that the records be not published until the judges shall have given in their decision. A new dispute arose concerning the selection of the judges ; and Carlstadt found it necessary to yield so far as to allow the judges to be appointed after the debate should be ended. Otherwise the opposite party said they should not proceed. Thus were we brought into a dilemma, and must either stop the proceedings or submit to partial judges. So you see the paltry practices whereby they wrested from us the promised freedom of discussion. For we know full well that the universities and the Roman pontiff will either not determine the question at all, or else they will decide it against us; and that is what our opponents desired.

"The next day I was called aside, and the same thing was propounded unto me. But not trusting the pope, and being, moreover, dissuaded by my friends, I refused all these conditions. Then they proposed to leave out the pope, and named other universities. I still demanded the promised freedom, [in respect to the disputation,] and since they would not allow it, I refused to take part in the discussion. Now it was rumoured abroad that I was afraid to debate, and, what was yet more untrue, that I would not consent to have any judges. These things were odiously and maliciously repeated, till all our friends were carried away with the rest, and our university was in danger of being brought into reproach. I finally yielded to the advice of friends, and accepted, though not without indignation, the proposals; with this condition, however, that I might appeal from the decision; that my cause should not be prejudged, and that the court of Rome should not be included among the judges.

" At first the disputation was begun with Carlstadt, and continued for a week, on the subject of the freedom of the will. He brought forward his authorities, and, with God's help, he stated and maintained his arguments exceedingly well and abundantly. When it came his turn to be assailant, Eck refused [to be respondent,] unless Carlstadt would promise to leave his books at home. He had produced them in order to prove that his quotations from the Scriptures and from the Fathers were correct, and that he did not wrest them, as Eck was found to do. Here a dispute arose, and it was finally determined that the books should be left at home. But who doth not perceive, that, if they were in quest of truth, they would desire rather to have all the books at hand? Never did envy and ambition show themselves more openly. At the close, the double-faced man conceded every thing, though at first he had contended earnestly to the contrary. He feigned that he agreed in every thing perfectly, glorying that he had brought Carlstadt over to his side !

" The second week he disputed with me. First we closed with each other right earnestly concerning the primacy of the Roman pontiff. . . . Then, toward the end, great stress was laid by Eck upon the Council of Constance, which condemned the opinion of Huss, namely, that the papacy was the creature of the emperor. . . . He also alleged that I was a heretic, and an abettor of the Bohemian doctrines. This sophist is as impudent as he is bold. With that accusation, the people of Leipsic were marvellously pleased, more than with the disputation itself. On my part, I brought forward the case of the Greek church for a period of a thousand years, and of the early Fathers, none of whom were ever subject to the Roman pontiff. I did not deny, however, that he was first in honour. I declared openly, and proved by direct and clear passages, that several articles, taught by Augustine, Paul, and by Christ himself, had been condemned. . . .

"The third week we disputed touching repentance, purgatory, indulgences, and the power of absolution by the priest. For he was not minded to debate with Carlstadt, but directed his aim only at me. Indulgences fell to the ground at once, as Eck gave up almost every thing. Though they were to have been the principal subject of debate, he attempted to maintain them only by way of sport and of jest. It is reported that he said, if I had not denied the power of the pope, he could easily have agreed with me in every thing. . . . He maintained one opinion in the hall and gave out another in the church; and, when he was questioned by Carlstadt, why he was so changeable in his teachings, he replied without shame, that what is here discussed ought not to be taught unto the people.

"When I was through with him, he took up the debate anew with Carlstadt for the last three days, in which he again yielded up and consented to every thing. Thus, in the whole disputation, nothing hath been worthily discussed, save my twelfth proposition. The people of Leipsic neither saluted us, nor visited us; but treated us as enemies; while they thronged about Eck, clung fast to him, feasted with him, invited him to their houses, made him presents of a tunic and a camlet robe, and rode out with him To be short, they did whatsoever they could to injure us. . . . Those who were friendly to us came to us privately. But Auerbach, a man of excellent genius, and the younger Pistoris, invited me to their houses. Duke George himself invited all three of us to his residence together."

It is here interesting to perceive that Luther was a guest with that very Auerbach whose cellar has become so celebrated in connection with the name of Faust.

The Leipsic disputation was chiefly useful to the cause of the Reformation, in opening the eyes of Luther himself on the whole subject of the authority of the Roman pontiff, and in drawing public attention to this point. It led to the overthrow of another pillar of the papacy. A few individuals of the papal party were won to the side of Luther; but most of the people of Leipsic, and of the duke's dominions, manifested, from this time, a deadlier hatred than ever to Luther's doctrines. Many of the vexations which Luther experienced for a year or two to come, were caused by men who were under the Leipsic influence.

Of the many broils and disputes which grew out of this debate, as they were mostly of a personal character, no particular account can be given in a brief biography. They are described in most of the histories of the Reformation, and to them the reader is referred. These disputes were with Emser, of the court of Dresden, with Duke George, with the Bishop of Meissen, with the Franciscan monk Alveld, and with men at Cologne and at Rome. Luther was almost everywhere denounced as a heretic. Even at the court of the elector, there was much displeasure with him. In these circumstances, the Prince of Dessau, and afterward the Franconian knight Schaumburg, and Francis von Sickingen, through Von Hutten, offered him protection, and invited him to their courts or castles. Luther wrote conciliatory letters to the new emperor, Charles V., to the Archbishop of Mainz, and to the Bishop of Merseburg. In Nüremberg, Spengler, a member of the city council, took up the defence of Luther. Œcolampadius wrote an anonymous work directed against Eck and Emser, which did admirable execution. Feldkirch and Melancthon joined in the defence, and all together prepared the way for Luther's address to the German nobility, which he wrote about this time, and which was the most magnificent and effective appeal which he ever made to the German nation. It united to his own religious spirit the glowing patriotism of a Hutten. A finer specimen of popular eloquence is scarcely to be found in the language.

SECTION III.—*Various Works of Luther on Practical Religion; and his Perilous Situation after the Disputation.*

IDST storms of controversy, where the polemic writer, situated as Luther was, must use that adroitness, point and wit which are likely to affect the popular mind, there is danger of losing the spirit of humility and charity. Luther was not always superior to such temptations. But as his polemical writings were but occasional productions, and his works on practical religion, commentaries, sermons, and catechetical writings were very numerous, we should be liable to do injustice to his piety, were we to over-look the latter class of his works, and judge of him exclusively from the former class. Although in re-spect to the great controversy, his heart, as he often says, was full of the matter, and he was only to open his mouth, and it would stream forth spontaneous-ly; still he took greater satisfaction in writing works purely religious for the spiritual improvement of the people. At that period of his life of which we are now treating, he was very active in this kind of labour.

The study of the Psalms afforded him very great de-light. He had twice delivered a course of lectures on them in the university, and had now recently publish-ed, on the first twenty-two Psalms, what he modestly called Labours on the Psalms, not presuming to pro-nounce it a commentary. *Labours* indeed they were. " You would not believe," he writes to Spalatin, " how much labour a single verse often makes me." It had been reported to him by Spalatin that the elector once said that sermons full of subtilty and human opi-nions were very cold and weak, but that the Scrip-tures had such a majesty and power as to overcome all the arts of disputation. In the dedication to Frederic, he refers to this incident, and says that the elector had thereby entirely won his heart, that he could not help loving the lovers of the Bible, and hating its enemies He could not presume to understand and explain all the Psalms. It was much to understand a few, and these only in part. The Holy Spirit reserves much to itself, wishing to retain us in the character of pupils.

In the same year (1519) in September, appeared his great work, the Commentary on the Epistle to the Galatians, in which he laid himself out to show, under every possible variety of form, the difference between the righteousness of the law and that of faith by which we are justified. This is the chief work in which the fundamental principles of the Reformation are carefully laid down, a work fully proving that his views were infinitely more scriptural than those of his opponents, but also showing that his own system was disfigured with some excrescences.

He next wrote a deeply religious work for the consolation of the elector in his sickness, entitled *Tesseradecas*, because it consisted of fourteen chapters, seven images or views of affliction, and seven of blessings. Erasmus said this production was highly approved even by those who were violently opposed to the doctrines of the Reformation.

He also wrote, in the early part of 1520, a sermon or popular treatise on Good Works, showing that outward acts of devotion, as prayers, fastings, almsgivings and mortifications, were of no avail, if they were performed without a living faith in Christ. "The Christian's faith and assurance makes every thing precious in the sight of God, which, in others, would be the most hurtful."

He wrote another work in October of the same year, dedicated to Leo X., on Christian Liberty, in which he maintains and illustrates the statement that "a Christian is a free man, lord over all and subject to no one; and yet is servant of all and subject to every one;" containing, (paradoxical as it may sound,) the great truth that Christ has set us free, allowing no man to be lord any longer over our conscience; and yet that the love of God leads us spontaneously to do good to all, and to be the servants of all. In the dedicatory epistle, Luther fulfilled, in his peculiar way, the promise made September 12th to Miltitz and others, that he would write once more to the pope, assuring him that the assaults he had made upon the papacy were not directed against his person. "Though I have been forced," he says, "by some of thy unchristian flatterers, to appeal in my affairs from thy seat and tribunal to a Christian and free council, yet has my mind never been so alienated from thee that I have not wished well to thee and to thy Roman see. . . . I have indeed fallen severely upon certain unchristian teachings, and been pretty nipping against my adversaries, not because of their evil lives, but because of their unchristian doctrines. Of this I do not repent, nor shall I leave off. . . . True it is, I have boldly impugned the Roman see, called the Roman court, which neither thou nor any other one can deny, to be worse and more scandalous than Sodom, Gomorrah, or Babylon ever was; and, so far as I see, there is no help nor remedy for it. . . . For it cannot be concealed from thee that, for many years gone by, from Rome nothing hath gone forth but perdition of soul and body and goods. . . . Thou sittest, holy Father Leo, like a sheep among wolves, like Daniel among the lions, like Ezekiel among the scorpions. . . . It were indeed thy proper business and that of the cardinals to stay this evil, but the disease mocketh at the remedy; the steed and the chariot give no heed to the driver. . . . Behold, the reason and ground of my setting myself so stiffly against this pestilential see. . . . Were I to retract, it would do no good. He who shall attempt to constrain me to do it, will only make bad worse. Besides, I must have no rule and measure laid upon me for interpreting the Scriptures : for the word of God, that teacheth freedom, must not be bound."

The tone of this epistle finds its explanation in the fact, that Luther had already gone so far in condemning the court of Rome, that he could not now either consistently or conscientiously speak of it in gentle terms.   He had, about a week before, published his work entitled the Babylonian Captivity of the Church, in which he retracted the concessions he had formerly made in respect to the papacy, and declared it to be "the kingdom of Babylon, and the power of Nimrod, the mighty hunter," alluding to the booty or prey taken by Tetzel and other "mighty hunters."   If any thing more were wanting to complete the rupture, it was supplied by the publication of the bull which Eck had procured at Rome against Luther.

October 11, Luther wrote to Spalatin : "The Roman bull, brought by Eck hath at length come to hand . . . I hold it in contempt. . . . Not only at Leipsic but everywhere, both the bull and Eck are despised. . . . I rejoice with my whole heart that I am made a sufferer for the best of causes, though I am not worthy of a suffering so sacred.   I am now more free than before, and I now feel assured that the pope is antichrist."

Although he regarded the bull as genuine, he treated it as if it were spurious, and wrote a work "On the new Bulls and Lies of Eck," and another "Against the Execrable Bull of Antichrist," and a third, called " Defence of all the Articles condemned in the recent Bull of Leo X."   A still bolder step was that of burning the bull, decretals and other books in the presence of the students before the Elster or eastern gate of the town.   Luther announced the occurrence to Spalatin in the following manner, as though he were a newspaper chronicler of the events of the week. "In the year 1520, the 10th day of December, at nine o'clock A. M., were burnt at Wittenberg without the eastern gate, near the Holy Cross, all the books of the pope, the decree, the decretals, the recent bull of Leo X.," and several other works, as Eck's, and Emser's, "in order that the incendiary papists may see that it requireth no great power to burn books, which they cannot refute."

Notwithstanding Luther's progress and increasing confidence in the truth, and the diffusion of his sentiments among the educated and intelligent classes, siorms of still greater violence from without seemed to be fast gathering against him. The mild and candid Emperor Maximilian had died; the interregnum during which Frederic was vicar of the empire had also passed away, and the new emperor, Charles V., who was elected the second day of the Leipsic disputation, and whose protection Luther sought in a patriotic but humble letter, showed signs of displeasure and hostility. Duke George of Saxony, the Bishops of Brandenburg, Meissen, Merseburg, and the Universities of Leipsic, Cologne, Louvain and even Paris, became Luther's bitter enemies; and now the pope had excommunicated him, and called on kings and princes to treat him as a heretic, and deliver him up to the papal emissaries. While these perils were coming on, Luther found new and unexpected support in the old chivalric spirit of certain Franconian knights. As early as May 13, 1520, he wrote to Spalatin: "Day before yesterday, I received a message from Silvester von Schaumburg, a Franconian nobleman, . . . offering me protection, if in any way the elector is endangered on my account. Though I do not despise this, yet will I rely on no protector but Christ, who hath, perhaps, put this into his mind." The knight hoped he would not think of going to Bohemia for safety, "For," he adds, "I, myself, and about a hundred other nobles, whom, with God's permission, I will gather around me, will honourably maintain you and defend you against all danger."

Francis von Sickingen, the magnanimous and powerful leader of the Franconian knights, repeatedly sent similar messages to Luther, inviting him to one of his castles a little south of Mainz. Ulrich von Hutten also, that fiery spirit, who kindled such a popular hatred against the Roman court and Roman tyranny, openly espoused Luther's cause. Luther wished the elector to let the cardinal, who had written to him, know, "that even should they succeed in their abominable measures to drive him from Wittenberg, they would accomplish nothing, save to make bad worse; for not only in Bohemia, but in the very heart of Germany, are to be found those who can and will, despite their malice, protect me against all their fulminations. . . . With me the die is cast; I despise alike the frownings and fawnings of Rome. I will never be reconciled with them, nor have part with them, let them condemn and burn my writings as they will." But Luther did not approve of appealing to the sword. He wrote in 1521 to Spalatin: "What Hutten hath in mind you see. I desire not that the gospel be made to prevail by violence and bloodshed, and so I have replied to him. The world hath been overcome by the word; by the word the church hath been sustained."

CHAPTER III.

LUTHER AND THE DIET OF WORMS.

SECTION I.—*Luther summoned to appear at Worms: and his Journey thither.*

HE new emperor, Charles V., who was in Spain at the time of his election, did not reach Germany till toward the close of 1520. Early in 1521 he held his first diet at Worms. No business that was to occupy the attention of the diet was beset with so many difficulties as that which related to the claims of the church of Rome. Not only were the religious sentiments of many changed by the writings of Luther, but the German princes and statesmen had long felt the galling yoke of Roman tyranny, and were desirous of freeing themselves both from ecclesiastical rule, and from the enormous tribute paid under various forms to the church of Rome.

The papal legate Aleander, and others in the interests of the pope, used their utmost influence to have the books of Luther burned by authority of the emperor. The latter had learned that the Elector of Saxony was not pleased with this procedure,—that he pronounced it unjust to condemn books to the flames which had not yet been proved to be false or heretical. On the 28th of November, 1520, therefore, Charles wrote to the elector, requesting him to bring Luther with him to the diet of Worms, that he might cause him to be examined before learned and able judges. At the same time, the elector was requested to see that Luther should write nothing against his holiness the pope, or the church of Rome.

Frederic replied, December 20, that while Luther's books, without being first refuted, had been burnt at Cologne and Mainz, Luther himself might have done something, [burnt the pope's bull and the decretals,] so that it would be difficult for him to appear at Worms. At the same time, however, the elector directed his secretary, Spalatin, to write to Luther, inquiring whether he would be willing to go, in case the emperor should insist on it. Luther replied, December 21 : "If I shall be summoned, I will, so far as it dependeth on me, be carried there sick, in case I be not well, sooner than refuse ; for, without doubt, I am called of God, if called by the emperor. If they intend to settle these matters by bare authority alone, as it seemeth, (for they have not probably produced this summons with a view to convince me,) then must the case be commended unto God. He still liveth and ruleth who preserved the three men in the fiery furnace. If he will not keep me, then my head is of little account, compared with the ignominious death of Christ, which was an offence to all, and the falling of many. For here we must have no regard to danger or safety, but rather see that we do not betray the gospel, which we have once received, and give it over to the contempt of the wicked, and our enemies have occasion to say, that we are afraid to acknowledge what we teach, and to shed our blood therefor, which disgrace on our part, and proud boasting on theirs, may God avert. . . . We cannot tell whether by our life, or by our death, more or less danger may accrue to the gospel. You know that divine truth is a rock of offence, set for the fall and rising again of many in Israel. Let it be our only care to pray unto God that the commencement of our emperor's reign be not stained with my blood, or that of any other man, in order to defend wickedness. As I have often said, I would rather perish by the hands of the Romanists, than that the emperor and his court should be involved in such an act."

The Roman party were strongly opposed to Luther's examination before the diet, as it would imply that one already condemned by the pope might still have a trial before a secular tribunal. They had procured a second bull from Rome, in which Luther was unconditionally excommunicated, and they made use of this as an argument to divert the emperor from his purpose, and succeeded so far as to induce him to write again to the Elector Frederic, and say to him, that, unless Luther was prepared to retract, he need not come, and at any rate, that he might come no farther than to Frankfurt, and there await further orders. But the elector prudently replied, that he himself was already on his way to Worms, and that he would there confer with the emperor on the whole matter. Meanwhile, he wrote to Luther, directing him to say how far he could comply with the emperor's orders.

The emperor viewed every thing through a political medium; truth and justice yielded to considerations of advantage. His advisers wished to moderate Luther, in order to make use of him in their negotiations with Rome. The two Roman nuncios, particularly Aleander, an intriguing man, resorted to bribery and every low art, in order to engage the emperor in their interest and secure his power against Luther. The emperor saw here the means of forcing the pope to support his policy against France, and determined to sacrifice Luther, but not without first securing every possible advantage. The princes did not enter into these views of Charles, but added their complaints to Luther's in respect to Roman tyranny, and therefore checked the emperor, though they were altogether disinclined to favour Luther's religious doctrines. The transactions at Worms all grew out of these conflicting interests, and form a singular series of intrigues and manœuvres, in order to reconcile and adjust them so as to secure the ends contemplated in the emperor's policy. Hence, the movements, counter-movements and suspensions which checker and confuse the proceedings of the diet.

During all these negotiations, in which Luther's safety was involved, he was labouring on at Wittenberg, as zealously and as laboriously as if there were nothing to disturb his mind He said in a letter to his friend Pellican, at Basle, who was superintending the printing of some of his books published there, "I am exceedingly occupied with business. I preach twice every day; I am engaged in writing my Commentary on the Psalms; I am working on the postils; I am fighting against the papal bull both in German and Latin, and defending myself against attacks; not to mention the letters I must write to my friends, and the conferences which I hold at home and elsewhere." When the citation and the safe-conduct from the emperor were brought to Luther by a herald sent to accompany him, Luther was in the very midst of those labours. Hence he apologized to Prince John Frederic, to whom he dedicated his commentary on the song of Mary at the annunciation, for sending him only a part of it, saying, " The remainder must be put off till my return; for you see that, being summoned to the imperial diet, I must drop every thing." Various expressions of his, both at this time and afterward, show that he expected his fate would, in all probability, be like that of Huss, and that he should never return alive to Wittenberg. Still he was not without hope. The straight-forward and honest, the bold and yet skilful movements of Luther, the prudence and increasing solicitude of the elector, the jealousy of the diet against the Roman nuncios and Italian intrigue, and the hesitancy of the emperor, a mere political calculator, to commit himself openly to the pope at the risk of offending the Elector of Saxony and his friends, these were the chief means employed by Providence for the preservation of Luther at this critical juncture. The imperial herald, Caspar Sturm of Oppenheim, reached Wittenberg, March 26th, and Luther commenced his journey about the 2d of April, the council of Wittenberg providing a conveyance for him. Amsdorf, Scheurl, and two or three other

friends accompanied him.   At Leipsic, he was merely
treated to wine by the authorities, which was regarded
as a cold reception, the same which he received at
the Leipsic disputation.   At Naumburg, the burgomaster entertained him and the herald; and a priest
sent him a likeness of Savonarola, an Italian reformer
and martyr, and exhorted him to stand firmly by
the truth, for God would be with him and uphold
him.   At Weimar, he was hospitably received by
Duke John Frederic, brother and afterward successor of the elector.   Here he received intelligence
that his books had been already condemned at Worms,
and saw the messengers who were to publish the imperial mandate in the cities.   The condemnation of
Luther, to which the emperor had once assented,
was, at the remonstrance of the German princes, put
off, and only the seizure of his books was insisted on
then.   The herald asked him if he wished still to
proceed, to which Luther replied in the affirmative.
Prince John furnished him with money to defray
the expenses of his journey.   At Erfurt, Luther was
welcomed with great pomp and ceremony.   Crotus,
then rector of the university, and the poet Eoban
Hess, and others, to the number of forty, on horseback, and a great multitude on foot, came out eight
miles from the city to escort him in.   The streets of
the city were thronged when he entered ; and, at the
request of many, he consented to preach in the Augustinian cloister, where he had once suffered so much.
Here Justus Jonas, formerly a student at Wittenberg,
but now professor at Erfurt, joined Luther and his
party.   At Gotha, also, he yielded to the urgency
of the people and preached.   At Eisenach he was
taken very ill, and did not entirely recover till after
he reached Frankfurt, from which place he wrote to

Spalatin, April 14th: "We have arrived here, my
dear Spalatin, although Satan hath endeavoured to
hinder me by more diseases than one. For all the
way from Eisenach I was sick, and am still so more
than I ever was before. I hear the mandate of
Charles is published for the purpose of terrifying me.
But Christ liveth, and I will enter Worms in spite
of all the gates of hell and the powers of the air."
Many undertook to dissuade him from his purpose;
his friends did it out of regard to his safety; his enemies to avoid discussion before the diet. It was said
to him at one time that he would be burned to powder,
as Huss was at Constance, to which he answered:
"Though they kindle a fire all the way between Wittenberg and Worms that shall reach unto the heavens,
I will, in the name of the Lord, appear, inasmuch as
I am summoned, and come between the great teeth
of the behemoth and confess Christ, and let him rule."

At the special instance of the emperor's confessor, who still, perhaps for good political reasons,
hoped to effect a reconciliation, Bucer was sent by
Francis von Sickingen from his castle at Ebernburg, inviting him to meet at that retired place such
men as Charles should send to confer with him.
But Luther, determined not to be turned aside by
frowns or flatteries, and knowing that the time of his
safe-conduct would soon expire, replied coolly, "If
the emperor's confessor hath any thing to say unto
me, he can say it at Worms," and proceeded on his
way. At Oppenheim, toward Worms, he received
a warning from Spalatin, who was with the elector
at Worms, not to venture into the city; to which he
made the well-known reply: "If there were as many
devils in Worms as there are tiles on the roofs of
the houses, I would still go thither." Just before

the close of his life, referring to this courageous state of feeling, he said : " I was then intrepid, and feared nothing. God can make one as it were beside himself. I do not know that I should be so confident now." "To-day," [*i. e.* April 16,] says an eye-witness, "came Doctor Martin hither, in an open Saxon vehicle, in company with three other persons, namely, a brother* of his, Nicholas Amsdorf, and a Pomeranian nobleman by the name of Von Suaven. Before the carriage rode the imperial herald on horseback, and in livery with the imperial escutcheon, attended by his servant. Justus Jonas and his servant followed next to Luther. Many nobles and courtiers went out to meet him. At ten o'clock he entered the city, and more than two thousand persons escorted him to his quarters." He stopped at a hotel called "The German Court," where the elector had provided lodgings for him. Two Saxon nobles of Frederic's court, and Pappenheim, the imperial marshal, lodged at the same place with Luther.

Section II.—*Luther before the Diet; his Return and Capture.*

EARLY the next morning, the marshal Pappenheim and the herald were sent with an order from the emperor, requiring Luther to appear before him and the diet at four o'clock in the afternoon, to answer to the matters that should then be presented. The interval of several hours was one of intense anxiety ;

---

* This was his brother Jacob Luther, who was with him also when he was seized and carried to Wartburg. Seckendorf, by an unhappy conjecture, explained the word brother as meaning a monk, and other writers have blindly followed him. So, too, have these writers made Von Suaven (Latinized, Suabenius,) a Danish, instead of a Pomeranian nobleman.

and it was on that occasion that he made the memorable prayer which has been recorded, and is to be found in the histories of the Reformation.

In order to understand Luther's position before the diet at Worms, we must glance at what had been done there previous to his arrival. January 16, just three months before Luther's entrance into the city, the elector wrote from Worms to his brother John, thus: "Every day, as I am informed, consultations are held against Doctor Martin, to put him under the ban of excommunication and outlawry, and to persecute him to the utmost. This, they of the red hat and the Romans with their party, do labour at. But there are many who regard him with favour." Leo X. wrote to Charles V. a letter dated Rome, January 18, but which did not come before the diet till February 13, in which he says, that as Luther had failed to appear at Rome to answer to his summons, he, the pope, had declared him a notorious heretic. Having learned through his nuncio that his imperial majesty was inclined to maintain the Catholic faith, he now implored him to issue a general edict that Luther, unless he retract his errors, suffer the penalties due to a heretic. February 13, the nuncio Aleander presented the apostolical brief above mentioned, and seconded its suggestions by an elaborate but haughty speech against Luther, beseeching the diet not to bear with the man, who was calling back from hell Huss and Jerome of Prague, who had been condemned and burnt. Glapio, confessor of the emperor, had several interviews with Pontanus, the elector's chancellor, during the month of February, seeking to effect a reconciliation, by inducing Luther to renounce the errors and hard sayings contained in his work on the Babylonian captivity. These errors

he pointed out, to the number of thirty-two. Glapio
admitted that the Roman party daily belaboured the
emperor to carry into effect the suggestions of the
papal brief, but that he had thus far manifested an un-
willingness to do so. Still we find a draught of an
imperial edict against Luther's writings, and against
his person, unless he should retract, as early as the
10th of February. This draught was laid before
the diet, together with the three following questions :
1. Whether Luther should be called to have a hearing—to Worms, or to some other place in the vicinity. 2. Whether his books, being full of heresy,
ought not forthwith to be burned and destroyed.
3. Whether, in case he should choose not to appear,
or, appearing, would not renounce his errors, he should
then be punished as a heretic.

The diet, near the beginning of March, replied
that, having taken the edict and questions laid before
them into consideration, 1. They must warn the emperor of the dangers of attempting by a new edict to
quell the excitement produced by Luther's preaching and writings; and, 2. They approve of citing
Luther to appear at Worms under a safe-conduct, not
however to discuss the points at issue, but simply to
reply to the questions whether he would retract or
not. When Luther was informed by Spalatin of
these counsels, he replied that he would not go to
Worms for such a purpose as that; he could as well
answer the question in Wittenberg as in Worms;
that he would never retract. The emperor informed
the diet that he should proceed according to their
advice.

After all this, and after Luther had (March 26)
received his citation and safe-conduct, dated March 6,
the emperor, nevertheless, issued his edict against

Luther's *books*, omitting that part which related to his person. This unjust and violent procedure, designed to prejudice the popular mind and to terrify the friends of Luther, induced the latter, and particularly Spalatin and the elector, to dissuade Luther from presenting himself for trial after his books were already condemned by the emperor.

We learn the state of feeling among Luther's friends, from a document of Pontanus, in which he recounts the considerations on both sides in respect to the safety of Luther's presenting himself under these circumstances. The chief objections were, that the cause was virtually prejudged, and that his safe-conduct would be no security, if he should refuse to retract, and should therefore be declared a heretic. There were in fact princes who were not ashamed to say that the emperor was not bound to keep his word with a heretic. But the house of Saxony and others rejected such a suggestion with scorn and with threats. The reasons urged by Pontanus in favour of Luther's coming were, that the edict itself, though it stated that Luther was cited to answer to the question whether he would retract what he had written or not, still expressly speaks of the safe-conduct to Worms *and back again*, without conditions or any reference to the kind of answer that should be given ; and that Luther's enemies would desire nothing better than to be able to say that he had not confidence to appear for trial. Luther knew the whole case perfectly, and decided with wisdom as consummate as his courage. It was here at Worms that he opened the eyes of many of the rulers of Germany, and actually drove a wedge which split the diet into two religious parties, not again for many centuries to be united. The scene which was opened at Worms did not close till the end of the Thirty Years' War, when the Protestants wrung from the Catholics a political equality.

When the hour arrived, Ulrich von Pappenheim and Caspar Sturm came and conducted him first to the Swan, the quarters of the Elector of the Palatinate, whence he was conveyed through secret passages to the Guild-hall, to avoid the concourse which had thronged the way from Luther's lodgings to the emperor's quarters. Many had climbed upon the house-tops to see Dr. Martin as he passed. As he was about to enter the hall, Freundsberg, a celebrated military commander, tapped him on the shoulder, and said, " Monk, monk, thou art about to make a passage and occupy a post more perilous than any which I and many other commanders ever knew in the bloodiest battle-fields. If thou art in the right and sure of your ground, go on in God's name and fear not; God will not forsake thee." Even after he had entered the hall, where, including those in the galleries and windows and about the doors, not less than five thousand were, according to the account of George Vogler, an eye-witness, assembled, many persons ventured to approach him and speak to him words of encouragement, saying to him, " Speak manfully, and be not afraid of them who kill the body, but have no power over the soul." He was instructed by Pappenheim to say nothing but when he was called upon.

Now the imperial orator, Dr. John Eck, (not the theologian, but the official or secular agent of the Archbishop of Treves,) addressed him, at the emperor's order, in Latin, and then in German, saying that he had been called before the imperial diet to an-

swer to these two questions : " First, whether you
acknowledge these books [a large pile of which lay
on the table] to be yours or not; secondly, whether
you will retract them or their contents, or whether
you will adhere to them still."

Before Luther replied, Schurf, his counsellor, said,
" Let the titles of the books be read." Then the
official read over the titles, among which were, Exposition of certain Psalms; Treatise on Good Works,
Explanation of the Lord's Prayer, and others which
were not of a polemical character.

Luther then answered, both in Latin and in German, " First, I must acknowledge the books just
named to be mine, and can never deny them. But
touching the next point, whether I will maintain all
these, or retract them, seeing it is a question of faith
and of one's salvation and of the word of God, which
is the greatest treasure in heaven and earth, and
deserving at all times our highest reverence, it would
be rash and perilous for me to speak inconsiderately,
and affirm, without reflection, either more or less than
is consistent with truth; for in either case I should
fall under the sentence of Christ, ' He that denieth
me before men, him will I deny before my Father
which is in heaven.' Therefore I beg of your imperial majesty time for reflection, that I may be able
to reply to the question proposed without prejudice
to the word of God or to my own salvation."

Hereupon the diet consulted, and returned a reply
through the official, "That although thou mightest
have known from the imperial summons for what
purpose thou wast cited, and dost not deserve the
grant of further time for consideration, yet his imperial clemency granteth thee one more day."

Whether we consider the serious nature of the

transaction, or the impression to be made upon such a national assembly, we shall perceive that Luther judged wisely in making such a request. The solemn suspense only heightened the solicitude of the multitude to hear the result.

As he was conducted to his quarters, he received many benedictions from the people, and nobles came to his lodgings and encouraged him. What his feelings were at this moment, we learn from a letter to Cuspinian, in which he says, " I have this very hour been standing before the emperor and his brother Ferdinand, and been asked whether I would retract my writings. I answered, 'The books laid before me are mine; but concerning the revocation, I will say what I will do to-morrow.' This is all the time I asked for deliberation, and all that they would give. But, Christ being gracious to me, I will not retract an iota."

About this time he received letters of encouragement from Ulrich von Hutten, the warrior-poet and patriot. He addressed a letter from Ebernburg, April 15, " to his holy friend, the invincible theologian and evangelist. Fight courageously for Christ," he says, "and yield not to wrong, but go forth confidently to meet it. Endure as a good soldier of Jesus, and suffer that the gift which is in you may be called out, and be assured that He on whom you have believed can preserve what you have committed to him till that day. I also will take strong hold of the work; but there is this difference in our undertakings, that mine is human, while you, far more perfect, cleave wholly to divine things."

On the following day, Thursday, the 18th, at four o'clock in the afternoon, the herald called again for Luther and conducted him to the emperor's court, where, on account of the engagements of the princes, he was obliged to stand waiting until six o'clock, with an immense crowd, which was gathered to hear his answer. The lamps were already lighted in the council hall. When the princes were ready to hear him, and Luther was standing before them, the official called on him to answer to the questions laid before him the previous day. Luther made his statement and defence in German, with modesty and calmness, but, at the same time, with a confidence and firmness that surprised those who expected nothing but a recantation. After bespeaking the indulgence of the diet, if, from his monastic and retired habits, he should fail in respect to any of the customary proprieties of courtly address, he observed that his published works were not all of the same character. In some he had treated of faith and works of piety with such plainness and Christian simplicity, that even his enemies were obliged to confess their harmlessness, usefulness and worth. To retract these would be to condemn the truth which all parties confessed. The second class of his works, were directed against the papacy and the Papists, as corrupting with their teaching and example all Christendom, both in body and soul. No one can deny nor conceal that by the papal laws and teachings of man, the consciences of Christians are held in bondage, burdened and tormented, and that goods and possessions, especially in Germany, are devoured by their incredible tyranny. They themselves have ordained in their own decrees, that the laws and doctrines of the pope which are contrary to the gospel and the teachings of the Fathers be regarded as erroneous. Were he to revoke this class of his books, he would but contribute to the strength of tyranny,

and leave open, not only a window, but a door and
a gate to wickedness, wider than ever; and by his testimony, especially if extorted by his imperial majesty and the whole German nation, their unchecked
tyrannical rule would be strengthened in its foundations. The third class of his books were personal
and written against those who undertook the defence
of Roman tyranny and the overthrow of the divine doctrines which he had inculcated. Against
these he had, he confessed, been more violent than
was becoming. He did not set himself up for a saint,
and disputed with his opponents not about his own
life, but about the doctrines of Christ. But even
these books he could not revoke, because he would
thereby give his influence in favour of Roman tyranny, which would trample on the people's rights
more mercilessly than ever.

But as he was a man, and not God, he could not
do for his books otherwise than Christ did for his
doctrines, who, when questioned in respect to them by
Annas, and smitten on his cheek by the servant,
said, "If I have spoken wrong, then show it to be
wrong." "Therefore," said he, "by the mercy of
God I beg your imperial majesty or any one else
who can, whoever he may be, to bring forward proof
against me, and overcome me by the writings of
the apostles and prophets. And then, if I am
shown to be in error, I will be ready and willing
to retract, and will be the first to cast my books
into the fire." But we cannot attempt to present
even an outline of this address. When it was
ended, he was requested, for the sake of the emperor and his Spanish court and others who did not
understand German, to repeat it in Latin. Though
exhausted with the effort he had made, he consented

to go over the ground again and rehearse the whole matter in Latin.

When he had finished, the imperial orator accused him of evading the point in question, and demanded that, instead of debating on articles which the councils had long ago settled, he should give a plain and direct answer, whether he would retract or not. To this Luther replied: "Since your imperial majesty and lordships desire a direct answer, I will give one, which has neither horns nor teeth, and it is this: Unless I shall be convinced by the testimony of Scripture, or by clear and plain argument, (for I do not believe either in the pope or in the councils alone, because it is plain and evident they have often erred and contradicted each other,) I am held by those passages which I have cited, and am bound by my conscience and by the word of God, and therefore I may not—cannot retract, inasmuch as it is neither safe nor right to violate my conscience. Here I stand, and cannot do otherwise, God be my help. Amen."

The electors and other members of the diet took the reply into consideration, whereupon Eck, the official of the Archbishop of Treves, took upon him to refute Luther, and to rebuke his immodesty. Luther rejoined, reaffirming and maintaining his positions, and entreated the emperor not to force a man to violate his conscience which was held bound by the authority of Scripture.

The next day, Friday, April 19, the emperor sent a written communication to the council of state, saying, that as Luther would not yield or move a finger's breadth from his errors, he, the emperor, must follow in the footsteps of his predecessors, and maintain and protect the Catholic religion, and inflict the penalty upon Luther if he should choose to come under the ban. But as a safe-conduct had been granted him, this must not be violated. He must first be allowed to return to his home. The remainder of that day and the whole of the following Saturday were consumed by the diet in deliberating upon this declaration of the emperor. In the mean time placards were stuck up, intimating that not less than four hundred knights had leagued together for the protection of Luther. Von Hutten and Von Sickingen were supposed to be the leaders.

Monday, the 22d, early in the morning, the Archbishop of Treves sent for Luther to come to his quarters and meet several princes there in a friendly conference. It was done, but all to no effect, both parties adhering to their principles. A private interview, which immediately succeeded, between the archbishop, Eck and Cochlæus on the one hand, and Luther, Schurf and Amsdorf on the other, was attended with no better success. Several other similar attempts were made to move Luther from his purpose, but without effect; and finally he was dismissed by the emperor with a safe-conduct extending to twenty days, with directions to refrain from agitating the minds of the people either by preaching or by writing. Luther submitted to the order without opposition, except that he claimed the right freely to confess and to teach the word of God.

The Elector Frederic was not displeased with the manner in which Luther acquitted himself on this extraordinary occasion. He had, even before Luther's arrival in Worms, expressed a desire to do something to protect him from unreasonable treatment. After Luther's address before the diet, the elector said to Spalatin, "The father, Dr. Martin, hath spoken well in Latin and German before the emperor, the princes and the estates. It was a bold step he took." "If it were in my power," he said afterward, "I would gladly procure justice for him." Such feelings led to the project of concealing him in the castle of Wartburg, and putting him under the protection of the commander of that place. The plan of a friendly capture was communicated to Luther the evening before he left Worms, and to his companion Amsdorf, though the time and place were unknown to them.

A graphic outline of the transactions at Worms is given by Luther in a letter to Albert of Mansfeld, written May 3, at Eisenach, the day before he was taken and carried to Wartburg. After the usual salutation, and an allusion to the count's request that Luther would send by a special messenger an account of the proceedings respecting him, he says, "First, my arrival at Worms was altogether unexpected. Therefore a prohibition was sent, and I, while under the imperial safe-conduct, was condemned before I came to the place or had a hearing. Afterward, that I might be quickly disposed of, I was asked whether I would cleave to my books or renounce them. Whereupon I replied as your grace hath, no doubt, already heard. Immediately the emperor, imbittered against me, issued a severe mandate and sent it to the estates of the empire. . . . Then certain persons were chosen out of the diet to admonish me, in a gracious and friendly way, to submit my books to the judgment of the emperor and of the diet. They were the Bishop of Treves, Margrave Joachim [of Brandenburg,] Duke George of Saxony, the Bishop of Augsburg, the Teutonic Master, the Bishop of Brandenburg, Count George of Wertheim and two deputies from the free cities. Then a doctor,

[Vehus,] chancellor of the Margrave of Baden arose
and gave unto me such a fine and well-arranged ad-
monition, that I must confess the official of Treves,
who spoke before the emperor, cannot hold a candle
to him. . . . When they failed to produce any effect
upon me, the Archbishop of Treves called me, Dr.
Schurf and Amsdorf, and also his official and
Cochlæus, before him apart. But it was an unprofitable dispute, and led to no good result. . . . After
ward the Chancellor [Vehus] of Baden and Peutinger were sent to me to persuade me to submit my
books unconditionally to the emperor. . . . I put it
to their consciences whether they could advise me
to commit myself wholly to the emperor and others
who had already condemned me and burnt my books.
. . . After this, the Archbishop of Treves sent for
me to see him alone. He showed himself in this
affair very kind and more than gracious, and would
gladly have quelled the difficulty. He set the
matter again before me, and I answered as before,
for I could not do otherwise, and so he dismissed
me. Soon after came the official, with a count, the
imperial chancellor, as a notary, saying to me in the
emperor's name, that inasmuch as I did not recede
from my purpose, I must return with twenty days
safe-conduct, and his imperial majesty would afterward do with me what was proper. I thanked his
majesty, and said, 'As it hath pleased the Lord, so
it is done, blessed be the name of the Lord.' They
enjoined it upon me not to preach or write by the
way. I replied, 'I will do all that his majesty
pleases, but the word of God I will have unbound,
as St. Paul says.' Thus I parted with them, and am
now at Eisenach."

Several days before, April 28, while at Frank

furt, he wrote to his friend Cranach, the painter : "I
shall suffer myself to be taken and concealed, I do
not myself know where. And though I would rather
suffer death from the tyrants, especially from the
furious Duke George, nevertheless I must not despise
the counsel of good friends, but must wait for the
proper time.

"My arrival at Worms was unexpected ; and how
the safe-conduct was observed you all know from
the prohibition which met me on the way. I had
supposed his imperial majesty would have assembled
about fifty doctors, and in a fair way have confuted
the monk. But only thus much was done. 'Are
these books yours?' 'Yes.' 'Will you retract them
or not?' 'No.' 'Away with you then.' O blind
Germans that we are ! How childishly we act and
suffer the Romanists so miserably to make us play
the ape and the fool. . . . Greet [professor and
burgomaster] Beyer and his wife, and express my
warm thanks to the council [of Wittenberg] for my
conveyance [to Worms.] . . . Farewell. I commend
you all to God, and may he keep the understanding
and faith of you all in Christ from the Roman wolves
and dragons and their rabble."

Luther left Worms, Friday, April 26th, at ten
o'clock in the morning, and was overtaken at Oppenheim by the herald, who followed after him. The
second day he went as far as Frankfurt, where, the
next morning, he wrote the above-mentioned letter
to Cranach. The third day he reached Friedburg,
whence he sent one communication to the emperor
and another to the diet by the herald, whose company, in view of the elector's project, was desired no
farther. The fourth day he arrived at Grünberg,
and the fifth at Hirsfeld, where he was received with

Wartburg Castle, and the seizure of Luther on his way from Worms.

great pomp. The sixth day, at night, he entered Eisenach, where, the next morning, he dismissed Schurf and his other travelling companions, except Amsdorf; while he himself and Amsdorf, after remaining another day, turned aside and went to Mora, on the other side of the Thuringian Forest, to visit his uncle and other relatives. The day following, a little beyond Altenstein, he was seized with feigned violence, and conveyed to Wartburg. He might easily have gone to this place when at Eisenach, but that would have divulged the secret.

In the church records at Schweina, a little south of Altenstein, is found the following entry: "Saturday, May 4, 1521, between four and five o'clock in the afternoon, Dr. M. Luther passed through this place on his way from Worms, and was taken captive about a mile beyond Altenstein, near Luther's Fountain, on the road to Waltershausen, and carried to Wartburg." This is the most romantic part of the Thuringian Forest. Luther had followed the winding mountain road southward to Schweina, and was passing through a sandy hollow at the bend of the road south-east of Altenstein, when the commander of that place, the Knight von Hund, and Berlepsch, the commander of Wartburg, seized him, according to a preconcerted plan. As it was not yet sunset, and as the utmost secrecy was necessary, they left the road and wandered about the forest to the north and west, till they came to a spring and a beech tree in a narrow glen, about a hundred and twenty rods from the castle of Altenstein. Here they sat down and rested, and refreshed themselves with the pure water. The spring is still called *Luthersbrunn,* and the beech, now six feet in diameter, *Luther's Buche.* A centennial celebration was held here in 1817.

In a letter to Spalatin, dated on the Mountain, [Wartburg,] May 14th, after speaking of "the papal yoke, which the people will no longer bear," and of his leisure time and his studies, he goes on to say: "The Abbot of Hirsfeld received me with a kindness which you would hardly believe. He sent his chancellor and his lord of the exchequer out five miles to meet me. He himself received me at his castle with a cavalcade, and accompanied me into the town. Within the walls we were received by the senate. The abbot entertained us [Luther and his companions] sumptuously in the monastery, and put me into his own chamber. The next morning they compelled me to preach. It was in vain that I objected, on the ground that it might cost the abbot his regalia, inasmuch as the imperial party might say that it was a violation of public faith, they having forbidden me to preach on the way. I indeed told him I did not consent that the word of God should be bound, and this was true.

"I preached also at Eisenach; but the timid parson was present with a notary and witnesses, protesting against it, and then excusing himself humbly, saying he did it out of fear of the tyrants which were over him. Perhaps you may hear at Worms [where Spalatin still remained] that I have herein not kept good faith; but it is not so. That the word of God should be bound was a condition wherein I had nothing to do, nor did I make any such promise; and even if I had done so, inasmuch as it is contrary to the will of God to make such promise, I should not be bound to keep it. The day following, the abbot accompanied us as far as to the [Thuringian] forest, and sent his chancellor forward to Berka to prepare a dinner for us.

"At length we entered Eisenach at evening, under the escort of the people, [among whom were many of Luther's youthful acquaintances,] who came out on foot to meet us. In the morning, Schurf and all my other companions [except Amsdorf] went on their way. I went across the mountain to visit my kindred, who inhabit that region. Leaving them and proceeding toward Waltershausen, soon after passing the castle of Altenstein, I was seized. Amsdorf necessarily knew that some one was to take me, but was ignorant of the place of my custody.

"My brother, seeing the knights in season, leaped from the carriage, and, without taking leave of me, went on foot to Waltershausen, which he is said to have reached in the evening, [followed, at length, by Amsdorf and the affrighted driver with the carriage.] So here I am, my own attire being laid aside, and that of a knight being put upon me, with long hair [as monk, he wore his hair shorn in the form of a crown of thorns] and long beard, so that you would hardly know me. Indeed, I have not for some time known myself. Here I enjoy Christian liberty, being set free from all the laws of that tyrant, though I would choose rather, if it were the will of God I should suffer for his word, that Dresden swine [Duke George] should be thought worthy to put me to death for preaching publicly. The will of the Lord be done."

CHAPTER IV.

Section I.—*Luther at Wartburg, May 4, 1521, to March 4,*
1522.

T was more than a week before Luther ventured to write any letters to his friends. On the 12th of May, he wrote one letter to Melancthon and another to Amsdorf. The one last quoted, giving an account of his capture, was written two days later. To Amsdorf he says, "I wrote lately to you all, my dear Amsdorf, but, on listening to a better counsellor, I tore the letters in pieces because it was not yet safe to send them. . . . The Lord now visiteth me with severe illness, [arising from costiveness.] But pray for me, as I always pray for you, that God may strengthen your heart. Be courageous, therefore; and, as you have opportunity, speak the word of God with boldness. Write to me how it was with you in your journey, [from Altenstein to Wittenberg,] and

what you heard and saw in Erfurt, [where a great
excitement was created by the attentions paid to
Luther on his way to Worms.]   With Melancthon
you will learn what Spalatin [still at Worms] hath
written to me, [concerning the violent proceedings
against me.]   The day I was torn away from you,
I, a new knight, weary from the length of the ride,
[about eight miles] came in the dark, nearly eleven
o'clock at night, to this mansion.   And now I am
here in a state of leisure, like one set at large among
captives.   Beware of the Dresden Rehoboam [Duke
George] and of Benhadad of Damascus, [the Elector
of Brandenburg,] your neighbour.   For a severe edict
hath been issued against us.   But the Lord shall
hold them in derision."

The Elector Frederic, in order to evade the questions with which the imperial and papal party would
be likely to press him, kept himself ignorant for a time
of the particular place where Spalatin, by his order,
kept Luther in custody.   We see, from the foregoing
letter, that his keepers dissuaded him from writing
so soon to his friends, lest the secret in respect to his
place of residence should be betrayed.   To Spalatin
he wrote, some time after : "I have with difficulty made
out to send you this letter, such is the fear entertained that it will be found out where I am.   Therefore, if you think it will be for the honour of Christ,
let it not be known whether I am in the keeping of
friend or foe ; for it is not necessary that any besides
yourself and Amsdorf should know any thing more
than that I am alive."

This design of concealment explains the indefinite
and amusing manner in which he dated his letters.
The above letter to Amsdorf, is dated "In the Regions of the Air;" that written to Melancthon the

same day, "In the Regions of the Birds;" others, "From my Hermitage;" "From the Isle of Patmos;" "Among the birds, which sing sweetly in the trees, and praise God with all their might, night and day."

As late as the 10th of June, he wrote to Spalatin : "It is the will of our gracious prince that my place of abode be not yet made known. Therefore, I do not write to him at all." Cochlæus and others of the Catholic party supposed that Allstedt was the place of his concealment. A few of Luther's intimate friends had learned where he was; but in a letter written September 10, we find him saying, "Duke John, the elder, at length knows where I am, but did not know before. My host privately made it known to him. But he will doubtless keep it to himself."

Luther poured out his whole heart in his first letter to Melancthon, May 12, probably the very first letter written from Wartburg. It is particularly interesting as revealing the state of his mind in that singular posture of public affairs. He writes thus : "And what, my dear Philip, are you meanwhile doing? Are you not praying that this withdrawal of myself, to which I have unwillingly given my assent, may turn out for the furtherance of the glory of God? I greatly desire to know how it pleaseth you. I fear I shall be accounted as deserting the field of battle, and yet I could find no way to resist those who desired and advised this course. I desire nothing more than to bare my breast to the fury of my enemies. Here I sit the whole day, with the visage of the church ever before me, and the passage, Psalm lxxxix. 47 : 'Why hast thou made all the sons of men in vain?' How horrible a form of God's anger is that abominable kingdom of the Roman antichrist! I abhor my own hardness of heart that I am not dissolved in tears, and that I do not weep fountains of tears for the slain sons of my people. But there is no one to arise and cleave to God, and make himself a wall for the house of Israel in this last day of his wrath. O, kingdom of the pope! worthy of the end and dregs of the world. God have mercy on us. Wherefore, be thou meanwhile instant as a minister of the word, and fortify the walls and towers of Jerusalem, till they shall assail thee. You know your calling and gifts. I pray earnestly for you, if, as I doubt not, my prayer can be of any avail. Do thou the same for me, and let us mutually bear this burden. Thus far I alone have stood in the front of battle. They will next seek for your life."

In another letter to the same, written May 26, he mentions, that "having composed his mind to quiet studies, he had reluctantly replied to Jacob Latomus," a sophistical theologian of Louvain, who had written in defence of the burning of Luther's books; that he had seen what his friends Faber, Œcolampadius, Hutten and others, had written against his opponents; that he was himself surprised at the boldness of Feldkirch, provost of Kemberg, in venturing at such a time to show his opposition to the celibacy of the clergy by actually entering into wedlock. He is generally represented as the first evangelical or Protestant clergyman who took this step; but two others preceded him in Saxony, and were imprisoned for their temerity.

Luther, though his personal situation was agreeable, proceeds to say: "Yet for the glory of God, and for the confirmation of myself and others, I would sooner be burnt over live coals than decay alone half-dead, not to say quite dead. But who knoweth whether, in this as in other cases, Christ will by such means effect a greater good? We have always been talking about faith and hope in things not seen. Come, then, let us for once make some little trial, especially since it is of God's appointing, and not of our seeking. Even if I perish, the gospel will not perish, in which you are now my superior, and Elisha succeedeth Elias with a double measure of the Spirit, which may the Lord Jesus in mercy grant you. Amen. Therefore, be not sad, but sing unto the Lord songs in the night season, and I will join with you. . . . Let the men of Leipsic glory, for this is their hour. We must go out from our country, from our kindred, and from our father's house, and for a time sojourn in a strange land. . . . I have not given up the hope of returning unto you, though I leave it to God to do what is good in his own eyes.

"If the pope shall fall upon all those who think and feel with me, there will be no want of tumult in Germany. The sooner he does it, the sooner will he and his perish, and I return. God so arouseth the spirit of many and the hearts even of the multitude, that it seemeth not likely to me that the thing can be put down by power; or, if it be put down, it will rise again with ten-fold force." The remainder of the letter, full of special references to the circumstances of his Wittenberg friends, though of the greatest interest to the historian, must be omitted here.

In another letter he says: "A certain Romanist hath written to the man of a red hat at Mainz: 'We have lost Luther, as we desired; but the people are so excited that I suspect we shall not save our lives, unless we seek for him everywhere with lighted candles, and bring him back.' He indeed joketh, but what if the joke should turn out to be a serious matter?"

The situation of Luther during the ten months of his residence at Wartburg is of a highly romantic character. The heroism he had lately shown, the perilous condition he was in when he left Worms, the mystery which hung about his present place of abode, all acted with visible effect upon the minds of the people. And now that we are let behind the curtain, his secluded life appears no less extraordinary than the wonderful missiles which, from his unknown retreat, he continually sent forth to the consternation of his adversaries. At one time we find him wandering for amusement, or picking wild berries, along the hill-sides and ravines east of the castle, toward St. George's gate, or the south gate of the city. Again, we see him out on a two-days' chase, busying himself with dogs and traps; but finding, in the hare caught by himself and wrapt in a garment to preserve him from the dogs—which nevertheless seized and destroyed him—an image of Satan and the pope murdering souls which others had endeavoured to save. Now he rides in disguise, under the direction of a wary knight, to the neighbouring towns and villages, to Gotha, Erfurt, Reinhardsbrunn, and Marksuhl. At the last-mentioned place, about five miles to the south-west of Wartburg, he saw his friends; but knight George, as he was then called, was not recognised in his knight's dress and long beard and hair. At Reinhardsbrunn, between Altenstein and Gotha, he was conducted hastily away by his guardian, when the latter perceived that his ward was known to the people.

The state of Luther's mind, at this time, was as peculiar as were his external circumstances. He was like a vessel that had outridden the storm, and was now moored by a desolate island. The waves had not so far subsided as not to rock his bark with some degree of violence. Partly from over-excitement and exhaustion, partly from unwonted inactivity, and too good living for one of his monastic habits, he suffered painful illness. It is not strange that he should, at times, be very much dejected. He complained of temptations sorer than he had ever experienced. This might all be so. But, when he tells of the devil's making such disturbance and noise about the premises that it was necessary to speak to him, we may well suppose that a little medical treatment and the poisoning of the rats would have aided essentially in giving him quiet nights.

It can hardly be doubted that his present seclusion was favourable to his character, both as a Christian and as a reformer. He needed time for reflection. Ever since he left the Erfurt convent, he had been very active, and often much excited by controversy. It was well that he could now commune with himself and with his God, and calmly contemplate the scene without. He had necessarily been much occupied with tearing down and destroying what was false; he now had opportunity to direct his mind steadily to what was true. The work of building up, which was soon to follow, was even more difficult than that of destroying.

At Wartburg, Luther, by translating the New Testament, made the best preparation for future usefulness. Not only did he hereby put the mighti-

est of Protestant weapons into the hands of all the
people, and in that way do immense service to the
Reformation, but, what was of no less importance,
he obtained that familiarity with the whole of the
New Testament, that thorough acquaintance with
biblical Christianity, which made it possible for
him to escape so many errors, and to incorporate
so much truth in his theological system.   It is
true, indeed, that on the subject of religious liberty,
his mind underwent a change.   After his return to
Wittenberg, and especially after the Peasants' War,
he was less inclined than before to the freedom of
the individual conscience in the interpretation of the
Bible.   Still, the progress he made in biblical
knowledge and in digesting and arranging his
various doctrines, as they had been disconnectedly
thrown out in his controversial and other writings,
seems to have been almost indispensable to him at
this time.

Though Luther was so occupied with inward
struggles and temptations and with the labours of
studying the Hebrew and Greek Scriptures, he did
not withdraw his interest or his view from the fortunes and the transactions of the religious party of
which he had become the leader.   With his friends
and former associates he kept up a diligent correspondence.   He requested them to communicate
to him all that was going on.   He was accurately
informed of the excitement that prevailed among
the nobles, of the disaffection of the common people
toward their ecclesiastical rulers; of the progress of
his doctrines at home and abroad, and of the de-
signs and plots of his enemies.   In these circumstances, he was the constant counsellor of his Wittenberg and other friends, giving them instructions

how to proceed in spreading the truth, and in warding off the attacks of the hostile party. He instructed Amsdorf how to reply to Emser. He is consulted about the best manner of organizing the Wittenberg Gymnasium, or Grammar-school. He urges Spalatin to compel Melancthon to preach, saying, "How I wish Philip would preach to the people in the German language, [he did not refuse to lecture on the Sabbath to the students, in Latin.] . . . Since he is called of God, what matters it that he has not been called by the tyrannical bishops? . . . But I know the temper and spirit of the man, that he will not yield to my entreaties. Therefore he must be compelled by the urgent demand of the whole [Wittenberg] church. Were I at Wittenberg, I should, as I think, move the senate and people to call on him to preach to them in German; and I greatly desire you should take the matter in hand. You can carry the measure in the senate through the influence of Cranach and Bayer."

He urged Justus Jonas, who, while at Worms with him, was made professor of canonical law at Wittenberg in place of Pollich deceased, to labour for the overthrow of the authority of the decretals, or laws of the pope. "Be an Aaron," he says to him, "clothed with sacred vestments, i. e. armed with the sacred Scriptures. Take the censer of prayer and go out to meet this destroyer. Place yourself in the very midst of the conflagration of the world, kindled by Rome, but soon to be extinguished by the coming of our Saviour whom we expect. Teach your pupils, my brother, that those things which it is your office to teach [the canon law] are to be unlearned, that whatsoever the pope and the papists enact and establish is to be avoided as a deadly poison. Since we are not able to remove this great evil by direct power, and are obliged to perform official service in these sacrilegious Babylonish provinces, it only remaineth for us to regard them as the devastators and plunderers of our Jerusalem." He advised Spalatin to favour the utter abrogation of the canon law. His host, Berlepsch, at Wartburg, had done well, he said, in treating this law as antiquated, and in prohibiting ecclesiastical jurisdiction. If the elector and other princes were not prepared to do as much, " let them, at least, take no notice of the courts and judges when they disregard the papal laws, for so will the abuse be insensibly corrected."

Luther's writings during this period were both numerous and important. The principal are those against Latomus, a learned theologian of Louvain, and this was one of Luther's best productions; against the University of Paris, which had given a judgment adverse to his cause; and against Emser; besides treatises on auricular confession, on the celibacy of the clergy, on private mass, on the abolition of cloisters, and on communion in both kinds, Commentaries on certain Psalms, and Postils on the Gospels. Perhaps the most characteristic of the productions of his pen during this period is the well-known letter which he addressed to Albert, Archbishop of Mainz. That prelate, as if triumphing in the decision of the diet of Worms and in the retirement of Luther from the scene of conflict, renewed the sale of indulgences at Halle, his favourite residence. Luther, who was fully informed of what was done, felt his blood boil within him as in 1517, when Tetzel was the direct object of his attack. He set himself to compose a tract which should fall like a thunderbolt upon the head of the archbishop. But Spalatin and Melancthon, who had been visited on the subject, in a friendly way, by two distinguished individuals from Albert's court, thought it too bold for the circumstances, and Frederic feared it would disturb his relations with the emperor and the Catholic princes; and the work was not, at that time, printed.

Luther reluctantly submitted, but, in place of publishing the pamphlet, he wrote the private letter above mentioned to the archbishop. If he, the archbishop, thought himself secure because Luther had retired from the scene, and supposed that, by the aid of the imperial authority, he could put down the monk, he would find himself mistaken. He himself would not fail to do what Christian love demanded, in spite of the gates of hell, not to mention popes, cardinals and bishops; and therefore requested him to cease from deceiving and plundering the people, and to act the part of a bishop, and not of a wolf; for it was notorious that indulgences were nothing but sheer knavery and fraud. The prelate would do well to remember what a great fire had been kindled by a little, insignificant spark; how a despised monk had given the pope himself enough to do, and, contrary to all expectation, carried his point so far, that what had been lost could never be retrieved, but, on the contrary, became worse and worse every day, so that God's hand must be recognised in the work. The same God still lives, and can resist and overcome a Cardinal of Mainz, though four emperors should undertake to protect him. That Divine hand took delight in breaking down the cedars of Lebanon, and humbling the proud and hardened Pharaohs. The bishop had better be cautious about despising and provoking that invisible power. "Let not your highness think," he goes on to say, "that Luther is dead. He will still joyfully trust in the God who hath humbled the pope, and will play a game with the Cardinal of Mainz, which few would expect. . . . I give you notice, that, unless the idol be removed, I shall feel bound, out of regard to divine truth and the salvation of souls, to assail your grace as I did the pope, and to speak plainly to a high dignitary, and to place all the abominations practised by Tetzel at the doors of the Bishop of Mainz, and to point out to all the world the difference between a bishop and a wolf. Your grace can hereby know what to do, and how to conduct. . . . I await your decision, and expect an answer within two weeks. If within that period none comes, then my book 'Against the Idol at Halle' will go to the public."

Strange as it may seem, a mild and submissive reply was received, in which the archbishop promised to stop the abuse. He did not care to be immortalized as Tetzel had been. He shrunk from a controversy which would be so little to his credit. The charm of indulgences had been broken; the eyes of the people had been opened, and the public sentiment fixed for ever in opposition to a practice so vile and contemptible.

SECTION II.—*Troubles at Wittenberg. and Luther's Return.*

MEANWHILE sentiments and principles were springing up among the friends and followers of Luther which were destined to make him great trouble. He had broken the bands by which the human mind had been so long fettered, and now men began everywhere to exercise freedom of opi-

nion and of speech.   Luther himself had not fully
considered how difficult it would be to stay the current after he had loosened the foundations and removed a portion of the dam which had hitherto
restrained it. How is this freedom to be controlled ?
Shall men be free to differ from the reformer himself ?   Is there to be no subjection to authority in
matters of religion ?   Shall differences of opinion,
when they exist, be adjusted by learned disputations,
with chosen judges to sit in arbitration ? or shall the
church be made again the ultimate authority ; or
shall the civil power be brought in as the protector
of the true faith ? It is not strange that so difficult a
problem should not have been solved by the reformers, and that, drifting along on the current of events,
they should sometimes be carried in a wrong direction.

There were two classes of subjects on which serious differences of opinion arose, the one relating
to what is true, the other to what is expedient.
Luther often agreed with his opponents in respect
to the former, and differed only in respect to the
latter.   The majority of the Augustinian monks of
Wittenberg agreed, in the absence of Luther, to
disband.   The step was a little too bold even for
Luther, though he himself had given the lesson.
Many would be shocked at such a wholesale violation of the monastic vow. The monks would rush into
wedlock, without either an income or a knowledge of
business sufficient to support their households.

The elector and all his ministers, and the university and the chapter, after innumerable consultations, found it difficult to settle this matter,
and still more difficult to manage the monks and
others who, in the exercise of their new freedom,
had abolished the mass service about the same time.

Finally, the subject of church ceremonies and church ornaments, altars and images, led to a controversy which ended in open tumult. On all these and kindred points, Carlstadt, who had joined the party of the monk Gabriel Didymus, took a different view from Luther. He insisted on bringing all things back to the pattern of the primitive church, without regard to men's prejudices, or to consequences. This controversy between Luther and Carlstadt is a delicate subject for the historian to dispose of. Men of equal intelligence and piety come to different conclusions in respect to it. So much, however, may safely be said, that Carlstadt, though a learned and undoubtedly a conscientious man, had neither the ability nor the discretion of Luther. He was excitable, somewhat changeable and fanatical, and perhaps ambitious. That his views of reform carried him at times to excess is undeniable.

But if, in respect to means and measures, he was too violent, and sometimes erred even when his principles were otherwise right, Luther was sometimes wrong in his principles. If the former laid too great stress on the reformation of external abuses, and did not rely sufficiently on well settled principles to work out their own results in due time, the latter went to the other extreme of undervaluing outward conformity to primitive Christianity, and of regarding the ceremonies introduced into the church in later times as a matter of comparative indifference. In this last respect, he differed widely from the Swiss reformers. Carlstadt was successively connected with two very different parties, both of which were at variance with the Lutheran church, namely, the Anabaptists and the Zwinglians. We are now concerned with the former only.

The name by which Luther and his associates designated these men was that of "Celestial Prophets," or "Zwickau Prophets," a clear indication that their leading characteristic was fanaticism, and that their peculiar views of baptism were regarded as subordinate or incidental. This view is supported by the fact that, for the first three or four years, they made no innovations in respect to this rite as practised by the church, or, at most, in but a few individual cases. The first clear instance on record of re-baptism by them was in Switzerland, in 1524, whereas the Zwickau Prophets commenced their movement near the middle of the year 1521. Muncer himself did not re-baptize, nor did his followers generally, during his lifetime.

Nor was there any dispute at that time about the mode of baptism, for the Anabaptists not only made no complaints of the practice of the church in that respect, but themselves ordinarily practised aspersion or pouring, and rarely immersion.

When, therefore, the men of Zwickau appeared at Wittenberg, in December of 1521, and confounded and alarmed Melancthon and Amsdorf, and, for a time, carried away with their persuasions Carlstadt and others connected with the university, their main doctrine was, that the people of God should follow an inward light; that they themselves possessed the spirit of prophecy, and spoke by immediate revelation; that the vain show and ceremonies of the church were all to be abrogated or changed, and the church restored to its apostolical simplicity. They professed to establish a spiritual church, regarding the Catholic church as carnal and corrupt, so that neither baptism, ordination, nor any thing else coming from it, could be recognised by a

Christian. Various extravagances were connected
with these views, of which none was more important
than their radicalism in respect to civil government.

Melancthon, Amsdorf and others represented the
perilous state of things at Wittenberg to the Elector Frederic, saying they were upon the very verge
of a violent insurrection, and, as Luther's authority
was appealed to by the insurgents, none but Luther
could have power with them. Their proposal to
recall Luther did not meet the elector's views. He
said he had purposely caused Luther to be conveyed
to an unknown place, and kept securely in secret,
so that he could truly say to the emperor, if required to deliver him up, that he knew not where
he was. Should Luther now make his appearance
openly at Wittenberg, he might be seized by his
enemies, and he himself, as elector, was subject to
the imperial authority, and could do nothing in opposition to it for Luther's protection. Luther, who
was informed of all these things, resolved to make
the bold experiment of going unprotected to the
place of danger, informing the elector of his purpose, but giving him no time to prevent the step.

No wonder that Luther was willing to risk his
life and his credit with Frederic, in order to allay
the tempest which he saw rising. He feared that
these disorders, springing up in the head-quarters
of reform, would bring the whole movement, with
which he was now identified, into discredit, and
prove more fatal to the Reformation than all the
opposition of the Papists. It must be conceded that,
in his general view of the case, he was substantially
in the right. Whether a little more sympathy with
the people in their longing for freedom, a little more
relaxation on points either debatable or compara-

tively unimportant, would have secured union, except with a few, as well as victory, and saved the people from the terrible catastrophe into which Muncer plunged them, is a question which no one can decide with certainty. But of this there can be no doubt, that Luther's abilities were equal to the exigency, and that he never manifested more consummate skill in management and discussion, nor a clearer insight into human nature, than on this occasion.

An incident occurred when he was at Jena, on his way to Wittenberg, which is too characteristic of his humour and of his social nature to be omitted. We have the account in the words of Kessler, of Saint Gall, one of the individuals concerned in the amusing scene. We will quote his language.

"Though it may seem trifling and childish, I cannot omit mentioning how Martin met me and my companion, when he was riding from the place of his captivity toward Wittenberg. As we were journeying toward Wittenberg, for the sake of studying the Holy Scriptures—and the Lord knows what a furious tempest there was—we came to Jena in Thuringia, where we could not, with all our inquiry in the town, find or hear of any place to lodge for the night, but were everywhere refused, for it was carnival, during which little heed is given to pilgrims or strangers. We, therefore, left the town again, to proceed farther on our way, thinking we might perhaps find a hamlet where we could pass the night. At the gate of the city we met a respectable man, who accosted us in a friendly manner, and asked us where we were going so late. . . . He then asked us whether we had inquired at the Black Bear hotel. . . . He pointed it out to us a little distance

without the city. . . . The inn-keeper met us at
the door and received us, and led us into the room.
Here we found a man at the table, sitting alone, with
a small book lying before him, who greeted us kindly,
and invited us to take a seat with him at the table; for
our shoes were so muddy that we were ashamed to
enter the room, and therefore slunk away upon a
bench behind the door. . . . We took him to be no
other than a knight, as he had on, according to the
custom of the country, a red cap, small clothes and
a doublet, and a sword at his side, on which he
leaned, with one hand on the pommel and the other
on the hilt. He asked us whence we were, but immediately answered himself, 'You are Swiss; from what
part of Switzerland are you?' We replied, 'St. Gall.'
He then said, 'If, as I suppose, you are on your way
to Wittenberg, you will find good countrymen of
yours there, namely, Jerome Schurf and his brother
Augustine;' whereupon we said, 'We have letters to
them.' We now asked him in turn, if he could give
us any information about Martin Luther—whether
he is now at Wittenberg or elsewhere. He said, 'I
have certain knowledge that he is not now at Wittenberg, but will soon be there. But Philip Melancthon is there, as teacher of Greek, and others teach
Hebrew.' He recommended to us to study both languages, as necessary above all things to understand
the Scriptures. We said, 'Thank God, we shall then
see and hear the man [Luther] on whose account we
have undertaken this journey.' . . . He then asked
us where we had formerly studied; and, as we replied
at Basle, he inquired how things were going on there,
and what Erasmus was doing. 'Erasmus is still there,
but what he is about no one knoweth, for he keepeth
himself very quiet and secluded.' We were much

surprised at the knight, that he should know the Schurfs, Melancthon and Erasmus, and that he should speak of the necessity of studying Greek and Hebrew. At times, too, he made use of Latin words, so that we began to think he was something more than a common knight.

"'Sir,' said he, 'what do men in Switzerland think of Luther?' We replied, 'Variously, as everywhere else. Some cannot sufficiently bless and praise God that he hath, through this man, made known his truth and exposed error; others condemn him as an intolerable heretic.' 'Especially the clergy,' interrupted he,—'I doubt not these are the priests.' By this conversation we were made to feel ourselves quite at home, and my companion [Reutiner] took the book that lay before him, and looked into it, and found it was a Hebrew psalter. He soon laid it down again, and the knight took it. This increased our curiosity to know who he was. When the day declined and it grew dark, our host, knowing our desire and longing after Luther, came to the table and said, 'Friends, had you been here two days ago, you could have had your desire, for he sat here at this table,' pointing to the seat. We were provoked with ourselves that we were too late, and poured out our displeasure against the bad roads which had hindered us. After a little while, the host called me to the door, and said, 'Since you manifest so earnest a desire to see Luther, you must know that it is he who is seated by you. I took these words as spoken in jest, and said, 'You, to please me, give me a false joy at seeing Luther.' 'It is indeed he,' replied my host, 'but make as if you did not know it.' I went back into the room and to the table, and desired to tell my companion what I had heard, and turned to him,

and said in a whisper, 'Our host hath told me that
this is Luther.' He, like myself, was incredulous.
'Perhaps he said Hutten, and you misunderstood
him.' As now the knight's dress comported better
with the character of Hutten than with that of a monk,
I was persuaded that he said it was Hutten. [Two
merchants now came in, and they all supped together.] Our host came, meanwhile, to us, and said in
a whisper, 'Don't be concerned about the cost, for
Martin hath paid the bill.' We rejoiced, not so
much for the gift or the supper, as for the honour of
being entertained by such a man. After supper the
merchants went to the stable to see to their horses,
and Martin remained with us in the room. We
thanked him for the honour shown us, and gave him
to understand that we took him for Ulrich von Hutten. But he said, 'I am not he.' Just then came
in our host, and Martin said to him, 'I have become
a nobleman to-night, for these Swiss hold me to be
Ulrich von Hutten.' The host replied, 'You are not
he, but Martin Luther.' He laughed and said jocosely, 'They hold me to be Hutten, and you say I
am Luther; I shall next be Marcolfus,' [a notorious
character in the monkish legends.] Afterward he
took up a large beer-glass, and said, 'Swiss, now
drink me a health;' and then arose, threw around
him his mantle, and, giving us his hand, took leave
of us, saying, 'When you come to Wittenberg, greet
Dr. Jerome Schurf for me.' 'Very gladly,' said we;
'but whom shall we call you, that he may understand us?' He replied, 'Say only this, he who is to
come, sendeth you greeting,' and he will understand
it. . . . On Saturday, we went to the house of
Schurf to present our letters; and when we were
conducted into the room, behold we found Martin

there as at Jena, and with him Melancthon, Justus
Jonas, Nicholas Amsdorf, and Dr. Augustine Schurf,
rehearsing to him what had taken place at Wittenberg during his absence. He greeted us, and smiling said, 'This is Philip Melancthon, of whom we
spoke.' Melancthon turned to us and asked us many
questions, to which we replied as well as we could.
So we spent the day with them with great delight
and gratification on our part."

SECTION III.—*Luther at Wittenberg again, and his First
Encounter with the turbulent Populace.*

LUTHER arrived at Wittenberg on Friday, the 7th
of March, and from Sunday the 9th harangued the
people eight successive days with overpowering eloquence. All his skill was put in requisition to save
from shipwreck the vessel laden with a freight, containing all that was precious to him. In his first
discourse, he went back and planted himself upon
the fundamental principles of the Christian religion,
and, carrying all hearts with him on these points, he
next proceeded cautiously, but firmly, to unfold these
principles, and to show their application to the case
in hand, which he approached with the skill of a
master. His main positions were so strong and clear
that one was the less disposed to call in question the
use he made of them. The following is a sketch of
what he said. "First, I maintain that we are all
children of wrath, and that all our works, thoughts
and feelings are sinful and nothing before God, so
that we cannot appear before him with them, how
excellent soever and fine they may be. Secondly,
that God, of his mere mercy and goodness, hath sent
his only-begotten Son into the world, that we might

believe and trust in him, and, believing, might be free from sin and become the children of God. In these two articles I find no defect or fault in you. They are preached to you pure and uncorrupt. Thirdly, we must have love, and by love serve one another, as God hath done unto us by faith, without which love faith is nothing, as Paul saith to the Corinthians. Here, on this point, dear friends, you are in fault; for I discover no trace of love in you, but observe that you have been unthankful to God, and that he hath, within these few years, bestowed upon you his treasures of grace in vain. Therefore let us beware lest Wittenberg become a Capernaum. I perceive clearly that you know how to discourse upon the doctrines which are preached unto you, such as faith and also love. But this is no great thing, though you could say much that is good about these virtues. Even the ass can be taught to sing. Cannot you, then, learn so much as to repeat the words of our faith? But, my dear friends, the kingdom of God standeth not in speech or words, but in power and in deeds. God will have not merely hearers and rehearsers, but followers and doers, who will keep his words, who will exercise themselves in faith, which worketh by love. For faith without love is nothing worth; nay, it is not faith, but its semblance only, just as one's face seen in a glass is not the face itself, but its image. Fourthly, we must also exercise patience. For whosoever hath faith, and trusteth in God, and hath love to his neighbour, and exerciseth himself therein, he shall not be without persecution. For Satan neither sleepeth nor is at rest, but maketh trouble enough for men. But persecution worketh patience; for if I am neither persecuted nor tempted, I can have little to say of patience. And patience worketh hope, which springeth up and flourisheth in God, and putteth one not to shame. Thus, by many temptations and persecutions, faith increaseth and is strengthened from day to day.

"Such a heart, wherein faith so increaseth, and so many virtues dwell, cannot rest, nor contain itself, but must pour itself out again, and do good to its neighbour as it hath received good of the Lord. Here, my dear friends, each one is not to do as he hath a right to do, but must relax from his right, and consider what is useful and profitable to his brother, as Paul did, who said to the Corinthians, 'I have all power; but all is not expedient;' and, again, 'Though I am free from all men, yet have I made myself the servant of all, that I might win many.' In these words of Paul, we are instructed how we, who have received faith from God, should conduct ourselves toward all, namely, accommodate ourselves to the weakness of our neighbour. For we are not all equally strong in the faith. He who is strong to-day, may be weak to-morrow; and he who is weak to-day, may be strong to-morrow. Therefore we must not consider our own faith or strength alone, but that of our neighbour, that we may condescend to him, and not offend him by our liberty. We must not forget how he hath borne with us, and had patience a long time with our weakness. We ought to do likewise unto our brethren, till they also shall become strong; not to storm at them, but treat them kindly, and with all meekness teach them, and not go to heaven alone, but endeavour to bring our brother with us. In this respect, I perceive you have erred, and some of you gone very far. I should not have gone so far, had I been here. The thing is right enough in itself, but there hath been too great haste. There are on the other side brethren and sisters who must be brought along with us. All those, therefore, have erred, who have given their consent and aid to doing away with mass; not but that the act itself was well enough, but that it was done violently, in disorder, and to the offence of others. They did not have recourse to the magistrates, nor make any inquiries of them beforehand. They had a good knowledge of the Scriptures, but had not the Spirit, else they would not have made a law out of that which is free. Therefore I say, and faithfully warn you, if we pray not earnestly to God and return to our duty, all the wretchedness which the Papists have suffered from us will be returned upon our own heads. For this cause, I could not remain away longer, but felt constrained to come and say this to you.''

This outline of his first discourse may suffice for a specimen of his manner. In his second, he carried out and illustrated the ideas with which he closed the first. In the six remaining discourses, he reasoned out, one by one, the various points on which he wished to correct the prevailing popular sentiment. Rarely has it happened that one man, unaided by power,—rather cramped by it,—by the mere force of his individual character and personal influence, should be able to stay such a popular excitement, which had already carried away all barriers, and shown itself superior to the control of the court and the university combined.

It is important that, at this critical juncture, when Luther's character was put to so severe a test, the turning point, as it were, of the whole work of the Reformation, we ascertain as accurately as possible the position from which he contemplated the extraordinary scene.

Happily we have ample means for such an investigation in the various letters written to his friends at the very time of these occurrences. On the day of his arrival, Friday, the 7th of March, he gave the elector, according to request made to him through Schurf, a statement of the reasons which induced him, contrary to his instructions, to leave Wartburg, and appear at Wittenberg. In this letter he says: "I may well suppose it will appear objectionable to you that, without your grace's consent or permission, I should return to Wittenberg again; for the appearance is, that out of it great danger will arise both to your grace, and to the whole country and people, and most of all to me, who, as one that is proscribed and condemned both by the pope and the emperor, am every hour exposed to death. But what shall I do? Necessity presseth, and God urgeth and calleth; it must and will be so; and so be it in the name of Jesus Christ, who is Lord over life and death. . . . The first reason is, that I received from the church at Wittenberg a written request, beseeching and begging me to come. Now, as no one can deny that the work was begun by me, and as I am bound to hold myself as the obedient servant of that church to which God hath called me, I could in no way refuse, without renouncing Christian love, fidelity and service. . . .

"The second reason is, that during my absence from Wittenberg, Satan hath broken in upon my flock, and hath, as all the world exclaimeth—and with truth—done mischief which I cannot by writing arrest, but must manage by personal presence, with living voice and ear. My conscience would allow no longer hesitation or delay. On this account, I was obliged to disregard your grace's pleasure or displeasure, and all the world's wrath or favour. For they are my flock, committed to me of God; they are my children in Christ; and there was no longer doubt whether I should come or not. I am bound to suffer death for them, which, with God's grace, I will cheerfully and joyfully do, as Christ requireth in the tenth chapter of John. . . .

"The third reason is, that I greatly fear, and alas! am but too certain, that a wide-spread insurrection will break out in Germany, wherewith God will punish this nation. For we see that the gospel pleaseth the people much, and they turn it to a carnal account; they see that it is true, and yet will not make a right use of it. To this end do those contribute who ought to quell such insurrection. They seek to quench the light, but do not consider that they thereby imbitter men's hearts, and drive them to rebellion, so that they act as if they would destroy themselves, or, at least, their children, [the next generation, by civil war,] which God no doubt sendeth as a judgment upon us. For the spiritual tyranny is weakened, for whose downfall alone I laboured, but now I perceive God will go further with it, and overthrow both the spiritual and the civil rule, as in Jerusalem. I have lately seen that not only the spiritual, but the temporal power must give way before the gospel, whether it be by consent or by constraint, as is clearly taught in all Bible history. Now, God requireth in Ezekiel, that we should set up ourselves in defence as a wall for the people. Therefore, I have thought it necessary to consult with my friends, to see if we could not ward off, or delay God's judgment."

To Spalatin he wrote the same day: Satan hath
attempted to do much mischief here in my fold, in
such a way that it will be difficult to meet the case
without offence to both parties. See to it, that no
innovation be allowed to be made either by common
consent or by violence. By the word alone must
error be assaulted, dislodged, overthrown and done
away, which our friends here, impelled by Satan,
have, in their first zeal, attempted to carry by storm.
I condemn as an abomination the papal mass, which
is made a sacrifice and a good work, whereby a man
is restored to favour with God. But I will not,
therefore, resort to force, or persuade one who is
without faith, much less compel him to do it away
with violence. Only through the word will I condemn the abuse of the mass. Whosoever will believe, let him believe, and follow unconstrained;
and whosoever will not believe, let him disbelieve
and go his way; for no one should be forced to faith,
or to any thing pertaining to the faith, but should
be drawn to it and won by the word. Then, whosoever believeth without constraint will freely follow.
I also reject the images which men worship; but I
do it through the word, not urging men to burn
them up, but rather not to put their trust in them,
as others have done, and still do. The images will
fall of themselves, if the people are instructed
through the word, and learn that they are nothing
before God. So likewise do I condemn the papal
laws about auricular confession, going at stated times
to the holy sacrament, praying to saints and fasting; but I do it through the word to free the conscience from these shackles. When that is done,
then they can either continue to use them on account of the weak who are still entangled with

them, or they can do those observances away, if others are already strong. Thus, charity may prevail in these outward works and laws. Now, I am most displeased with our people, (and the populace who are drawn with them,) that they let the word and faith and charity go, and glory that they are Christians, simply because they (not without offence to the weak) can eat meat, eggs, milk, &c., lay hold of the eucharist with their own hands, and omit the fastings and prayers.''

Luther went further, however, than to censure violence instead of persuasion in matters of religion. He condemned the removal of images from the churches, the omission of the mass ceremonies, of the prescribed fastings and prayers, and the touching of the bread and wine, on the part of the laity, with their own hands, because such things, though innocent in themselves, shocked the feelings of many pious persons. If, in these respects, we grant that Luther acted, as he did, not wholly without reason, we must also concede that the new practice which he censured in the other party, was neither unnatural, nor altogether unreasonable. High authority could have been pleaded on the other side, as in fact it was pleaded.

SECTION IV.—*General Narrative of Events from* 1522 *to* 1525.

HE who is accustomed to recognise the presence of a superintending Providence in human affairs, will not fail to perceive the hand of God in the peculiar direction given to public affairs in Germany about the time of Luther's return to Wittenberg. Luther himself was defenceless, and both the papal and imperial authority was arrayed against him and employed to put in execution the severe edict of Worms. The cause of the Reformation seemed, moreover, to be weakened by the disorders prevailing at Wittenberg and in several other towns, and destroying the confidence of men in respect to the tendencies of Luther's great enterprise.

George, Duke of Saxony, and the Elector of Brandenburg, were ready to execute that bloody edict, and seize Luther and his associates; but the great influence of the Elector Frederic, his caution and wisdom had hitherto preserved Luther from a violent death. And now, when the elector's plans were all baffled by what seemed to him the imprudence and rashness of the reformer, and when he could find no plausible ground for refusing, if the pope and the emperor should demand that Luther be delivered into their hands, behold Leo X. was removed by death in December of 1521, and was succeeded by Hadrian VI., who for nearly two years continued to maintain a new policy entirely against the views of his court; and Charles V. was, meanwhile, so occupied in his war with France as not to be able to visit Germany, but was obliged to intrust its government to his brother Ferdinand. Under these remarkable circumstances, Frederic was relieved from his embarrassment, and Luther could go on undisturbed in his work.

Though the edict was still nominally in force, yet in most of the middle of Germany the sentiments of the intelligent and virtuous were so on the side of truth and justice that the edict was disregarded. This period, therefore, was the very one in which the public mind was enlisted in the cause of the Reformation. The unjust and cruel, but unsuccessful attempts of the Catholic princes, instead of terrifying men into submission to their authority, had the contrary effect, and aroused the indignation which always follows an attempt to do violence to the moral sense of the people.

From this time onward, Luther's labours, at home and abroad, were greater than ever. Wherever a town or even an individual manifested a love for the evangelical doctrines, there Luther was either personally present to aid by public preaching and private conversation, or sent letters of encouragement, consolation and counsel. Wherever the radical party spread their doctrines and made disturbance, there none but Luther could appear either with safety, or with any hope of success, to quell the difficulty. Wherever the Catholics made an attack or exercised cruelty against the converts to the doctrines of the Reformation, there Luther, as the bishop of all such flocks and individuals, was quick to show his sympathy and extend his powerful aid.

In April, 1522, he went to Zwickau, and was obliged to pass through the dominions of Duke George, at no small hazard, to reduce to order the excited population of that town, where Muncer and his colleagues made their first attempts to revolutionize the church and the state. On the way thither, he preached at Borna, and at Altenburg.* He lodged in Zwickau with the burgomaster, and preached in the town-hall, in the castle, and in one of the churches. It was said that twenty-five thousand people from the adjoining towns came to see

---

* Borna is fifteen miles, Altenburg twenty-five, and Zwickau forty-five south of Leipsic. Eilenburg is fifteen miles north-east of Leipsic.

and hear him. On his return, he preached twice at Borna, and then proceeded to Eilenburg, and thence to Wittenberg.

For similar reasons, he made a journey to Erfurt in October of the same year. The same spirit of speedy, if not violent reform, in respect to doing away with images, mass and the invocation of saints, which had manifested itself at Wittenberg, was early active in Erfurt. After several letters on the subject, Luther, in company with Melancthon, Agricola and two others, visited the place in person. The day before reaching it, he preached at Weimar. On approaching Erfurt, Luther descended from the carriage, and passed through the gate privately, in order to avoid the crowd which came out to welcome him or to see him. In the evening, which was passed at the parsonage of one of the churches, he was visited by multitudes of persons. He preached there three times the two following days, and then returned to Weimar, where he remained some time, preaching every day.

Of his numerous writings published in 1522, no particular account can be expected here. Besides writing the interesting letter to the knight, Von Kronberg, son-in-law of Von Sickingen, he had a very violent controversy with Duke George and Henry VIII., of England, or rather with Sir Thomas More. Though these potentates, who undertook to dabble in theology and to instruct Luther therein, deserved no better treatment than they received from his hands, Luther himself suffered in the estimation of many wise and good men from the intemperate violence, and even ribaldry, in which he freely indulged.

The history of the diet of Nüremburg, which was

in session during the whole winter of 1523, while it is too complicated to find a place in a brief biography, is too important and too closely connected with Luther's fortunes to be omitted altogether.

The Turks had broken in upon Hungary, and were approaching the frontiers of the German empire. Charles V., who had undertaken to check them, was obliged to hasten to Spain to put down the insurrections which had sprung up there during his residence in Germany. His brother, Ferdinand, whom he had appointed vicar of the empire, called the diet above mentioned, in the emperor's name, to engage the estates in a war of defence and reprisal. The emperor, in a letter from Valladolid, endeavoured to persuade the pope to contribute from the ecclesiastical funds to support the war, adding as a special inducement, that the same military power might, before being disbanded, be employed to destroy the Lutheran sect by the sword.

Hadrian paid little regard to the emperor's chief object; but resolved to make use of the diet to further his own ends in eradicating the Lutheran heresy. After taking the preliminary measures, and inviting the co-operation of the princes—and even threatening the Elector Frederic, if he should refuse to unite—the pope, through his legate, urged the diet no longer to suffer the edict of Worms to remain without effect, but to crush the heresy of Luther by the arm of the civil power, if milder measures did not succeed. To give new weight to his arguments, which met with opposition, he confessed the corruption not only of the priests and prelates, but of the cardinals and popes themselves; and promised (with all sincerity) to institute a reformation which should, in a proper manner, accomplish all that Luther undertook to effect in an improper manner. This concession and promise, so far from promoting his object, served only to defeat it. The Roman courtiers and prelates desired no such reform. The party which sympathized with Luther turned the confessions to a good account. A committee was appointed to draft a statement, in reply to a communication of the legate, and John of Schwartzenburg, a man of learning and talent, and warmly in the interest of the evangelical party, was chairman of the committee. With great moderation and judgment was that document prepared, which stated, that it was impossible to put in execution the edict of Worms, in respect to Luther, so long as the court of Rome, which Luther had justly exposed to contempt, remained in its corruption, and unreformed. It recommended referring the whole matter to a general council, the preachers meanwhile adhering to the doctrines of the ancient church, and Luther and his friends refraining from writing and publishing. With slight modifications, advocated by the Archbishop of Mainz and others, the draft prepared was adopted by the diet, to the great mortification and indignation of the legate. Plaunitz, the deputy of the Elector of Saxony, who was not present, was the chief diplomatist in the interest of Luther, and well did he and Schwartzenburg concert their measures for baffling the papal counsels. Felitzsch, the ambassador of Frederic, would not yield so much as his associates did, and protested, in the name of his prince, against the prohibition laid upon Luther in respect to publishing his opinions. Luther himself, however, was very well satisfied with the main features of the order passed by the diet, pronouncing it "remarkably liberal and acceptable." Inasmuch as the enemies of Luther interpreted this *recess*, as it is called, so as to make it appear condemnatory of the cause of the Reformation, and confirmatory of the decision passed at the diet of Worms, Luther addressed a public letter to the vicar and government of the empire, in which he gave a different interpretation. Thus the plans and schemes of the pope and his ministers, to engage the German diet in a crusade against the new heresy, failed utterly of their object. The Protestant writers, who complain of the doings of the diet, do not, perhaps, sufficiently consider how many chances there were of coming to a result incomparably worse, and how much skill and effort it required, in a few, to take such advantage of the circumstances to ward off the evil.

The result above mentioned was merely negative. Luther and his friends were in the same state of insecurity as before. The elector was often alarmed, and it required all the ability and boldness of Luther to inspire him with confidence. In such a state of things, it was to be expected that the followers of Luther, in Catholic territories, should be bitterly and cruelly persecuted. To this class of sufferers, Luther directed his particular attention.

Three ladies had been dismissed from the court of Henry, Duke of Saxony, for having read the writings of Luther. Henry himself, who then resided at Freiberg, was favourably disposed toward Luther; but he was forced to this measure by his brother George, the reigning duke. Luther, though a stranger to these ladies, addressed to them [June 18, 1523] a consolatory letter, urging them to Christian fortitude and patience. "Submit patiently," he says, "and let Christ work. He will abundantly avenge you of your wrong, and raise you higher than you could wish, if you will only leave the matter, and commit it all to him."

In July of the same year, he writes to his friend Crotus: "Two brethren have already been burnt at Brussels, and a third has been degraded (as they call it) and sent into some unknown Assyria or Babylon. The papal priests rage with incredible madness against Christ. Some of them write accursed and blasphemous things. This is their obedience to the imperial [Nüremberg] edict, referring our dispute to a future council. Thus far, I have kept quiet, [as the edict required;] but, if they go on thus, I too shall bid adieu to the edict—not to burn, imprison, or do any violence—for this is not the part of Christians—but to defend, by word of mouth and by writing, the glory of the Scriptures, and to expose still further the abominations of the papacy."

He addressed a letter, worthy of Tertullian or of Cyprian, to the Christians in Holland, Brabant and Flanders, congratulating them "that God is causing his marvellous light to shine again, and that the voice of the turtle-dove is heard, and the flowers appear on the earth." The correspondence of Luther, in the years 1522 and 1523, is very rich in such specimens of Christian sympathy; the instances in which he intercedes for the poor, the afflicted and the outcast, being almost innumerable. At one time, he asks of the elector charity for an aged and feeble monk, who, from conscientious scruples, has abandoned his cell; at another, for nine nuns, who were abandoned by their relations for having laid aside the veil. Now, he takes the part of a pious preacher, who has been driven from his post for having preached evangelical doctrines, or having taken a wife; and now, he writes letters of encouragement to the handful of believers who venture to confess Christ, in various towns and cities. Besides, his opinions were asked on so many questions, laid before him by princes and nobles, by magistrates and town-councils, by scholars and theologians, by ecclesiastics, monks and nuns, on all points connected with the change he introduced in respect to man's ecclesiastical and social relations, that he was often obliged to excuse himself for want of time, and refer them to his writings, to other religious teachers, and to the Bible.

Hadrian VI., the reforming but narrow-minded pope, lived less than two years after his accession to the apostolical chair. He was succeeded (Nov. 19, 1523) by Clement VII., a wily politician of the family of the Medici, whose intriguing policy better pleased the corrupt Roman court. At the next German diet, held in the beginning of 1524, Campegius, the papal legate, and Haunart, the orator sent from Spain by the emperor to represent his views, acted in concert against Luther, as Charles at that time felt the need of the pope's assistance in his war with France. Though their councils prevailed in part in the diet, the resistance of the Elector Frederic and some others was so decided, that the danger of Luther was but slightly increased. So far was he from being terrified by the new Nüremburg edict, which enforced the edict of Worms, while it provided for the settlement of the religious differences at the next diet to be held at Spire, that he published the two edicts together, with satirical comments, under the title of "Two Irreconcilable and Contradictory Imperial Orders respecting Luther." In the preface, he says, "It is scandalous that the emperor and the princes deal openly in falsehood, and, what is more scandalous still, issue contradictory commands, as you here see. I am to be seized and punished according to the decision made at the diet of Worms; and yet, at a future diet, to be held at Spire, my teachings are to be examined. So I am at one and the same time condemned and referred to a future trial; and my countrymen are to treat me as an outlaw, and then wait to see me condemned."

Of the controversies in which Luther was engaged at the close of this period, or from 1523 to 1525, we will mention only those which tended to check the progress of the Reformation, namely, his controversies with Erasmus on the freedom of the will; with Carlstadt on the real presence in the eucharist; and with Muncer and the peasants on civil government.

The controversy with Erasmus derived its immediate importance from his great personal influence, and from the support he had indirectly given to the cause of the Reformation. Both parties had been eager to claim him, and it was long doubtful which side he would espouse. But, from our point of view, we are led to attach still greater importance to the remoter consequences, those which are connected with the subject of the controversy; for, at a subsequent period, both Melancthon and the Lutheran church abandoned the predestinarian view maintained by Luther, and became converts, in part, to the doctrine advocated by Erasmus.

Luther had long been suspicious of Erasmus, and, in a letter to Œcolampadius, (June 20, 1523,) he gave utterance to his impressions of him in these words : "Although I here and there feel his sharp arrows, yet, as he pretendeth not to be my enemy, so I pretend not to understand his manœuvres, though I see through him better than he supposeth. He hath accomplished that to which he was called. He hath introduced the languages, and recalled men from their impious studies. Perhaps, with Moses, he is to die in the land of Moab, for, to better studies, which pertain to piety, he doth not advance. I could most earnestly desire that he would abstain from treating of the Scriptures and from his paraphrases; for he is not equal to this task, and only impedeth his readers in a knowledge of the Scriptures. It is enough for him to have pointed out what is evil; to reveal what is good, and to lead to the land of promise, is, as I now see, more than he can do."

A letter of his, written in May, 1522, had been injudiciously published, in which he had said : "I knew before that Mosellanus agreed with Erasmus on predestination. But I think Erasmus knoweth less of predestination than the sophistical scholastics knew. Nor do I fear that I shall fall, if I do not change my sentiments. Erasmus is not formidable in this matter, nor is he generally in what pertaineth to Christianity. . . . I will not provoke him to combat, nor, if he provoke me once and again, will I immediately resent. Nevertheless it seemeth to me not good for him to try the powers of his eloquence on me. . . . If, however, he will have a hand in the game, he shall see that Christ is afraid neither of the gates of hell, nor of the powers of the air; and I, though a stammerer, will boldly meet the eloquent Erasmus without regard to his authority, name, or favour. . . . Salute Mosellanus in my name.

I am not estranged from him because he followeth Erasmus rather than me. Tell him to be a lusty Erasmian. The time will come when he will think otherwise."

Referring to these two letters, he says, (Oct. 1, 1523:) "My private letter concerning Erasmus, and another written to Œcolampadius, have been published, which he taketh very ill. Although I have not a single word to take back, if called to defend myself, I am nevertheless not well pleased that letters, written in confidence to intimate friends, should be made public by informers. But the writings of Erasmus will not harm me, if directed against me; neither will they give me confidence, if they support me. I have one who will defend my cause, though all the world rage against what Erasmus calleth my pertinacity. . . . I am resolved not to defend my manner of life and character, but the cause only. Let whosoever will mangle my character as heretofore. . . . I am sorrowful and afraid when I am praised, and joyful when reproached and maligned. If this seemeth strange to Erasmus, I do not wonder. Let him learn Christ, and bid adieu to human wisdom. The Lord enlighten him and make another man of him."

Luther knew that the Papists, and particularly the pope himself, had urged Erasmus to come out against him. He was long kept in painful suspense, expecting either an open attack or a private expostulation, and yet receiving neither. He finally broke the silence in a letter to Erasmus, holding out the olive of peace, but in a way that did not flatter the vanity of the man who had long been regarded as an oracle.

"I have long kept silence," he writes, (April

1524,) "that you, as the greater and older, might
break it. But, having waited so long in vain,
Christian charity, I think, compelleth me to make
the beginning. First, I will not complain that you
have stood aloof from me, in order to be on better
and safer terms with the Papists, my enemies. Nor
do I take it ill that you have, in some passages in
your published works, for the sake of securing their
favour or mitigating their wrath, used some bitter
and biting expressions relating to me; for I perceive that the Lord hath not yet given you the fortitude and courage to join me in cheerfully and
boldly meeting those monsters with which I have to
contend. I am not one to exact of you what is above
your powers and your measure. But I tolerate your
weakness, and honour the measure of the gifts bestowed on you of God. The whole world must own
that it is a great gift of God in you, and one for
which we ought to be thankful, that through you
letters have been made to flourish and prevail, to
the manifest aid of the study of the Bible. It was
never my desire that you should desert or neglect
your gift, and mingle in my combats, wherein your
genius and eloquence would, indeed, avail much.
But, as you lack the courage, it is safer for you to
cultivate your own gift. I have only feared this,
that my adversaries would persuade you to assail my
doctrines, which would compel me to resist you to
the face. . . . So much did I wish to say, as evidence of my candid feelings toward you; and I desire
that a spirit may be given you of the Lord, worthy
of your name. But if it should not yet be given
you, I beg you, if you can no nothing more, to be a
mere spectator of my tragedy, and not join my adversaries with your troops, and especially to publish

no books against me, as I will publish none against you."

That so sensitive a man as Erasmus should feel keenly on the reception of this letter is what might be anticipated. He replied with evident emotion, repelling the charge of timidity and dissimulation, and claiming to have served the gospel far better than many infatuated writers who make themselves important under its abused name. The influence of Henry VIII., his patron, being added to that of the papal court, prevailed; and in September, 1524, Erasmus opened his batteries upon Luther, who replied with unsparing severity. Whatever be the merits of this controversy—and it was conducted with distinguished learning on the one side, and distinguished ability on the other—Erasmus confesses that he was influenced not wholly by a love of truth, but also by the fear of his enemies, the monks; who were exciting against him, as a secret favourer of Luther's doctrines, the ill-will of the court of Rome and of several potentates, whose protection and patronage he could not consent to lose. Here, as everywhere, the otherwise virtuous and well-disposed Erasmus calculated nicely his own personal interest. Thus these two great and, for the most part, good men, became inveterate enemies of each other. Luther never loved those who taught differently from himself. Carlstadt, Erasmus and Zwingle, when they opposed any of his views, were no less heretical than Muncer. This was a fault in Luther's character.

A few words from Luther's letter to a friend (March 30, 1522) will be sufficient to remind us of his relations to Carlstadt at that time. He there remarks: "I have offended Carlstadt, because I have put a stop to his measures, though I did not condemn his doctrines, except that I did not approve of his labouring so for mere ceremonies and external forms, while the true Christian teaching, that of faith and charity, is neglected. For, by his foolish manner of preaching, the people were led to think they were Christians from the sole consideration (which is nothing at all) that, in the communion, they partook both of the bread and the wine; that they handled them; that they did not go to confession; and that they broke down the images. Behold Satan's malice, in resorting to this new expedient to destroy the gospel!"

Carlstadt had explained his position thus: "That we are sometimes at variance, is because we do not stand by the word of God, and think we may, by our reason, devise something that will please him. On this wise are we disagreed on the article of confession. For my part, I have followed the Scriptures, and appeal to my candid hearers. I have also requested the magistrates to forbid, under a severe penalty, preaching any thing which the Scriptures do not contain and teach. Death itself shall not drive me away from the Scriptures. For I know that nothing pleaseth God but what doth conform to his holy word. . . . Therefore I shall build exclusively on the word of God, not regarding what others teach. I know that I shall offend only those who are not Christians." These words have been pronounced, by historians, haughty and insolent. Had Luther uttered them, they would have been pronounced heroic.

If Carlstadt did not act according to this standard —if he was fanatical, envious, or unkind in his opposition to Luther—that is quite another matter. Carlstadt was at first compelled by the elector to promise not to preach to the people in the way he had done. After restraining himself about three months, till April, 1522, he resolved to publish his views in opposition to Luther. The latter writes, (April 21,) "I have this day suppliantly entreated Carlstadt in private not to publish any thing against me, for, in that case, I should be obliged to contend with him earnestly. He solemnly affirmed that he would write nothing against me, though the six sheets now in the hands of the rector and judges for examination speak otherwise. Certainly I will not so disregard public scandal as to pass over what he hath written. They are endeavouring to persuade him to retract or to suppress what he hath written; I shall not urge it." Melancthon writes to Spalatin a few days afterward, "It hath been decided that Carlstadt's book shall be suppressed."

It would appear that the intimation made by Luther against Carlstadt's good faith was not at this time justified by the result, for the latter returned to the ordinary discharge of his duties, much to the satisfaction of the former. In January, 1523, Luther speaks of Carlstadt's lectures in most flattering terms.

For three centuries, Carlstadt's moral character has been treated somewhat as Luther's would have been, if only Catholic testimony had been heard. The party interested has been both witness and judge. What if we were to judge of Zwingle's Christian character by Luther's representations? The truth is, Carlstadt hardly showed a worse spirit, or employed more abusive terms toward Luther, than Luther did toward him. Carlstadt knew that in many things the truth was on his side; and yet, in these, no less than in others, he was crushed by the civil power which was on the side of Luther. Luther was so zealous to maintain the doctrine of justification by faith, that he was prepared even to call in question the authority of some portions of Scripture, which seemed to him not to be reconcileable with it. To the Epistle of James, especially, his expressions indicate the strongest repugnance. Indeed, so intemperate was his language in reference to this subject, that we cease to wonder why Carlstadt should complain of "the audacity, the unreasonable severity, the violence, the false reasoning, the immodesty and shameless decisions of his *friends*." "Still," says he, "I will challenge no one, but if I am challenged for the defence of the canon of the Scriptures, though I cannot do it as it should be done, I will contend with all my might."

He had so far restored the sacrament of the Lord's supper as to distribute the wine as well as the bread to the laity. Luther, " in order not to offend weak consciences," insisted on distributing the bread only, and prevailed. He rejected the practice of elevating and adoring the host. Luther allowed it, and introduced it again. Carlstadt maintained, that "we should not, in things pertaining to God, regard what the multitude say or think, but look simply to the word of God. Others," he adds, "say that, on account of the weak, we should not *hasten* to keep the commands of God; but wait till they become wise and strong." In regard to the ceremonies introduced into the church, he judged as the Swiss reformers did, that all were to be rejected which had not a warrant in the Bible. " It is sufficiently against the Scriptures, if you can find no ground for it in them." Luther asserted, on the contrary, " Whatever is not against the

Scriptures is for the Scriptures, and the Scriptures for it. Though Christ hath not commanded adoring of the host, so neither hath he forbidden it." "Not so," said Carlstadt, "we are bound to the Bible, and no one may decide after the thoughts of his own heart."

Carlstadt differed essentially from Luther in regard to the use to be made of the Old Testament. With him, the law of Moses was still binding. Luther, on the contrary, had a strong aversion to what he calls a legal and Judaizing religion. Carlstadt held to the divine authority of the Sabbath from the Old Testament; Luther believed Christians were free to observe any day as a Sabbath, provided they be uniform in observing it. But Carlstadt was also a mystic, following an inward light. Hence his sympathy with the Zwickau Prophets. He was a singular compound of Zwinglian, Lutheran and Anabaptist ingredients.

The most important difference between him and Luther, and that which most imbittered the latter against him, related to the Lord's supper. He opposed not only transubstantiation, but consubstantiation, the real presence, and the elevation and adoration of the host. Luther rejected the first, asserted the second and third, and allowed the other two. In regard to the real presence, he says: "In the sacrament is the real body of Christ and the real blood of Christ, so that even the unworthy and ungodly partake of it, and 'partake of it corporally,' too, and not spiritually as Carlstadt will have it." After Carlstadt had been compelled to keep silence, from 1522 to 1524, and to submit to the superior power and authority of Luther, he could contain himself no longer. He, therefore, left Wit-

tenberg, and established a press at Jena, through
which he could, in a series of publications, give
vent to his convictions, so long pent up. He also
preached in several places in that neighbourhood,
but chiefly at Orlamunde, a little above Jena, on
the Saale. A furious controversy ensued. Both
parties exceeded the bounds of Christian propriety
and moderation.

Carlstadt was now in the vicinity of the Anabaptist tumults, excited by Muncer. He sympathized
with them in some things, but disapproved of their
disorders. Luther made the most of this. The work
which he wrote against him, he entitled "The Book
against the Celestial Prophets." This was uncan-
did; for the controversy related chiefly to the sacrament of the supper. In the south of Germany, and
in Switzerland, Carlstadt found more adherents than
Luther. Banished as an Anabaptist, he was received
as a Zwinglian.

No doubt this circumstance did much toward producing that intolerant spirit which Luther ever afterward manifested toward Zwingle and his associates.
It is not for us to decide the doctrinal question.
It is enough to say that those men were as much
entitled to the respect and charity of Luther, as he
was to their's. We pass over this whole controversy, and the numerous colloquies and debates
growing out of it, as inappropriate to the character
of this work.

Against the peasants, who, on the one hand, were
driven to desperation by the oppression of their
rulers, and, on the other, were intoxicated with the
new ideas of liberty that had just begun to be proclaimed, Luther wrote and spoke in terms of unmi-
tigated severity. He was a better theologian than

politician. He held to the divine right of kings, and, consequently, to the doctrine of passive obedience on the part of their subjects. He was justly alarmed lest the fair name of the Reformation should be stained by deeds of violence and blood.

In Thuringia, particularly, and under Muncer's influence, the political movements were linked in with fanaticism which led to the wildest disorders; though, in the south-west of Germany, the insurgents acted more wisely and intelligently. That Luther should, in these circumstances, employ his pen, and even travel from city to city, to allay the excitement and put down the peasants, is not strange. But that he should proclaim doctrines subversive of all principles of freedom, and be the means of riveting more firmly the already galling chains of despotism, and of exciting the despots to a bloody revenge, is a matter of regret, if not of wonder.

The recent revolutions of Germany are very similar to those attempted in the sixteenth century. The cause was as sacred then as it is now : we do not say that the means were justifiable. Certainly the theories of government were extravagant and grotesque. The failure of the undertaking of Von Sickingen and Von Hutten, the tragic scenes of Alstedt, Frankenhausen and Mühlhausen, and the counter-revolution in Suabia, and the character given to the Reformation as hostile to all political revolutions, retarded the cause of liberty for three centuries.

Perhaps it is well that it was so. Perhaps there was not, in that age, a sufficient preparation for the enjoyment and preservation of freedom ; and so the want of enlarged, rational and philosophic views of the nature and functions of civil govern-

ment, which we observe in Luther, is the less to be
regretted.   To be, at the same time, a religious and
a political reformer is more than can reasonably
be demanded of one individual.   Of the strict integrity and high moral principles of Luther, in all
his transactions, both with princes and with peasants, during these unhappy times, there can be no
question.

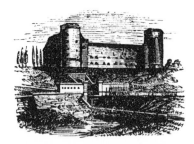

CHAPTER V.

LUTHER'S CHARACTER AS IT APPEARS IN SOME PARTICU-
LAR SPHERES OF ACTION NOT INCLUDED IN THE GENERAL
NARRATIVE.

SECTION I.—*Luther's Marriage and Domestic Life.*

 O fully con-
vinced had Lu-
ther been for a
long time that
a monastic life
was an evil, that
he published a
tract, showing
that nuns, who
had taken the
veil, could with
a good con-
science before
God lay it aside
again. The
monks were beginning to disband, and it was to be
expected that many nuns, who had, by parental influence or authority, taken the rash vow in their early
youth, would feel the tedium of their monotonous
life and the fetters which robbed them of their
liberty, and, consequently, eagerly read those
writings which aimed at restoring them to their
natural rights, and introducing them unto those

KATHARINA VON BORA

WIFE OF LUTHER

American Sunday School Union

social and domestic relations for which nature designed them. A little to the south of Grimma and not very far from Leipsic was the Cistercian nunnery of Nimptschen, whose inmates were of noble birth. Luther was at Grimma, with Staupitz and Link, in 1516; and again he spent some time there in 1519.

The next year the Reformation was introduced into Grimma. Thus the light that was beginning to shine must have cast some of its rays upon this convent, and Luther's name was well known to the nuns who were there pining away in their solitude. They, at length, entreated their parents and friends to take them from the cloister, and restore them to their homes. But such were their ideas of the sanctity of the monastic life, and of the inviolability of the vow, when once taken, that these entreaties of their children were of no avail. Nothing remained but to appeal to the sympathy and humanity of the liberator of the oppressed, to the straightforward, honest-hearted reformer. He listened to their petition, and formed the plan of sending Koppe, a distinguished and prudent citizen of Torgau, to deliver them from their captivity.

The project was one of great difficulty. It would shock the superstitious multitude, and arouse the wrath of monk and priest. Besides, the journey from Torgau to Nimptschen—about sixty miles in a southern direction—led through the territory of Duke George, the bitter enemy of Luther, though both these towns belonged to the elector. Koppe was assisted by his nephew and a man by the name of Tommitsch. The plan was put in execution on the evening of April 4, 1523. Tradition says, that, at the time agreed upon, the nine virgins descended from the window of Catharine von Bora's cell, which was on the south side of the nunnery, into the court, where Catharine herself left one of her slippers, and were lifted over the wall and put into standing barrels in a wagon, and thus escaped detection. It is said in the Chronicle of Torgau that when an individual, meeting Koppe, asked him what he had there, he replied, " Barrels of herring." April 8, Luther writes to his friend Link, " Yesterday I received from their state of captivity, nine nuns belonging to the Nimptschen convent, among whom were the two Zeschaus and [Magdalene] Staupitz." This last was a niece of Luther's spiritual father, and the two Zeschaus were near relations of Luther's friend of the same name, prior, and afterward also reformer, at Grimma.

After announcing the same fact in a letter to Spalatin, he says, " But you will ask what I am intending to do with them. First, I will inform their parents, and request them to take them home. If they will not do so, then I will see that they be otherwise provided for. I have already received promises in respect to part, and I will get the rest married, if I can." After mentioning their names, he adds, " These need our compassion, in showing which, we do service to Christ. Their escape is quite wonderful. I beg you to exercise your charity, and, in my name, beg some money of your rich courtiers to sustain them one or two weeks, until I can either deliver them to their parents, or to others, who have given me promises." Luther urged Spalatin to persuade the elector to contribute something for this object, and promised to keep it secret, that it might not give offence to George and to the Catholic clergy.

This unheard-of adventure, this breaking up of conventual life, and the temporary settlement of the fugitive nuns in Wittenberg, produced an extraordinary excitement. No attempt of the priesthood could succeed in concealing it. The example was the more dangerous, as the same discontent prevailed in other convents. Soon the abbess of Zeitz and four nuns followed the example; and six from another, and eight from a third, and sixteen from a fourth, many of whom belonged to the Duchy of Saxony, or the territory of Duke George. The consequence was, that Luther was bitterly assailed as being the author of all the mischief. He was spoken against and written against, till he found it necessary to reply, which he did to the cost of the opposing party. He portrayed the darker side of life in the nunnery, spicing his productions with striking narratives of inhumanity and cruelty. He published an account of Florentina of Upper Weimar, who passed through many sufferings before she succeeded in making her escape from a monastery in Eisleben. She had been sent there by her parents at the age of six; was, without her consent, consecrated, or made to take the veil, at the age of eleven. Feeling discontented, she made her complaints to the abbess, who replied that she must remain a nun for better or for worse. She wrote to Luther; but the letter was intercepted, and she was kept in a cold prison, in an inclement season, for four weeks. She next wrote to a relative; this letter, too, was seized, and she was beaten by the abbess and four others till they gave over from fatigue. Luther made an appeal to the Counts of Mansfeld, in whose dominions these cruelties were practised, to put a stop to such flagrant abuses.

Koppe was exposed to popular indignation still more than Luther, for he had performed the daring act of rescue, and was very anxious that his agency in the matter should be kept as secret as possible. Luther thought and felt otherwise, and made the whole transaction known; and then wrote to Koppe, bidding him lift up his head and not shrink from the honour of so noble a deed. "They, indeed, will say, that the fool Leonard Koppe hath suffered himself to be caught by a condemned heretical monk, and then drove to the place and carried off the nuns and aided them in breaking their vows. . . . But I have made all this known for the following reasons;" and then he goes on to justify the transaction.

Luther was not at that time, nor in the following year, (1524,) when he abandoned the cloister himself, inclined to marry. In a letter to Spalatin, dated November 30, he says: "For what Argula writes respecting my getting married, I give her my thanks. No wonder such things are tattled about me, as many others are in like manner. Thank her in my name, and tell her I am in the Lord's hands as his creature, whose heart he can change, and whose life he can save or destroy at any hour or moment. But with such a mind as I have hitherto had, and still continue to have, I shall not take a wife; not because I am by nature averse to matrimony—for I am neither wood nor stone,—but I am disinclined to it, because I am every day expecting death as inflicted upon a heretic. I do not wish to obstruct God's work in me, nor rely upon my own heart for comfort. It is my hope that I shall not be permitted to live long."

But within five months, we find him writing the

following playful letter to Spalatin : "As to what you write me touching my marriage, I would not have you wonder that I, who am so famous a lover, do not marry. Be surprised rather that, since I write so much about marriage, and mingle so much in female society, I am not turned into a woman, not to say married. For I have had three wives at once, whom I loved so desperately that I have lost two of them, who are already engaged to others. The third I just hold by the left arm, and she, too, will be snatched away from me soon. But you, a cold lover, dare not be the husband even of one. Look out that I, with all my reluctance to marry, do not get the start of you, who are already affianced, as God is wont to do what you least expect. Without joking, I say this to urge you on in the way you have taken." In another place he says : "Had I become a lover before, I should have chosen Eve von Schönfeld," who was one of the nine nuns above mentioned, and who, at his own suggestion, was married to a medical student, afterward royal physician. What he said jestingly to Spalatin turned out to be true, for Luther was actually married first.

Catharine von Bora, having no home to which she could go, was, on her arrival at Wittenberg, received into the family of a distinguished citizen by the name of Reichenbach, where she showed herself worthy of the paternal interest that had been taken in her, both by him and by Luther. Luther used his influence to form a matrimonial connection between her and Baumgärtner, a theological student from Nüremberg, who became a distinguished man, and enjoyed, in a high degree, the confidence of Luther and Melancthon. A mutual attachment seems to have existed between the two parties; but when the young Nüremberger returned to his native city, the attachment appears to have faded from his memory. Luther, therefore, wrote to him, October 12, 1524: "If you intend to have your Katy von Bora, you must be quick about it, or she will be another's, who is already at hand. Her love to you remaineth unaltered. I should certainly rejoice to see you united to her in wedlock." The acquaintance, however, was not renewed. The other individual referred to was Glatz, pastor at Orlamünde. For Luther, who had never lost sight of providing for the settlement in life of the nine nuns, had selected this individual for Catharine, in case he did not succeed with Baumgärtner. But she had a mind of her own, and would listen to no such proposal, and, in respect to Glatz, her judgment proved to be correct. She entreated Amsdorf to divert Luther's mind from his purpose, adding, however, by way of conciliation, that if Luther himself, or Amsdorf, were to become suitor, she would make no objection!

At first, Luther was not particularly pleased with Catharine, because he "supposed she was proud and haughty." Learning upon a more perfect acquaintance, that what had so appeared was in reality a certain womanly dignity and independence, he came to entertain other feelings toward her. "And, thank God," he says, "it hath turned out well: for I have a pious and faithful wife, to whom one may safely commit his heart." He was married to her without much publicity, June 13, 1525, when he was at the age of forty-two, and she at the age of twenty-six. The ceremony was performed by Bugenhagen, in the house of Reichenbach, in the

The interior of Luther's dwelling.

presence of Professor Apel, Justus Jonas, Cranach
and his wife, without the knowledge of his other
friends. The cause of concealing his marriage from
the elector, Melancthon and others, till it was actually performed, was the alarm it would give them.
At a time when the public mind was agitated by
the Peasants' War, and when the Catholic princes
were greatly imbittered against Luther and even the
elector, the marriage of a monk to a nun would, on
account of the two-fold violation of the monastic
vow, do utter violence to the feelings of the community, and Luther supposed they would endeavour
to prevent so daring a step. How offensive such a
marriage was to the superstitious sentiments of even
good men at that age, may be seen from the remark
of Erasmus, who, when he heard of the occurrence,
said: "When a monk marrieth a nun, we may expect antichrist will be born." The next day, when
it became generally known that the marriage union
had been formed, the city government, according to
the usage of that age, honoured Luther with a present of fourteen cans of wine, of different sorts;
and the newly-married pair had the right of free
access, for the space of one year, to the wine cellar
of the city. A principal ceremony, at that time,
was the festival following the wedding, on the occasion of conducting the bride to her new home, where
a large company were treated to a dinner. The
apartment, known as Luther's dwelling, in the Augustinian cloister, was undoubtedly the scene of this
solemnity. Seven of the invitations sent to different individuals have been preserved, and give us a
view of the peculiar and somewhat awkward position of Luther, as well as a picture of the times.
The first is that written to Chancellor Rühel, Lu-

ther's brother-in-law, and two other Mansfeld court-officers, and reads as follows: "According to the wish of my dear father, I have taken me a wife; and on account of evil-speakers, and that no hindrance might be placed in the way, I have hastened the act. It is my wish that the festive occasion of bringing my bride home take place a week from next Tuesday, and that I may enjoy your presence and receive your blessing. Since these are times of commotion [the insurrection of the peasants] and danger, I cannot urge your attendance; but if you have a desire to come and can do so, and bring with you my dear father and mother, you can easily understand that it would give me great joy, and whatsoever [presents] you may receive from good friends for my poverty, will be very welcome." Another invitation, sent to Dolzig, the elector's marshal, is written with characteristic humour. "No doubt," he says, "the strange rumour hath reached you, that I have become a husband. Though this is a very singular affair, which I myself can scarcely believe, nevertheless, the witnesses are so numerous that I am bound in honour to believe it; and I have concluded to have a collation next Tuesday for my father and mother and other good friends, to seal the same and make it sure. I therefore beg you, if it is not too much trouble, to provide venison for me, and be present yourself to help affix the seal with becoming joy." At this time the city presented to Luther several casks of beer; and the university gave a large silver tankard, plated with gold on the outside and inside, weighing five pounds and a quarter. It was purchased in the year 1800, from the heirs, by the University of Greifswald, for one hundred rix dollars.

Catharine von Bora was born, January 29, 1499, probably at her father's estate, now called Mildenstein, not far from Bitterfeld, between Wittenberg and Halle. We know nothing of her parents; but Luther often speaks of John von Bora, her brother, who was in the service of Albert of Prussia, and afterward in that of Henry, Duke of Saxony. There was once a nunnery in Catharine's native place, and she is said to have entered that at first. Her monastic life was probably without incident. She appears to have been prominent among the nine fugitive nuns; and Luther's early treatment of her, even before he was pleased with her manners, shows the consideration in which she was held.

Luther himself often speaks of his marriage as a happy one. True, the sex did not then receive the same delicate regard which is shown it among us at the present time. Luther, too, was a man who told all his private thoughts and feelings; and it would be strange indeed, if a man of such a temperament should never see nor mention a wife's little imperfections. He at one time remarks, "Katy is kind, submissive in all things, and pleasing, more so, (thank God,) than I could hope, so that I would not exchange my poverty for the riches of Crœsus." The epistle of Galatians was a favourite epistle with him. "It is my epistle," he says, "to which I am betrothed; it is my Catharine von Bora." Again, he says, in 1538, thirteen years after his marriage, "Even if I were a young man, I would sooner die than marry a second time, knowing what I do of the world, though a queen should be offered me after my Katy." "A more obedient wife," he observes again, "I could not find, unless I were to chisel one out of marble." And again, "I prize her above the kingdom of France, or the state of Venice; she is a pious, good wife, given me of God."

Hers, too, was a happy life. Not only was she the wife of the great man of the age, but of one whose domestic feelings were as tender as his public character was masculine and strong. From the personal dangers of Luther, and from his frequent illness she had much to suffer. To Spalatin, who had invited him to his wedding, he said, "The tears of my Katy prevent me from coming; she thinks it would be very perilous." He had just excited the fury of some nobles by delivering several nuns from their prison houses. In February, 1526, she went with Luther to visit Carlstadt at Segrena, a little west of Kemberg, where he was then living as a shop-keeper and farmer. Here Carlstadt's wife was born. Luther, who never recovered entirely from the effects of his early austerities, and who was worn down with excessive labours, saw so much trouble spring out of his perpetual controversy on the real presence of Christ in the supper, that his cheerfulness was much abated and his temper somewhat soured. It was then that Catharine proved of inestimable value to him.

In his temporary illness of 1526, and especially in 1527, when it was expected he would leave her a widow with her infant child, she showed remarkable fortitude as well as faith and patience. "You know," he said to her, "that I have nothing to leave you but the silver cups." "My dear doctor," she replied, "if it is God's will, then I choose that you be with him rather than with me. It is not so much I and my child that need you, but many pious Christians. Trouble not yourself about me."

When Luther was depressed, his considerate wife often sent privately for Justus Jonas, whose cheerful conversation was known to be a good remedy in such cases. Luther somewhere says, "I expect more from my Katy and from Melancthon than I do from Christ my Lord, and yet I well know that neither they nor any one on earth hath suffered, or can suffer, what he hath suffered for me." Molsdorf, a former member of Luther's household, says, "I remember that Dr. Luther used to say, that he congratulated himself with all his soul, that God had given him a modest and prudent wife, who took such excellent care of his health." "How I longed after my family," says Luther, "when I lay at the point of death in Smalcald! I thought I should never again see my wife and child. How painful would such a separation have been!"

When Luther was at Coburg, in 1530, he heard of the illness of his father, and yet his own life was in such peril that he could not safely make the journey to see him. At this, both he and Catharine were much distressed. Soon afterwards, the news of his father's death reached him. "I have heard," he says to Link, "of the death of my father, who was so dear and precious to me." Catharine, to comfort him, sent him a likeness of his favourite daughter Magdalene, then one year old. "You have done a good deed," says Veit Dietrich, Luther's amanuensis, "in sending the likeness to the doctor; for by it many of his gloomy thoughts are dissipated. He hath placed it on the wall over against the dining-table in the prince's hall."

The foregoing are only a few of the evidences of conjugal affection and domestic happiness in the family of Luther, which are to be found in his

writings and in those of his contemporaries. They
have been thought necessary in this connection, on
account of the contrary representations which were
made by his enemies, and which have been so often
repeated by Protestant writers. That no differences
of opinion or of feeling between Luther and his wife
ever manifested themselves in an unhappy manner,
is more than need be said. This is rarely the lot of
humanity, especially where there are those mental
qualities which give force and energy to character, as was the case with them But aside from
these common frailties, found in the great and the
good no less than in others, there appears to have
been nothing to interrupt the personal happiness of
these individuals in each other.

There are two facts, often overlooked, which lead
superficial observers to a false conclusion. The one
is the plain and simple honesty which, in striking
contrast with modern French manners, characterized
the age of the Reformation; and, connected with
this, the decided tone in which the husband was
then accustomed to speak as the master of the
household. The obedience of the wife was a matter
of direct and simple reality, and was spoken of as
such without circumlocution or ambiguity. In this,
Luther should be judged, not by a modern standard,
but by that of his age. On any other principle,
neither Paul nor Moses would be able to pass the
ordeal of modern criticism. The other particular
alluded to, is the playfulness and vein of drollery
that run through nearly all Luther's correspondence
with his intimate friends. Many of his pleasant
sallies have been taken in earnest, and thus made to
signify what was never intended. It may well be
conceded that many of those expressions were half

in joke and half in earnest. But the man who sets them all down as the serious statements of a formal witness, betrays an utter ignorance of the character of Luther. Thus, when, in his humorous letters, he addresses her as, "my Lord Katy" (meus Dominus Ketha, mea Dominus Ketha, meus Domina Ketha, &c.) he furnished pleasant amusement to his university friends and the students, some of whom were generally members of his family. He once gave out a similar phrase in German to a student in his examination to translate into Latin, and the answer contained such a ridiculous blunder that it long continued a by-word. Luther closes one of his letters to an old friend by saying, "My lord and Moses [the lawgiver] Katy most humbly greeteth you." He also, in a letter to his wife, addressed her as "My kind and dear lord and master Katy Lutheress, [Lutherinn,] doctress and priestess at Wittenberg." Stupid, indeed, must he be who construes all these freaks of the reformer's pen into so many serious charges against his wife!

If we wish to see his creed in respect to a wife's place in a household, we have it undoubtedly in these words, addressed once to his Katy, as he was fond of calling her: "You may persuade me to any thing you wish; you have perfect control;" to which was added, by way of explanation, "*in household affairs* I give you the entire control, my authority being unabated."

Luther was charitable and benevolent, perhaps to a fault, and would have been reduced to absolute suffering but for the frugality and economy of his wife. Some have turned this to her reproach. But what would have been the condition of the family if she too had been above considerations of economy?

Luther had reasons for being as far removed as pos·
sible from suspicions of selfishness, for the honour
of the Reformation, which, in the private life of his
companion, had not the same significance and public
importance. Of his pecuniary affairs, Luther speaks
thus, on different occasions: "I manage my house·
hold affairs strangely, and consume more than I
receive. I expend five hundred gulden* in the
kitchen, to say nothing of clothing, ornaments and
alms-giving; while my annual income is but two
hundred gulden." "I am a very poor manager of
pecuniary matters. By giving to my poor relations
and to other persons who make daily application for
aid, I am myself made very poor." "As you know,
I am oppressed by being obliged to entertain so
much company. I have run into debt by my im-
providence more than a hundred gulden this year.
I have pawned three goblets in one place for fifty
gulden. But the Lord, who thus punisheth my
imprudence, will deliver me. Besides, Lucas [Cra-
nach] and Christian [Aurifaber] will no longer take
my name for security, either because they see it is
of no use, or think it will all be sponged away from
me. So I have given to the former a fourth goblet
for twelve gulden, which have gone to that fat
Herman. . . . But why is it that I alone am so
drained of my money, or rather involved in debt?
I think no one can accuse me of penuriousness or
avarice, who am so free with what is not properly
my own." "I have with my income and presents
built and purchased so much, and entertained so
many in my house, that I must account it as a won·

* See page 111.

derful and singular blessing that I have been able
to meet it all."

Many individuals often remained for several
weeks, and even months, in his family. Had it
not been for the many presents which he received,
especially from the Elector John of Saxony, he
could never have become the owner of so many
little patches of land. His property, at the time of
his death, amounted to about nine thousand gulden.

His father left him about two hundred and fifty
gulden. In 1526, the elector gave him the cloister
building, in which he lived, with the adjoining
garden, free of taxes, together with twelve brewings
of beer annually. This place was sold to the university by his children, in 1564, for three thousand
seven hundred gulden, and made into a college building, to which a new one was added. It was here that
those students resided who received the stipends,
one hundred and fifty in number. Since 1817, it
has been occupied by the Theological Seminary.
Luther's garden was made a botanical garden. In
1541, he purchased, for four hundred and thirty
gulden, the small Bruno House and lot, adjoining
the former place. In his will he gave this to his
widow for her place of residence. On this spot the
new university building above mentioned was erected. He had before purchased a nursery near the
swine market, and also a small estate called Wachs-
dorf, near the village of Pratau, which last was
estimated at one thousand five hundred gulden, and
sold to the younger Cranach, the painter, to whose
family it continued to belong for about a century.
Two years before his death, Luther purchased a
garden adjoining the Speck, or celebrated grove of
oaks, nearly a mile to the east of Wittenberg, and

one of the most common places of resort for the students and others. But the most interesting purchase was that of the estate of Zöllsdorf, two miles from Borna, made in 1540 by Luther for his wife, at the cost of six hundred and ten gulden. The elector agreed to furnish gratuitously any timber she should need for building. To Spalatin Luther writes, November 10, 1540: "Katy now asks for that, of which she spoke with you when you were lately here. She wishes, that when you give the letter to the elector's questor, you will join her in requesting him to give her the oak timbers which she needs." To another person he writes: "Katy has just been in her new kingdom." Two years later, he wrote to Spalatin: "To-morrow, my Katy purposeth to go to Zöllsdorf, and will take with her a load of timber, and attend to some other matters." She frequently repaired to this place, and generally passed her time there when Luther was from home. Luther jocosely called her, at times, Catharine Luther von [of] Bora and Zöllsdorf. In the last year of his life, he addressed a letter, when away from home, "To Catharine Luther, the Zöllsdorf doctor," (alluding to his own title as Dr. Luther.) It is to be hoped that no one will attempt to make out that Luther reproached his wife for leaving his house and being a quack doctor in a retired village by herself.

Some persons have represented Catharine as extravagant, in expending so much on buildings at Zöllsdorf. May it not, with more propriety, be regarded as a proof of laudable enterprise to help support the family, inasmuch as the timber was given her, and her rents were of course increased? How different from this thrifty, calculating woman does Luther himself appear in the following incident! A student, who had finished his course of study, and was about to leave Wittenberg penniless, came to Luther for a little aid. But Luther's pocket was empty, and his wife, who was present, was as destitute of money. Luther expressed his regret that he was unable to render him any assistance. But as he observed the sadness of the young man, his eye fell on a silver goblet, which he had received as a present from the elector. He looked at his wife inquiringly, and she returned a look which meant, " No." He, however, took the costly gift, and gave it to the student. The latter refused it, and Katy seized the opportunity of interposing another significant look. Luther said, " I have no need of silver cups; take it to the goldsmith, and get what you can for it, and retain the money."

Their ordinary style of living, when without company, was simple. The wife was economical, and the husband, who had been trained a monk, could almost dispense with food, and frequently ate nothing during the day but bread and salt, and was always content with his favourite dish of pea-soup and herring.

Luther complained of being invited so often from home. He preferred to be more in his own family circle. He loved to sit in his own garden, his wife with her work at his side, and his children enjoying their sports. When he journeyed, his wife accompanied him, if she could. She was often his companion in his study, taking an interest in his writings, and reminding him if he forgot to reply to the letters he received. When he had important works in hand, he chose to seclude himself. On one occasion, when writing his commentary on the twenty-second Psalm, he shut himself up, with nothing but bread and salt, for three days and nights, till Catharine was alarmed for him, and caused a locksmith to open the door, and there they found Luther lost in deep meditation. He had a weekly family entertainment in singing and playing on instruments, to which other practised singers were invited. Christmas was always a joyful evening in Luther's house. And rarely did a fair go by without furnishing something for the gratification of his children.

Luther was delighted with his first-born, John or Jonny (Hänschen) as he loved to call him. It was to this darling boy, when he was but four years old, that he addressed, from Coburg, in 1530, the letter which has so often been referred to as illustrating his extraordinary power to adapt himself to persons of every variety of capacity and condition. It is as follows: " Grace and peace in Christ, my darling little son. I am glad to see that you study and pray diligently. Go on doing so, my Jonny, and when I come home I will bring with me some fine things for you. I know of a beautiful, pleasant garden, where many children go, and have little golden coats, and gather from the trees fine apples and pears, and cherries and plums; they sing and play, and are happy; they have beautiful little horses with golden bits and silver saddles. I asked the owner of the garden, whose children these were. He replied, 'They are children which love to pray and learn, and are good.' I then said, 'Dear sir, I, too, have a son, whose name is Jonny Luther. May he not also come into the garden, that he too may eat these beautiful apples and pears, and ride on these fine horses, and play with the boys?' The man said, 'If he loves to pray and learn, and is good he shall

Painted and Engraved by C. A. Schwerdgeburth of Weimar, 1846

Luther on Christmas Eve

come into the garden, and Philly and Jussy [Philip and Justus] too; and when they are all together, they shall have fifes and drums and lutes, and all kinds of music, and dance and shoot with their crossbows.' And he showed me a fine grass plat in the garden for dancing, and there were hanging nothing but golden fifes and drums and fine silver crossbows. But it was early, and the children had not yet dined; and as I could not wait for their dancing, I said to the man, 'O, my dear sir, I will hasten away, and write all about this to my dear little Jonny, that he may pray and learn diligently, and be good, and then come into this garden. He has an aunt Lene, [Magdalene,] and she must come too.' The man said, 'That is right, go and write to him so.' Therefore, my dear little Jonny, learn and pray well, and tell Philip, [Melancthon's son,] and Jussy, [Justus Jonas's son,] to learn and pray too, and then you may all come together into the garden. And now I commend you to God. Greet aunt Lene and give her a kiss for me. Your dear father, Martin Luther."

This John Luther was first instructed by his father and by private tutors, and was then sent to the Latin school at Torgau, and afterward studied law at Wittenberg and Königsberg, married the daughter of Professor Cruciger, and entered the Prussian service, and died at Königsberg at the age of fifty. Luther's second child, a daughter, lived less than a year. Upon her death, he wrote to a friend: "My little daughter Elizabeth is taken from me, and hath left me with a bleeding and almost womanly heart, so sad am I on her account. I never thought the heart of a father was so tender toward his children Pray the Lord for me."

His favourite child was Magdalene. She was born in 1529, and died, very pious, at the age of thirteen. The parting scene was very touching. Luther, full of agony, fell on his knees at her bedside, and prayed earnestly for her. "I love her dearly," he exclaimed, "but as it is thy will, gracious God, to take her hence, I will gladly give her up to be with thee." He then rose and bent over her, and said, "Magdalene, my dear daughter, you would be glad to remain here with your father; are you willing to depart and go to that other Father?" "Yes, dear father," she replied, "just as God will." He turned away to conceal his tears, and, looking upward, said, "If the flesh is so strong, how will it be with the spirit! Well, whether we live, or die, we are the Lord's." She fell asleep in his arms. As she was placed in her coffin, he said, "You, dear Lene, how well is it with you!" and again, "Ah, dear Lene, you will rise again, and shine like a star, yea, as the sun." To his sympathizing friends, he said: "You should not lament; I have dismissed a saint, yea, a living saint for heaven. O, that we could so die! Such a death I would willingly accept this very hour."

His fourth child was Martin. Luther was accustomed to moralize over the sports of his children. One day, as Martin was playing with the dog, the father exclaimed, "This boy preacheth God's word by his deeds and acts; for God saith, have dominion over the fishes of the sea, and over the beasts of the field. See how the dog putteth up with every thing from him." At another time, joining his amusements, he said: "Such was our state in Paradise, simple and upright, without guile or hypocrisy. . . . . Therefore, such natural sports and jests are the best for children." "How must Abraham's heart have beaten when he was about to offer up his son! He would not mention it to Sarah. I might contend against God, if he should make a similar demand upon me." Catharine, with a mother's feelings, said, "I cannot believe that God can desire parents to destroy their children." "And yet," replied Luther, "he could give up his own Son to die on the cross." Martin studied theology, and was married, but led a private life in Wittenberg in consequence of continued ill health, and died childless at the age of thirty-three. Paul Luther, the fifth child, studied medicine, and after being a short time professor in Jena, was court-physician. He married a lady of rank, and left four children. He was the ablest and most distinguished of Luther's sons. So robust was he as a boy, that Luther said of him, "He must fight against the Turks." Through him most of the branches of the family now living have descended. Margaret, the youngest of the family, was married to George von Kunheim, and became the mother of nine children.

Section II.—*Luther as a Preacher.*

WE should overlook one of the most essential traits in the character of Luther as a reformer, if we were to omit the consideration of his pulpit oratory In his university lectures, which contain the earliest germ of his reformatory measures, he laid the foundation of his work, by leaving upon a small but influential circle of young men the impress of his own mind. By his university disputations, and by frequent conversations, he won over his opponents with a few exceptions, in the theological faculty. By the numerous learned treatises which he had occasion to publish in defence of his Ninety-five Theses, he made known the doctrines of the Reformation to the literary world, both at home and abroad. But his pulpit eloquence was a powerful auxiliary to all his other efforts in this cause; and, moreover, it carried the Reformation beyond the walls of the university and the barriers of the Latin tongue, (of which the people knew nothing,) to the popular assembly, to the men of all trades and professions. When we consider that he preached almost every day, and several times in a day in the towns and cities through which he passed in his journeys, and that his unsurpassed eloquence always called out throngs to hear him, we shall not be surprised that, in his own times, so much public importance was attached to his preaching.

To most men it was a novel spectacle to behold the crowded assembly, eagerly listening to warm and earnest preaching in the native language. Not that the church had been wholly destitute of able evangelical preachers; for though there was then no Chrysostom to charm and enlighten metropolitan audiences; no Basil or Gregory eloquently to maintain the faith; no Augustine to be the Edwards of his age; no Bernard to sway the popular masses, and to castigate and subdue princes and even popes; there had been such men as Tauler and Suso among the Mystics, and a few of similar character among the Brethren of the Life in Common, who were truly spiritual preachers, and who discoursed to the people in the native dialect. But these were rare instances of popular and evangelical preaching, and the influence thus exerted was mostly of a local character. The greatest preacher at the close of the fifteenth century was, undoubtedly, Geiler of Kaisersberg, who produced extraordinary effects at Strassburg and along the Rhine, by the earnest and captivating, though rude eloquence of his sermons, delivered to great concourses of the people. After his death, in 1510, Luther was for a period of about thirty years, not only the most celebrated, but actually the greatest pulpit orator then living.

The Catholic religion is a religion of show and ceremonies. It aims not so much to unfold the intellectual and rational part of our nature, by means of doctrinal truth, as to excite our wonder at its mysteries; our veneration for the church, the priesthood and the sacraments; our imagination by its legends of a saintly mythology, and our sensibilities by its gorgeous ritual. Preaching is but an incidental appendage to that system; the mass and its attendant ceremonies are the central point of attraction. Luther revived the primitive spirit of Christianity, which demanded that all ceremonies should be subordinated to "the preaching of the word." This was the watch-word of the Protestants—the preaching of the pure word of God to the people. The altar of the priest gave way to the pulpit of the preacher. Every thing conspired to make Luther an illustrious example of what he taught on this subject. He was of that physical organization which fitted him to command attention. His manly form, his piercing, fiery eye, his penetrating voice, and natural manner and action, were all favourable to eloquence.

Still deeper were the foundations for distinguished pulpit oratory laid in his mental constitution. His intellect was powerful and acute, sometimes pouring a flood of light around a subject, and sometimes

astonishing and delighting his audience by the ease
and celerity with which he would penetrate through
the crust of scholastic learning to the very core of a
disputed doctrine, and expose it from an interior
point of view. His logical talents, which were of a
high order, and which were admirably cultivated by
study and discipline, were wonderfully aided by his
strong vein of plain and practical sense, bringing
him into immediate sympathy with every sound
mind, whether cultivated or not.

There was also a large poetical ingredient in his
composition. He had an eye for every thing that
was beautiful and attractive in nature. There was
not a tone in all nature's harmony which did not
find an echo in his heart. Though his poetical
compositions are not of the first order, his sermons
and other prose writings glow and sparkle with
poetic fire. To speak more truly, it is genius, with
its nameless attributes, that distinguishes Luther
from so many other good preachers. Besides, he
was deeply sincere and truly in earnest in all his
preaching. He was not a mere professional man,
aiming to elevate and adorn his profession. Preaching was with him what the military art was with
Napoleon, not an end, but a means, valued only by
the effect produced.

Luther had also experienced the power of the
truth which he preached, and had, in early life,
suffered immeasurably for want of it. Saved, as he
was, by its efficacy, he proclaimed it as the only
means of salvation to others. The genuine warmth
of his own feelings, and the singular capaciousness
of his soul for every natural and every pious emotion, gave him almost absolute dominion over the
emotions of others. The feelings of his heart, and

The market place at Wittenburg—on the left, the City Hall—in the rear, the City Church where Luther was accustomed to preach—and in front, Luther's monument.

the fact that he always spoke from it, and stopped when his discourse had reached the height of its interest, must be considered as one of the causes of his uniform success.

But, more than all, it was the gospel, of which his sermons were so full, that gave a divine power to his preaching. He had studied the Bible, and digested its varied truths, as no other man of that age had done. He had translated the whole Bible, and revised the translation frequently; he had delivered exegetical or expository lectures in the university; he had written commentaries; and when he came to preach, he opened a Bible, every verse of which he had carefully studied. In his own peculiar language, "he had shaken every tree in this forest, and never without gathering some fruit." If we add to all this, quickness of memory, self-possession, vivacity, wit, a rare knowledge of human nature, and an unequalled power over the language of the people, charming alike to the ruler, the scholar and the peasant, we can account for it that all the men of the age, friends and foes, pronounced him the prince of pulpit orators.

It was the preaching of Luther that endeared him to Frederic the Wise, even when he saw his own superstitions unsparingly exposed. It was his preaching that made him as absolute ruler over the people at Wittenberg, as Chrysostom was at Antioch and Constantinople, or Calvin at Geneva. It was his preaching that so often stilled the tumult in the many towns and cities he visited during the first five years after his return from Wartburg. Luther was not, properly speaking, a pastor. He preached statedly for Bugenhagen, the pastor of the city parish in Wittenberg, in 1528 and 1529, while the latter was acting as a sort of missionary in Brunswick and Hamburg; also from 1530 to 1532, three times a week, (Wednesdays, Saturdays and Sundays,) while Bugenhagen was acting the part of reformer in Lubeck; and again from 1537 to 1540, while the same pastor was employed in organizing the church in Denmark. The sermons preached at this time were not committed to paper by himself, but were written down by note-takers, after the manner of reporters of the present day. A part of them are now, for the first time, after a period of three centuries, in a course of publication. What are called his Domestic Postils were preached at home to his own household, when he was so ill as to be unable to go to church. His Church Postils were written for the benefit of the churches and of the clergy while he was confined at Wartburg, and when there were few evangelical preachers to be found, and those few were so ignorant of the Bible as to be unqualified for their work. All the rest of Luther's preaching (and the amount was very great) was either occasional, or was limited to the cloister.

SECTION III.—*Luther as a Promoter of Education.*

IN Germany the church and the schools have always been connected, and the idea of their separation was not even conceived of till the late revolution. But schools are an essential part of Protestantism. It admits of no church to think and decide on all matters of religion for its members, no priesthood to interpose as interpreter of the divine will for the laity, no pope nor council to settle the controversy. The reformers, in giving the Bible to the people, and in relying on its grammatical and true explanation as the only authority in religion, made the study of the Bible, and whatever other studies are preparatory to it, indispensable. Not only the education of the clergy, but a high degree of intelligence among the people, is involved in the very theory of Protestantism. No man ever felt this more deeply than Luther.

The education of the young, next to the preaching of the gospel, lay nearest to his heart. In a letter to the elector in the year 1526, he says: " Since we are all required, and especially the magistrates, above all other things, to educate the youth who are born and are growing up among us, and to train them up in the fear of God and in the ways of virtue, it is needful that we have schools and preachers and pastors. If the parents will not reform, they must go their way to ruin ; but if the young are neglected and left without education, it is the fault of the state, and the effect will be that the country will swarm with vile and lawless people, so that our safety, no less than the command of God, requireth us to foresee and ward off the evil." He maintains in that letter, that the government, " as the natural guardian of all the young," has the right to compel the people to support schools. " What is necessary to the well-being of a state, that should be supplied by those who enjoy the privileges of such state. Now nothing is more necessary than the training of those who are to come after us and bear rule. If the people are unable to pay the expense, and are already burdened with taxes, then the monastic funds, which were originally given for such pur· poses, are to be employed in that way to relieve the people." The cloisters were abandoned in many cases, and the difficult question, What was to be

done with their funds, Luther settled in this judicious manner. How nearly did he approach to
the policy now so extensively adopted in this country, of supporting schools partly by taxation and
partly by funds appropriated for that purpose !

As early as 1520, three years after the beginning
of the Reformation, he laid special stress on the necessity of reforming and improving the schools, in
his eloquent address to the Christian nobility of the
German nation. In 1524, he wrote a remarkable production entitled " An Address to the Common Councils of all the Cities of Germany in behalf of Christian Schools," from which a few passages may here be
extracted. After some introductory remarks, he
comes directly to his point, and says to his countrymen collectively :

" I entreat you, in God's behalf and that of the
poor youth, not to think so lightly of this matter as
many do. It is a grave and serious thing, affecting
the interest of the kingdom of Christ and of all the
world, that we apply ourselves to the work of aiding
and instructing the young. . . . If so much be expended every year in weapons of war, roads, dams,
and countless other things of the sort for the safety
and prosperity of a city, why should we not expend
as much for the benefit of the poor, ignorant youth,
to provide them with skilful teachers ? God hath
verily visited us Germans in mercy and given us a
truly golden year. For we now have accomplished
and learned young men, adorned with a knowledge
of literature and art, who could be of great service,
if employed to teach the young. . . . Surely it is not
meet to neglect this divine favour, and let God
knock in vain at our door. He now standeth at
the door, and happy shall we be if we open unto

him. He now greeteth us, and happy is he who returneth the salutation. Let us recall to mind our former wretchedness and the darkness in which we were enveloped. . . . If we let this season pass, manifesting neither gratitude nor interest, there is reason to fear that still greater darkness and misery will come upon us. Beloved countrymen, buy while the fair is held at your door; gather the harvest while the sun shineth, and the weather is fair. Avail yourselves of the grace and word of God while they are at hand. Know that they are a passing shower, which doth not return where it hath once been. . . . Therefore seize at it, and lay hold of it whosoever can. Idle hands will reap a slender harvest. . . .

"Why else do we older persons live, but to take care of the young, to teach and train them? It is not possible that giddy childhood shall provide for its own instruction. Therefore God hath committed them to us who are old and have experience, and he will call us to a strict account.

"It is, however, a sin and shame that it has come to this, that we must stir up one another to educate our children and the young. Nature impelleth us to do it, as the example of the heathen abundantly showeth. Even the irrational brute traineth its young to what is needful. . . .

"What though we had and did all else, and were ourselves *saints*, if, in the mean time, we should neglect that for which we chiefly live,—the care of the young? Of all outward sins, I think none greater before God, or more punishable than even this which we commit in respect to children, in that we neglect their education. Alas! that children are born and left to grow up as they will, with no one to feel anxiety for them, or train them up! But, you say, all this concerneth parents. What have magistrates and rulers to do about it? True, but what if parents neglect it? Who shall attend to it then? Must they go uncared for, and untaught? . . . The causes for the neglect of children by their parents are numerous.

"1. There are those who are so wicked and brutish that they would not educate their children if they could. They leave them as the ostrich doth her young. And yet they grow up among us and live in the same place with us. How can reason and Christian charity allow them to grow up uneducated, to become a poison and pestilence, corrupting a whole town? . . .

"2. The greater part of parents are, alas! unqualified, and know not how their children ought to be educated. They themselves have learned nothing but how to gratify their appetites. Therefore there must be those who make it a business to instruct and train children well.

"3. Even if the parents were qualified, and were also inclined to teach, they have so much else to do in their business and household affairs that they cannot find the time to educate their children. Thus there is a necessity that public teachers be provided. Otherwise each one would have to teach his own children, which would be for the common people too great a burden. Many a fine boy would be neglected on account of poverty; and many an orphan would suffer from the negligence of guardians. And those who have no children would not trouble themselves at all about the whole matter. Therefore it becometh rulers and magistrates to use the greatest care and diligence in respect to the education of the young."

In what estimation he held the teacher's office we learn from his own lips. "The diligent and pious teacher," he observes, "who properly instructeth and traineth the young, can never be fully rewarded with money. If I were to leave my office as preacher, I would next choose that of school-master, or teacher of boys; for I know that, next to preaching, this is the greatest, best and most useful vocation; and I am not quite sure which of the two is the better; for it is hard to reform old sinners, with whom the preacher has to do, while the young tree can be made to bend without breaking."

In pleading so earnestly for public "Christian schools," Luther by no means overlooked the importance of domestic education, but rather insisted on it no less strenuously. He taught that the beginning in education must be made at home, and that domestic influences must constantly be employed in support of the discipline of the schools. Indeed, with Luther education consisted not merely in the acquisition of knowledge, but in the formation of character. The former stood in the relation of means to the latter. His views of some of these points may easily be gathered from the following truthful observations. "Where filial obedience is wanting," he somewhere remarks, "there no good morals, no good government can be found; for, if in families obedience be not maintained, it is in vain to look for good government in a city, or province, or kingdom, or empire. For the family is the primary government, whence all other government and dominion on earth take their origin. If the root be not sound, then neither the tree nor the fruit will be good." "See to it," he says in another place, "that your children are instructed in spiritual things, that you surrender them first to God, and then to worldly occupations. But, alas! this order is commonly reversed. . . . The whole power of the Christian church lieth in the young, and if they are neglected, it will become like a garden that is neglected in the spring season." Again, he says, "Are we not unwise? We can merit heaven or hell in our children, and yet we regard it not. Of what use will your acts of piety be to you, if you neglect the training of your children? . . . Believe me, it is much more important that you bestow care and attention upon the education of your children, than that you buy indulgences, repeat prayers, perform pilgrimages, or make many vows. . . . Those who knowingly neglect their children, and let them grow up without the nurture and fear of the Lord, are the destroyers of their children."

In 1530, Luther published a discourse, the object of which was to enforce the obligation of parents to send their children to school. In this, he says, "God hath given you children and the means of their support, not merely that you may find your pleasure in them, or bring them up for worldly splendour, but he hath strictly commanded you to train them up for his service."

In 1527, a visitation was made of the churches and schools of the electorate of Saxony, in which more than thirty men were employed a whole year. The result in respect to education was, that "the Saxon school system," as it was called, was drawn up by the joint labours of Luther and Melancthon; and thus the foundation was laid for the magnificent organization of schools to which Germany owes so much of her present fame. The reformers were the fathers of the German system of education, improved indeed, but never radically changed by their successors for a period of three centuries. The traveller, that visits Eisleben, sees in a flourishing condition the very gymnasium which was established by Luther as the last act of his life. The school of Pforta, near Naumburg, where a greater number of accomplished classical scholars have been educated than in any other gymnasium or grammar school in the world, had a similar origin. It was in consequence of Luther's counsels that the old monastery of that name, was, with all its funds, converted into a learned school.

In the Saxon schools, founded upon the plan of Luther and Melancthon, the languages took the precedence of all other studies. The forenoon session was two hours every day; the afternoon three, except Wednesdays and Saturdays, when only the musical exercise of one hour was held, as it was every other afternoon. The catechism was taught every Saturday forenoon. Thus, of the twenty-six school hours in the week, eighteen were devoted to the languages, six to music, and two to the subject of religion. There was, however, further provision made for the religious education of the pupils. They went to the village church or to the public chapel every morning, at about five or six o'clock, sung hymns in Latin and German, and read the Scriptures and the catechism aloud, in Latin and then in German, and repeated prayers. They had a similar evening service. Besides, the schools were kept seven days in the week; or, in other words, there were regular Sunday-schools then, as now, only the teachers were the same as on other days of the week. The pupils were, early on Lord's day mornings, conducted to the church for the matins, as all such morning services were called. Next, they had a lesson from the Bible, or the catechism, in the school-room. At eleven or twelve o'clock, they attended on the principal public service of the day. Sometimes, the younger classes remained at the school-room, where they received religious instruction better adapted to their capacities than that given in the pulpit. The older pupils were carefully examined upon the sermons which they had heard. The order was varied in different schools, as well as the exercises themselves; but the above general statement is sufficiently accurate to illustrate the way in which the day was passed in the schools. From all this, it will appear that the nineteenth century has made less advance than is commonly supposed upon the sixteenth, in respect to the religious education of the young. In respect to books and organizations, there is a great difference; in respect to the thing itself, the object sought, the comparison would not be discreditable to the reformer. A volume might be made up of Luther's views of education, beginning with domestic training, and ascending through the lower schools to the university; but enough has been said to indicate his comprehensive views in respect to schools.

SECTION IV.—*Luther as a Lover of Music.*

ALLUSION has frequently been made in the foregoing account to Luther's musical tastes and talents. He was early known as a melodious singer; and it was in this capacity that he had won the kind regards of Madam Cotta, his first patroness. His last evening before entering the cloister was devoted to musical and social pleasures. It was to be expected, therefore, that, when the work of the Reformation was moving successfully on, sacred music should be called in to its aid: so it was in point of fact. Luther early employed his poetical talents in composing original hymns, and in translating and adapting to his use the better Latin hymns. A version of the Psalms, generally, was never made for public worship in Germany. Of hymn-books the Lutheran church has a plentiful supply; of psalm-books none, though a few psalms were versified by Luther and appended to his collection of hymns. In 1524, the first hymn-book of Luther, accompanied by the music set to the words, in which Walther lent his assistance, was published. Within twenty years from that time, one hundred and seventeen collections of hymns, by Luther and his friends, were printed. "These hymns," he says, in the preface, "are set to music in four parts, for no other reason than because of my desire that the young, who ought to be educated in music as well as in other good arts, might have something to take the place of worldly and amorous songs, and so learn something useful, and practise something virtuous, as becometh the young. . . . I would be glad to see all arts, and especially music, employed in the service of Him who created and made them."

This book, which is so great a curiosity that it was reprinted in 1840, was used in families and social circles and schools, as well as in churches. In the history of the city of Hanover, we read that the Reformation was first introduced there, not by preachers, nor by religious tracts, but by the hymns of Luther, which the people sung with delight. In his second edition, in 1533, he complains that his hymns had been altered, and others published under his name. In this new collection, therefore, he added two to his own hymns (which, at first, were twenty-nine in number) and several old hymns from the Middle Ages, and, finally, fifteen new ones by his friends and contemporaries, remarking, at the same time, in respect to the last, that, of the many which were in circulation, only a few deserved a place in the collection.

Luther himself composed music for several of his hymns, which was not only good in itself, but agreed beautifully with the sentiment expressed by the words.* The same Walther, mentioned above, says: "I have spent many a happy hour in singing with him, and have often seen the dear man so happy and joyful in spirit, while singing, that he could neither tire, nor be satisfied. He conversed splendidly upon music. Forty years ago, when he was arranging the mass [communion] service in German at Wittenberg, he sent for the elector's old chorister, Rupf, and myself, to confer with us about the music for the Epistles and Gospels. . . . He himself composed tunes for the epistles and gospels, and the words of Christ at the institution of the supper, and sung them to me, and asked my opinion of them. He kept me three weeks at Wittenberg, writing the notes for a few gospels and epistles, till the first German mass was sung in the parish church. I was obliged to stay and hear it, and to take a copy of it with me to Torgau, for the elector, at the doctor's command." We select the following from a large mass of Lu-

---

* There appears to be no evidence that "Old Hundred" was composed by Luther.

ther's sayings in regard to music: "It is a beautiful and lovely gift of God; it hath often so excited and moved me, as to give me a desire to preach. I have always been fond of music. He who understandeth this art is the right sort of man, and is fit for any thing else. It is needful that music be taught in schools. A schoolmaster must be able to sing, or I do not think much of him. Music cometh near to theology; I would not exchange my little knowledge of it for much money. The young should be constantly exercised in this art, for it refines and improves men. Singing is the best of arts and exercises; it is not of a worldly character, and is an antidote for all contentions and quarrels. Singers are not gloomy, but joyful, and sing their cares away. There can be no doubt that, in minds which are affected by music, are the seeds of much that is good; and those who are not affected by it, I regard as stocks and stones. . . . Music effecteth what theology alone can effect besides—it giveth peace and a joyful mind. . . . Therefore the prophets have employed no art as they have music; inasmuch as they have put their theology, not into geometry, or arithmetic, or astronomy, but into music. Hence it cometh, that, by teaching the truth in psalms and hymns, they have joined theology and music in close union."

CHAPTER VI.

THE PRINCIPAL EVENTS OF LUTHER'S LIFE, FROM HIS MARRIAGE IN 1525 TO HIS DEATH IN 1546.

SECTION I.—*From Luther's Marriage to the Completion of the Augsburg Confession in* 1530.

OTH the enemies and the friends of Luther had been much astonished by his selecting such a time as the very midst of the turmoil of the Peasants' War to celebrate his marriage with a fair nun. His friends censured his imprudence, his foes interpreted the act to his ignominy. The papal writers represented the great beauty of Catharine von Bora as proving a snare to Luther, while the Protestant writers, in defence of the reformer, detracted quite as much from her beauty as is consistent with the likenesses taken of her by Cranach.

The death of Frederic, Elector of Saxony, had

emboldened the Catholic princes, who hoped that
the fall of this pillar of Protestantism would greatly
weaken the cause of Luther. The latter, not yet
knowing the firmness of the new elector, who proved
himself so heroic at the presentation of the Augsburg Confession to the diet in 1530, thought it prudent to attempt a reconciliation with Henry, King
of England, and George, Duke of Saxony, the bitterest of his enemies on the throne, and therefore
wrote them respectively very humble letters, which,
however, instead of answering their purpose, were
received with scorn.

The year 1527 was one of sadness to Luther.
His friends were persecuted, and some of them put
to death, and he himself fell into a state of melancholy and despondency, of which Bugenhagen and
Justus Jonas have left us a memorable detailed account. How far all this was the effect of bodily
disease and other natural causes, or how far it was
a visitation from the evil spirit, as Luther himself
believed, it is not our province to determine. About
the same time an epidemic, or the plague, as it was
termed, raged so at Wittenberg that the university
was temporarily removed to Jena. Near the middle of the year 1527, the great work of visitation
was begun by Melancthon and others, and ended in
1529. The surprising ignorance which Luther
found as well among the priests as the people, induced him in the following year to write those monuments of his genius as a popular and catechetical
writer, the Larger and the Smaller Catechism. What
he did for schools need not here be repeated. Meanwhile, the controversy on the real presence of Christ
in the eucharist, between Luther and Zwingle and
their respective adherents, had grown so warm and

threatened such serious consequences, that Philip Landgrave of Hesse, a man of enlarged views and enlightened policy, more so perhaps than any other of the Protestant rulers, proposed to have both parties meet for friendly conference, and such a meeting finally took place in the Marburg Colloquy, October 1, 1529, but to no very good purpose.

The diet of Spire, which was held in the same year, had come to a decision unfavourable to the interests of the evangelical party, which called forth the Protest that has since given name to the opposers of papal error and corruption. As there were now ominous indications of a combined hostility of the Papal rulers against the Protestants, it was proposed by the latter to enter into a league for mutual defence. Luther opposed the measure, saying, "He would rather die ten times than have the consciousness that the gospel preached by him was the occasion of bloodshed;" a fresh proof that Luther trusted not in the power of the sword, but in the power of truth; yet what (to human view) would have become of the Protestant states of Germany, if they had followed his views in respect to defensive war?

Early in the spring of 1530, the elector wrote to Luther and other Wittenberg theologians, informing them that the emperor had called a diet to be held at Augsburg, April 8, at which his majesty was to be present in person. Inasmuch as it was intended to make this diet answer the purpose of a council in settling the difficulties between the religious parties, the elector said : "It is necessary that we have a clear understanding among ourselves, touching the articles to be maintained as well of rites and ceremonies as of faith, so that both we and other members of the diet who have embraced the pure evangelical doctrines, may know how far we can, with propriety and a good conscience, be a party in the transactions." He directed, therefore, that they draw up such articles as should seem to them best, and appear with them before him at Torgau, on the 20th of March. He also instructed Luther, Jonas and Melancthon to make arrangements to be absent from the university, and to accompany him, together with Spalatin and Agricola, as far as Coburg, on the way to Augsburg. They entered upon this journey, April 3, and Luther preached on the way at Weimar, Saalfeld, Gräfenthal, Neustadt, and frequently at Coburg. On the 21st, the elector and the rest of the company proceeded to Augsburg, while Luther, for reasons unknown to him, was left behind to remain at Coburg. The elector thought it more prudent to employ the mild and peaceful Melancthon in negotiating with the Papists, having Luther, at the same time, within reach, to be consulted whenever it should appear necessary. Luther was accordingly conducted to the electoral palace, situated on a bold eminence, for a residence of nearly six months. He, his companion Dieterich, and his servant Cyriac, resided here alone with no company but the keepers and attendants and occasional visiters, and had the whole of the great building which crowns the hill and the fortress to themselves. Being here without books for several weeks, he amused himself in a playful description of a diet held by the birds which congregated about his lofty abode.

Here the old complaint from which he had suffered so much, that of a roaring noise in his head, especially in his left ear, returned upon him; and, as usual, Satan came with it, armed with the fiery darts of temptation. Notwithstanding Luther's ill health and dejection, he translated the prophetical writings, wrote the well-known sermon enforcing upon parents the duty of sending their children to school, and other treatises, besides a great amount of letters to the elector and to his friends concerning the proceedings of this diet. Though Melancthon was the chief agent in drawing up the Augsburg Confession, and the Apology or defence of it, it was Luther, standing behind the curtain, that exercised control over the minds of the evangelical princes and theologians. As formerly in his Patmos, so here in his Sinai, as he called it, his was the ruling spirit.

The letters of Luther, from the time of his marriage to that of his death, are so numerous and so abound in incident that they serve well as a substitute for a minute journal. It will be proper, therefore, to take advantage of this circumstance, and follow him through some of the scenes already alluded to.

In a letter to Amsdorf, now pastor at Magdeburg, written June 21, 1525, after saying that the report of his sudden marriage with Catharine von Bora is true, and that he took this step partly in compliance with the wish of his father, partly to confirm his own teaching by example, and partly to show some degree of boldness at a time when everybody is terror-struck, adding, incidentally, that he loves his wife, though he is not enamoured or fired with passion, he thus speaks of the Peasants' War, which was then raging: "Meiningen, Mellerstadt, Neustadt, and Marstadt, with ten other towns, [in the southwest of Saxony,] have surrendered to the elector, and he is restoring peace and order there. It is ascertained that in Franconia, about eleven thousand peasants are slain in three different places, sixty-one

bombs taken, and the citadel of Wirtemberg liberated.
The Margrave Casimir [of the house of Brandenburg, which possessed one or two principalities in
the vicinity of Bayreuth] is proceeding furiously
against his subjects, for having violated their faith.
In the duchy of Wirtemberg six thousand have
been slain; in other parts of Suabia ten thousand.
The Duke of Lorraine, it is said, hath put to the
sword twenty thousand in Alsace. Thus the miserable peasants are everywhere cut down. How it is
in Bamberg, we shall soon hear. But in Breisgau
[Baden] the insurrection is still in progress, and
also in the Tyrol, so much so that from Inspruck to
Trent all is in a state of commotion, and the
Bishops of Brixen and of Trent are put to flight.
Duke George is about to hold a conference at Dessau
with the Margrave and the Archbishop of Mainz.
The report is, that, inflated with his success, he will
pursue me. He thinketh me to be like unto Muncer
in doctrine. But Christ will bestow his grace. See
that he do not make an attack upon Magdeburg."

In the following letter to the elector (July 20)
are some interesting facts relating to Spalatin:
"George Spalatin hath informed me that he is
called on by your grace to take into farther consideration the proposal to make him preacher at
Altenburg, and desireth me to write your grace on
this behalf. I therefore humbly submit unto you,
that I remain of the same opinion as before. For
he is a man of learning, a comely speaker, of good
manners and morals, and, what affecteth me most,
is of a pure and upright heart, and will deal faithfully with the word of God and with souls. Whether
his health is too feeble, the experiment must show."

To Brismann, of Königsberg, he writes, Aug. 16:

"If the poison of Carlstadt or Zwingle concerning the sacrament reacheth unto you, be on your guard against it. . . . Muncer and the peasants have so prostrated the gospel with us, and so aroused the Papists, that it seemeth as if it must all be built up again. For which reason I have testified to the gospel not only by word but by deed, in marrying a nun in the face of my enemies, who are triumphing and crying 'Io!' 'Io!' that I might not, though old and unsuitable, seem to yield up the ground; and I shall do some other things, if I am able, which will trouble them and make known God's word.

"Duke George, the Elector of Brandenburg, and the two Dukes of Brunswick have sworn to each other that they will restore the old order of things. Our Elector John, though much belaboured by George, standeth firm, so that the latter is almost beside himself and bursting with anger. The Landgrave of Hesse is also believed to stand firm, though he hath been visited and urged by the Duke of Brunswick, as delegate from the council of princes. The imperial cities are now consulting how they shall stand by the gospel, although threatened by angry princes."

That the university should not prosper under such circumstances was almost a matter of course. Luther wrote to Spalatin, September 6, not a little alarmed : "The report hath come to our ears that the elector's mind is alienated from our university, and that he is displeased with our movements as unjustifiable. We have great difficulty in keeping our students, who will rush forth at every gate and go into all the world, if these reports are found to be true."

The next week he wrote to the elector: "Although I and all the rest confidently rely on your grace's promise concerning the university, still we perceive that you are hindered by other necessary occupations, and particularly by the assembly of the estates. I cannot, therefore, omit to remind you of it, and to beg that you will send some one to us, or write and inform us of your purposes. Otherwise, since many lectures are dropped, and some not being yet paid for are likely to be discontinued, there will be reason to fear that we shall be unable to retain the students."

To his friend Stiefel he wrote, September 29: "I have this night caused thirteen nuns to be removed out of Duke George's dominions, and thus snatched from the raging tyrant the spoils of Christ. Our princes [the elector and his son] have openly espoused the gospel. Master Eberard [prior of the cloister at Wittenberg] is made Bishop at Altenburg with Spalatin. The income of the monastery we have resigned to the elector, and I live as a private householder, remaining in the monastery."

On occasion of Spalatin's marriage, Luther wrote, December 6: "Grace and peace in the Lord, and joy in your sweet wife, also from the Lord. As disagreeable as your marriage is to your Baalitish brethren, [the priests of Altenburg,] so agreeable is it to me. God hath granted me nothing more agreeable, the gospel excepted, than the privilege of hearing and knowing that you are a husband. With what feelings and for what causes I was detained from attending your joyful wedding, Master Eberard will explain. I cannot now travel so safely as I could under a prince who had not declared his views. . . . I, in my poverty, would have sent you that gold cup which you gave me at my marriage, had I not feared it would offend you. I therefore send you all that remains of those presents, not knowing whether it came from you or not. My affection you will regard as much in a small gift as in a great one." So violent was the opposition of the canons and priests at Altenburg to this infraction of the papal law, requiring celibacy in the clergy, that it was necessary for Luther to request protection for his friend of the elector.

The following letter to Link of Nüremberg, written near the close of December, shows what different cares and thoughts often occupied Luther's mind: "The King of England, to whom, at the instance of the King of Denmark, I wrote an humble and suppliant letter, with pleasant anticipations and good and pure intentions, hath replied to me with a bitterness which showeth that he, like Duke George, rejoiceth at an opportunity for revenge. So impotent and womanly are the minds of these tyrants, so sordid and vulgar, that, thanks to Christ, and joy to myself! it is sufficient revenge for me to despise Satan, their god, together with themselves.

"I rejoice at the promise you make of sending me garden seeds in the spring. Send as many as you can. I desire them, and shall expect them. If there is any thing I can send you in turn, order it and it shall be done. For while Satan and his subjects rage, I will laugh and contemplate gardens, which are God's blessings, and enjoy them to his praise.

"Because with us barbarians there are no arts nor exercise of the ingenuity, I and my servant Wolfgang have taken up the art of turning. We send you this gold piece, that you may, at your convenience, procure some instruments for hollowing and turning, together with two or three screws for the lathe, which any turner will show you. We have instruments here, but we wish to get some more elegant, after your Nüremberg fashion. If they cost more, the money shall be sent, though I think all such things are cheaper with you than with us. Thus, if the world shall be unwilling to support us to preach the gospel, we will learn to live by the labour of our hands, and then, after the example of our heavenly Father, serve the unworthy and ungrateful."

In a similar strain he wrote to Amsdorf, at the beginning of the new year, January 3, 1526 : "By Bruno, the bearer of this, I send you seven florins, my dear Amsdorf, to pay for the butter and dried fish. For though I have lost your letter, I recollect that this is about the amount due you. I wrote to Duke George a very humble and candid letter, and he answered me, according to his character, with that stolidity and rustic ferocity which runs in his Bohemian blood. The letter is every way worthy of himself. You shall see a copy of it. It is currently reported that you have taken that Suabian damsel, my former flame, for your wife. It will be odd if you retaliate upon me by such a secret movement."

Of the use he made of his influence with the elector, we have a good example in a letter, written about the middle of April : "First," says he, "I present a request from a young singer by the name of Holzwart, whom your grace hath supported one year, with the encouragement that you would do better by him, if you could, afterward, as the petition showeth. He appeareth to have good talents All which is referred to your good pleasure.

"Secondly, a request already made for a nun of Nimptschen, near Grimma, by the name of Alsey Gaudelitz, that she may recover something from the cloister to which she gave much. No answer hath yet been received.

"Thirdly, God hath sent us two guardians [superiors in a monastery] from France. They were plundered on their way, as they were coming hither to study theology. The pastor and myself are supporting them, relying upon your gracious aid, hoping you would give them five or six gulden. If you cannot, then we must dismiss them after giving what we can, and, after all, beg it again from your grace. God sendeth us many poor, and we are poor ourselves, and yet are provided for.

"Fourthly, the request of a pious man, whom I have thought of sending as preacher to Arnstadt. . . . He hath been here three years, and I have helped him what I could; for what I do is from your grace's bounty, for I have nothing of my own to give. I wish your grace would grant him something, for he possesseth piety, learning and talents, but is poor and destitute, and I cannot do so much for him as is necessary. I refer it to your good pleasure.

"Finally, I entreat for myself, as formerly, that your grace will not suffer the singing to be so neglected. The persons belonging to the choir [boys] are growing up, and the art of music deserveth, moreover, to be sustained by princes and lords. More than enough to support them here is applied elsewhere, without so great need. The monastic funds might usefully, and with the approbation of God, be applied to support such persons.

"Enough for once; please receive it graciously."

The history of a certain cup or vessel, presented
to Luther, is not only amusing, but strikingly illustrative of the times and of the character of the parties concerned. Luther, in a note to his friend
Hausmann, pastor at Zwickau, dated March 27,
1526, says: "I thank you for the vessel. I did not
expect it would be done up with so much labour
and care, for it was well enclosed in a wicker-work
of vines. But you excited the desire of my Katy
too much, as is wont to be the case with these women. I am delighted with the minerals, but am
unwilling to take them away from you. You have
others to whom you can give them. If there is any
thing else, don't waste it upon my curiosity." In
a letter, written about three weeks afterward to
Agricola, at Eisleben, recommending a young man
about to open a school there, he says: "That vessel
from Zwickau, oh! how changed it is since you saw
it, and how beautiful! But concerning this and the
cup presented me by Meinhard, at another time.
For of these magnificent things I cannot write to
day, and so briefly" A month later he writes to
the same: "I send you that pewter and glass vessel
before it finds another owner." And then in a postscript, adds: "Behold, when I was ready to give
the letter to the messenger, and looked for the cup.
my Katy, that enemy in ambush, had carried it off.
I would have got hold of it, but our provosts and
plebeians, [probably certain members of the household,] who, perhaps, have taken it in charge, conspired together and hindered me. It must be put
off, therefore, till she gets up from childbed, and
when she brings it forth I will seize it for you."
The end of the story is given in a subsequent letter
to Hausmann: "My chain [wife] tenaciously holds

the glass vessel ornamented and presented me by yourself. Otherwise, Agricola of Eisleben would have begged it away from me."

A day or two afterward, we find him writing to the elector the following request, in behalf of an old schoolmaster of his: "The bearer of this, Mr. Bigand, hath given up his parish at Waltershausen to the town-council, in consequence of an agreement, made by yourself, to allow him thirty florins annually from the church funds. Now the money doth not come, perhaps the council have not those funds in charge, and this old man must wander abroad for his living. As he was my schoolmaster, whom it is my duty to honour, I humbly beg your grace not to suffer my old schoolmaster to be deprived of his money, but graciously to aid him, that he may not be left to beg in his old age."

At the close of a note to his brother-in-law, Rühel, he thus announces the birth of his first-born: "Please say to Agricola, for me, that my dear Katy hath, by the great blessing of God, borne me a son, John Luther, yesterday, at two o'clock, the very day when *dat* [he gives] standeth in the calendar; and that he must not wonder that I storm him so early with this intelligence, for he himself ought to think, about this time, what it is to have sons. Greet the dear mother of your children, and Agricola's Elsey. My sick Katy is the cause of my sending you only this scrawl." Referring to the same event in a letter to Spalatin, he speaks of being a "happy husband, and having, by the great blessing of God, been presented with a son from the best of wives and the most excellent of women;" and closes by saying, "When you come to see us,

will you still find the old monuments of our friendship and intimacy? I have planted a garden, and
built a fountain. Come, and you shall be crowned
with lilies and roses." To Agricola he writes again,
" I have received your letter, in which you say my
mother was hindered from coming to me. Let
Christ do what he pleaseth, and it will be well.
Little John Luther is doing well, though he is a
slender child, and hath too little nourishment from
his mother."

As a specimen of his ecclesiastical correspondence,
we will present a letter, addressed August 8, 1526,
to the Council of Mühlhausen, which was the head-
quarters of Muncer's army the previous year:
" Grace and peace in Christ, honourable, wise and
dear sirs. At the command of our gracious lord,
Duke John, Elector of Saxony, I have selected a
preacher for his grace to send to you. That individual,
John Mantel, reader in our church at Wittenberg,
now cometh to you, who, as far as God giveth unto
men to do, will, I hope, take the care of you, as a
learned, affable, quiet, pious man. I beg you,
therefore, to receive and regard him in a Christian
manner, as I doubt not you will. And may Christ
graciously look upon you and help you, after all your
wretchedness, that rebellion may cease, and that
you may learn to follow his pure and holy word.
I would gladly have come with him, but our circumstances here would not allow it."

August 28, he replies to an inquiry of Link, respecting parental authority, and maintains that it
ought always to be asserted, though not always exercised, and then subjoins the following intelligence:
" The diet of Spire is held as the Germans are wont
to hold diets, with drinking and sports, and nothing

more. Here there is nothing new, save that Wittenberg is fortified with such great labour, that, comparing the past with the present, you would hardly know it. I am now lecturing on Ecclesiastes, which is stubborn and refuses to be explained, so full is it of Hebraisms and of the obscurities of an unknown tongue; nevertheless, by the grace of God, I shall break through the obstacles. Pray for me; and farewell, both you and your rib, whom may God bless in her approaching crisis. My son is, by the mercy of God, living and well. Philip [Melancthon,] who is a little better, and would be better still if he could have a respite from his labours, saluteth you."

An interesting and lasting friendship commenced with the incident referred to in the subjoined note: " April 22. To Frederic, abbot at Nüremberg. Grace and peace. Though we are unknown to each other, I write to you, most excellent sir, because of what Link, my friend, and more than a friend to you, hath done in sending to me, in your name, a brass clock, a most acceptable present. This hath compelled me to become a disciple of our mathematicians, to learn the forms and rules of one single clock; for I never before saw such an one, so little am I acquainted with mathematical affairs. Would that I had the power to respond in like manner to the kindness expressed by this gift; nothing would please me more."

In other letters, which cannot be quoted, he speaks of having received garden-seeds, ("all of which, except the melons and cucumbers, grew well,") and the turning instrument for which he wrote, together with a quadrant and a wooden clock. " Send me," he says, in another letter, " seeds for

my garden in as great variety as you can; for, if I
live, I will be a horticulturist."

Many of Luther's letters refer to schools, and
show an intense interest in teachers, both in the
higher and in the lower, in public and in private
schools.   A letter written May 2, 1527, to Elsey
von Kanitz, requesting her to open a girl's school in
Wittenberg, presents the reformer in an interesting
light.   " My dear friend in Christ," he says, " I
wrote to your dear aunt Anna von Plausig, requesting her to send you to me for a time ; for I have
desired to employ you in teaching young girls, and
through you to give an example for others to follow.
You shall be in my house and sit at my table, so
that you shall have no risk nor trouble. I beg you,
therefore, not to decline the proposal."

Luther and his wife appear to have been tenderly
attached to the wife of John Agricola, school-
teacher at Eisleben.   A letter written to Agricola,
in May, 1527, contains expressions of tenderness
such as are often found in Luther's correspondence.
" It seemeth to us best," he says, at the close,
" that your Elsey should come and spend some days
with us, for the sake of a change in the climate,
[Wittenberg was about seventy miles to the north-
east of Eisleben.]   Consult together concerning this
matter, for we will gladly do whatsoever can in any
way be beneficial to the wife who is so ageeable to
you, and to the woman who is so sincere and virtuous. My Katy, who is troubled again with vomit-
ting, nausea, and dizziness of the head, but not
very ill, heartily saluteth you and your Elsey. My
little Johnny is lively and robust, and eats and
drinks like a hero."

This amiable lady appears to have suffered much

and to have become dejected, especially as her husband was at that time called from home; for we find
Luther writing to her, June 10th, thus: "Dear
Elsey. Grace and peace. I had it in mind lately to
write to you, but Mr. Matthes was away before I was
aware of it. By this time I suppose your husband
hath returned home, so that it is not so ill with you.
You must not be so desponding and fearful, but remember that Christ is near to help you to bear your
sufferings. For he hath not so forsaken you as your
flesh and blood suggest. Cry unto him earnestly,
and be assured he will hear you; for you know it is
his way to help, strengthen and comfort all who
desire it. Be comforted then, and consider that he
hath suffered more for you than you can ever suffer
for him. We will also pray, and pray earnestly,
that God will accept you through his Son, and
strengthen you in body and in soul. Greet your
husband and all yours in our name."

Luther's heart was full of benevolence, and no
opportunity for benefiting the poor was allowed to
pass unimproved. The Franciscan cloister, which
had been the burial-place for the electoral family
time out of mind, was now vacant, the monks having
left their cells. The elector had given a part of the
grounds and buildings to a man by the name of
Bürger. Luther wrote to the former: "We have
conversed with Bürger about it, and he is willing to
give the place up for the benefit of the poor, in the
hope that you will bestow upon him another in its
place. Since, then, the cloister, as the burial-place
of princes, cannot be better used . . . than in the
service of God and for the relief of the poor, in whom
Christ himself is served; therefore I humbly request,
in conjunction with the city-council, that your grace

will grant that the cloister, together with the grounds
and buildings of Bürger, be given to our Lord Jesus
Christ as a retreat and residence for the poor, as the
members of his body.''

A melancholy period in Luther's life now ensues.
The plague appeared at Wittenberg, and the people
fled in terror; the university was removed to Jena,
and Luther, overcome in body and in mind, passed
through a scene of deepest gloom, agony and despair.
He writes to Melancthon, August 2: "For more
than a week I have been tossing in death and hell,
so prostrate in body as to tremble all over.   Christ
hath been almost wholly lost, and I have been agitated with the billows and storms of despair and blasphemy against God.   But God, moved by the prayers
of the saints,* hath begun to have compassion on me,
and hath delivered me from the lowest hell.   Pray
continually for me, as I do for you.   I believe my
conflict will concern others as well as myself.   The
plague is here, we are fully persuaded, but we hope
it will be mild and gentle with us, the tender flock
of Christ, already afflicted with the hatred of the
whole world and our own sufferings, to say nothing
of our poverty and other humbling circumstances.''
Ten days later, he writes to Justus Menius: "Cease
not to pray earnestly for me and to comfort me, for
this conflict is above my power.   Thus far Christ
hath been a faithful Saviour, nor do I despair that
he will be so for evermore.   I have been sick, not
only in body, but much more in soul, Satan and his
angels have, with the permission of God my Saviour,
so vexed and tormented me."   To Spalatin he says,
in a letter dated August 19th: "The plague hath

---

* His Christian friends.

indeed begun here, but it is mild, though with the people there is a wonderful fear and fleeing away, so that I never saw the like of Satan's work before. He rejoiceth that he can so terrify men's hearts as to disperse and ruin this our university, which he, not without cause, hateth above all others. Still, in all this time, there have been but eighteen deaths in the town, including children. In the fisher's quarter [south] it hath raged vehemently; in our quarter [east] there hath been no death, though all are buried here. . . . Justas Jonas's little son John is dead Jonas himself hath gone to his native place, . . . so that Bugenhagen and I are here alone with the chaplains."

An evangelical preacher at Halle, George Winkler by name, had been murdered, at the instigation, as some supposed, of the Archbishop of Mainz, who was unwilling that the light should break in upon this favourite residence of his. Luther, though still troubled with fierce temptation, wrote a letter of encouragement to the Christians of Halle: " I have long purposed," he says, "my dear friends, to write to you a letter of consolation for the calamity which Satan hath brought upon you by the murder of the good and pious Master George, thereby depriving you of a faithful preacher, and of the word of God; but I have in divers ways been hindered, chiefly by my own illness; and though I am not yet through with my difficulties, I can wait no longer. For though we would not be comforted, still it would be wrong to be silent concerning such a scandalous and treacherous murder, and so let it pass, and leave the blood, whereby the word of God hath been testified, to be buried in the ground. Therefore I will publish it, and help it to cry unto heaven, so that, as much as in us lieth, such a murder shall not keep silence, till God, the merciful father and the just judge, hear it, as he did Abel's; and take vengeance on the old enemy, murderer and traitor, who hath instigated this act, and cause that the blood of Master George be a seed sown in the earth by Satan and his emissaries, which shall bring forth a hundred fold; so that, instead of one murdered George, a hundred true preachers shall spring up, who shall do Satan a thousand times more harm than one man could do."

The following letter to Amsdorf has a peculiar interest, as being written on the tenth anniversary of his attack upon Tetzel's indulgences: "Grace and peace. It pleaseth the Lord, my dear Amsdorf, that I, who have formerly comforted so many others, should myself now be destitute of all comfort. One thing I ask, and do you ask the same with me, namely, that my Christ do with me what he will, only that he leave me not to be ungrateful and to become his enemy, whom I have heretofore preached and adored with such zeal and fervour, although I have, in the mean time, offended him with many and great sins. Satan seeketh to have another Job given over to him . . . My house beginneth to be an hospital. Anna, wife of Augustine [Schurf,] hath had the plague, but is recovering. . . . For my Katy, who is in critical circumstances, I have great fears. My little John is sick, and hath eaten nothing for three days. . . . Thus we have fightings without, and fears, great fears within; Christ visiteth us One solace remaineth, which we can oppose to Satan, namely, that we have the word of God for saving the souls that believe, however it may be with our bodies. Commend us to the brethren, and pray for us, that we may patiently bear the hand of the

Lord that is upon us, and conquer the power and devices of Satan, whether by our death or by our life. Wittenberg, All-saints' day, the tenth year from the trampling down of indulgences."

The last day of the year 1527, he says: "We are all well, except Luther himself, who, though well in body, suffereth without from all the world, and within from Satan and all his angels." The following letter, in which he playfully rebukes Justus Menius and his other Erfurt friends for not visiting him when he was at Weimar, near by them, brings the author before us again in his old and easy attire: "I expected some of you would come and visit me here, and wonder what could hinder you, since there was no obstacle in the length nor breadth nor height of the way, for the sky and sun were serene above. I will excuse you for this neglect, if you will some time explain to me the reason of such a breach of the laws of friendship, charity and humanity. Erfurt is Erfurt; Erfurt will be Erfurt; Erfurt always was Erfurt. What else can I think or say? Greet the brethren for me, and your Eve and Abels and Seths."

We have already had occasion to speak of Nüremberg as a renowned and refined city, which shone like a bright star in the time of the Reformation. There lived Pirkheimer, the patrician and scholar; there preached Link and Osiander; there was the great Dürer, the painter, and Eoban Hess, the elegant scholar and poet, and Camerarius, the classical teacher, and Baumgärtner and others. Dürer died April 6, 1528, and his death called forth a beautiful elegy from his friend Hess, a copy of which Luther thus acknowledged: "I have received a second letter from you, together with an Elegy on Dürer, and

thus, contrary to my expectation, you are in advance
of my reply to your former letter. For I had resolved to reply by the first carrier I should find. As
to Dürer, it is a pious act to mourn over the loss of
so excellent a man. But it is yours to pronounce
him happy that Christ hath taken him away so well
prepared, and by so peaceful an end, from times so
turbulent, and to be, perhaps, more turbulent still,
lest he, who was worthy of the happiest times, should
live to see the most wretched. Let him rest in peace,
then, with his fathers. I thank you next for the
love which breathes, or rather flames and burns in
every word of both your letters. Not that I am
worthy of such praise or love, but because I cheerfully suffer myself to be exalted by the testimony
and favour of the good against Satan and his ministers, who diligently and incessantly seek my blood
and extinguish me, so that I can boast of going the
way of Paul, through honour and dishonour, through
good report and evil report. . . . Blessed be my
Lord Jesus Christ, who hath willed I should be
such, not that I should boast, but that many through
me should be saved from these pestilent spirits. . . .
When I see this prayer, which I breathe every hour,
fulfilled, I think myself happy; and regard it as an
abundant reward of my labours to know that I live
only to serve others. I rejoice, therefore, not so
much in the praise which you, in your partiality,
abundantly bestow, as in the truth to which you
testify by your candour and too great affection for
me, and thus with great openness and simplicity
confess Christ. For what can be more delightful to
hear than that you, and others like you, stand strong
against Satan by a substantial and pure knowledge
of Christ, when so many, whom we hoped would

be pillars, fall, and are now worse enemies to us than the Turks? I therefore pray the Lord Jesus Christ, that he will crown you with his benedictions, and preserve you, with us, perfect and unblamable to his glorious appearing. Of news I have nothing to send you to your emporium, for Nüremberg itself is the eye, as it were, and ear of Germany, which seeth and heareth every thing, a part of which, perhaps, never cometh to our knowledge. Salute your dearest doe, together with your dear fawns. The blessing of the Lord be upon you." How beautifully does Luther here place himself almost within the soul of the Nüremberg poet, and appropriate to himself, for the time being, the qualities of his mind!

To a letter to Spalatin, dated Wittenberg, "in the aerial and ethereal house," (in allusion to the name of the owner Luft, which means *air*,) he appends this postscript: "Pomeranus, [Bugenhagen, of Pomerania,] who goeth to Brunswick, saluteth you, and desireth you to pray for him. Justus Jonas, fighting against the gravel, saluteth you, and desireth you to pray that he may get the victory. Casper Cruciger saluteth you, and desireth you to pray for him that his hopes may be realized; that is, if you do not understand it, that Duke George may be converted to Christ, or be bruised by Christ. John Mantell saluteth you, recently bereaved of a little son, the same day on which Bugenhagen lost his elder son Michael, having lost his younger son John two weeks before, and desireth you to pray that for one son he may receive many. My Eve, joyful and well, with all of this convivial company, saluteth you, and desireth you to pray for her that her third offspring may come safely to the world."

The visitation of the churches for the purpose of

doing away the evils of the papal system, and intro ducing the evangelical in its stead, continued after several interruptions into the year 1529. In February, Luther, who was still engaged in that work, in which more than thirty men had been employed, wrote to Spalatin the following lines, which give us some idea of the state of the people at that time: "We desire to know what you are doing in the visitation and how you succeed, and we are surprised that you do not mention this in your letter. We, on our part, confer a living when it is necessary; and though it is small, yet it is an aid to the poor pastors to have two acres to cultivate. Furthermore, we strenuously require a contribution from each individual. But the condition of the churches is most wretched; the peasants learn nothing, know nothing, pray for nothing, do nothing, except abuse their liberty, neither confessing nor communing, just as if they were set free from all religion. For they have neglected their own papal ordinances; they despise ours; so that the administration of the papal bishops is horrid to contemplate."

Luther, who believed that all physical evils, bodily pains, diseases, epidemics, earthquakes and calamities of every sort, were produced by a direct invisible agency of Satan, and who had full faith in astrology, was led by the strange and frightful character of the times, and by singular appearances in the heavens, to believe that the end of the world was at hand. After describing the Northern Lights, as they appeared on a certain evening, he says, "God knoweth what these signify." At another time, referring to the same and to a meteor which was seen at Breslau, and to some other peculiar appearances in the heavens, he says, "I believe these

signify that the end of the world is at the door."
This opinion is often repeated in his letters, but it
is unnecessary to accumulate quotations.

The following letter to Matthias, Bishop of
Dantzic, gives us a more pleasing view : "Reverend
father and venerable in the Lord, your letters and
present were very agreeable and acceptable to me in
the Lord, since I thereby learned that, in your old
age and before the end of life, you have been capti-
vated and illuminated by the gospel of Christ, which
I regard as the miraculous grace of God, knowing
as I do how dignitaries of your order are wont to
resist the word of God. The Lord Jesus, who hath
begun a good work, perfect it. As you have a desire to see me, so it would give me in turn great
joy in Christ to see your venerable gray hairs confessing Christ amidst this herd of hostile dignitaries,
who dare to oppose. It is not in my power, however, to go to see you. May God, who is able to
do it, grant that we may meet at least once ; and
may he mercifully bless and keep you."

A letter to Amsdorf, dated May 31, 1529, breathes
the same pure spirit of love. He there says : "There
is nothing new with us which you do not already
know. These ministers of the word at Goslar, [the
old capital of Hanover,] I send to you, that they
may relate to you the condition of the church there.
I beg you to receive, and hear them kindly. They
seem to be good men, who deserve the favour of the
pious; and it is meet for you to know these things,
inasmuch as you first laid the foundations of piety
there, and have not unsuccessfully built thereon.
It will animate these trembling believers to perceive our agreement and joy in this matter ; and
it will confound Satan and his instruments, or, at

least, impede them. Therefore cherish and comfort them in the bowels of Christ. They who dread offences and are so solicitous for peace cannot but have great confidence in Christ."

To the Christians in Goslar he wrote in the same spirit, saying, "I rejoice over you from the heart, and pray God, the Father of all grace, to uphold and prosper you in this way." June 14, Luther wrote to Justus Jonas, who was then occupied abroad in the work of visitation thus : "The wall of your house [in the west part of the town] must wait for bricks to be made in the senate's furnace. We have betrothed Dr. Augustin [Schurf's] sister to [professor] Milich. Bugenhagen writes that he will soon return [from Hamburg,] and when he cometh, I [his substitute as city preacher] can act with you in the work of visitation, if it shall still be necessary. Philip [Melancthon] is wasting away under his anxiety for the church and the state."

How perfectly overwhelmed Luther was with labours and cares, may be learned from the closing part of a letter to Link, in which he says, "You complain in your last letter that I have not replied to your inquiry. Be not surprised. If you wish for a reply, write and admonish me again. For I am every day so overwhelmed with letters, that my table, benches, foot-stools, desks, windows, cases, boards and every thing are full of letters, inquiries, causes, complaints, petitions, &c. On me falleth the whole weight of the church and the state, as neither the ecclesiastics nor magistrates perform their duties. You at Nüremberg sit and play in Paradise, because you have magistrates who provide all things for you to enjoy in security and peace."

We find another striking proof that Luther took

a deep interest in education, and that his opinion was of great weight on this subject, in the following instructive letter, written to Margrave George of Brandenburg, July 18, 1529.: "I have long delayed, though unwillingly, to reply to you, for at first I had not the time, when the messenger was here, and afterward I had no way to send. . . . But now I will tell you what Melancthon and myself, upon mature consideration, think best to be done.

"First, we think the cloisters and foundations may continue to stand till their inmates die out. . . . Secondly, it would be exceedingly well to establish in one or two places in the principality a learned school, in which shall be taught, not only the Holy Scriptures, but law, and all the arts, from whence preachers, pastors, clerks, counsellors, &c. may be taken for the whole principality. To this object should the income of the cloisters and other religious foundations be applied, so as to give an honourable support to learned men, two in theology, two in law, one in medicine, one in mathematics, and four or five for grammar, logic, rhetoric, &c. . . . Thirdly, in all the towns and villages good schools for children should be established, from which those who are adapted to higher studies might be taken and trained up for the public."

For a present of garments from the elector, Luther makes this singular acknowledgment, under date of August 17: "I have long delayed to thank your grace for the clothes and garments which were sent to me. I humbly beseech your grace not to believe those who represent that I am in want. I have, alas! more, especially from your grace, than I can with good conscience receive. It is not meet for me, a preacher, to have abundance, neither do I desire it. Therefore, when I perceive your grace's too great liberality to me, I am not without fear; for I do not wish to be found here in this life among those to whom Christ saith, 'Wo! unto you that are rich, for ye have received your consolation.' And, furthermore, to speak after a worldly manner, I desire not to be burdensome to your grace, knowing you have so many occasions to give, that you cannot have much to spare; for, if there be too much, it rendeth the sack. Though the brown cloth would of itself be too much, yet I will, out of gratitude and honour to your grace, wear the black garment also, notwithstanding it is too valuable, so that I would never wear it, if it were not a present from your grace. I beg you, therefore, wait till I complain and ask, so that I may not, by your forwardness to me, be prevented from begging for others, who are far more worthy of such favours. For your grace hath already done too much for me. May Christ graciously and abundantly repay it."

We must not omit to give, at least one specimen out of a hundred, of Luther's contempt for the Zwinglian party, with what reason the reader can judge. While at Marburg to see if there could be a union formed with that party, he wrote to his wife this charitable letter: "Dear lord Katy, know that our friendly colloquy at Marburg is ended, and that we were nearly agreed in all points, save that the other party will recognise nothing but bread in the supper, and will not admit that Christ is present except spiritually. To-day the land-grave trieth to see if we cannot be agreed, or, if not agreed, that we recognise each other as brethren and members of Christ　He laboureth

hard for this; but we want nothing of this brother-
ing and fellowship, though we are for peace and
good-will. . . . Say to Bugenhagen the best arguments were those of Zwingle, 'That a body cannot
exist without space; therefore the body of Christ
is not in the bread;' and of Œcolampadius, 'That
the sacrament is a *symbol* of the body of Christ.'
I think God hath blinded them that they could
bring forward nothing better. I have much to do,
and the messenger is in haste. Say good night to
all, and pray for us. We are all safe and sound,
and live like princes. Kiss Lene and Jonny for
me."

Luther's father, who had reached to an advanced
age, was taken ill, and his sickness was the occasion
of a letter from his son, full of tenderness and love.
He begins thus: "To my dear father, John Luther,
citizen of Mansfeld, grace and peace in Christ Jesus
our Lord and Saviour, Amen. Dear father, my
brother Jacob hath written to me how that you are
dangerously sick. Since the air now is bad, and it is
everywhere dangerous, and your time of life is such,
I am made very anxious about you. For though
God hath given you a firm and strong body and
hitherto preserved it, yet your age [probably not
less than eighty] giveth me, at this time, anxious
thoughts, although, aside from such things, none
of us are sure of life, or ought to be. I should be,
beyond expression, glad to visit you personally, but
my good friends oppose and have dissuaded me, and
I myself must remember that I ought not to rush
into danger, presuming on God; for you know what
kind of favour I have, from both lords and peasants.
It would be the greatest joy to me if it were possible for you and mother to come hither to us, which

my Katy desireth with tears, as do we all. I have therefore sent [my servant] Cyriac to you to see whether your health will allow you to come. For in what way soever God shall dispose of you, whether for this life, or for another, I desire heartily, as I ought, to be present with you, and, by filial faithfulness and attention, according to the fifth commandment, to show myself thankful unto God and unto you." He then goes on to comfort his father with "those divine truths which God had already given him to know," and to express the desire and hope that God would " carry on to its completion, in the life to come, the work which had been begun in him." " For," he adds, " he hath already sealed in you these doctrines and this faith, and confirmed them by signs, inasmuch as you have with us all suffered much abuse, reproach, scorn, contempt, hatred, enmity and peril."

Luther has been accused of inhumanity toward the Anabaptists; and when we compare him with the mild Brentz, who opposed putting them to death for their sentiments, and with religious men of modern times, we must, in part at least, admit the charge. But in this he was not alone. Most of the Reformers, having been brought up in the papal church, were led to countenance, to some extent, her revolting doctrines and practices in respect to those whom she denounced as heretics. They conscientiously held opinions which would be repudiated by all enlightened Christians at the present day. Without dwelling on these painful details, we will adduce one brief letter, as giving a fair specimen of Luther's feelings, and thus dismiss the subject. The letter is addressed to Menius and Myconius in 1530. " I am pleased," he says, "that you intend to publish a book against the Anabaptists as soon as possible. Since they are not only blasphemous, but also seditious men, let the sword exercise its right over them. For this is the will of God, that he shall have judgment who resisteth the power. Let us not, therefore, think better of these men than God himself and all the saints have done." Yes, the saints made themselves like unto God, and assumed the prerogative, not only of punishing those who were actually guilty of sedition, but of putting to death heretics whose sentiments were judged to be seditious in their tendency.

The diet of Augsburg, so important in the history of the Reformation, is first alluded to by Luther, in a letter to Justus Jonas, March 14, 1530, in these words: "The elector hath written to us, that is, to you, Bugenhagen, Melancthon and myself, instructing us to lay all other business aside and come together, and, before next Sunday, prepare whatever is necessary for the coming diet of April 8. For the Emperor Charles will come thither in person, as he writeth in his mandate, to adjust, in a friendly manner, all our religious differences. Wherefore, though you are absent, we, the other three, shall do to-day and to-morrow what we can. It will be your duty, in order to comply with the will of the elector, to put your work [of visitation] into the hands of your associates, and be with us here to-morrow. Every thing must be hastened. May Christ breathe upon us, that all things may be done to his glory."

He says to another friend, April 2: "I am about to go as far as Coburg with the elector. Melancthon and Jonas will also go, and we shall wait there till it shall be known what will be undertaken at Augsburg." The same day he writes to his young friend Cordatus, who had experienced much trouble at Zwickau, and was now, moreover, afflicted with the loss of a son : "As to what I hear of your purpose to hasten away to the diet, I would say, I disapprove of it altogether. First, I have not been cited thither, but I am to go with the elector only to the border of his dominions. Secondly, the cause of the gospel will be managed in a very dilatory way, if at all ; for princes are not wont to act with despatch in matters of religion ; and the Turkish question will, moreover, have the precedence there. You might, if you should wish, make a flying excursion thither, at a suitable time, and let your Zwickau men get a little cool and gentle. Salute the companion of your grief, and endeavour to rejoice rather in a living Christ than mourn over a son deceased, or rather living, but removed. My Katy and all the family salute you."

His next letter is dated at Coburg, April 18, and directed to Hausmann, pastor at Zwickau : "Say to Cordatus," he writes, "that we still remain here, not knowing when we shall proceed farther. Yesterday, a messenger and letters reached us, informing us that the emperor was at Mantua, where he was to pass the festival of Easter. It is, moreover, said, that the Papists are labouring to prevent the meeting of the diet, out of fear that it will pass decisions against them. The pope is angry with the emperor for wishing to meddle with ecclesiastical affairs, and to give the parties a hearing ; for they had hoped he would act the part of executioner for them, and restore all things. They wish not to change, nor to lose any thing. nor even to be

judged or examined, but simply that we be condemned or destroyed, and they reinstated, and thus
destroyed. So they will go to utter ruin. . . . I
am commanded by the elector to remain at Coburg,
I know not why, while the rest proceed to the diet
Thus, every thing groweth, from day to day, more
and more uncertain."

To Melancthon, after he had left Coburg for
Augsburg, Luther writes: "We have come at length
to our Sinai, my dear Philip; but we will make of
this Sinai a Zion, and build here three tabernacles,
one for the Psalms, one for the Prophets, and one
for Æsop, [three works to be prepared for the
press.] But this last is temporal. The place is
exceedingly lovely and convenient for study, save
that your absence maketh it gloomy. . . . I pray
Christ to give you quiet sleep, and to liberate and
keep your heart from cares, that is, from Satan's
fiery darts. These things I write because of my
leisure, for I have not yet received my desk, papers,
&c., nor have I seen either of the keepers. Nothing is wanting to make the solitude complete.
That immense building which towers over the whole
fortress is all ours, with the keys to all the apart-
ments. More than thirty persons are said to take
their food here, of whom twelve are night guards,
and two watchmen in the different towers. But
what of all this? Why, simply, that I have nothing else to write."

A mind like Luther's could not remain inactive,
and, for want of other employment, he suffered his
fancy to picture to itself a diet of birds, as he saw
them congregate before his window, much as he saw
persecuting bishops in the huntsmen and hounds
while engaged in the chase at Wartburg. The reader

will easily recognise the satire. The sportive letter which we are about to present was addressed to his table companions at Wittenberg, and reads thus: "Grace and peace in Christ, dear friends. I have received your joint letter, and learned how you all are. That you may know, in turn, how things are here, I give you to understand that we, that is, I, Master Veit Dietrich and Cyriac, do not go to the Augsburg diet, though we are attending another one in this place. There is, directly before my window, a grove where the jackdaws and ravens have appointed a diet; and there is such a coming and going, and such a hubbub, day and night, that you would think them all tipsy. Old and young keep up such a cackling, that I wonder how their breath holds out so long. I should like to know if there are any of these nobles and knights with you, for it seemeth to me that all in the world are gathered together here. I have not yet seen their emperor, but the nobles and great ones are all the time moving and frisking before us; not gayly attired, but of one uniform colour, all black and all gray-eyed. They all sing the same song, though with the pleasing diversity of young and old, great and small. They pay no regard to the great palace and hall, for their hall hath the high blue heavens for its ceiling, the ground for its floor, the beautiful green branches for its panelling, and the ends of the world for its walls. They don't trouble themselves about horses and wagons, for they have winged wheels wherewith they escape from fire-arms. They are great and mighty lords; but to what decisions they come I know not. But, so far as I can learn through an interpreter, they meditate a mighty crusade against wheat, barley, oats, malt, and all kinds of corn and grain, and there is here many a hero, who will perform great deeds. . . . I consider all these nothing but the sophists and Papists, with their preachers and secretaries, and must have them all before me thus at once, that I may hear their lovely voices and their preaching, and see how useful a class they are, to devour all that the earth bringeth forth, and cackle for it a long while."

Perhaps Luther and his family were nowhere more intimate than with the family of Jonas. The wife of this friend of Luther seems to have been the one to whom all domestic anxieties and interests were freely unbosomed by Luther and his household. On the 24th of April, 1530, while at Coburg, midway between her, at Wittenberg, and Jonas, now at Augsburg, he wrote to her as follows: "Dear friend, I have read your letter to your husband, and was glad to learn that God hath given you a more cheerful mind touching your delicate situation, and the injury which has befallen your house. Your husband is not so cheerful, but is very anxious for you, and is quite angry and scoldeth about the breaking of the wall, and is as near to being offended with Mr. Blank as your house is near to his. But be not troubled; there will be no difficulty about the house, for an arrangement is already made to remedy the evil. . . . You will, I think, be blessed with a daughter, they have now become so seldom and are so shy, a single house not being large enough for them; just as their mothers can hardly get along with a husband and the whole world besides. Salute your dear [son] Justus, the grandmother, and accept a salutation for yourself." The child alluded to died in May, while the father was still at Augsburg. The following letter to Melancthon on the occasion explains itself: "I have directed this letter to be delivered to you separately, for there was no other way of broaching the matter to Justus Jonas. See that in the gentlest way possible he be informed of the loss of his infant child. His wife and servant have written to him that the child is ill, but in language removed from all ideas of death. My wife writeth that she was present when it died. It was with the same disease that carried off her little Frederic. . . . I was unwilling to write to him about it, lest his sorrow should be too great; and I wish to keep it back from him, and write him another time. Perhaps this is the hour when our gospel is also in child-birth; but we will, when the sorrow is over, rejoice that a man is born into the world. If our word is true, which the rage and fury of our enemies sufficiently declare, our cause is safe. . . . Do you, therefore, solace the man, who so sinketh in worldly trouble, that he may be able to rejoice while we are sad." A few days later, he writes a letter of condolence to Jonas, full of tenderness, saying, among many other things, "You have many great blessings to set over against this calamity," and then mentions the excellent character of his wife.

Luther's engagements and state of mind were such that he was disinclined to see so many visitors as were constantly calling upon him. "Yesterday," says he to Melancthon, under date of June 2, "John Reineck of Mansfeld [his old school companion at Magdeburg] and George Römer were here; and to-day Argula von Staufen. As I perceive that this place will be too much frequented, I am determined, after the manner of your Stromer, to pretend to go away, or actually go for a single day, that the report may go out that I am no longer here. Do you and your friends, therefore, tell people not to call on me so much. I wish to be secluded."

Near the end of May, Luther's father died. With what feelings he received the intelligence we may best learn from his own words in a letter to Melancthon: "To-day," he there remarks, "John Reineck hath written to me that my dearest father departed this life, Sunday, the 29th of May. This death hath plunged me into deep sorrow, being affected not only by nature, but by the most tender love, for through him my Creator gave me whatsoever I am and have. And though what he writeth to me, namely, that 'strong in the faith of Christ, he sweetly fell asleep,' nevertheless my sorrow for him and the memory of his most delicious intercourse shake my whole frame. . . . I now succeed next in the family name, and am the senior Luther in my family. . . . It is right and fit that I, a son, should mourn for such a father, . . . by whose sweat I was supported and made whatsoever I am. I rejoice that he lived in these times, when he could behold the light of truth."

At a later period when, for four days, he could, as he says, neither read nor write, he chanced to find in the ditch a mutilated piece of music in three parts. He corrected and altered it, added a fourth part, and composed words for it, and sportively sent it to his friend, Agricola, to show to his chorister as the song with which the emperor and his brother were greeted on their entrance into Augsburg. He amused himself by seeing whether he could thus mislead the chorister, and, to make the attempt the more successful, he requested Agricola to praise the piece.

During Luther's absence, a student by the name of Weller became private tutor to his son John, now

four years old. To him Luther wrote, June 19
"I have received your two letters, both of which
are very agreeable, but the last by far the most so,
because, in it, you write concerning my John, saying that you have become his teacher, and that he
is a sedulous and diligent pupil. I wish I could
make you a suitable return, but what I cannot, may
Christ repay. Master Dietrich hath signified to me
that you have a spirit of melancholy, which is very
hurtful to a young man."

If we consider what the habits of our fathers
were, as compared with those of most Christians of
the present day, in respect to temperance, we shall
hardly expect to find Luther or any man of that age
conforming to all our stricter views or practices in
this regard. There was indeed a society formed
among the noblemen of Austria against drunken-
ness and profane swearing in the year 1517. But
it was only when a member drank more than seven
glasses of wine at one dinner that he was regarded
as a transgressor, and was then to pay the fine of a
horse. Luther drank wine and beer habitually, but
with moderation. He one time apologizes to some
young men present for taking wine in the evening,
by saying that old men sometimes need it to induce
sleep. At Coburg, he wrote, June 19, to a friend:
"I am well and live splendidly, save that I have
for a month had, not a tinkling, but a thundering
in my head, whether it be from the wine, or whether
Satan thus playeth his game with me. I have
finished Ezekiel, and now shall proceed to translate
the other Prophets. Be diligent both you and the
church in praying for the elector. Pray for him
and for the whole diet, and be assured that prayer
is not in vain The power thereof is manifest and

great" This was the time that tested the character of the Elector John, and well did it pass the ordeal. An expression of Luther's, the following January, states more explicitly one cause of his illness. "The Wittenberg beer," he says, "hath not yet conquered the disease of the head contracted at Coburg by the old wine. I must therefore moderate my labours, and give my head its Sabbaths, a great evil to me and to the printers." He was then superintending the printing of the various works prepared at Coburg.

Although Luther approved of Melancthon's draft of the Augsburg Confession, and said of it, in a letter to the elector, "It pleaseth me exceedingly well. I know not what improvement or change to make, nor would any alteration of mine be in place, for I cannot step so softly and gently;" yet he disapproved of Melancthon's caution and prudence as excessive. Therefore he writes to Jonas, (June 20 :) "I greatly and wonderfully exult in the abundant grace of God, in that our elector is of so firm and calm a mind. I think our prayers for him have been heard. . . . This my joy is increased as I learn that you also are confident in God against this fury of Satan, [the violent proceedings of the diet.] Melancthon is swayed by his philosophy, and by nothing else; for he will have the whole matter in his own hand. . . . I would not have it in mine, nor would it be best. I have had much in my own hand, and lost it all, and saved nothing. But what I have put out of my hands, [and into the hand of the Lord,] that have I secured and saved. . . . I have here [in Coburg] become a new pupil of the decalogue, and am making myself a boy again, and learning it by heart. . . . I begin to consider the decalogue as the logic of the gospel, and the gospel as the rhetoric of the decalogue; and Christ as having all that is in Moses, though Moses hath not all that is in Christ." To Brentz, he expressed his feelings (June 30) more fully in regard to Melancthon's over-much solicitude. "From your letters, and from those of Melancthon and others, my Brentz," he observes, "I perceive that you are all in like manner troubled by that idolatrous diet. It is the example of Melancthon that so affecteth you. For he is anxious for the public peace and tranquillity, and that piously too; but his zeal is not according to knowledge. Just as if our forefathers by their care and solicitude made us what we are, and not rather the counsel of God alone, who will be Creator after us, as he was before us. He will not die with us, or cease to be God, governing the thoughts of men. . . . These things I write to you and to others that, by the persuasion of Brück, [Pontanus,] or some other one of you, Melancthon may cease to desire to be ruler of the world, that is, to excruciate himself. If I should die, or be slain by the Papists, I shall still mightily defend our posterity, and be revenged upon those ferocious beasts enough, and more than I desire; for I know that there will be one to say, 'Where is thy brother Abel?' and he will make them fugitives in the earth. . . . If there is a God, we shall live not only here, but where he liveth also. And if this is so, what, I ask, are all these furious threats of idols, which are already, not barely mortal, but dead? He who created me will be the father of my son, the husband of my wife, the ruler of the people, the preacher of the parish, and will be, after I am dead, more and better than I am while alive."

The important and yet delicate relations which the two reformers, Luther and Melancthon, sustained to each other, are perhaps nowhere more apparent than in the letter of the former to the latter, written June 29, 1530. Neither the gentle influence of Melancthon upon Luther, nor the invigorating, emboldening influence of Luther upon Melancthon, could safely have been dispensed with. But, at this time, unfortunately, both were in a state of nervous excitement and irritability.

"I have read your rhetoric," says Luther, "by which you excuse your silence to me. In the mean time, I have written to you twice, explaining the cause of my silence. To-day I have received your last letter, in which you admonish me of your labours, perils and tears, so that I seem unworthily to add sorrow to sorrow by my silence, as if I were ignorant of these things, or were sitting here upon a bed of roses, not bearing your cares with you. Unless your letter had reached me last night, . . . I should have sent you a messenger at my own expense. . . . I have received your Apology, [the Augsburg Confession,] and wonder what you wish or desire,—what and how much is to be conceded to the Papists. How much is to be yielded to the elector, if he is in danger, is another question. For myself, more than enough is already conceded in the Apology; and if they refuse this, I see not how any thing more can be conceded, unless I can see better reasons and clearer passages of Scripture than I have yet seen. I am occupied with this subject day and night, thinking, revolving, reasoning and surveying the whole Bible, and my assurance in our doctrine increaseth, and I am more and more confirmed, so that, God helping me, I will suffer nothing more to be

taken from it, come what may. . . . I am not pleased
with your saying in your letter, that you 'follow
my authority.' I do not wish to be, or to be called
an authority in this cause; and even if it could be
so explained, I do not like the term. If it be not,
at the same time, equally your cause, I am unwilling
it should be said to be mine and imposed upon you.
If it be mine, I will act for myself. . . . It is the
result and issue of this cause that troubleth you,
because you cannot grasp it. If you could grasp it,
I would have nothing to do with it, much less be
the author of it. God hath put it into that chapter
which is not included in your rhetoric nor philosophy. That chapter is called faith, in which are
placed all those things 'which are not seen and do
not appear;' and if any one attempt to render them
visible, apparent and comprehensible, as you do, he
will have troubles and tears as the reward of his
labour, such as you now complain of, notwithstanding all our persuasions.

"*Postscript.* After closing my letter, the thought
hath occurred to me, that I might seem to you not
to have replied specifially to your inquiries, how
much and how far we should concede to our opponents. But your inquiries are general; you do not
signify what and how much you think will be demanded of us. I am ready, as I have always said,
to concede every thing, if only the gospel be left
free unto us. But any thing repugnant to the gospel, I cannot concede."

He also said, "I wish I could be allowed to come
to you; I burn with desire to come unbidden and
uninvited." The elector knew why he would have
Luther not so far from the diet as Wittenberg, nor
so near as Augsburg.

The first paragraph of the above letter is well interpreted by another, written in a more playful mood, the day after, to Spalatin. Five long letters to his friends at Augsburg, to Brentz, to Spalatin, to Agricola, to Melancthon, and to the elector, bear date June 30. To Spalatin he writes: "You said you would not suffer yourself to be called dilatory in correspondence, and yet you are obliged to do so. You promised me and the Wittenberg friends that you would write abundantly by the messenger of Jonas and of Dr. Apel, so that we might both expect and fear a whole forest of letters, which should be more obstreperous than my jackdaws. But when the messenger came, bringing letters from Jonas alone for Wittenberg, I said, 'Do you bring any letters for me?' Reply, 'No.' 'How is it with the men there?' Answer, 'Well.' Of this case I have just made complaint to Melancthon. Afterward came a messenger on horseback sent to Torgau, with letters from the elector. I asked him, 'Do you bring any letters for me?' Reply, 'No.' 'How is it with the men there?' Reply, 'Well.' Then, when a wagon was going to Augsburg with flour, I wrote again to Melancthon, and that returned bringing no letters. Now I began to have gloomy thoughts, and to suspect you wished to conceal something from me. A fourth person came. I asked him, 'Do you bring me any letters?' Reply, 'No.' 'How is it with the men there?' Answer, 'Well.' I will not tell you how often our questor has, in the mean time, had letters from his brother Falkenstein, while we have been kept for more than three weeks hungering and thirsting by the favour of your silence. From his letters have I been obliged to learn what I would know. Now I ask if you would not call me a dilatory correspondent, if I were to do so to you. I confess I was offended and alarmed, knowing, as I did, the anxiety of Melancthon and the trials of the elector. . . . But enough of this. Do not dispute, nor think any more about it."

If we desire still more light on this temporary ruffling of the feelings of the two reformers, it can be found in the letters of Melancthon and others. On the 25th of June, he wrote to Luther: "The letter in which you complain of my silence giveth me great pain. I have written very fully every week. I know not how it happeneth that this evil should be added to the great and distressing cares which I have in this place, namely, that I should be judged so much in fault that you will not write to me." The next day, he wrote to Veit Dietrich, [Vitus Theodorus :] "I cannot express how much it distresseth me that, in your letter, you say the doctor is so angry with me that he will not even read my letters. You know how I am situated, and in what peril we all stand. We here are in greatest need of his counsel and consolation. I have, therefore, hired a special messenger to take this letter, that I may appease him and make some inquiries. I have left it unsealed, in order that you may read it and repeat it to him, if he will not read it." The letter to Luther commences thus: "I am here in a wretched state of anxiety and in perpetual tears. Besides this, a strange consternation hath to-day seized my mind on reading Dietrich's letter, in which he saith you are so angry, &c. . . . I will not, my father, exaggerate my sorrow to you; but I beg you to consider what is my condition, and what are my perils, where I have no solace but in your consolations. Every day the sophists and monks are flocking to the emperor to imbitter him against me. The bishops already hate me. Friends, if I ever had any, are now away. Alone and deserted, I am here struggling with great dangers. I entreat you to consider either me, who follow your authority in the most important matters, or the public, and not refuse to read my letters and reply, both that you may govern my conduct and comfort me." Osiander wrote to his Nüremberg friends, July 4, saying, among other things: "Melancthon, worn out and exhausted with many labours, vigils and cares, is sometimes troubled with melancholy and almost desperation, without any good reason, which greatly dejecteth most of our party. I soon perceived, and learned from others, that he hath a natural inclination to melancholy. In such a state of mind, he thinketh, speaketh, writeth and acteth, which doth not help our cause, so that he must be watched and chided, that he do nothing which will make us all repent. Luther, knowing this, took occasion to write pungently to him, and to exhort others to chide him." Melancthon thanks Luther, July 8, for answering his letters, and from that time the current of good feeling flows clear again.

Luther had just finished his commentary on the 118th Psalm, which he dedicated to Frederic, abbot at Nüremberg, of whom mention has been already made. In the dedicatory epistle, dated July 1, he says: "Venerable and dear friend and patron, I have desired to manifest my gratitude for your love and favour; but, in worldly estate, I am a poor beggar; and had I ever so much, your condition is such that I could effect but little. I have, therefore, turned to my wealth, my treasure, and taken from it my favourite psalm. I have put my thoughts upon it on paper, because I had so much leisure here in my desert, and because I wished, at times, to rest and relieve my mind from severer labours, namely, the complete translation of the Prophets, which I hope soon to finish. These thoughts of mine I have desired to dedicate and present to you, having nothing better to give. Though some may regard it a profuse and, perhaps, useless expectoration, yet I am sure it containeth nothing evil or unchristian. For it is my psalm, the one I love. Though all the psalms and the whole Bible are very dear to me, as my only consolation and life, still I am wonderfully attached to this psalm, so that I may call it mine. For it hath often done me great service, and helped me out of many sore troubles, when neither emperors, kings, sages, nor saints could have helped me. I value it more than I should the favour, wealth and power of the pope, the Turks, the emperor and all the world; and I would not exchange this psalm for them all together."

To Spengler he thus describes the device which he had decided to have for his seal: "First, a black cross in a heart of the natural colour, to remind me that faith in him who died on the cross saveth us. . . . Though the cross is black, mortifieth and giveth pain, still it leaveth the heart in its own colour, doth not destroy nature, doth not kill, but maketh alive. . . . Such a heart is enveloped in a white rose, to show that faith giveth joy, comfort and peace. It is set in a white rose, and not a red one, because it giveth peace and joy not as the world giveth. . . . This rose is placed in an azure field, to signify that such spiritual joy is the beginning of future heavenly joy, already apprehended and included in hope, but not yet manifest. In the azure field is a gold ring, to signify that the bliss of heaven is everlasting, and the most precious of all possessions, as gold is the most precious metal."

SECTION II.—*From the Diet of Augsburg in* 1530 *to Luther's Death in* 1546.

THE purpose for which the emperor had summoned the diet was not answered. On his part, there was to be seen nothing of that clemency mentioned in his summons, but, on the contrary, a close adhesion to the papal party, and a menacing severity toward the Protestants, and most of all toward the Elector of Saxony. But the latter, together with Philip, Landgrave of Hesse, manifested a firmness and courage superior to all such intimidations. Indeed, the excessive violence of the emperor and the severity of the decision of the diet, both bound the Protestant princes more closely together, and provoked an opposition, which, when organized at successive conventions at Smalcald, became too powerful to be despised, and the emperor, at last, saw the necessity of coming to an agreement with them. At the Nüremberg pacification, in 1532, articles were agreed upon and signed by both parties.

The course pursued by Luther during this busy period of two years, in which he was consulted in respect to all the public measures adopted by the Protestant statesmen, was somewhat peculiar, presenting a singular compound of opinionated pertinacity and of submissive compliance. In his uncharitableness toward the Zwinglian party, he persisted so far as to exclude them from any participa-

tion in the Protestant cause, neither admitting them
as associates at Augsburg, nor as members of the
Smalcald confederacy for mutual protection and
defence.   The Landgrave Philip, who sympathized
with Zwingle in his view, exhausted all his influence
upon Luther, in endeavouring to persuade him that
the differences of opinion which prevailed respecting
the Lord's supper were not so fundamental as to
require the utter rejection of the Swiss churches
But it was all in vain.   Luther's pious abhorrence
of their doctrines was as deeply and as immovably
fixed in his mind as was that against the Anabaptists.
On the other hand, he maintained that the Protestant rulers had no right to combine together for
mutual defence, if the emperor should make war
upon them for their religion.   When the Saxon
jurists decided, that, according to the constitutional
principles of the empire, the electors and other
princes had, clearly, the right to protect themselves
against the illegal encroachments of emperors, Luther merely admitted that it might be so according
to the civil law; but adhered to his original opinion
in a theological point of view.   But what is still
more strange, he resisted nearly all the statesmen
of his own party, who insisted, that, not only those
who had already embraced the Protestan. doctrines
but those who should hereafter embrace them,
ought to have their rights secured in the articles of
pacification with the emperor.   Luther said it was
but reasonable that the emperor should insist
on excluding the latter from the benefits of the
articles of agreement.   If men will not come out
and show themselves openly in times of danger,
they are not entitled, he maintained, to the quiet
and security acquired by others at their peril, and

so he prevailed against the landgrave, who main
tained the contrary.   However great we may admit
the urgency to have been to secure a peace with
the emperor, and to avoid a religious war, the principle here avowed by Luther savours little of that
brotherly love which is an essential part of true
religion.

The emperor was obliged to be often absent from
Germany, in order to attend to his affairs in Spain
and Italy.   As he had taken decided ground against
the Protestants, and as the dukes of Bavaria were
jealous of the house of Austria, it seemed necessary to the emperor to have some one on whom he
could rely to protect his interests in Germany during his absence.   The Elector of Saxony was,
properly, the vicar of the empire ; but he was the
leader of the Protestants, and a league between
them and the disaffected Catholic dukes of Bavaria
might endanger the emperor's interests.   Charles
decided to secure the coronation of his brother
Ferdinand as King of Rome, the effect of which
would be to make him successor to the imperial
throne, thus establishing his own family in power,
and excluding the rival Bavarian family ; and also
to place the government of Germany in Ferdinand's hands, whenever he himself should have
occasion to be absent.   Luther, with less wisdom
and less knowledge of political affairs than the
advisers of the elector, advocated the propriety of
yielding this point to the emperor, greatly to the
grief of the elector.

The latter part of Luther's life is not susceptible
of the same treatment as the former.   It has less
unity, and must either be presented without a very
consecutive chain of events, or must be spread out

into a general history of the times, so widely as to lose the character of a biography. The choice between the two courses cannot, in the present work, be doubtful. Leaving, therefore, the tenor of general history, we revert to the narrative of events of a more personal character.

The irregular and harsh proceedings of the magistrates of Zwickau, in relation to the clergy of the place, were doubly wounding to Luther's feelings. He was grieved that such an example should be set to the newly-organized churches; and he almost regarded it as a personal injury that the pastor, Hausmann, his confidential friend, should be treated with such indignity. He, therefore, used his influence with the elector in favour of Hausmann's removal from "the beastly inhabitants of Zwickau" to a people of a more congenial spirit; and the result was, the settlement of his friend in Dessau, where he enjoyed the confidence of the princes of Anhalt.

In the same year, that is, in 1531, Luther was afflicted by the death of his mother. He was not able to visit her in her last illness, but wrote her an affectionate letter to confirm her faith and to prepare her mind for the event that was near at hand, and closed by saying, " All the children and my Katy pray for you. Some of them weep, and some eat and say, ' Grandmother is very sick.' The grace of God be with us all."

The next year was made one of sadness to Luther by the death of the Elector John, surnamed the Constant. He went to Schweinitz, a summer residence a few miles to the east of Wittenberg, for the purpose of indulging in the chase, and was taken suddenly ill. Luther, Melancthon and Schurf arrived a short time before his death. "Alas!" said Luther, "how a great prince dieth here alone, without the presence of a son, relative, or friend to witness his departure! The physicians say he died of the cramp. Just as children are born without sorrow, live without sorrow, and die without sorrow, so will our dear prince, at the last day, come to himself, as if fresh from the chase in the Lochau Forest, and will not be conscious of what happened to him." His son, John Frederic, then in his twenty-ninth year, succeeded him. Though a firm and faithful friend of the Reformation, and already conversant with public affairs, he had not the high qualities of wisdom and firmness which characterized his predecessors, Frederic and John.

Many of Luther's letters, written about this period, were letters of consolation to the afflicted, the tempted and the persecuted, or of warning to rulers and magistrates against disturbers of the public peace, particularly the Anabaptists, who were beginning, at Munster and other places, to lift their heads again. In 1533 and 1534, he was employed in preparing a new edition of his hymns, in completing his translation of the Bible, in comforting and aiding Christians who had been banished from Leipsic by Duke George, and in other labours of piety and charity.

Luther, from the beginning of his public career as a reformer, had always desired and demanded that a general and free council of the church should be held, before which both religious parties might bring their complaints for adjudication. The German diets had joined with Luther in this request, and even the emperor promised that such a council should be held. But the Roman pontiffs had opposed the project, or, if they seemed to yield, they required that it be held in Italy, be constituted and organized by the pope, and, moreover, that it decide the questions submitted to it by the traditions and usages of the church. The Protestants, on the contrary, demanded that the council should be held in Germany, where the troubles existed; that it should not be subject to the authority of the pope, but that he, as one of the parties, should be subject to the authority of the council; and that its decisions should be formed, not according to human traditions, but according to the word of God. Charles V., on his way to Spain in 1532, had an interview with the pope, Clement VII., on the subject, in consequence of which a papal ambassador and an imperial orator appeared with the proposal before the elector at Weimar, but were referred by him to the assembly of Protestant princes to be held the year following at Smalcald. At that meeting they received answer, as stated above, that the council must be held in Germany, that the pope must not be both party and judge, and that the Scriptures, and not human opinions, must be ultimate authority.

Two years later, in 1535, the project was renewed by Paul III., Clement's successor, and the elector asked the opinion of Luther whether any other answer should be given to the pope than that given before. Luther replied that he believed the whole matter to be a mere feint, and therefore was not disposed to trouble himself about the conditions. Luther had good reasons for such an opinion, for the previous proposal for a council on the part of the pope was undoubtedly made for no other purpose than that of preventing a German diet which, he feared, would meet to act on the same subject, at that unfavourable time, when the Protestant power was strong. The papal legate, Vergerio, came, in this instance, to Wittenberg, to hold an interview with Luther himself, and the morning after his arrival invited Luther and Bugenhagen to break fast. Early in the morning, Luther sent for a barber to prepare him for the occasion, who, when he had come, said, "How is it that you wish to be shaved so early." "I am to go," replied Luther, "to the legate of his holiness the pope, and I must adorn myself, so as to appear young; and the legate will then say to himself, 'Zounds! is Luther so young, and yet hath done so much mischief? What then will he yet do?'" When his head was dressed, he put on his best clothes, and laid his jewel, set in gold, around his neck. The barber said to him, "Doctor, that will be offensive to them." "For that reason I do it," said Luther; "they have conducted offensively enough toward us; and we must manage in this way with those serpents and foxes." "Go, then, doctor," said the barber, "in God's name, and the Lord be with you, that you may convert them." "That," said the doctor, "I shall not do; but it may be that I shall read them a good lesson, and let them go." He then mounted the carriage with Bugenhagen and drove off to the castle, to the legate. On the way, he smiled and said to his companion, "Here go the German pope and Cardinal Bugenhagen; these are God's instruments and artillery."

On arriving at the place, he was announced and immediately admitted and kindly received, and he greeted the legate in turn, but not with the high-sounding titles which were formerly used on such occasions. They soon began to speak of a council, and Luther said, "You are not in earnest about holding a council; it is only a trick; and if you were to hold one, it would concern itself only about cowls, shorn heads, meats, drinks, and such-like foolish things, and others still more useless, which we know, at the outset, to be nothing. But of faith and justification, and other useful and weighty matters, such as how believers may be united in spirit and in faith, you do not wish to confer, nor would it be for your interest. . . . But if you desire to have a council, very well: have one, and I will come, though I should know you would burn me at the stake." "Where?" answered the legate. "In what city will you have the council?" "Where you please," was the answer, "at Mantua, or Padua, or Florence, or wheresoever you please." "Will you come to Bologna?" said the legate. "To whom does that place belong?" inquired Luther. "To the pope." "Gracious Lord, hath the pope got his clutches on this city, too! Well, I will come," said Luther. The legate added, "The pope would not refuse to come to you at Wittenberg." "Well, then," said Luther, "let him come; we should like to see him." "How would you like to see him," replied the legate, "with an army or without?" "Just as best pleaseth him," said Luther; "we will be ready for either." Then the legate asked, "Do you consecrate priests?" "To be sure," said Luther, "for the pope will not consecrate or ordain any for us. Here you see a bishop, (pointing to Bugenhagen,) whom we have consecrated." After the interview was over, and when the legate was seated upon his horse, he said to Luther, "See that you are prepared for the council." Luther replied, "I will come, sir, with this neck of mine."

Through the influence of the Landgrave of Hesse

and Bucer, who were extremely desirous for the union of the two Protestant parties, efforts were made in 1534, 1535, and 1536, to agree upon articles of concord relating to the eucharist. The cities of Strasburg, Augsburg, Ulm, and Esslingen in particular, which were situated in the south-west of Germany, along the borders, between the Lutheran influence on the one side, and the Zwinglian on the other, were inclined to the extreme views of neither party, and were anxious that both should agree on some common intermediate ground. A convention was finally held at Wittenberg, May, 1536, for the purpose, and Luther succeeded in bringing the Upper Germans, as they were called, to subscribe to his views.

Toward the close of the year 1536, as the pope had proposed to the Protestants to hold a general council, the theologians of Wittenberg were directed by the elector to draw up articles in respect to it, which might be presented to the convention about to be held on that subject at Smalcald. This is the origin of the Smalcald Articles. Luther, Melancthon, Bugenhagen and others from Wittenberg attended this convention, which resulted in a refusal on the part of the Protestants to participate in the council. Luther and his companions, who went by the way of Grimma, Altenburg and Weimar, arrived at Smalcald, near the south-western border of Saxony, the 7th of January, 1537. The first week he had little to do, and complained that business proceeded so slowly. The second, he suffered so severely from the stone that he did not expect to live to return home. The elector, Melancthon, Spalatin and Myconius were often at his bed-side The elector said to him : "If, contrary to our hopes,

it be the will of God to take you from us, be not
concerned about your wife and children, for they
shall be my wife and children." Getting no relief
for more than a week, he decided to be removed
from Smalcald, as medicines could not be procured
there.   At Tambach, he experienced relief; but
while at Gotha he had a return of his excruciating
pains, and six stones, one of nearly the size of a
bean, passed from him.   He was able to proceed to
Erfurt, and then, after a pause, to Weimar.   At Altenburg, he stopped at the house of Spalatin.   Melancthon wrote afterward from Grimma that Luther
had some rest and could take a little food ; and, after
a little more than two weeks from the time of leaving
Smalcald, he reached home in extreme weakness.

The following year was imbittered by one of the
severest trials which Luther had been called to endure.   Agricola, of Eisleben, one of his dearest
and most confidential friends, led on, perhaps, by
some of Luther's unguarded and unadvised expressions, became an avowed Antinomian, and maintained
that Christians had nothing to do with the law of
God, but were to concern themselves simply with
Christ crucified.   The enemies of Luther rejoiced
in this new schism, and maintained that it was the
legitimate fruit of his doctrines.   He wrote six
elaborate disputations in the course of four years to
disprove the positions of Agricola, and took from him
the license to preach which he had formerly given him.

For twenty years, ever since the Leipsic Disputation in 1519, Duke George had been among the
bitterest of Luther's enemies.   He imprisoned and
put to death Luther's followers, and at one time
banished eight hundred souls from Leipsic.   But,
connected as his territories were with those of the

elector, it was impossible to keep them free from the influence of the Reformation. Even his brother Henry, who held his court at Freiberg, favoured the evangelical doctrines. Finally, Prince John, son of the duke, on whom he relied for the maintenance of the Catholic faith after his death, died before him, and afterward another son; and the Protestant Henry was the next heir to the throne. Just at the time that a dangerous league of Catholic princes was expected to open an attack upon the Protestants, George, a leader among them, suddenly died, and all their plans were destroyed in a moment.

Luther and his associates were now called upon by Duke Henry of Saxony to introduce the Reformation into his dominions, beginning at Leipsic. Luther preached his first sermon on this occasion, May 24, 1539, in the chapel of the same palace where, twenty years before, he had held his debate with Eck. This was in fulfilment of his own prediction:—"I see, that Duke George will not cease opposing the word of God and the poor Lutherans. But I shall live to see him and his whole family perish, and shall one day preach God's word in Leipsic." The next day, when he preached in St. Nicholas' church, there was such a crowd that all the space about the pillars and railings and passages was full, and many stood out of doors and heard him through the windows. The hearers fell upon their knees, and with tears thanked God that the day of their deliverance had come!

It was at the close of the same year, that the unhappy consultations commenced about the bigamy of the Landgrave of Hesse. Luther and Melancthon were involved in inextricable difficulties by the false principles on which they suffered themselves to act.

That they acted hypocritically, out of fear of offending the landgrave, as has often been said, is hardly
credible; that they were misled by their ill-advised
casuistry, is but too evident. Nothing was ever
thrown into their teeth with more bitterness and scorn
by the Catholics, than their secret approval of this
flagrant violation of Christian morals. A sufficient
apology for their conduct in the unhappy affair cannot be given. It so wore upon Melancthon's feelings as to bring on a sickness which came very near
proving fatal.

Conventions, conferences and diets were still held,
during the next succeeding two or three years, at
Smalcald, Worms, Ratisbon and Spire, to settle the
difficulties between the Catholics and Protestants;
but Luther, who was tired of these useless endeavours, excused himself from attending them, and
the task was imposed upon Melancthon and others,
whom Luther aided by his counsels. The last years
of Luther's life were rendered cheerless, partly by
the death of many dear friends, and partly by the
unhappiness which sprung up between himself and
the living. These events will be sufficiently presented in the extracts from his letters which follow.

Although more than thirteen hundred octavo pages
of letters were written by Luther after his return
from Coburg in 1530, only a small part of them
relate to his private history. The remainder are
connected with public transactions, of so complicated
a character, that a full explanation of them would of
itself constitute a general history of Germany for
the times. Only a few selections, therefore, can, in
accordance with the plan of this work, find a place
here.

The third letter written after his return to Wittenberg was addressed to Amsdorf, his confidential friend. In this he says: "In complaining unto me of my silence, most excellent Amsdorf, you do but furnish me with an occasion of justly expostulating with you for yours, which hath been so obstinate and persevering. For when you did know of my solitude, you were not only wanting in commiseration, so as not to comfort me with your letters, but you added grief to grief, by afflicting me with perpetual silence. And now you even add to your sin by gratuitously reproving and censuring me for a fault, not my own, but yours. You compel me to suspect that you have meanwhile, perhaps, been made Archbishop of Magdeburg and Primate of Germany, so that you easily forget me in my poverty, and proudly censure me. Hence it cometh, I think, that you complain of my calling the Archbishop of Mainz 'most reverend father,' lest I may thereby detract somewhat from your honour; though I only used the language of courts, in which even ferocious demons are called 'gracious lords.' In one thing you gratify me, namely, in approving the books I have published this summer. More I could not write, by reason of my poor health; and on those which were written, only half, or a little more, of the time I was in my solitude, stolen with difficulty from sickness, could be employed. The printers proceeded with a pace equally slow, for they still have in press two books written long ago. Of the rest I will speak when you come to visit me, which I hope will be very soon, in order that we may refresh ourselves in each other's company, before we are separated for ever. For I feel that I am fast growing old, at least, am losing my strength. A messenger of Satan hath severely buffeted me. The Lord be with you in grace and truth."

The name of Jerome Weller has already been mentioned as a tutor to Luther's son, and as a young man of fine talents, but of melancholy disposition. His brother Peter was also a friend of Luther, and even lived in his house. To the former, in a state of despondency, Luther, whose experience well qualified him for the office, wrote the following words of encouragement, under date of November 6, 1530: "My dearest Jerome, you ought to consider that this temptation of yours is from the devil; and that he thus vexeth you because you believe in Christ. For you see how secure and joyful he lets those be who are most hostile to the gospel, as Eck, Zwingle and others. . . . You ought to rejoice in this temptation of the devil, because it is a sure sign that God is propitious and merciful to you. You will say, 'The temptation is heavier than I can bear,' and will fear lest it so prostrate and oppress you that you will fall into desperation and blasphemy. I know this art of the devil: whom he cannot by the first assault lay prostrate, he endeavoureth assiduously to harass and debilitate, that he may fall and confess himself vanquished. Wherefore, as often as this temptation cometh upon you, take care that you do not debate with the devil, or indulge in these deadly cogitations. For this is but to believe the devil, and to yield to him. But rather boldly despise these cogitations suggested by the devil. In this kind of temptation contempt is the best and easiest means of overcoming the devil. Laugh your adversary to scorn, then, and seek for a companion or friend. Flee solitude, for he then lieth in wait for you, and catcheth you when you are alone. This devil is overcome, not by resistance and disputation, but by ridicule and contempt. Indulge, therefore, in playfulness and face-tiousness with my wife and others, and by that means delude those diabolical machinations, and be of good cheer. This temptation is more needful to you than your meat and drink. I wish to relate what happened unto me when I was about your age. When I first went into the monastery, it happened that I was always falling sad and melancholy, nor could I lay this sadness aside. Wherefore I consulted Dr. Staupitz, and confessed to him, whom I love to mention, and disclosed to him what horrid and terrific cogitations I had. He said: 'You know not, Martin, how useful and necessary this temptation is to you. For God doth not so exercise you in vain; you will see that he will employ you to do great things.' And so it hath turned out. For I am become (this I may justly say of myself) a great doctor, which at that time, when I was under the temptation, I would never have believed. So, beyond all doubt, will it be with you. You will become a great man. See that you be of good heart, and be assured that such words, coming from the lips of learned and great men, are a sort of oracle and divination."

To Veit Dietrich, now in Coburg, he writes: "I have succeeded to the labours of Bugenhagen, [the city pastor;] I preach, lecture [in the university,] am distracted with causes to be decided, and am busy in writing letters, so that I can do no more. Salute all in my name. I must seize time by force, if I would do any thing out of my line of duties. My head still roareth, especially in the morning."

As pastor, he had occasion to perform new duties, one of which, relating to a breach of promise, we find represented in the following official letter: " I,

Martin Luther, doctor of the Holy Scriptures, and
preacher at Wittenberg, do you, Brosius Heinrich of
Dittersdorf, to wit, that the honourable lady Anna,
widow of Wetzel of Zernegal, hath appeared before
me, and entered complaint that you promised her
proper marriage, and was therefore publicly affianced
to her; and, notwithstanding this, have abandoned
her, and refused to fulfil, according to promise and
duty, (which are binding before God and all the
world,) to consummate the marriage with the afore-
said lady. Wherefore she hath called upon me, as
pastor, for the time being, at Wittenberg, to protect
her in her rights. In place, therefore, of the pastor,
I hereby peremptorily summon and cite you to appear before me and others, who have such things in
charge, here at Wittenberg, to hear said complaint,
and whatever else is right and proper."

The deliberation of Luther with his young friend
Jerome Weller, in regard to his marriage celebration, is not without interest to us. "I have learned
with satisfaction," says Luther in a letter to him,
"that you have become a man, and have obtained a
companion. . . . May Christ bless you and your
spouse, and grant that you may always live together
with kindness and affection. I do not entirely approve of your plan for the wedding. You know the
difficulty under which we labour here because of our
market, so that neither I nor my Katy can conceive how, in such a destitution of all things, we
can provide a suitable dinner for such a multitude.
I would not like to leave any stain upon your
honour or mine. I think it would be better to celebrate the marriage in Freiberg, [Weller's residence,]
or, if that cannot be done, to take leave of your
friends there with a splendid entertainment for as

many as would be convenient, and then come hither
with a small company, as Cruciger, Dr. Brück and
others did, and prepare a collation or dinner of two
or three tables. . . . If you were to invite all the
university and the families of the professors, and
others, who could not on my account be omitted,
you would need nine or twelve tables. You remember that on receiving your doctorate, you invited the
men without their wives and children, and yet seven
or eight tables were filled." In another letter, he
says such a public wedding in Wittenberg would
cost one hundred gulden.

In January of 1537, Luther wrote to his son
John, who was at school, these affectionate and judicious lines : " Thus far, my dearest John, your
studies and the letters you have written please me.
If you go on thus, you will not only gratify me, a
tender father, but will chiefly benefit yourself in not
becoming degenerate. Wherefore proceed diligently
as you have begun. For God, who commandeth
children to obey their parents, promiseth blessings
to obedient children. See that you regard this
blessing only, and that you do not allow yourself to
be misled by bad examples. For the same God
threateneth disobedient children with cursing. Fear
God, then, who blesseth and curseth, and who,
though he delay his promises and threatenings to
the destruction of the wicked, fulfilleth them soon
enough for the salvation of the good. Fear God,
then, and listen to your parents, who desire nothing
but your good, and flee base and evil conversation.
Your mother heartily saluteth you, as also aunt
Lene, with your sisters and brothers, who also all
look forward to your happy career and the end of
your studies Your mother biddeth you salute your

preceptor and his wife. If they wish to come with
you this carnival or vacation, very well, though I
shall be absent.   Aunt Lene desireth it very much.
Farewell, my son ; learn and practise the counsels
of good men.   The Lord be with you."

The Smalcald convention was held in February
of this year.   A few words from Luther's letters
will sufficiently represent to us the character of that
convention, and the feelings which he cherished in
respect to it. "Although, my dear Jonas," he writes
to him from Altenburg, "this letter, as I suppose,
will not come to hand immediately, nevertheless I
desire to say that I hope you are by this time recovered from the gravel, and that my prayers are
heard.   It is rumoured that the holy legate, [Peter
Vorst,] Bishop of Aix, is on his way from Nüremberg to visit our prince.   This hath been written to
him from Coburg, whereunto he replied, that the
legate must come to Smalcald, if he desired to see
him. . . . The imperial chancellor, Matthias Held,
will be there.   The convention will, perhaps, be
greater than either party expected.   God grant that
it may be a true council. . . . I miss your company
exceedingly.   Visit my family, and also the Pomeranian Rome [the family of Pomeranus, or Bugen-
hagen] and its Quirites, [citizens.]   We are well
and happy, and have been sumptuously entertained
by the prince in his castles at Grimma and Altenburg.   We had hoped to be guests of that old
Pylades [true friend] and Theseus, [namely, Spalatin ;] and therefore amused ourselves, after our
manner, which you know, in making Latin verses
on him.

"I wish to write to you while I have leisure ; for
after a little time we shall be engaged in delibera-

tion. . . . Many think there will not be as many men at the council of Mantua as here, though there may be more mules, asses and horses, with riders like themselves. . . . Yesterday the Landgrave of Hesse and the Duke of Wirtemberg made a splendid entry into the city. To-day, the princes are in secret council, while we are at leisure, and can write. What will be done I do not know, nor can I divine. Yesterday Spalatin preached; to-day I shall do the same before the princes, in the lofty and spacious parish church, which is so large that our voices will sound like that of a mouse in it. The place and the climate are healthy, and we are well. You only are missed. You would like to see so many great men, and to be seen among them. Yesterday I suffered from the gravel." The dangerous illness, already described, immediately ensued.

In May, 1538, he wrote to Duke Albert of Prussia, on the Vistula, in behalf of his brother-in-law, who wished to enter again into the service of that excellent prince. "My brother-in-law," he says, "John von Bora, who was formerly in your service at Memel, [near the borders of Russia,] hath desired me to write to you. He was forced to stay away from you long, to marry and settle on his estate, in order to hold possession of it; but hath never wished to abandon your service. He hath always spoken in your praise, and desired to be in your employ; and now it is his request that you will take his long absence in good part, which was caused only by the necessity of securing his own and his brother's estate." This brother of Catharine von Bora, Luther's wife, is often mentioned by Luther in his letters. In 1539, failing of an appointment in the service of Duke Albert, he was made overseer of a Benedictine nunnery in Leipsic, by Henry, Duke of Saxony. Afterward he obtained from the Elector John Frederic, a small estate, a little south of Altenburg, which he retained from 1545 to 1560.

Not long after writing the letter quoted in part above, he wrote the following lines to a judge in Torgau: "'Serve the Lord with fear, and be instructed, ye judges of the earth.' These words should be the judge's daily motto; and it is, I think, yours. For you are such a pious and Christian judge, as all who know you testify. I thank you, my dear Judge Antony, that you gave your assistance to Margaret Dorste, and did not allow the nobles to take away her property and her very blood. You know that Dr. Martin is not only a theologian and a champion of the faith, but a defender of the rights of the poor people, who come to him from all quarters to get help before magistrates, so that he would have enough to do, if he had no other business. But Dr. Luther loveth to serve the poor, as do you also; for you fear the Lord; you love Christ; you study the word of God, and still learn your catechism daily no less than the children in the school. Christ, the Lord, will remember this of you. But, dear Judge Antony, it was not enough for you to listen to my request and entreaty, and to give me pleasing intelligence of your love and readiness to grant my request, but you must honour me with a present—with a whole cask of Torgau beer of your own brewing. I am unworthy of such kindness; and, though I know that you are not poor, but that God hath blest you with abundance, still I should have liked better that you should have given it to the poor, and from their prayers have received a greater blessing than you can from poor Martin's alone."

The following touching allusion to the death of the companion who went with him, when a boy, to the school at Magdeburg, will be read with interest. "It is strange," says he, in writing to a citizen of Mansfeld, "how carefully all my friends and relations concealed from me the death of John Reineck, your brother-in-law, and my best friend. Neither my brother Jacob nor my Katy was willing that I should know any thing of it in my sickness. Yet I rejoice that he died so happily and piously, though I bear with reluctance and grief the loss of such a man."

Under date of 1539, we find a letter of Luther to his sister, whom he addresses as "Lady Dorothy, wife of Balthasar Mackenrot, in the service of the elector at Rossla," in the vicinity of Nordhausen. He there says: "Dear sister, I see from your letter to me that your highly burdened conscience longs after the comforting preaching of the gospel, and that you desire it to be introduced into your church at Rossla. Rejoicing thereat, I have resolved to be with you at Christmas, if God shall spare my life and health, and to introduce, with God's help, the first evangelical preaching myself both at Rossla and Upper Rossla, and to establish it as a memorial. Greet your husband, and your little daughter Margaret, for whom I will bring some present." This sister survived Luther several years.

When his daughter Magdalene was apparently near her end, Luther wrote to Torgau, September 6, 1542, for his son John, who was attending school there. "I request you," he said to Marcus Crodel, "to keep from my son John what I now write you.

My daughter Magdalene is drawing near to death, and will soon be with her true Father in heaven, unless it shall seem best to God that it should be otherwise. But she longeth so much to see her brother, that I am constrained to send a carriage for him, hoping she may live till he returneth. They were very fond of each other. I do whatsoever I can, that my conscience may not afterward reproach me. Direct him, therefore, without mentioning the reason, to hasten home in this carriage, by which time she will either be with the Lord, or be restored." · The daughter lived but two weeks. He says, in a letter to Justus Jonas, after her death, that, notwithstanding her peaceful and happy departure, "The power of parental affection is such, that he cannot suppress his sighs and groans." "The countenance, words and motions of the living and dying daughter, so obedient and reverent, remain deeply fixed in my heart."

The same year, Jonas experienced a great bereavement in the death of his wife, the most intimate of all the friends of Luther's family. The latter wrote to Jonas thus: "What to write I know not, so suddenly hath your calamity stricken me down. We have all lost one of the sweetest of companions. She was not only beloved by me, but her countenance was always pleasant and full of consolation, so that we had all our joys and sorrows in common, and bitter indeed is the separation. I had hoped she would survive me, as the best and first comforter among women for my wife and children."

In 1545, the year before his death, Luther became dissatisfied, as he had often done before, with the people of Wittenberg for their luxury and wanton pleasures. He even resolved to leave the place and spend the remnant of his days elsewhere; and in May actually forsook Wittenberg, and went first to Löbnitz to his friend Ernest von Schönfeld; then to Leipsic to see a mercantile friend by the name of Scherle; afterward to Morseburg to the provost, Prince George of Anhalt; and finally, to Zeitz to visit Amsdorf, now bishop. But the entreaties of a deputation from the elector and from the university induced him to return. His last work was the completion of his Commentary on Genesis, on which he had laboured diligently ten years. The closing words are: "I am weak, and can do no more. Pray God that he may grant me a peaceful, happy death."

The Counts of Mansfeld had been for several years at variance with some of their subjects, whom they wished to deprive of their furnaces. Luther's brother-in-law, Mackenrot, was in danger of losing his. Luther had written to Count Albert on the subject in 1540 and in 1542, and also to the other two counts, Philip and George. These counts were in controversy also with each other, in respect to what is called the right of patronage. Luther, who had advised them to settle the matter by a reference, was himself requested to be one of the referees, and gave his consent. Though it was contrary to his custom to intermeddle in secular disputes, he yielded in this case, because he was a native of Mansfeld, and owed it a service. He left Wittenberg, January 23, 1546, with his three sons, John, Martin and Paul. On the 25th he reached Halle, and stopped with Jonas the three following days, on account of the flood in the river Saale. From this place he wrote to his wife: "Dear Katy. We came hither at eleven o'clock, but did not proceed to Eisleben; for a great Anabaptist met us with his waves and blocks of ice. We could not return on account of the river Mulda. Therefore we were forced to remain at Halle between two floods, not that we were thirsting for these waters, for we have good Torgau beer and Rhenish wine, and indulged in these till the wrath of the Saale should cool off."

On the 28th, Luther, his three sons and Jonas, crossed the river in a boat, not without danger, that they might proceed to Eisleben. No sooner had they reached the boundaries of the county of Mansfeld, than the counts met them with an escort of one hundred and thirteen horsemen. Before reaching Eisleben, Luther was very ill, but recovered after being rubbed with warm cloths. From January 29th to February 17th, he was engaged every day at Eisleben with the counts in settling their difficulties. He became impatient at his apparent want of success, and often wished himself at home again.

February 6, he wrote as follows: "To the profoundly learned lady, Catharine Luther, my gracious housewife at Wittenberg. Dear Katy. We continue here in a state of vexation, and wish ourselves away; but that cannot be, I think, within a week. You may tell Melancthon to correct his Postil, for he did not understand why the Lord called riches *thorns.* This is a school for learning to understand that. . . . Your sons are at Mansfeld. We have enough to eat and to drink, and should have good times, were it not for these disagreeable transactions."

While at Eisleben, his native place, he communed twice, ordained two priests, and preached four times. Three days before his death, he preached in the pulpit, which is still standing, his last sermon, from

Matt xi. 25–30, and closed by saying: "This, and much more, may be said from the passage, but I am too weak, *and here we will stop.*" During his stay at Eisleben, his conversation was unusually rich and impressive, both on religious and other subjects. He experienced all that exhilaration which an old man is wont to have in visiting the place of his birth. Every evening, for those twenty-one days, he retired, about eight o'clock, from the great hall, where the company transacted their business and took their meals, to his private apartment, and, standing by the window, prayed for a long time so earnestly that Dr. Jonas, M. Cœlius, preacher at Mansfeld, his servant Ambrose, and Aurifaber of Weimar, often overheard him.

On Wednesday, the 17th of February, the Princes of Anhalt and Count Albert of Mansfeld and his friends generally entreated him not to enter the great hall during the business in the forenoon, but to take repose in his own room. He did so, lying a part of the time upon his leathern couch, walking the room a part of the time, and going to the window at times, and praying so that Jonas and Cœlius, who were with him in the room, could hear him. At noon he left his own apartment, and dined in the great hall with the company. At table he was heard to say: "If I could only reconcile the rulers of my native place with one another, and then, with God's permission, make the journey, I would go home, and lay myself down to sleep in my grave, and let the worms devour my body." In the afternoon, before supper, he complained of a painful pressure at the breast, and requested that he might, according to his custom, be rubbed with warm cloths. He experienced a little relief, and was able to take his supper in the hall. His conversation at this time, which is recorded, related to death, eternity and the recognition of friends in a future state. As he arose from supper, he went to his room, accompanied by his two sons, Martin and Paul, then fourteen and thirteen years of age respectively, and Cœlius. Soon the latter left the room, and Aurifaber entered. Luther now complained of a pain in the breast, as before. Jonas and Cœlius were immediately called, who rubbed him with warm cloths, and Count Albert, who brought with him the shavings from the tooth of a sea-unicorn, a favourite medicine in those days, and Luther took it. He slept till ten o'clock in the evening, and Jonas, Cœlius, his host Albrecht, and his wife, Ambrose and Luther's two sons watched with him. At ten he arose, and attempted to walk, but was obliged to return to his bed. He afterward slept till one o'clock, and when he awoke he requested Ambrose to make more fire, although the room had been kept very warm. As Jonas asked him whether he felt weak, he replied: "Oh! how I suffer. Oh! my dear Jonas, I think I shall die here at Eisleben, where I was born and baptized." The friends were awaked and called in. When Jonas spoke encouragingly of his profuse sweat, Luther said, "It is a cold death-sweat; I must yield up my spirit, for my malady increaseth." He then prayed fervently, and commended his soul confidently to God. After taking a little medicine, and assuring his friends that he should die, he repeated three times quickly the words: "Father, into thy hands do I commend my spirit; thou hast redeemed me, thou faithful God." He then became quiet. The attendants shook him, rubbed him, and spoke to him, but he closed his eyes and made no reply. Jonas and Cœlius then spoke very loud, and said, "Venerable father, do you die trusting in Christ and in the doctrine which you have preached?" and he answered distinctly, "Yes," and turned upon his right side and seemed to sleep for nearly a quarter of an hour. His friends were encouraged, but the physician told them that it was no favourable symptom. A light was brought near his face, and it was evidently turning pale; and his forehead, face and feet were becoming cold. After one gentle breath and sigh, with folded hands, he quietly died, on Thursday, the 18th of February, 1546, between two and three o'clock in the morning, at the age of sixty-two years, three months and eight days. He was laid out upon a bed till a lead coffin could be cast; and two painters were employed to take his likeness.

On the 19th of February, at two o'clock, a funeral discourse was preached by Justus Jonas before a large audience at St. Andrew's church, which stands nearly opposite the house where Luther died. The corpse remained over night in the church, guarded by ten men. The Counts of Mansfeld desired that he might be buried at Eisleben, where he was born and where he died. But the Elector of Saxony was desirous that his remains should be brought to Wittenberg, and deposited in the collegiate or electoral church, and the counts yielded to his wishes. Another funeral discourse, however, was pronounced by Michael Cœlius, of Mansfeld, before the body was removed from Eisleben.

The same day, between twelve and one o'clock, the corpse was removed, a great company following it to the gate of the city, and the Counts of Mansfeld with about fifty-five horsemen proceeding with it to Wittenberg. As they passed along the way

to Halle, the bells were tolled in the villages and
many people came to express their grief. At five
o'clock, as they approached Halle, the clergy, civil
authorities, citizens, schools, matrons, virgins and
children in great multitudes came out in mourning,
and singing funeral hymns, to meet the procession.
At one of the churches, to which the body was conveyed at seven o'clock in the evening, one of Luther's hymns was sung amid a flood of tears, and
then a watch was stationed there for the night. The
next morning, which was Sunday, the procession left
the city in the same manner in which they entered
it, and reached Bitterfeld at noon, where they were
received with becoming ceremony. Here they were
met by the delegation from Wittenberg sent by the
elector. They came as far as Kemberg, and it was
evening. The next morning, they approached the
eastern gate of Wittenberg, and were joined by the
widow and sons of the deceased, and a great multitude from the university and the city, and passed
amid crowds of people to the church at the other
end of the town. Here the funeral ceremonies took
place, and a funeral sermon was preached by Bugenhagen, and an address was delivered by Melancthon,
after which the remains of Luther were deposited
near the pulpit where he had preached, where they
still lie to attract the attention of the thousands
who, after three centuries, still continue to visit
Wittenberg, THE SEAT OF THE REFORMATION.

THE END.

INDEX.

THE END.